D0850072

KING ZOG AND THE STRUGGLE FOR

STABILITY IN ALBANIA

BY
BERND JÜRGEN FISCHER

EAST EUROPEAN MONOGRAPHS, BOULDER
DISTRIBUTED BY COLUMBIA UNIVERSITY PRESS, NEW YORK

1984

EAST EUROPEAN MONOGRAPHS, NO. CLIX

this work is dedicated to my parents

Emil and Gertrud Fischer

TABLE OF CONTENTS

ACKNOWLEDGEMENTS

My study owes much to the financial assistance available for projects of this nature. The University of California at Santa Barbara made extensive European research possible by providing a Patent Fund Research Grant. Central Michigan University through the Faculty Research and Creative Endeavors Committee helped in the final stages by extending a generous publication subsidy.

I would of course like to thank the many people without whom this work would never have been completed. Professors Stavro Skendi and Nicholas Pano, the two leading Albanian scholars in the United States, provided useful suggestions with regard to my search for material. Since there is a serious dearth of secondary sources concerning this topic, I spent many months in various archives. The staffs of the National Archives in Washington, the Public Record Office in London, the Auswärtiges Amt in Bonn and the Haus-Hof und Staatsarchiv in Vienna showed kindness and patience as I am sure they always do.

I would like to thank Queen Geraldine for adjuring her twenty-year self-imposed silence in order to share with me her invaluable personal insights concerning her late husband the King. Professors Joachim Remak and Abraham Friesen were good enough to read the manuscript and provide constructive suggestions. Lastly and most importantly, I would like to thank my mentor and friend Professor Dimitrije Djordjevic. Not

only did he suggest the topic pointing out that while there were a significant number of works dealing with Albania prior to World War I and after
World War II, very little had been done on the important interwar period,
but he also guided me through the maze of difficulties associated with this
project. I am extremely grateful for his inspiration and encouragement.

ABBREVIATIONS USED IN THE NOTES

AA	Auswärtiges Amt (Germany)
CAB	British Cabinet Papers
DDI	documenti diplomatici italiani
FO	Foreign Office (Great Britain)
HHStA	Haus-Hof und Staatsarchiv (Austria)
USDS	United States Department of State

NOTE

Many Albanian names and place-names have various spellings. I have used the Albanian spelling whenever available. With regard to Albanian place-names, I have kept the indefinite forms used in the country itself, e.g., Durrës, Shkodër, Vlorë, etc. An exception has been made in the case of the capital. The more familiar form Tirana is used throughout. In many of the documents cited, Western spelling is used. The following are the most frequent:

> Durazzo for Durrës
> Scutari for Shkodër
> Valona for Vlorë
> Sesseno for Sazan

CHAPTER ONE

THE ORIENTAL-WESTERN EDUCATION OF A CHIEFTAIN

Ahmed Zogolli, second son of Xhemal Pasha chief of the Mati tribe, was born on October 8, 1895, at the castle of Burgayet which overlooked a small village of 150 houses. The 15th century castle was built in an almost impregnable defensive position, surrounded by four mountains and extensive pine forests. The physical surroundings of Burgayet are indicative of the lifestyle of the Albanian mountaineer in general and of Zogolli's Mati clan in particular.

The origin of the clan is shrouded in mystery and legend and has become the subject of tales handed down from generation to generation. Officially, Ahmed liked to think that the Zogolli family first gained its prominence in the late 15th century when Princess Mamica of Krujë, sister of the Albanian national hero George Castrati Skanderbeg, wedded Zogolli, the lord of Burayet castle.[1]

A much more romantic Arthurian tale has it tha the family originated in the small village of Zogai at the foot of the Tarabosh Mountains on the shore of Lake Shkodër. It chanced, so the story runs, that some four hundred years ago a Zogolli of the period happened to be in the Mati country on a day when the Turkish Kaimakam gave an order that the daughters of the leading families should come and dance before him. The affront aroused the wrath of the Mati tribesmen. The young Zogolli put himself at their head and routed the Kaimakam's retinue. The chieftain of the clan gave to the hero of the occasion his daughter in marriage and from that day on, the leadership of the Mati clan remained in the Zogolli family.[2]

1

While little credence can be lent to these stories, existing Turkish records show that the family sprang from the north of Albania and settled towards the end of the 15th century, the beginning of the Turkish period, in the untamed Mati country in the midst of a series of indigenous tribes.[3] The family was Catholic, warlike, and lived from plundering coast dwellers in the vicinity of Shkodër. The archives of the Porte mention a major uprising in 1631-1632 led by a member of the Zogolli family who managed not only to burn Tirana but was able to fight his way to the gates of Durrës before Sultan Murad IV could gather the forces of Sandschakbegs of Ohrid, Shkodër and Elbasan. With these armies the Sultan succeeded in crushing the revolt and extracting Zogolli from his mountain stronghold in Mati. Zogolli and two of his lieutenants were beheaded in Ohrid in 1633 while his sons became Moslems, thereby saving the position of the house and the lives of its adherents.[4]

The family does not become prominent again until Xhelal Pasha Zogolli, grandfather of Ahmed, led his small tribe in an abortive uprising against the Turks near the end of the 19th century. A man of some culture and political acumen, he went so far as to appeal to the Austrian Kaiser Franz Joseph for aid but the movement proved to be premature, and he was forced to flee.[5] He was eventually captured by the Turks and kept in exile in Constantinople while his son, Xhemal Pasha, succeeded him as chief of the tribe.

Xhemal Pasha continued the warlike pastime of most northern chiefs until he had successfully gained control of the entire Mati district from the Kruja Mountains to the Mirditë. For his efforts, he was officially recognized as leader of Mati and neighboring Dibra by the Porte.

An astute mountain politician, Xhemal Pasha recognized that force of arms was but one method by which to extend his power and influence. Much like happy Austria, Xhemal contracted a number of marriages with neighboring chiefs, the second one with Emin Bey Toptani, the scion of a powerful Tirana family with control over much of central Albania. Sadije Toptani proved to be an excellent choice for a number of reasons including her remarkable gift for statesmanship and extraordinary keen judgement. These attributes served her well when on the death of her husband, she took control of the tribe. She was responsible for keeping the clan independent and united while her sons grew to manhood.

By Western standards, the world in which Ahmed grew up was primitive, violent and extremely patriarchal. The father of the family had life and death powers over his wife and children. Following tribal custom, the Albanian husband had a simple and efficacious remedy against a faithless wife: he shot her and that was the end of it. Not until the 1920s and early 1930s was this right even questioned by the central authorities.[6]

Women were generally betrothed in infancy or even before birth by the head of the house to which they belonged, and in consideration of the prospective transfer of services, a purchase price was agreed upon part of which was paid on betrothal, and the balance when the bridegroom took possession of his bride. If the bridegroom refused her, which was seldom the case, a feud resulted. The bride could escape only by swearing lifelong virginity in which case she was treated with the greatest respect.[7]

This unhappy manner of betrothal was a frequent cause of abduction and consequent feud between the abductor and his family on the one side and the families of the betrothed couple on the other. Though the abductor and bride might escape abroad, the feud continued and twenty or thirty might be slain before the matter was settled.[8]

Once a part of the family, however, wives often assumed male attire and carried guns. They frequently acted both as advisers to their husbands and as workers since a great deal, if not most of the work, was done by the women while the men, as they had been since time immemorial, were enmeshed in the ramifications of the blood fued. Despite this significant role, women had no social standing.

Because of their savage love of independence, the chief of the tribe acted as judicial, political and military leader. He decided on matters of war and peace and led the tribe into battle. He administered Albanian mountain justice based upon the Canons of Lek Dukagjin, a legendary chieftain who lived during the 14th century. Lek was evidently of such insistent individuality to have so influenced the people that "Lek said so" obtained far more obedience than the Ten Commandments. The teachings of Islam and Christianity, the Sheriat and Church law all yielded to the Canon of Lek which was probably little more than old tribal law with a few new provisions designed to check or reform old usage by enforcing punishment. The Canon of Lek inflicted only two forms of punishment, fines and the burning of property. Neither death nor imprisonment could be inflicted because prisons did not exist and death simply led to further blood feuds, that peculiar Albanian custom which for centuries sapped the strength and manhood out of northern Albania.[9]

The chief also determined how far a blood feud should be pursued. Since the preservation of unblemished honor was the principal aim of the tribesman's existence, blood feuds originated over the merest trivialities such as an accidential blow. Once started carnage usually resulted, but carnage under strict rules. A man could not shoot for vengeance when his target was with a woman or with a child. (Women were never liable for blood vengeance since female blood was not considered of any value.) A man could not shoot when he was met in company or when a besa (oath of peace) had been given. The two parties often swore an oath for a few weeks for business purposes or to repel the attack of a common foe.

To have shot four men in defense of honor was no exceptional record. Since tribesmen felt incomplete without their weapons, the opportunity for defending one's honor was always close at hand. Although many Albanians recognized that the feuds were the scourge of the land, their fear and distrust of any central government drove them to settle disputes in their own way. Even in the 1920s, the death toll from blood feuds was astonishingly high. In some areas, as many as 40 percent of all deaths resulted from feuds.[10]

This indigenous social organization and all of its attributes, including the belief that personal and political problems could best be handled with violence, left a deep impression on Ahmed and became a rather substantial part of his political method. The young boy absorbed Albanian tribal customs, watching his father give justice under a tree. He would most likely have developed into little more than a copy of his father, had it not been for the early death of Xhemal Pasha in 1908.

Ahmed, then eight, was sent off as a hostage to Constantinople while his mother assumed leadership of the tribe. Up until this point his education had consisted of little more than an occasional conversation with a Moslem holy man in Mati. While in Turkey, Zogolli was given the opportunity to receive a formal, if somewhat truncated, education. He studied first at the Galata-Serail Lycium for notables and later at a school for officers in Monastir, both of which were considered progressive Young Turk schools.[11] His three short years in school taught him Turkish and some French but left him in complete ignorance of the world beyond southeastern Europe. He did not seem to have the desire, or as it turned out, the time to further develop his education along these lines.

Despite his lack of formal education, Zogolli learned a good deal on his own while in Turkey. Europe was in the midst of troubled times.

Zogolli witnessed the Young Turk revolt and the last gasp of the Ottoman Empire. Although he was still young, these events did not fail to impress him and give him some concept of the workings of Oriental politics.

Zogolli's personal experiences taught him something about poverty and survival and gave others an example of some of his stronger character traits. Geraldine, his future wife, maintains that shortly after his arrival in Constantinople, he was given an interview with Sultan Abdul Hamid because of the influence of some highly placed Albanians. As the story goes, the Sultan took a liking to the boy and offered to make him an adjutant to his youngest son. Ahmed refused, angering both the Sultan and his uncle under whose auspices he was to live. The Sultan cut him off from communication with Mati and his uncle refused him support.[12]

Although it is difficult to say whether any credence can be lent to this story, it is clear that the boy experienced difficult times while in Constantinople. The Albanian guards of the palace took him in and supported him for some time. Zogolli was eventually able to regain his financial independence by extracting some funds, which he believed rightly his, from his uncle at gunpoint.[13]

His stay in Constantinople abruptly ended in 1911 when he was called back to Albania to lead his tribe in a revolt against the Young Turks who had attempted to centralize their authority in Albania. Although Zogolli had an elder half-brother, Xhelal Bey, Albanian tribal law never followed strict primogeniture and his mother had quietly pushed Xhelal aside, claiming that he was basically incompetent and a drunkard.

Ahmed Bey raised his clan and joined the Kosovo Albanians under Hasan Bey Prishtina, Reza Bey Kryeziu and Bajram Curri. Although this first encounter turned out to be little more than a skirmish, this event constituted Ahmed Bey's first direct involvement in Albanian internal affairs.[14]

Had the international situation been similar to the previous 500 years of Albanian history, Ahmed Bey would probably have remained another tribal leader fighting for the expansion of influence, lost somewhere in the inaccessible mountains of northern Albania. But the situation was different than it had been for his father and his grandfather. The Ottoman Empire, which for five centuries had been both an oppressor and a protector, was finally on the verge of collapse and the Albanians were forcibly extracted from their long Medieval sleep and thrust into the 20th century.

The dangers and uncertainty would possibly have discouraged a lesser man, but Ahmed Bey recognized that the opportunities were boundless for those with proper qualifications, for those with the ability to manipulate a situation until it became advantageous and then to effectively take advantage of it.

As a military state, the Ottoman Empire began to decline as soon as it stopped expanding in the 16th century. This decline, however, was gradual and did not reach crisis levels until the 20th century. In 1912, perceiving its weakness and taking advantage of the disagreement among the Great Powers, the small Balkan states decided to dismember the rest of European Turkey, including the territory inhabited by the Albanians. Forming together in a Balkan League, the Balkan states attacked the Ottoman Empire. Most Albanians as usual fought with the Turks against the Slavs, having always feared and hated the Slavs as a neighboring stronger power.

At the same time a number of Albanian intellectuals, realizing that the Albanians were far from ready for independence and yet aware that the Ottoman Empire was no longer strong enough to protect the Albanian territories, felt that the only way to prevent absorption by the neighboring Balkan states was to declare independence and hope for the support of the European powers at the councils of peace which would follow the Balkan wars.

Accordingly, Ismail Kemal Bey, a southern intellectual and member of the Turkish Parliament, proclaimed the independence of Albania at Vlorë on November 28, 1912, despite the fact that a considerable degree of local autonomy had already been granted by the hard pressed Young Turk government after its unsuccessful Ottomanization campaign. Ismail Bey set up a provisional government and called a Congess which was attended by delegates from various districts including Zogolli from Mati. The Albanian leader also appealed to the powers for protection from external and internal enemies.

Internally the new government was faced with the opposition of a Turkish army near Vlorë and the forces of Esad Pasha Toptani, Zogolli's uncle, a feudal lord from the Durrës area who commanded part of the Turkish army in the north. Esad was an able commander but rather prone to be carried away by his own vaulted ambition.

External forces, in the meantime, presented an even more dangerous obstacle to the survival of the new state. Not surprisingly, the Balkan states

engaged in the desperate struggle against Turkey paid no heed to the declaration and continued to consider the Albanian vilayets to be part of European Turkey. The Montenegrin army, led by King Nicholas, attacked
Shkodër, defended by Esad Pasha who was assisted for a time by his
nephew. Zogolli, who had been armed for the occasion by the Turkish
Kaimakam of Dibër, soon withdrew after losing 200 of his best men. He
returned to Mati which was at that point under seige by the Serbs who
were attacking from the east.[15]

Esad Pasha, under somewhat dubious circumstances (he was later accused of having sold Shkodër to King Nicholas), marched out of the city
on April 21, 1913, despite the fact that the Powers had already ordered
Nicholas to cease hostilities. Esad Pasha took with him 40,000 men, their
guns and the support of Montenegro for his political aspirations in Albania.
Both Montenegro and Serbia continued their advance into Albanian territory playing the old game of inciting the primitive xenophobic tribes
against each other in order to take advantage of the ensuing choas.

The new government, meanwhile, had won the recognition of Austria-
Hungary. This enabled the Albanians to present their case at the Conference of Ambassadors representing the Great Powers which was convened
in London in December 1912 to attempt a general settlement following
the first Balkan war.

The principal support for the Albanian cause at the Conference came
from Austria-Hungary, whose policy had always been to deny Serbia access
to the Adriatic, and from Italy who also feared Serbian and Greek expansion. Italy proposed that the region be left under nominal Turkish suzer-
ainty while Austria hoped to create an independent and great Albania
which would include peripheral regions containing not only Albanians
but other nationalities as well.[16]

Because of the strenuous opposition from Russia and the Balkan states,
the Conference accepted a compromise proposal recognizing the independence of Albania but deferring the question of frontiers until 1913 when
borders were finally delineated. In terms of the construction of a government for the new state, the Conference proclaimed Albania to be "an
autonomous principality sovereign and hereditary by order of primogeniture under the guaranty of the six powers."[17] Its neutrality was guaranteed and control of its civil administration and budget was vested in an
international Control Commission composed of an Albanian delegate and
delegates from the six powers.

The selection of a prince for the new state proved to be an arduous task. At the heart of the problem was the question of whether Albania was to be oriented towards the East or the West. The Turks argued that Albania could only be preserved as a vassal state of the Ottoman Empire and therefore urged the acceptance of a member of the Imperial Ottoman dynasty. Ismail Bey and his colleagues were resolved, however, that Albania should become part of Europe and de-emphasize its Ottoman heritage which had proved for centuries to be an obstacle to progress.

Ultimately, Austria-Hungary and Italy were entrusted with the selection of a prince. As one of the leading figures in Albania, despite the grave mistrust which Ismail Bey harbored for him, Esad Pasha was appointed as a Albanian delegate on the search committee. Many were considered for the throne, including Prince Ghika of Rumania, Duke Ferdinand of Montpensier, Prince Karl von Urach, Prince Moritz von Schaumburg-Lippe, the Count of Turin and Prince Arthur of Connaught.

While the process continued, Esad Pasha resolved to take advantage of the power vacuum and uncertainty and make a bid for leadership, claiming that the existing provisional government was hostile to Moslems.[18] Ismail Bey sent representatives to negotiate with Esad but to not avail. The discontented Moslem holymen, who had gathered around Esad, proclaimed him the savior of Albania and the champion of Islam. Esad announced his intention to overthrow the provisional government and formed an opposition government at Durrës.

By force and bribery, the two primary methods of achieving results in Albania at the time, Esad managed to establish himself firmly between the Mat and Shkumbin rivers, commanding most of central Albania, including the towns of Tirana, Krujë, Kavajë, Shijak and Durrës. Ismail appealed to the Powers for a quick decision on a prince fearing that his government would not last long under the pressure from Esad. In November of 1913, the Powers informed Ismail Bey that they had chosen the Protestant Prince William of Wied, the third son of William Prince of Wied and Mary, Princess of Holland, nephew of Queen Elizabeth of Rumania and grand-nephew of Emperor William II of Germany.

William had accepted the post, much to his later chagrin, without becoming fully aware of what he had done. He apparently had never really been interested in the throne but rather was persuaded to accept by his aunt and uncle. Queen Elizabeth and King Charles of Rumania convinced him that the task was not an impossibility despite the Prince's complete lack of knowledge concerning the Balkans. The Prince was primarily a soldier, a man with a high sense of honor and duty who had no concept of or experience with intrigue and diplomacy. As a result, he was incapable of holding his own against the flock of opportunists who hoped to take advantage of the Prince's weaknesses.

Foremost among the latter was Esad Pasha who had by this time overthrown Albania's first government under Ismail Bey and had transferred the capital to his stronghold at Durrës. Upon receiving news of the Prince's appointment, Esad completely changed his Moslem oriented policy and even went so far as to lead the delegation to Neuwied in February, 1914. He obviously saw this as a rare opportunity to assume the role of the power behind the throne and indeed was appointed to the crucial positions of Minister of War and Minister of the Interior in Wied's first government.

Esad hoped to dominate the cabinet with his large force of retainers while at the same time emasculating his rivals by using the authority of the Prince. Because Zogolli controlled one of the largest fighting forces in Albania, namely his fiercely loyal Mati tribesmen, and because Zogolli had refused to help against Ismail Kemal Bey, Esad was convinced that this nephew constituted one of the major obstacles on the road to complete dominance of Albania. Esad once remarked to Ekrem Bey Vlora, an Albanian notable "did you take a good look at this young man, he will do well in his country and push us all aside if I don't shorten his legs at the right time."[19]

In pursuit of this end, Esad attempted to have Ahmed arrested as the young chieftain came down from Mati to pay his respects to the Prince and present proposals for the convocation of a National Assembly. Wied intervened and Ahmed returned to Mati with his family feeling for his uncle undoubtedly considerably diminished. Once back in his mountain fastness, Zogolli resolved to turn on the government. He came to the conclusion that the Prince would not last long under any circumstances and that Esad would quickly step in and attempt to assume power.[20]

Zogolli's uncle soon found himself in serious difficulty. He had not only overstepped his bounds but he had also seriously overestimated his support. The Prince was finally convinced that Esad was a traitor and planned for his arrest. The Prince had to move carefully, however, since

Durrës was still Esad's stronghold and, as with most prominent Albanians, he travelled with an armed retinue at all times. Deciding on the direct approach, on the night of May 19th Wied placed a battery in the garden of the palace and trained it on the residence of his Minister of War and Interior who happened to live next door.[21] The officer commanding the guns called for Esad to surrender. After it become clear that the Minister was making extensive preparations to resist, which included sending a dispatch to nearby loyal tribesmen, the Prince's men fired three shells, one exploding in the bedroom. Realizing that the Prince had the capacity to blow the house to pieces, Esad's wife appeared at the window waving a white sheet.[22]

Ahmed's uncle was thereupon escorted out of the country on an Italian cruiser, to the relief of most of the political elements in Albania with the exception of the Italians who had been subsidizing his activities in the hope of extending their influence. Esad, despite this rather serious setback, did not, however, abandon his quest for power, reappearing on the Albanian political scene during World War I.

Esad's departure did not have the desired effect; political choas did not subside. Quite to the contrary, unabated insurrection dragged on. Moslems had been stirred up against the Christian Prince and Wied's reliance on the conservative landowning class alienated the peasantry. Some of the chieftains, including Ahmed with his 2,000 tribesmen, now supported the Prince, however, and moved to stop the predominantly central Albanian unrest.[23]

Zogolli occupied Krujë for the government and subsequently took up a strong position overlooking Tirana which had since fallen to the insurgents. Because his men, like the Catholic Mirditë, showed reluctance to shed blood in civil strife in which they had no personal interest, and because Ahmed Bey saw that he was heavily outnumbered, he began negotiating with the insurgents, presumably offering them his services in exchange for a powerful position in the cabinet. The negotiations broke down, and despite a personal appeal from the Prince, Ahmed returned to Mati, convinced that the Prince's position remained untenable.

From Mati Ahmed Bey issued a manifesto, supposedly in the name of 150,000 Albanians to the effect that the insurgents comprised only a small minority. He maintained, somewhat hypocritically, that the majority was loyal to the Prince and willing to support him; moreover, since the insurrection had been prompted by foreign agitation, no self-respecting Albanian should identify himself with it.[24] This was as far as the Mati chief would go for his European Prince.

If the insurgents comprised only a small minority, then the Prince's supporters comprised an even smaller and weaker minority. The rebellion was successful in setting the Prince to flight at the end of May, 1914. The Italians seem to have played a role here as well, suggesting that the insurgent force was actually much bigger and advising the Prince to embark on an Italian warship.[25]

Although Wied was to return and hold out until September, he had little support either inside or outside of Albania. Of the many powers that had guaranteed their support, only Rumania, because of family ties, and Austria-Hungary, because it suited its policy, remained faithful to the Prince. The other six powers either completely ignored him because of more pressing problems or, like Italy which considered him a tool of Austria-Hungary, actively worked to destabilize his regime by supporting his opponents. An astute observer, M. E. Durham commented, "We may blame Wied for incompetency but only a man of unusual force of character and intimate knowledge of the land could have made headway against the powers combined against him."[26] Such a man had not yet surfaced.

During World War I Albania was occupied by the armies of several of the belligerent powers including the Serbs, Montenegrins and Greeks who remained for a short time, and the Italians, French and Austro-Hungarians who remained for a longer period. For lack of any central authority, each region of the country acted on its own behalf, throwing in its lot with whoever was there and whoever could offer the most at any given time.

The southern leaders rallied to Ismail Kemal Bey who had returned to Albania to oppose Greece which hoped to annex portions of southern Albania containing large Greek minorities. Central Albania was in the hands of Moslem insurgents who entered Durrës after the final flight of Prince Wied and raised the Turkish flag declaring themselves for the Sultan. As soon as a Senate was called to order, however, the many differences among the insurgents became obvious.

Under these unstable conditions, Esad Pasha, with Italian and Serbian military support, was able to raise a force in Dibër while his supporters convinced the Durrës government to send troops to the south to oppose the Greeks. Surprisingly they complied, thus allowing Esad to take the city unopposed on October 2, 1914. On October 5, by threatening to shoot every member, he compelled the frightened Senate into proclaiming his President and Commander-in-Chief.[27]

Outside of Durrës in the rest of central Albania, opposition to Esad was widespread and eventually joined together in what became known as the Union of Krujë under Haxhi Qerim. This group hoped either for a reincorporation into the Turkish Empire or for the election of one of the Ottoman princes as king of Albania. The group also attracted many tribal leaders who opposed Esad primarily because he was threatening to construct a central government which might compromise their fiercely defended independence. The Union did not, however, extend its authority into Mati or Dibër.

A military stalemate existed between the two opposing camps until June, 1915, when the Serbs attacked central Albania. Ahmed Bey and his tribesmen manned the passes at Mati but were unmolested, probably because Ahmed's half-brother Xhelal was at that moment an important official in the government of Esad Pasha. The Serbs did, however, open military operations against the Union of Krujë which was quickly scattered. Haxhi Qerim, Musa Kazim and a few other leaders of the Union were captured by the Serbs and sent as prisoners to Durrës. Here they were tried by a court under the presidency of Zogolli's brother and executed by order of Esad Pasha.

Ahmed's uncle remained dictator of central Albania as long as the Serbs remained in control of the areas he administered. He made some attempts to extend his influence, sending a small army to attack Ahmed Bey in Mati. He might have succeeded in defeating his nephew, but in January of 1916, Austro-Hungarian troops drove the Serbian army out of Albania. Esad found himself in a rather awkward position, realizing that Austria-Hungary would never recognize him and for that matter might do him harm. Believing that his star was irrevocably attached to the Allies, he declared war on Austria-Hungary and left with the Serbs.

Esad arrived at Salonika in August, 1916, in a French warship and was recognized by General Sarrail, the French commander, as the President of the Albanian Republic. He was given a villa in which he set up a court, a government, a ministry of war, a ministry of foreign affairs and even a ministry of agriculture. The Allied powers were not completely willing to trust him, however, so they each sent a Minister Plenipoteniary to watch him and each other.[28]

While he and his 500 men actually did contribute to the war effort on numerous occasions, Esad was generally considered in terms of comic relief with his uniform and myriad of medals which made him look like a general in anybody's army.

With the Serbs and Esad gone, new opportunities presented themselves in Albania, particularly for those who had opposed Esad earlier. As one of this number, Ahmed Bey welcomed the Austro-Hungarians, recognizing that Vienna was the only major power which had consistently supported the idea of a strong independent Albania. Before entering the country, the Austro-Hungarians had issued a proclamation claiming that their army was entering Albania only to drive out the Serbs and the Italians. Many prominent northern leaders called upon the Albanians to recognize the Austrians as liberators. Vienna encouraged this by sending representatives to the major chieftains in an attempt to outbid the Bulgarians who also hoped to extend their influence in Albania. Sophia assumed presumably that with a victory for the Central Powers it might eventually share a common border with the Albanians. Zogolli was considered a prime target for such activity.

Ahmed Bey decided to remain aloof for the time being, however, having learned from his uncle's experience that to be identified too closely with a foreign power could be disastrous. Although the Austro-Hungarians were not despised as much as the Serbs because they represented a power with whom the tribesmen had rarely come in contact, xenophobia was still rampant. Ahmed Bey understood this very well and decided to see how far he could get without compromising himself.

As soon as Esad had departed, Ahmed Bey initiated a movement to bring back the Prince of Wied, reasoning presumably that as a foreigner and a Lutheran, Wied might at least represent a nationwide symbol. Ahmed could control the symbol, provided he act with more circumspection than his uncle had.

In a more active vain, Ahmed Bey rallied his tribe and marched on Elbasan in central Albania which had been occupied by the 23rd Bulgarian Infantry Regiment under Captain Serafimoff on January 29. The Bulgarians, in an effort to win him over, allowed him to take over the administration of the city. Elated with his success, Ahmed Bey immediately marched on to Durrës which had been evacuated by the Allies. He telegraphed to his supporters: "Today we raised the national flag in our Prince's palace at Durazzo . . . ."[29]

While Ahmed Bey was extending his influence, his followers at Elbasan constituted yet another provisional National Assembly and elected a "Commission of Initiative" under the presidency of Ahmed Bey. On February 18, the Commission, with the unanimous approval of the Assembly, passed a resolution in favor of a National Congress of duly accredited representatives to be convened as soon as possible. In the meantime they invited Aqif Pasha Elbasani, the Minister of Interior and War in Wied's last government to call together his colleagues since they had never formally resigned. Aqif Pasha was rejoined by Midhat Bey Frasheri and Luigj Gurakuqi. Zogolli too was asked to join the provisional government but refused because of his position on the Commission.[30]

Ahmed Bey soon announced that the National Congress would be held on March 18, 1916, in Elbasan and he further suggested that Vienna and Sophia be sent letters of gratitude for allowing the national flag to be raised in Albania.

Ahmed's gratitude was somewhat premature and his elaborate plans were never carried out due to the extremely fluid situation which the war had caused. At the beginning of March, the Austro-Hungarians occupied Durrës which they turned into a naval base and held until the end of the war. At the same time, they occupied Elbasan, replacing the Bulgarians who moved further south. The Austrian commander immediately cordoned off the city, claiming that the danger of a spreading epidemic of cholera necessitated this action. The city was not reopened until March 21, after the Congress was to have been held.

The commander further announced that during times of war, political assemblies were not allowed in territories occupied by the armies of Austria-Hungary. Ahmed Bey and his followers were offered positions on the Albanian Civil Administrative Council, the Austrian occupation regime which had been formed at Shkodër with Auguste Kral, the former Austro-Hungarian consul, as president.[31]

The provisional government had little choice but to heed the wishes of the Austro-Hungarians. Aqif Elbasani resigned on April 14 and advised his officials to carry out their duties in conjunction with the instructions received from Vienna. Ahmed too decided that he would have to at least nominally cooperate with the Austrians. Through the efforts of their agent Prince Ludwig Windischgrätz, the Austrians convinced Ahmed Bey to recruit and command Albanian volunteers for action against the Italians, in exchange for 50,000 levas and the rank of colonel in the Austro-Hungarian army.[32]

Zogolli was not very successful in this endeavor and indeed the Austrians probably did not really expect him to be. They were hoping merely to keep him busy. His commission was of course little more than a sophisticated device to ensure that he did not join the Allies.[33]

It was not long before the Austrians realized that Zogolli was attempting to beat them at their own game. While ostensibly recruiting troops, he was secretly engaged in negotiations with the Bulgarians in the hope of rekindling his military and administrative plans for an independent Albania. The Austro-Hungarians soon tired of Zogolli's machinations and finally decided that his presence has become prejudicial to their policy in Albania. Not wanting to simply arrest him for fear of repercussions among his followers, they invited him to Vienna to receive a decoration and to participate in a war council of some sort.[34] Once in Vienna, Zogolli was received as an ally, generously decorated and then simply informed that he was going to remain as a guest of the government. Zogolli's forays into the arena of international events resulting from World War I had come to an end. He was to spend the rest of the war in Vienna.

This enforced stay proved to be quite important for Zogolli in a number of respects. First it gave him a chance to become acquainted with Western society and culture. As a dashing, young, rather mysterious, colonel from the remote mountains of Albania with a considerable amount of money, Zogolli made the rounds of Viennese social events and gaming establishments. Vienna dazzled Zogolli; he had never before seen a European capital. The sophistication of the city and the opulence of the coronation of Karl, which Ahmed Bey witnessed, impressed him.

He was apparently very popular with the ladies who admired his uniform and his generally dapper appearance, including his bright red hair and highly waxed moustache.[35] Ahmed Bey spent a good deal of his time in more worthwhile pursuits as well. His stay in Vienna provided him with a chance to learn German and eventually led him to become something of a language enthusiast.

Undoubtedly the most important result of his two years in Vienna was the opportunity to study Western politics. Up to this point his political experience and training was limited to Oriental Ottoman politics, tempered by Young Turk modernization and tribal intrigue. In Austria, Zogolli was able to add Western constitutionalism to his collection of political doctrines. He learned a certain respect for outward constitutionality as well as a healthy regard for the matter of form in politics. Zogolli's time in Vienna contributed substantially to the political duality of Western constitutionalism combined with Oriental despotism with which he would operate in the future.

He now possessed everything he needed to reenter the battle for Albanian political dominance. Apart from his political duality, he commanded a natural intelligence and an intimate knowledge of his people. He was quiet and dignified and held himself in complete control in all circumstances. When political danger appeared, however, he became passionately jealous of potential rivals. He would nevertheless conceal his feelings beneath a feline gentleness of manners until he could strike.

He was generally aware of his limitations, as evidenced by the circumspection he had shown during the Balkan Wars. If he considered the risks too great and the rewards too small, he would simply withdraw to gather his strength for another occasion. Despite his frequent tactical retreats in the early days, he maintained a reputation for personal dash and fearlessness.

He had an uncanny talent for summing up and playing upon the foibles of the Albanians around him. He possessed a flair for intrigue and for making others serve him, enabling him to utilize in his own interest, forces which would never have aided him, had they been conscious they were doing so.[36]

His outstanding quality and the force that drove him onward, as with his unfortunate uncle, was a relentless ambition ably seconded by an instinctive esprit de suite which determined the tortuous but logical deviations necessitated by his steady opportunism. This lack of concern for political scruples had already found him fighting for and against the Serbs, Turks, Austro-Hungarians, Prince Wied and his uncle. Only with the Italians had he been consistent; he had never fought for them. Consistency, however, was not required at this point. Military experience was, and in this regard, it was not without reason that the Austro-Hungarians had gone out of their way to insure Zogolli's removal from the field.

Ahmed Bey of course was equally well endowed with disadvantages. His rather limited education and lack of knowledge concerning the world outside the Balkans produced a certain childishness which was apparent in his vanity and in his confidences and his suspicions. This crucial lack might also be considered at least partially responsible for his inability to coordinate and delegate his work, as well as for his susceptibility to needless alarms.

His most serious fault and the one which would cause him the greatest difficulty was his inability to judge his subordinates and his unwillingness to jetison loyal supporters even when they proved to be harmful to the furtherance of his career. This unfortunate weakness might well have been brought on by his habit of shrinking from unpleasant truths. In his personal intercourse with people, Zogolli had a sincere desire to please, which led him sometimes to preach a magnanimous doctrine which he was not always able or willing to apply in practice.[37]

Zogolli, then, as he prepared to reenter Albanian political life might be described as the quintessential Albanian, imbued with many of the advantages and faults which characterized Albania after World War I. Arbitrary and self-assured, lacking many of the attributes which Western Europeans would consider necessary for statesmanship, Zogolli was nevertheless endowed with many of the proper qualities required for success under the unique situation presented by Albania in 1919.[38] Time, circumstances and sheer luck naturally played a significant role in Zogolli's political career, as they do in the rise of any politician. But unless one is able to effectively take advantage of the opportunities presented, all of these considerations are of little value.

CHAPTER TWO

THE STRUGGLE FOR POWER:
THE MAKING OF A PRIME MINISTER

The Albanian genius for combination appears to lie in uniting for sudden hostilities rather than for a common effort to develop the country along peaceful lines. This was demonstrated first by the movement to prevent the dismemberment of Albanian territory following the Balkan Crisis of 1875-1878, then by the insurrection which eventually led to the proclamation of independence and again immediately after the war.

When Zogolli returned to Albania in 1919, the country was occupied by the British, Italians and French in Shkodër, the Serbs in the east, and the French and the Greeks in the south. The Italians, who in 1917 unilaterally had declared a protectorate over a united Albania, occupied the rest of the country. Albanian xenophobia not having diminished as a result of the war, there was a considerable amount of agitation to have these occupation forces removed.

A provisional government had been set up in Durrës in 1918 under the auspices of the Italian government by M. Frasheri, but it commanded little respect because it was essentially controlled by the Italians. In exchange for their sponsorship, Rome received a series of valuable oil and asphalt concessions.[1] Nevertheless, the government was not recognized by any of the other powers because the Italians controlled the flow of information to and from Durrës and decided to keep Europe in the dark about its existence, as well as keep the provisional government completely isolated from events outside of Albania.

Recognizing that the provisional government was little more than a puppet, a group of Albanian leaders decided to convene a congress at Lushnjë to organize a temporary government to deal with the threat posed by foreign troops on Albanian soil. The congress, dominated by Ahmed Bey, Aqif Pasha of Elbasan and Eshref Frasheri, met in late January under the presidency of Syleman Bey Delvina and by the beginning of February had adopted the Lushnjë Statutes. The Statutes declared the principality in abeyance and constructed a High Council of Regency composed of one member from each of Albania's four religious communities, one Bektashi, one Sunni, one Catholic and one Orthodox.

These provisions resulted from the conviction that the Prince had hopelessly compromised himself by fighting in the German army during the war. It was believed that as a result many of the powers would object to his return. The Congress also realized that the expenses of the court were beyond Albania's capabilities. The most telling arguments against Wied's return revolved around the primary aim of the Congress. The gathering hoped to establish some kind of unity to deal with a specific problem, and the Prince, if he returned, would again become the powerless axis of unlimited intrigue.[2]

The Congress set up a single Chamber of seventy-nine deputies to be elected by a unique electoral system which, although it might have seemed democratic, left the power in the hands of the few leaders who had organized the system. Voting was conducted on the electoral college principle, every 200 males, 90 percent of whom were illiterate, chose one representative; fifty such representatives in turn voted for the candidates on the lists furnished from above; voters in both categories blindly following orders given to them. As an example, in the first election in Shkodër, one of the most enlightened centers in Albania, the entire list of Catholic nominees agreed upon by the party leaders was changed at the last moment; this proved no obstacle to the election in toto of the fresh list submitted at the eleventh hour.

The entire Chamber, then, consisted of the nominees of the leaders of the Congress who could count on the perfect obedience of the deputies without having to be concerned that the latter would ever contemplate consulting their constituents before following their instructions.[3]

After the first parliamentary election in March, a cabinet was formed consisting of Syleman Bey Delvina, a rather weak inoffensive man as Prime Minister, and Ahmed Bey as Minister of the Interior. As one of the most powerful leaders in Albania and the most active element at the Congress, Zogolli was the logical choice for the number two spot in the cabinet.[4] His tribe had been responsible for the protection of the Congress throughout its deliberations and with the provisional capital in Tirana, close to Mati, his tribe could be relied upon to protect the new government.

Having forced the provisional government in Durrës to resign following a series of intrigues, including the murder of a member of the Congress, the new Tirana government turned to its primary function, the dispersal of foreign troops on Albanian soil. The government had at its disposal a meager force consisting of eight battalions of gendarmerie (total 3,200 men), three battalions of infantry (total 1,200 men) and one battalion of engineers (total 600 men), who were commanded by Italian, French, Austro-Hungarian and Turkish officers. Supplementing this small force were the tribes controlled by the Minister of the Interior.

Zogolli moved immediately, replacing the prefects appointed by the Durrës government with men answerable directly to him. His first military move was to rapidly occupy Shkodër along with the Minister of Justice, Hoxha Kadri, after the inter-allied occupation of that city ended in March 1920, with the departure of General de Fouton. The Serbs apparently had planned to occupy the city but were forestalled by the quick action of Zogolli.[5] The Minister of the Interior impressed his colleagues, who rewarded him with the title of Governor of Shkodër. Shortly thereafter, the government successfully settled part of the southern problem by signing a temporary protocol with Greece calling for the status quo and postponing the Epirus question until another time.

Much to the annoyance of the government, Esad Pasha chose this time to make another bid for power in Albania, since the collected delegates of the Great Powers seemed disinclined to pay any attention to him in Paris. His primary agent in Albania, the band leader Osman Bali, successfully recruited a considerable force and was able to occupy a rather strong position around the capital. Zogolli suggested that the government treat with Esad while it built up its own forces. An agreement was signed with the rebels, and a delegation was sent to Paris to find out what Esad had in mind.

Under the agreement, most of the insurgents were convinced to disperse. Those who refused were forcibly removed by troops under the leadership of Bajram Curri, under the orders of Zogolli who gained further prestige as a result of this episode.[6] The long-range problem was effectively solved by Esad's assassination in front of the Hotel Continental in Paris on June 13, 1920. This rather opportune death was laid at Zogolli's door, but the fact that Ahmed would later have serious trouble with the assassin, Avni Rystem, tends to belie this conclusion.

The major problem, of course, remained, for the Italians were still in control of most of the country. Despite their military superiority, their position was actually rather tenuous. The government in Rome was faced with opposition not only from the Albanians but from its own people as well. To further compound matters, Italian policymakers began making a series of errors in judgement. Attempts to prohibit the Lushnjë Congress in favor of the puppet government in Durrës brought the Italians considerable discredit. In a last desperate effort to influence matters in Albania, Italy financed Esad Pasha's abortive attempt to overthrow the Tirana government.

Time was running out for the Italians. Not only were they faced with demoralized troops who were becoming easy prey for leftist agitators, but strong protests from the large Albanian colony in Italy caused the government considerable difficulty. The uncompromising attitude of President Wilson, who refused to support any Italian move in Albania, added to these difficulties. Finally, the Albanians themselves were becoming extremely hostile and were beginning to move against Italian troops. In May the Italians were dislodged from the fortress at Tepelenë after being attacked by Albanian irregulars.[7]

Although the Tirana government did not instigate these movements, they strongly supported them once they had begun. Under the circumstances, the Italian High Command felt it best to withdraw all of its troops to Vlorë, which it hoped to retain because of the strategic importance which the city possessed in relation to the Adriatic.

The Albanian government was not satisfied and requested that the Italians continue their evacuation while Albanian irregulars, under the orders of Zogolli, took up positions surrounding the city. The Italian commander, General Pracentini, with 15,000 troops and 200 guns at his disposal refused, and fighting ensued.[8] Before long, much to the chagrin of the Italians, the citizens of Vlorë joined in the fight against the occupation forces.

The Italian government immediately complained to Tirana. Hoping that a compromise might still be reached, the Albanian government disclaimed responsibility for the guerrillas attacking Vlorë, adding that since it did not have control of the administration in that region, it could not be held responsible for what occurred in that area. The government asked to be given control over the administration in exchange for insuring order. At the same time, Tirana was aiding the insurgents with what meagre supplies and equipment were available. The Italians ignored these suggestions and continued to resist strenuously. With Albanian forces now numbering over 10,000, a stalemate was reached.[9]

Under normal circumstances, the Italian military could have held out against the Albanians almost indefinitely, but internal Italian affairs finally decided the situation in favor of the Albanians. While the Italian Prime Minister, G. Giolitti, would have preferred to retain Vlorë, condition which had forced the Italians to withdraw initially had worsened considerably. The Italian troops in Vlorë were ridden with malaria and were becoming even more susceptible to Communist agitation. Leftist organized railway and dock strikes prevented the government from resupplying Albania. Finally, soldiers refused to board troopships at Bari and Brindisi.

The Italian Minister of War answered urgent pleas for reinforcements with the confession that, "Internal conditions of country (Italy) do not permit sending of troops to Albania. Attempt to do so would provoke general strikes, popular demonstrations gravely injurious to solidarity of Army, which must not be exposed to such hard tests."[10]

Giolitti was left with no alternative but to negotiate, sending Baron Aliotti, who had been the Italian representative to Prince William. The Baron was not well received, however, because of the extensive intrigue of which he had been one of the focal points during the reign of Wied. The Italian terms, which included the permanent occupation of points commanding Vlorë Bay, were also unacceptable. The fighting was renewed and continued until Giolitti and his Foreign Minister Count Sforza decided to back down. Sforza sent a new negotiator, Count Manzoni, to Tirana with new terms which the Albanian government eventually accepted in August, 1920.

In exchange for the Island of Sazan and the temporary occupation of points commanding the Bey from the land, Italy agreed to evacuate Vlorë and renounce the 1917 self-proclaimed protectorate. The Italians also extended the new government official recognition within the frontiers delineated in 1913 by the Conference of Ambassadors and encouraged other nations to do the same.[11]

Sforza reasoned that:

> What else could we have done? Incur the enormous expense of an expedition altogether out of proportion to the problematic benefits to be derived from it? By so doing we should also, in all probability, have been playing the game of other people, and we should have seen the Albanians going off to throw themselves into the arms of their neighbors on the north and south. The necessity for military occupation having come to an end with the war, we will not and can not pursue towards the Albanians any policy but one of friendship.[12]

Not all Italians agreed with Sforza's view of the situation, however. Benito Mussolini, writing in the *Popolo d'Italia* on August 5, 1920, commented:

> Valona was to be the recompense for Italy's suffering and blood which she shed. Valona was to be the threshold of our pacific penetration into the Balkans. We admit that, from the strategic standpoint, the possession of Sasseno makes up for the loss of Valona. . . . But all this does not attentuate the extent of the Albanian catastrophe which is essentially of a political and moral character . . . . The real facts of the case will appear to the peoples of the Balkans and to others in this schematic but true aspect: A few thousand Albanian rebels have thrown a Big Power like Italy overboard.[13]

Mussolini's assessment here was basically correct. Italian prestige suffered considerably while the prestige of the Albanian government and that of Zogolli in particular had risen precipitously. The Albanians congratulated themselves on having defeated a major European nation. This myth created a false sense of strength which would eventually do considerable harm in dealings with Italy in the following decades. Zogolli did nothing to dispel this false impression, realizing that a reputation for military invincibility would be of considerable use in the advancement of his career.

With every success Zogolli became more powerful, more determined and somewhat more ruthless. He preferred to be feared, arguing that great men and active politicians are never loved or respected because of the power they wield. Zogolli was determined to strike fear into his opponents by calculated acts of violence.

During the 1920 campaigns one Mon Pitza, a well-known band leader who held an important post in the mountain line of defense, appalled at the Albanian inferiority in numbers, returned hurriedly to Tirana and explained to the Prime Minister in the presence of Zogolli, the reasons which rendered further resistance futile. Zogolli congratulated Pitza on his military acumen and invited him to discuss matters further at his office.

Pitza, elated, walked unsuspecting into Ahmed's office to find himself covered by two revolvers; he was placed under arrest, a Court Martial was instantly summoned, within half an hour he was condemned to death for desertion. An hour later placards in Tirana invited the population to witness his execution. This event and its silent rapidity awed the people considerably. Zogolli's open preference for "suppression" to imprisonment added to his fearsome reputation.[14]

At the beginning of August, Zogolli confidently hurled his motley armies against the forces of the newly created Serb-Croat-Slovene state. Yugoslav units had been allowed, by General Franchet d'Espey, to advance to a strategic line inside the 1913 frontiers, pending the decision of the Conference of Ambassadors which had reconvened to review its work.

Zogolli's troops, supported by his tribes of Mati and Dibra, were initially successful, forcing the Yugoslavs to retreat beyond the 1913 line. The Yugoslav forces quickly recovered, however, pushing the Albanians back beyond their original positions, burning Zogolli's castle during their advance. Zogolli's overconfidence had gotten the better of him, so he resorted to intrigue and diplomacy, opening negotiations with the Yugoslavs while at the same time advising the government to address urgent notes to the powers.

Both tactics were basically successful. Italy and Great Britain asked the Yugoslavs to halt their advance since the question of the Albanian boundaries had not yet been decided. In direct negotiation Zogolli used his personal and family connections in Belgrade to assure the Yugoslavs that he would personally work against Kosovo irredentism in exchange for a secession of hostilities. By this politically realistic and extremely politik move, Zogolli was able to defuse the Yugoslav situation.[15]

The Yugoslav Foreign Minister, M. Trumbic, agreed to bow to the will of the powers, at least for the time being. Delicate negotiations for the conclusion of the Treaty of Rapallo were in progress, and Belgrade was having some difficulties with the Albanians already inside its borders.

Fearing further difficulties and being aware of the necessity of recognition, the Albanian government applied for admission to the newly formed League of Nations. Pandeli Evangjeli who had been sent by the government to represent Albania at the Peace of Paris but had not been heard, addressed a formal request for admission to the League. In his request he argued that Albania had been declared an independent state by the Conference of Ambassadors and that this declaration had never been rescinded. Evangjeli further argued that although the work of consolidating its independence had been interrupted by the war, Albania was now ready to assume that task.

There was considerable opposition to the admission of Albania coming mainly from the Greeks and the Yugoslavs. Their representatives argued that a postponement should be approved because of the unsettled frontiers, the questionable stability of the government and finally because the government had not been widely recognized.

Despite these arguments, Albania was finally admitted as a full member in December, 1920, due largely to the South African delegate, Lord Robert Cecil, who argued that the existence of the state was obvious and that it clearly desired to fulfill its international obligations.[16] Albania's admission brought rapid international recognition for the new government.

Although Albania's general condition was by no means stable, the immediate crisis was over and the Albanian leadership was left in a state of relative peace which could presumably have been used to put the country on a tranquil course towards modern development. Nothing of the kind occurred; with the foreign threat gone, the Albanians were left alone to resume quarrelling among themselves.

The new political system contained no provisions for the arbitration of old tribal animosities. In fact, the new situation complicated matters further. The makeshift democratic government which had been organized at the Congress of Lushnjë was basically temporary, and it soon began to show its limitations. Because of its rather weak construction, the same old tribal warfare started up again, only this time under a superficial veil of parliamentary democracy. Ironically, in many cases the quarreling began as a direct result of playing to the fiction of Western political institutions.

The reality of politics in these early years immediately after the war came down to what it had always been, individual personalities and raw power based ultimately on the number of guns a leader could muster. The followers of any particular chief remained with him because of who he was, not because of the policies he pursued, and the power which the leader wielded depended not on votes but on rifles. During this initial period the various chiefs paid homage to Western ideals of democracy by observing the parliamentary methods of opposition, but only as long as success by these means was anticipated. As soon as this was no longer the case, violence was readily used.

The game commenced as soon as the foreigners were gone. Syleman Bey Delvina's government fell almost immediately after the Yugoslavs had been persuaded to halt their advance. His resignation on November 20, 1920, was due ostensibly to quarrels among the ministers, but it was most likely engineered by Zogolli who hoped to make his move in the ensuing crisis.[17]

Delvina's government has generally been credited with a number of successes including the raising of a domestic national loan of two million gold francs in order to raise an army, organize a gendarmerie and create a civil service. Although these officials lacked efficiency, a start had to at least been made.

The government also was able to begin a system of education where none had existed in the past. Over 500 elementary schools were established and efforts were underway for the development of schools at more advanced levels.[18] Possibly the most significant achievement of Albania's first postwar government was its successful handling, due primarily to Zogolli, of internal insurrection and the foreign threat.

Zogolli had perhaps been somewhat too successful. He had frightened the Regents enough to appoint Iljas Bey Vrioni as the next Prime Minister. Vrioni came from a prominent landowning family and his government consisted primarily of the Beys who controlled the Christian and Moslem peasantry in the western and central plains as well as people who became known as bureaucratic Beys who had served in one capacity or another in the Ottoman administration or the army.[19]

With the proclamation of independence, they had hurried back to Albania hoping to take advantage of the primitive political conditions. They came to power with Vrioni primarily because they were the only people in Albania with any concept of administration, even though it was of the wasteful and inefficient Turkish variety.

Politically they were interested in maintaining the status quo and feudal land tenure. They were violently opposed to any attempt at social, political or economic reform, particularly agrarian reform, but then no one in a position of power would have actively supported such a program at that time. They were primarily interested in keeping others out of power and in this they were considerably successful. Zogolli was kept out of office for ten months. Vrioni and his coalition were ultimately doomed to failure however, since the government lacked significant tribal support.

Zogolli was, of course, not idle, using his influence to create one of Albania's first political parties. During the Vrioni administration, two such organizations came into being, the Progressive Party and the Popular Party. They could not be considered political parties in the Western sense, however, since both presented identical vague programs supporting reform, education and the material development of the country. Initially they could not even be told apart by the type of member, being that elements of all facets of Albanian life could be found in both. Support for one or the other was based once again on personalities.

As they began to develop, however, the Progressive Party, dominated by Shevket Verlaci, the richest landowner in the country who was allied for the time being with the Prime Minister, became known as the Bey's party. The Popular Party, which included Zogolli and Bishop Fan Noli whose Orthodox deputies had initially supported the Progressives, developed a more Western orientation. Members continued to shift back and forth, however, depending on the personalities each party could attract.[20]

Almost as soon as the parties were formed, Zogolli became dissatisfied with is position in the Popular Party and decided to search for other means to reach his goal of political power. He found such a vehicle in the "clique," a secret society very similar to the Turkish Committee of Union and Progress, formed well before 1914. Although it is difficult to determine who was involved in this group at any given time since there did not seem to be any particular criteria for membership and since the kaleidoscopic combinations, unions and disintegrations are rather difficult to follow, it is clear that the clique, when Zogolli gained control of it in 1920, included members of the intellectual classes of southern Albanian reinforced by such prominent Kosovo chieftains as Bajram Curri and Hasan Prishtina.[21]

The original purpose of the organization was to suppress Christian groups and the old tribal system and its laws. Its goals, like its membership, however, were extremely flexible. Because Zogolli would eventually use it to oppose Vrioni's government of landowning and bureaucratic Beys, the organization acquired an anti-Turkish complexion.[22] Not surprisingly, however, the clique generally included members of groups and organizations which it supposedly aimed to destroy, in this case, ex-Ottoman officials and Beys like Zogolli himself.

In the final analysis, this nebulous group was basically opposed to those in power, whoever they happened to be, and its primary aim was the acquisition of power and wealth for its own members by any means available.[23] Zogolli and the clique consumated their marriage of convenience and hoped to use one another temporarily.

One of Albania's significant minorities which remained aloof from all of these political machinations was the Catholic population in the north. Although they leaned somewhat naturally towards the Popular Party, they refused to join because they feared the increasing power of Zogolli.[24] Their abstention created a dangerous situation because by the rules of the new political game, if one saw no hope of gaining power through the workings of the parliamentary opposition, one was left with only one alternative. Mark Gjonmarkaj and his Mirditë tribe decided to make a bid for power and took to the field in July, 1921.

Mark had successfully convinced his followers that the predominantly Moslem government was on the verge of launching repressive measures against Christians. The government, of course, had planned nothing of the sort being at the time hard pressed simply to survive the internal quarrels and the pressure from outside forces.

Gjonmarkaj took the opportunity to proclaim the establishment of the Mirditë Republic. As he was illiterate and probably had no concept of what a republic was and because he spend considerable time in Prizren just before the declaration, the action has been laid, not altogether unreasonably, at Belgrade's door. With the support of Belgrade, units of General Wrangel's refugee army and some ex-supporters of Esad Pasha, Mark opened operations against Albania. With the addition of his 2,000 tribesmen, Mark controlled a formidable force.

The government was at a loss as to how to proceed. Zogolli, in an unofficial capacity, suggested two options: either send a commission to treat with the Mirditë or send a force of at least 8,000 men to crush them. At first the government decided to send a commission but then went back on its decision and sent some 1,200 men, not enough to effectively deal with the situation.

Nevertheless, at first all went well and Orosh, the capital of Mirdita, was captured, and Mark fled to Yugoslavia. Shortly thereafter, a certain Halil Leshi, a renegade in Yugoslav pay, pushed across the Drin with a large force made up, it was alleged, partially of Yugoslav regular troops disguised as irregulars. While the Albanian commander was able to drive him back, he was forced to leave only a small garrison at Orosh which quickly fell to the Mirditë. In the process of dislodging these tribesmen, the Albanians were fired upon by artillery supported by Yugoslav troops.25

The Albanians succeeded in driving the insurgents and the Yugoslavs back once, but in September Orosh and the surrounding area was overrun. The Yugoslavs and their allies remained in possession of this territory until November when they withdrew once again under international pressure. Having lost their main base of support, the Mirditë were eventually forced to come to terms with the government.

The already hard pressed Vrioni regime was weakened by the Mirdite crisis with much of the blame falling on Selaheddin Bey Shkoza, the Minister of War. Selaheddin Bey was accused of botching the military operations as well as harboring Kemalist sympathies. It was also rumored that he had conspired to bring 120 officers from Turkey to fill the highest posts in the militia. Parliament had turned against him and the cabinet would not give him up.

The situation deteriorated to the point where the government commanded about as little influence as Wied had been able to muster. Albania had essentially reverted back to what it had been before the war; brigandage was again rampant and tribesmen again invaded the fertile valleys of Macedonia.26 Although Iljas Bey was an honest man, a patriot and even something of a liberal, his weakness of character and inability to make decisions had created an intolerable situation. Zogolli did not wait long to take advantage of the chaos and drew up plans to overthrow Vrioni.

As the young Mati chieftain moved to consolidate his support within the clique, a point of serious contention arose which eventually split the organization. The problem was Kosovo. Zogolli and many of the southern leaders including Eshref Frasheri believed that Albania should first establish itself as a viable state before pursuing irredentism. Many of the Orthodox southern leaders also feared the massive influx of Moslems. These leaders preferred to put the question off with the hope that it would be forgotten entirely.

The Kosovo chieftains in the group, Curri and Prishtina, naturally took exception to this position. These people had been fighting all their lives and even though the prospects seemed dim, they felt they could not abandon their fellow countrymen. They did not overlook the fact that if somehow they were able to succeed, their own positions in Albania would be immeasurably strengthened.

These leaders hoped that by direct or indirect association with the chain of intrigue continually being carried out against the Yugoslavs, they might succeed in regaining Kosovo at an early date. In pursuance of this policy, they disassociated themselves from Zogolli's attempt to overthrow Vrioni and aligned themselves with those forces, primarily the northern Catholics under Gurakuqi, who were being financially supported by Italy.[28] The break came as no surprise, what was more surprising was that Zogolli had been able to hold the various unruly elements of the clique together as long as he had.

Undaunted by this setback, Zogolli and his truncated clique decided to attempt to overthrow Vrioni regardless. It soon became clear, however, that he could not do so alone. Zogolli thereupon allied himself with another coalition known as the "Sacred Union" which had formed in order to oppose Vrioni. This new group was made up of elements which had remained out of the clique and even included some of the Kosovo chieftains who had recently withdrawn from the clique. Basically, everyone, except for those who belonged to the Bey's party, participated in this shaky coalition.

Vrioni, who had attempted to hang on to his position by rearranging his government, quickly fell as a result of pressure from this new group. The question of who was to succeed him caused considerable difficulty. Zogolli had hoped to dominate the group but found his opposition led by the Regent Aqif Pasha and Hasan Prishtina to be too strong. A compromise, hardly foreseen in the Statutes of Lushnje, was finally agreed upon.

Pandeli Evangjeli, the weak but honest Albanian representative to the Paris Peace Conference, formed a cabinet chosen by three agreed upon arbitrators who apportioned the ministerial posts equally between the two groups. The three, Bajram Curri, an opponent to Zogolli, Kazim Bey Koutzouli, the Prefect of Tirana and Avni Rystem, the assassin of Esad Pasha, accordingly constructed a cabinet with Zogolli as Minister of War.[29]

The unorthodox compromise initially worked quite well for Zogolli who, much to the regret of Aqif Pasha, took command of an expeditionary force to go and treat with the Mirditë concerning the still unresolved Mirditë Republic question. The Regent was particularly concerned since Zogolli had for some time been attempting to gain the support of the Mirditë for his own cause. Given the circumstances created by the Evangjeli cabinet, with Zogolli in a position of considerable power, Aqif was afraid that since Zogolli now had more to offer, the Mirditë would join with him. This would have left Aqif in an extremely disadvantageous position. While he had widespread influence, he could muster no more than 1,000 men.

Aqif's problems were further complicated when his supporters in the cabinet resigned. He refused to allow Pandeli to fill the vacant ministries unless he first approve the choice, again in complete violation of the statutes. Since Evangjeli was unable to replace the ministers, he had to rely more heavily on Zogolli, who, by December 5, was the only remaining cabinet minister.

Aqif Pasha decided on a coup, a rather unfortunate move which led to an entire series of coups. He hoped to immediately convoke a Constituent Assembly and then choose a sovereign. Aqif managed to convince one of the other Regents, Mgr. Bumci, a northern Catholic bishop, to join him in demanding the resignation of the Prime Minister.[30] Aqif Pasha explained that this move had become necessary because Evangjeli had lost the confidence of the people. On being asked how he had discovered this since the Chamber was not sitting, Aqif explained that as the Regents had originally been appointed at the wish of the people to represent the absent sovereign, they therefore were in point of fact themselves the people and consequently fully entitled to act without reference back to anyone.[31]

Evangjeli, who was not at all convinced by Aqif's rather curious conception of representative democracy, refused to resign, reminding the Regent that he was acting completely unconstitutionally. At this point, Aqif decided to dispense with formalities and on the night of December 11 sent a body of armed men to Evangjeli's bedroom at the Hotel International. They surrounded the bed, awakened him with the muzzles of their guns and demanded his resignation. Evangjeli obliged and subsequently left Tirana immediately on horseback.[32]

Although Evangjeli was gone, Aqif Pasha's troubles were by no means over. On December 7 he chose Kazim Bey Koutzouli as the next chief actor somewhat haphazardly without determining the strength of his support. Kazim Bey accepted the task and became Prime Minister but found it impossible to form a cabinet since those he approached felt that the entire project was doomed to failure. Aqif had dismissed Evangjeli in a coup and now found that he was having difficulties replacing him. Grudgingly and despite himself, he turned to Hasan Bey Prishtina.

Prishtina's appointment created an even more volatile situation. Not only was he a rabid Kosovo irredentist with violent pro-Italian and anti-Yugoslav sentiments, but since the breakup of the clique, he had become violently anti-Zogolli. Prishtina announced that a dangerous secret society existed in Albania which sought to ruin the country and that it must be stopped.[33] That he had until recently been a member of this dangerous secret society was not mentioned. Living up to his reputation of being reckless and daring, Prishtina immediately proceeded to take steps against the clique. He gave orders for a series of arrests and replaced Zogolli with Bajram Curri.

Zogolli in the meantime had enjoyed a good deal of success dealing with the Mirditë. He convinced the sub-leaders of the tribe that Mark was acting as a Yugoslav agent and that their loyalty should remain with Albania. He was joined, on November 19, by a League of Nations Commission of Inquiry which basically came to the same conclusion regarding Gjonmarkaj. On November 28 Zogolli had been authorized to extend a general amnesty to those who had taken part in the abortive Mirditë Republic. The sub-leaders, accepting Zogolli's word of honor, agreed to this amnesty and made their submission to the government.[34]

Hasan Prishtina's coup jeopardized Zogolli's work among the Mirditë since it diminished their faith in Tirana's promises. Zogolli and his supporters moved quickly to remedy the situation. Even before they had received specific orders from Zogolli, numerous officers, members of the clique, fled Tirana with several thousand troops to organize armed resistance in the provinces.

Zogolli's supporters within the capital, by arguing that Evangjeli had been illegally and forcibly removed and that Hasan Bey and his entirely Geg or northern cabinet were in the pay of the Italians, were able to stir up widespread opposition to the new government. While steps were taken to call together opposition deputies to form a Constitutional Parliament in some southern city, demonstrations, protests and strikes effectively shut down Hasan's two day old government.[35]

Before Hasan could even react to this crisis, he was faced with Zogolli and several thousand followers marching on Tirana. By dint of forced marches, he and his army of government troops, Mati tribesmen and as Aqif Pasha had feared, Mirditë tribesmen, had been able to reach the capital in four days. Hasan pinned his hopes on Bajram Curri who with 500 government troops had been instructed to guard the Yugoslav frontiers. Curri, a patriot who was always more ready to fight external rather than internal foes, informed Hasan that he could not leave the frontiers. Had Curri supported Hasan, many others would have followed because of his prestige, but once he decided to abstain, Hasan's cause was lost. Realizing this, the Kosovo chieftain was left with no alternative but to quit Tirana and did so twenty-four hours before Zogolli arrived. Once again it became clear that retention of power ultimately belonged to whoever could command superior armed forces.

Following Hasan's departure, an inoffensive Christian commission agent from Durrës was installed as interim Prime Minister by one of the Regents. The new Prime Minister sent three successive messengers to Zogolli begging him to enter the city alone since all was quiet. Zogolli was unwilling to relinquish this opportunity to play the savior of the fatherland, so he refused to treat with the new government and following ancient precedent, ordered the messengers to follow on in his troop.

On December 12, Zogolli and his army entered Tirana unopposed. For a few days Zogolli reigned as virtual dictator, issuing proclamations to the people and substituting his own men for the government gendarmerie who were temporarily imprisoned against the mild protests of the tactful interm Prime Minister. After laying plans for the reconstitution of the government along his own lines, Zogolli gradually allowed the existing authorities to resume their posts.[36]

Once in control of the immediate situation, Zogolli moved to legally devest his already vanquished opponents of any status they might have had. The elections from the river Drin district, which included those of

Hasan Bey and his followers were annulled. The remaining members of Parliament were recalled, and the clique, through the votes of the Popular Party, then set about carrying through a series of so-called "national measures."

Zogolli and his followers illegally called on Aqif Pasha and Mgr. Bumci to abdicate from the Regency which the two prudently agreed to do. This resulted in the resignation of the other two Regents who protested the dismissal of their colleagues. Their resignations were accepted by Zogolli who took the opportunity to appoint four of his minions to the vacant posts.

Their first action was to accept a law which the Chamber had passed setting up a High Court with retroactive powers to judge any minister or deputy acting against the Statutes of Lushnjë. The Court consisted of six persons, five appointed by the Regents and one by parliament. The Court dutifully impeached the ministries of Evangjeli, Koutsoulis and Prishtina, the first for not using force, the third for using force and the second for having taken advantage of an illegal situation. The ex-Regents were not impeached because it was decided that they were irresponsible before the law.[37]

On top of the first illegality committed by Aqif Pasha when he refused to sign the decrees for the ministers presented to him by Evangjeli, then, so many subsequent abuses of the Statutes followed including many committed by Zogolli, that a veritable legal embroglio had been created. This fact did not really disturb anyone, however, since it was clear that Zogolli and the government he constructed held office by virtue of the physical force which had been exercised to obtain it. It was equally clear that Zogolli's opponents, who had fled to the hills with their supporters, would attempt to overthrow him as soon as they felt they were strong enough.

A new cabinet was elected on December 25 headed by Xhafer Bey Ypi, a member of the clique and basically a figurehead for Zogolli, who again became the Minister of the Interior, a post which emerged as the most powerful. The first act of the new government was to further postpone the calling of a Constituent Assembly, thereby delaying any decision on the question of sovereign power.

Realizing that he had many enemies waiting for an opportunity to do away with him, Zogolli moved immediately to stabilize his position by extending his influence to include groups that had hitherto been opposed to him. Since the Kosovo chieftains were irreconcilable and the Western educated intelligentsia still feared Zogolli as an unscrupulous uneducated mountaineer who hoped to establish Oriental despotism, Zogolli slowly turned to the feudal Beys and the remaining northern chieftains for support. His first move in this direction was to sign a marriage contract with Shevket Bey Verlaci who, although an elderly fop, was of considerable importance because of his wealth.[38]

With regard to the chieftains, Zogolli resorted to the time honored tradition of "peace-money," a method which had been used by Austria, Serbia and Montenegro to influence the clans. Since Zogolli himself had received payments and honors during the war, it was not long before he became a master of the tactic. Chieftains of major tribes were given the rank of colonel in the army and paid on a regular basis. Each month large groups of unreconstructed highlanders would descend upon the capital, weaponed to the teeth and collect their gold on warrants issued by the War Department. These payments appeared in the budget as Army Allowances since technically at least, the chiefs were being paid to maintain a certain number of irregular troops in reserve at the disposal of the government.[39]

In reality, of course, the chieftains were being paid simply to refrain from rising up against the government. In return for their gold, the tribal leaders declared recurrent besas which set aside blood feuds for a prescribed period of time. In addition, the chiefs took an oath to Zogolli personally, rather than to the country, a concept which was basically still foreign to them. Zogolli was recognized as an over-chieftain and they subsequently looked to him personally for their money.

This system had many disadvantages. Zogolli was often put in a position where he had to arbitrate between two opposing tribes. Whatever he did, he would invariably gain the emnity of one of the two parties. Although the system would eventually work, the situation in Albania in the spring of 1922 did not lend itself to control.

The Kosovo chieftains were so determined to move against Zogolli that they were perfectly willing to do so on their own without the support of the remaining northern tribes. Zogolli was, of course, quite aware of this and he initiated steps which he hoped would forestall the inevitable attack. Zogolli reasoned that the best way to do this was simply to disarm them.

Accordingly, the Minister of the Interior launched a program to disarm the population in general. Had he succeeded, he would have not only secured his own position but would have been able to reduce the endemic violence which continued to plague the country. It was a bold move with considerable risk. The importance of guns to the mountaineer cannot be overestimated since they represented his means of livelihood on the one hand and freedom and the only protection against personal and foreign enemies on the other. A rifle was part of a mountaineer's dress. His thoughts in the spring turned first to his rifle and then to his woman.

Zogolli's move, however, must be considered somewhat premature and certainly haphazard and arbitrary in its execution. Zogolli had hoped initially to be selective as to who was to be disarmed, allowing his tribe of Mati to keep their weapons while demanding that rival tribes, particularly the Kosovites, surrender theirs. Although the program was successful in the lowlands and the south where in a matter of months in excess of 35,000 weapons were collected, most of the northerners, in particular the irredentists, refused to participate. They rightly saw the move as an effort to suppress their liberties and feared that Zogolli was attempting to follow in the footsteps of Esad Pasha.[40] Rather than prevent a northern uprising, Zogolli's move convinced the irredentists to move even sooner.

At the end of February, Prishtina and a number of his followers, including Bajram Curri, Zia Dibra and Elez Jusuf, demanded the reconstruction of the Sacred Union government. Upon receiving no satisfaction from Zogolli, they resolved to overthrow him by force. Collecting a considerable army among those who felt that Zogolli's attempt to disarm them was motivated exclusively by sinister goals, Prishtina quickly arrived at the gates of Tirana and threatened the city from three sides.

Fearing the wrath of the mountaineers, the Prime Minister, most of the government and most of the deputies fled to Elbasan. Once safe, many of them, including Fan Noli, took the opportunity to resign, thereby disassociating themselves from Zogolli's policies. Tirana was defended by the Minister of the Interior and a few of his followers who had barricaded themselves up in the offices of the government. Street fighting ensued with Zogolli's forces being led by a certain Captain Osman Gazepi, nicknamed the terrible, who with his five gunbelts across his chest and his revolver and machinegun hailed his opponents with inflamed speeches and bullets.[41]

Zogolli's position seemed hopeless; as a last resort, he asked the newly appointed British Minister, Sir Harry Eyres, to attempt to dissuade the rebels from finishing off the government. Sir Harry, who most recent post had been British Consul in Constantinople, had considerable experience working with the Balkans. In a remarkable feat of diplomacy, he was able to convince Jusuf, whose men had occupied most of Tirana by this time, to withdraw. With the primary threat gone, Zogolli was able to quickly defeat the remaining rebel forces.

Eyres had saved not only the government but, more than likely, Zogolli's life as well. Although Zogolli rarely confided in anyone, as a result of Eyres' efforts on his behalf, Ahmed Bey elevated the British Minister to a position of personal advisor. Much to the displeasure of the other foreign legations, this honor was transferred, to a certain extent, to other British Ministers as well.

Zogolli gained a considerable amount of prestige from this eposide since heroics in the face of overwhelming odds are much valued by Albanian chieftains. Zogolli did not fail to capitalize on this stroke of good fortune by taking the opportunity to do away with many of his opponents by way of the military court set up to deal with the insurgents. In short order, thirty-two rebels were executed for their participation in the uprising. Zogolli's swift and rather ruthless methods did not go unnoticed by his opponents, many of whom fled abroad.

Zogolli's repression was not without its positive results. A certain amount of peace and tranquility was achieved. Although the situation was still extremely tenuous, for the first time in 500 years the government was obeyed in almost every section of the country.[42]

The Regency and the remainder of the government had been discredited by their behavior during the irredentist crisis. Nevertheless, Zogolli decided that it was in his interest to reconstitute the Ypi government. Since those elements which might conceivably have opposed Zogolli within the government had resigned, Zogolli hoped to completely dominate. Undoubtedly, the thought also occurred to him that every government since the war had fallen to a coup, and reconstituting the Ypi government might, therefore, establish an element of continuity. Not more than a few months passed before rumors of new problems emerged for Zogolli, however, primarily because the reconstituted cabinet was unable to effectively rule Albania.

With the exception of the Minister of the Interior, the government lacked talent. The Prime Minister, Ypi, who had also become Foreign

Minister after the resignation of Fan Noli, was a man of very limited intelligence who was overly suspicious and a bad judge of character. He was unable to hold his cabinet together and generally had no knowledge of what was going on in his ministries, nor did he really seem to care. He shied away from work and did not bother taking the time to discover the facts before he made a decision. Subsequently, his decisions were hasty, impulsive and invariably ill-directed. Zogolli or the British Minister frequently had to intervene to prevent some disastrous proceeding and they unfortunately were not always on time.

As Minister of Foreign Affairs, Ypi refused to write his own notes, allowing other ministers to add material of their own. As a result, the documents coming out of the Ministry were rather inept.[43] Although Zogolli had often stated that he knew nothing about foreign affairs, he was so frequently reminded of the incapacity of his colleagues that he insisted on being consulted before an important step was taken.

The other ministers were equally ill-suited for their particular positions. The Ministers of Finance and Justice were basically non-entities who achieved little or nothing in their departments. The Minister of War was completely ignorant of all matters except those relating to the military and therefore added nothing to the rather meagre collective wisdom of the cabinet.

Bishop Fan Noli, despite his well deserved reputation at the Conference of the League of Nations, was something of a disappointment as Foreign Minister, although he was by far one of the most intelligent people on the cabinet. That he sent in his final resignation from Rome was certainly not to his credit, nor was it to the credit of the government. Possibly the most indolent of all cabinet members was the Minister of Public Works who, with his equally idle clerks, literally produced no effect whatever.

A cabinet of this level of incompetence could exist only for so long. Rumors of unrest were rife and the government, with the exception of Zogolli, became unpopular among even the common people of the south, even though southerners made up most of the government.[44]

To forestall a crisis, Zogolli began eliminating the more incompetent members of the cabinet. Ypi was replaced as Foreign Minister by Evangjeli, a basically good administrator and an old supporter. This was not nearly enough, however, particularly since Zogolli's problems were being multiplied by severe economic difficulties and the machinations of neighboring states.

Expecting a collapse, Zogolli contemplated carrying on the government on a feudal basis by calling together the tribal chiefs and forming a government with their approval and assistance. Although fifty or sixty deputies called on Zogolli to take matters into his own hands, he remained reluctant to do so, fearing the effect such a move might have on Albania's already shaky image abroad. He also feared that one of the surrounding powers might use the opportunity to attack Albania.[45]

The leaders of the clique slowly saw their hold on the situation slipping. It was becoming more difficult to restrain northern and central Albania from rejecting a government and administration consisting so largely of men from the south. Despite their preponderance not only in the civil government but also in the army and gendarmerie, they could not hold on to power. By December they had ceased to even command the fear of the people, which they had so carefully nurtured through repression, terrorism and even torture.[46]

Although Zogolli was not convinced that his acceptance of the post of Prime Minister was in his best interest at that particular time, the corruption and incompetence of the Ypi government was on the verge of destroying his own influence. Some sort of change was required or a crisis would occur and it was generally agreed even by those who distrusted him that Zogolli was probably the only one who could hold the teetering structure of Albanian democracy together. On December 16, 1922, then, Zogolli replaced Ypi as Prime Minister, retaining the crucial position of Minister of the Interior. At the age of twenty-seven, Zogolli had atained the highest post his country had to offer.

Zogolli (who, as a token of his dedication to Westernization changed his name to Zogu, dropping the Turkish "olli" or "son of") had learned a great deal in these first two years of participation in Albanian national politics. He came to the realization that he was particularly well suited for Albanian politics, his political duality had stood him in good stead. His ability at intrigue was clearly superior, his military prowess in terms of strategy, but more importantly in terms of attracting followers, was unsurpassed. Indeed, Zogolli's early experiences in Albanian politics brought him to the inescapable conclusion that there were few people in Albania competent enough to play a role on the national scale.

Zogolli was determined to look elsewhere for competent men to help him stabilize the chaotic conditions which had plagued Albania since its premature declaration of independence. The new Prime Minister was left with little choice but to seek outside help, despite the inherent dangers of foreign rivalry and unwanted influence. The need for aid was particularly urgent. While the various tribal groups had clawed at one another from 1920 to 1922, serious problems had been obscured. Once the political dust had partially cleared as a result of Zogolli's efforts, these difficulties became much more visible.

CHAPTER THREE

POLITICAL INTRIGUE AND TRIBAL WARFARE

Zogu was able to hold on as Prime Minister for over a year. While by Western standards this might seem a rather insignificant claim, by Albanian standards it certainly was not, considering that from 1920 to 1922 Albania endured no less than seven heads of government. Although Zogu too, like all of his predecessors, would eventually fall to tribal warfare disguised by Western political garb, his administration was able to make modest strides towards national unity and the alleviation of Albania's appalling poverty and general lack of economic development, two of Albania's most pressing concerns.

Not only was Albania seriously disunified but the small state even lacked many of the necessary preconditions generally associated with unity, including advanced centralization, religious and linguistic unity, leadership of a self-conscious class, foreign intellectual stimulus and discontent with foreign rule.[1] Instead, a combination of indigenous Albanian circumstances and conscious Ottoman policy succeeded in burying any national sentiment until the late 19th century.

Racially and to some extent linguistically, the country was divided between the Tosks in the south and the Gegs in the north; there were three major religious groups including both Sunni and Bektashi Moslems, Catholics and Orthodox. Social and economic disunity was fostered by the coexistence of three conflicting stages of civilization, the mountain clains in the north, the feudal Beys in the south and the more educated and urbanized population of the Hellenic and Catholic fringes.[2]

41

Before the invasion of the Turks, the Albanians had been religiously split between Catholicism and Orthodoxy. During the Ottoman period approximately 70 percent of the population converted to Islam, generally out of material considerations rather than conviction since tax advantages were accorded followers of the Prophet. While most Albanians remained orthodox Sunni, Bektashism, an offshoot of the Shiite sect, soon made considerable inroads into central and southern Albania.

Bektashism is a peaceful and positive strain of Islam very unlike the reactionary and intolerant Sunni. Although the rank and file were outwardly indistinguishable from other Moslems, the Dervishes stand out by their costume, which includes tall rigid white felt hats, and by their behavior. Their mental and bodily functions were slowed down by opium, judiciously given out each morning by the abbot, and by copious quantities of native gin at night. The gentle, slightly bemused creature that resulted had little capacity for positive good or evil.[3]

The Catholics largely remained a compact minority in the north, led by an influential clergy, and extended their influence only as far as the Mirditë tribe. The remaining Catholics resided in and around Shkodër and they joined forces from time to time with the Orthodox Christians of the south who made up 10 percent of the population.[4]

Despite these extensive religious differences, the importance of this element should not be overestimated for the religious feeling was generally not strong. Unlike in other Balkan countries, religion was not identified with nationality. Many links more or less transcended the bounds of religion; the Catholic and Moslem mountaineers for example lived in the same tribal society and were regulated by common laws. In the south the social system was basically a patriarchal one as well, which applied equally to the Moslems and Orthodox Christians.

Much more important than the religious divisions were the differences in social development among the various groups within the country. The northern tribesmen remained the most primitive, fiercely indepedent, concerned exclusively with blood feuds, land and cattle, ignorant to the extent that the belief in witchcraft and vampires was widespread.[5]

This was contrasted with the highly urban Orthodox and Catholic communities in the north and south where most of the brighter intellects and the majority of Albanian commerce could be found. These people were for the most part Middle Class and included many who had either studied or lived abroad. And yet within Albania they were at a distinct disadvantage for being almost unarmed among the armed. They were also without a common program or policy since a good deal of friction existed in the south concerning the question of a national Albanian church and the schools.

In between the extremes of the Christians and the Moslem mountaineers were the lowlanders, also Moslem but generally not Sunni like the mountaineers. Here the leading families had ruled for the Turks retaining Medieval privileges and feudal rights in exchange for conducting local administration and cooperating with the Ottomans in the collection of taxes and recruitment of men for military service.

The land which these central Moslem Beys received from the Turks for the above services was farmed under the tenant system, which placed the unfortunate Moslem peasant completely under the control of his landlord and gained for the peasant the disdain of the mountaineer who considered him fair game for brigandage.[6]

The Ottomans were quick to add their own obstacles to unity alongside the already existing indigenous ones. In classic carrot and stick fashion, the Turkish authorities subverted Albanian nationalism through outright repression as well as by means which amounted to little more than bribery.

The Turks realized that language was one of the chief factors which could threaten their position, accordingly they placed severe restrictions on the teaching of the Albanian language. They were quite successful in this endeavor as witnessed by the fact that an alphabet for the promulgation of literary Albanian was not agreed upon until 1908.

The Porte was careful to physically divide the Albanians by sectioning their territory into four vilayets, making certain that each contained people of varying nationality. The Turks took advantage of and frequently instigated discord between the tribes in the north. They used the same approach with the feudal Beys in the south and assumed the role of arbiter, to which the various opposing factions would turn for support.

On the other hand, the Ottomans realized, particularly as their empire entered the final stages of disintegration, that the Albanians were of considerable use. Sultan Abdul Hamid often commented that his empire depended on the Albanians and the Arabs.[7] The Sultan's weakness for the Albanians was due largely to the fact that his bodyguard consisted of Albanians, upon whom he knew he could rely. Since most Albanians were Moslems they were offered opportunities for education and advancement. Subsequently, many Albanians served in the Turkish military and administration.

Although official ties with the Ottomans were severed in 1912, a strong rather negative Ottoman legacy remained, elements of which were detectable in all three levels of Albanian civilization. A unique Weltanschauung was created and it included a strong distrust of the government and of the city as well. This suspicion was coupled with a cleverness used to cheat the authorities, a practice which was considered not only completely normal but admirable.

A generally accepted fatalism, derived from the Koran, resulted in a very complacent attitude towards progress in general and work in particular, which was considered as a means to an end, that end being leisure. The love of leisure, the whiling away of countless hours in coffeehouses, was complemented by widespread hedonism. Celebrations were extremely important, often lasting for extended periods. Zogu's father's wake, for example, lasted for forty-one days. Fatalism also contributed to a general attitude of submission, which was seen as the one way to survive.[8] The result was the creation of isolated stagnant communities, a situation which by no means lent itself to unity or modernization.

As with other facets of life, Abania was still in the Middle Ages economically. Five centuries of Turkish domination had created none of the necessary bases for modern economic development and indeed, had retarded such development. In 1922, over 90 percent of the population was engaged either in agriculture or animal husbandry. Given the makeup of the countryside, with 67 percent scrub, woodland and eroded mountain slope, 24 percent forest and only 9 percent usable for agriculture, the average Albanian lived in a state of extreme poverty.[9]

On the little land available for farming, Medieval techniques of crop rotation as well as wooden plows were still being used. The irrigation system in most parts of the country dated back to the Middle Ages. Approximately 40 percent of the peasants were landless and lived under the chiflik system of land tenure, a holdover from Ottoman times which strongly resembled serfdom.[10]

Under this system, the Moslem landowner required that the peasant bring his crop to the square of the chiflik village where the state tax and seed cost was deducted. The remainder was divided equally between the landowner and the peasant, leaving the peasant usually about 30 percent of his crop. Since this was generally not enough to live on, the peasant was forced to borrow from the landowner to feed his family and animals. Although under the chiflik system the peasant was nominally free to leave, few were ever out of debt considering the yearly deficit and the high interest rates.11 As a result, the Albanian peasants were bound to the land in a deplorable state of ignorance and poverty.

What little was produced rarely reached a wider market because of the primitive transportation system. Proper road linking the major inland cities and the coast were basically nonexistent. Although some roads had been built by the Austrians and Italians during the war, they were constructed rapidly for war purposes of rather poor material. Due to climatic conditions and lack of maintenance, even these roads had deteriorated. On the few roads that did exist, wheeled traffic was possible only during the summer months because they were basically mud paths that became impossible in bad weather. With few exceptions, travel was possible only by foot or packtrain. Subsequently, some areas of the country were cut off for months at a time. Some areas were cut off completely as few bridges remained, most having been blown up during the war or carried away by floods.

In terms of motorized traffic, Albania was completely without it. The country's entire rolling stock in the early 1920s consisted of three miserable old Fords left behind by an American relief mission.[12] Although the Austrians had constructed a narrow gauge Decauville railroad from Durrës to Elbasan and from Tirana to Durrës, it had been completely neglected and by 1922 was no longer salvageable. Albania had entirely passed over the railroad age and would not have its first functioning train until after World War II. Coastal shipping before the war had been divided between the Austrians and the Italians, and during the post-war period it was controlled exclusively by the latter.

This extremely weak transportation network did a great deal to hamper the development of industry and the extraction of raw materials. In 1922 industry was either nonexistent or of the handicraft variety. What little production did exist was limited to gold and silver filigree work done by skilled artisans, tanning and dying of saddle and shoe leather by a primitive vegetable process, rough ovaliform tiles and a small amount of heat treated and sundried bricks.[13]

None of these products were exported and little was sold within the country. Everything that was needed in an Albanian household could be produced at home. Flour was ground by hand or by small water driven mills, and wool was spun in the home. Albanians were able to produce most of their food and about 75 percent of the clothes they needed.[14]

Apart from the lack of transportation facilities and the weakness of the internal market, industrial development was also plagued by a paucity of raw materials, or at least available raw materials since few statistics existed and few surveys had been done. During the war, the Austrians and the Italians had discovered coal, silver, copper, petroleum, asphalt and bitumen, but exploration ceased as soon as the troops left.

The search was not resumed until the foreigners came back to buy concessions, which they did in a scramble beginning immediately after the war. Since little statistical material existed, only those organizations with enough money to take considerable financial risk came to bid for the concessions. Subsequently, most of them went to Western powers including Italy, Germany, the United States and Great Britain.

Six organizations received large concessions to drill for oil, the largest parcels leased to the Anglo-Persian Oil Company, Ferrovia della Stato Italiano, the Standard Oil Company and the Deutsche Erdöl AG. Other foreign groups presented plans for railroad, airline, forestry, mining and banking concessions, many of which were never approved because the bribe had been insufficient or the Albanian official in charge had simply assured the foreign representations of ratification and then forgotten about it.[15]

What little foreign investment managed to survive the Oriental bureaucracy, did the country almost no good in any case. The money paid for the concessions rarely turned up inside the state treasury. The concessions which had the possibility of providing Albania with both raw materials and capital in the end provided neither, demonstrating the difficulties involved in applying 20th century finances to a Medieval economy.

Superimposing Western economic practices on the primitive Albanian economy had other negative effects as well. As with other Balkan states, Albania discovered credit. In a less developed society, credit is initially seen as something of a panacea, capable of rectifying all possible evils, both on the individual and the national level. With the introduction of a monied economy, peasants were faced with the possibility of possessing products like tea, coffee and sugar which had previously been considered as luxury goods. The peasant bought but was unable to repay because he lacked the knowledge and capital to increase his productivity. He was more often than not forced to turn to a well-to-do peasant who had become a merchant and moneylender for a loan at rates anywhere from 10 percent to 100 percent. Western economic influence led to serious peasant indebtedness.[16]

Substantial peasant purchasing showed up in the economic figures released by the government in the early 1920s. On the surface the figures for government intake and expenditure for 1921 seemed reasonable and could be broken down as follows:

Government Services	gold francs (19½ cents)
Ministry of War	8,168,740
Ministry of Public Instruction	2,141,710
Ministry of Foreign Affairs	2,678,245
Direction General of Public Works	1,163,520
Ministry of Justice	824,170
Ministry of Finance	733,540
Direction General of Posts and Telegraph	575,600
Direction General of Public Hygiene	493,850
Direction of Public Safety	405,570
Direction of Customs	359,610
Direction General of Monopoly	334,120
Chamber of Deputies	273,180
Sherjat Tribunals	263,480
Direction of Agriculture	243,760
Council of Regency	86,540
Presidency of Council of Ministers	51,820
Total	18,797,455[17]

The receipts for the same period can be broken down as follows:

Agricultural tax	6,000,000
Customs receipts	5,000,000
Various monopolies	2,000,000
(alcohol, tobacco, salt)	
Taxes on animals	2,000,000
Surplus from previous year	2,000,000
Internal loan	1,500,000
Total	18,500,000[18]

Despite the extremely heavy burden of the army on the budget and the fact that most of the revenue clearly came from the already impoverished peasants and an overreliance on customs duties, the 1921 budget, in strictly economic terms, did not seem unhealthy. The deficit was very small. They did not, however, show the real problem, namely the adverse balance of trade through which the country was rapidly losing its gold reserves and incurring an enormous debt. The balance of trade figures for 1921 are typical of the figures for the early 1920s.

	Imports	Exports
Italy	12,730,691	1,613,503
Greece	2,124,414	487,803
Great Britain	1,135,344	———
Austria	669,465	———
Turkey	665,141	———
Yugoslavia	334,741	88,490
Totals	17,659,796	2,189,796[19]

Zogu's first priority was to attack the immediate economic problem. His initial step to curb this disastrous trend took place in February 1922, when the government implemented a hastily drawn customs tariff which significantly increased import duties making the cost of foreign goods on the Albanian market almost prohibitive. Had this move succeeded, Albania's modest gold reserves might have been saved.

Before any positive effect could be generated, however, Italy, the principal supplier of Albania's needs as well as the main customer for her products, exerted pressure on the government to recall the prohibitive duties.

Rome used a number of methods to achieve this effect, including the threat to restrict shipping between Albania and the rest of the world. Since all of Albania's shipping was handled by the two Italian shipping companies, the Puglia Line and the Lloyd Triestino Line, the government felt constrained to accommodate the Italians.

With the failure of unilateral action in the face of hostile moves by those countries that might be affected, Zogu applied to the League of Nations for financial assistance. The League Commission of Inquiry which had been sent to Albania to investigate the Mirditë Republic question in December 1921, had already made preliminary suggestions regarding the economic problems in Albania. Dr. J. J. Sederholm, the financial expert on the commission, submitted his final report in May 1923, strongly supporting Zogu's application for a loan. He concluded that:

> Albania has achieved independence at a time when the whole world is impoverished and she finds herself therefore financially at a disadvantage in comparison with the situation in which the other Balkan states found themselves when they achieved independence. In their case they generally found some Great Power able and willing to befriend them and to afford them financial assistance. Albania depends on the League for impartial political support.[20]

Sederholm insisted that without foreign assistance and foreign advisors, Albania had little chance of retaining its independence. His final recommendation was that if Albania was to stand any chance of survival the League would have to loan the government twenty million dollars at the very least.[21]

The League took Dr. Sederholm's recommendations under advisement but turned down the proposal for a loan. Money was tight and even if some had been available, the creditors would have required some form of collateral, something of which Albania had very little. Apart from its customs revenues, the only securities of tangible and potential value which the country possessed consisted of public domain, extensive state-owned agricultural land and forests and its unknown mineral wealth. Albania was in a position to offer as security for a loan nothing more than its natural resources as a state. Considering these circumstances, the League did little more than to invite members to participate in the establishment of a bank

of issue but since only Italy, Belgium and Switzerland responded, the proposal was dropped.

Having exhausted all avenues of direct assistance, the League simply suggested that the Albanian government be more frugal with its meagre financial resources. In an effort to assist the government to this end, the League
appointed Mr. J. Hunger of Holland as financial advisor. Hunger, who was
given a five-year contract to be paid by the Albanian government, arrived
in June 1923, by which point the economic condition of the country had
weakened considerably. Not only had the balance of payments problem
gotten worse but government expenditures had greatly exceeded the
revenue intake. The proposed budget for 1924 was reported to have a
three million gold franc deficit but on closer examination, Hunger discovered that the deficit would be at least three times as large.[22]

Albania's financial experts had made a three million franc mistake in
receipts, and arrears of payments of claims against the government, and
conversion of treasury bonds were not included in the estimation of expenditures, resulting in a further three million franc deficit. In addition,
no provisions for unforeseen expenditures like free food distribution in
case of bad harvest, added another one million to the deficit. Ultimately,
the final figures showed receipts of about fifteen million, with twenty-two
million in expenditures.[23]

Hunger submitted a series of reports both to the League and the Albanian government in which he called for far-reaching changes. His first priority was extensive income tax reform in order to level the burden of taxa-
tion somewhat. As it stood the peasants, who were already subjected to
extreme poverty, paid 76.2 percent of the taxes.[24] Hunger suggested that
the wealthy Moslem landowners who controlled 80 percent of the best
land and paid only 6 percent of the taxes be required to assume a heavier
burden. What Hunger suggested, then, was agrarian reform.

Hunger went on to point to alarming abuses within the government and
the state bureaucracy. After careful study he concluded that the number
of officials could be significantly reduced and that the work of those remaining could be increased. He argued further that the army should be
abolished entirely since it was too small and would not be able to resist
an invasion from any of Albania's neighbors. Finally, he saw a need for
the complete reorganization of the Ministry of Finance, particularly the
department which controlled expenditures, which was understaffed and

lacked the necessary independence to effectively do its work. Hunger's figures showed that with these changes the deficit could be reduced from seven to 2½ million francs. The remainder was to be procured through an internal loan.[25]

Hunger's far-reaching suggestions would have been extremely practical and wise for a state with a considerable degree of political stability. For Albania in 1923, however, they would have undoubtedly resulted in the immediate overthrow of Zogu's government. Hunger probably did not realize that Zogu was still courting Shevket Verlaci and the reactionary Moslem Beys who paid so little tax. An attack on Albania's primitive agrarian structure, the basis of their privileges, would have thrown all of their wealth over to political groups who could assure the status quo.

In suggesting that the army be disbanded, Hunger was probably unaware that it was not meant for external but primarily for internal use and that much of the money spent by the War Department went for bribes to the northern chieftains or back to Zogu for use in other fields. Hunger had looked at the situation through the eyes of a Westerner, unable to comprehend the complexities of Albanian politics and the connection between expenditures and the longevity of Zogu's government. The Prime Minister was looking for financing, not Western lessons in frugality.

Hunger was subsequently either ignored or faced with obstructions. Important road contracts were granted without his knowledge and concessions were sold to foreign investors without his advice. While he was conducting investigations intending to reduce the overblown bureaucracy, foreigners were being appointed to lucrative posts.

Hunger was also faced with accessibility problems. Initially he had been guaranteed access to all cabinet meetings but as the gap between the Prime Minister and his financial adviser widened, the cabinet scheduled meetings and convened without Hunger's knowledge. His suggestions did not conform well to the existing circumstances and would not be implemented.

It only remained to do away with him altogether. Accordingly, in May 1924, Hunger's contract was terminated, four years before it was due to expire. Much to the chagrin of the League, the government claimed that because of increasingly adverse financial conditions, it could not longer afford to pay his salary. So ended Albania's brief experience with the League and its last chance to receive impartial foreign aid.

Zogu had actually come up with many of Hunger's conclusions independently, well before the financial adviser's arrival. He had even gone so far as to pledge attention to them in the ambitious program which he laid out for himself in his first speech to Parliament in December 1922. He had promised to cut the budget, reduce the number of officials, reorganize the administrative system and appoint prefects with some knowledge of the districts with which they were entrusted. He had even suggested that the army might be reduced, the legislature reformed and more roads built. He had hinted at social and agrarian reform. It was not long, well before the arrival of Hunger, that the Prime Minister came to the realization that much of what he had promised could not be implemented, at least not in the foreseeable future.

In the meantime discontent grew. In southern Albania the people waited for their agrarian reform. The commercial Middle Classes were also unhappy. Because the south was the most developed and prosperous, it paid a great deal of the taxes, little of which was ever returned in the way of services. Discontent grew among the Orthodox community which was angered by what it perceived as advantages granted to Moslem landowners supported by Moslem officials who were accused of being arbitrary. Christians were reportedly imprisoned on the slightest provocation and sometimes through personal motives.[26] Many of these accusations had foundations. Dr. Sederholm had stigmatized the south as a "little Turkey."[27]

Despite these various problems, Zogu's personal reputation seems to have suffered a good deal less than those of his entourage and his associates in the clique, who were universally condemned. Surprisingly, this was particularly true in the south where many among the Orthodox population were convinced that if Zogu were given a free hand, he would make it his business to purge the country of its reactionary Moslem elements in the sphere of internal politics.[28] Judged in comparison with his colleagues in the government, it is not surprising that Zogu was developing the reputation of a patriot.

These rumors, taken in conjunction with other grievances, produced anxiety among the elements of the clique within the government, particularly the Moslem elements in control of the southern administration. They had never trusted Zogu and were further confirmed in their suspicions by his actions as Prime Minister. It was clear that he was using his power to enrich himself, a fact which would not have bothered the southern clique members except that Zogu effectively employed his wealth for the consolidation and increase of his own prestige. He acted arbitrarily without consulting the cabinet. In a move to stabilize his own power base he had appointed Colonel W. F. Stirling, lately Governor of Jaffa District, as adviser to the Ministry of the Interior. The Colonel had been retained without the knowledge or approval of any of Zogu's colleagues. The Prime Minister had so effectively manipulated men and events that his intervention was indispensible on all occasions, a situation which opposition groups within the government would not tolerate indefinitely.[29]

At the end of September 1923, a number of Kosovite deputies who favored a chauvinistic policy towards Yugoslavia precipitated a crisis and ultimately a second split within the clique. The Minister of War, Colonel Hakki, and a number of his supporters, accused Zogu of pro-Yugoslav activities and of failing to reform the internal administration. The group declared themselves against Zogu, hoping to remove him either from the Prime Ministership or from his position as Minister of the Interior by a vote of no confidence in the Chamber. Their effort failed.

Zogu, encouraged by his parliamentary victory and the knowledge that his prestige was still higher than that of his opponents, felt that the time was ripe to further stabilize his position by the election of a Constituent Assembly to establish a capital, decide on the nature of the government and revise the Statutes of Lushnjë. With control over these proceedings, the Prime Minister could essentially create the ideal state.

In pursuance of this goal, Zogu could count on support from the mountains as well as from much of the center and the south. He was even confident of a considerable amount of support from Shkodër. When he dissolved the Chamber at the end of September, there was reason to believe that after the new elections had taken place his position would become more secure than it had been.

The possibility that Zogu might realize his goal had not escaped the members of the clique who opposed him. Zogu had been able to count on twenty-five deputies who would follow his lead under any circumstances. During the campaigning, which began in November, he appealed for the formation of one strong party based upon military discipline to direct the affairs of the nation. This state party would "check all abuses rising from personal influence in whatever place, at whatever time and under whatever government."[30]

Zogu was clearly attempting to put an end to the system of party squabbling and form a government completely under his control. The members of the clique in opposition consorted together to frustrate the Prime Minister's plans, first through propaganda and failing that, through a coup d'etat.[31]

The opposition campaign was begun by Shevket Korca, a prominent member of the clique and the head of the gendarmerie. Korca let it be known that Zogu was making arrangements for the return to Parliament of a great number of candidates who were in no way fit to represent the country in the Constitutional Assembly. He concluded that Albania could be saved only if public spirited individuals moved to insure that Zogu would not become another Esad Pasha.

Korca took the initiative and declared that he would not obey the orders of the government, unless he felt that they were in the interests of the country. He sent instructions to his subordinate officers throughout various parts of the country to do everything in their power to prevent Zogu's adherents from winning seats.

Before the Prime Minister could move effectively against Korca, a much more serious plot, engineered by Colonel Hakki, had come to his attention. Hakki, who had resigned his post after his unsuccessful attempt to oust Zogu in September, in cooperation with other highly placed officers and certain officials, had prepared a coup d'etat for November 28, the Albanian national holiday. The plan included the assassination of the Prime Minister and the proclamation of a military government.

Zogu planned to move quickly against Korca and the conspirators but was prevented from doing so by members of his own government and one of the Regents. The Ministers of Public Works, Education, War and Justice, along with the Regent Sotir Peci, all announced that they would resign if any action was taken against the conspirators.

It was in Zogu's interest to prevent such a mass resignation since such an action would have necessitated the recall of the old Parliament thereby indefinitely postponing the new elections. Legally, Zogu was also in something of a bind, since no proceedings could be taken against the ministers who supported the conspirators because no court except Parliament was competent to judge them. Also, many of the officers involved were lieutenant colonels, the highest rank in the Albanian army, who could be tried by no one except superior officers. Therefore, they were responsible to no court unless special powers were obtained from Parliament. A legal deadlock had been created.

While negotiations to break the deadlock ensued, each side prepared for what it saw as the inevitable armed conflict. Shevket Korca took to parading the town with a band of irregulars and called to Tirana from various places in the south, large numbers of gendarmerie on whom he could depend. Within a few days, patrols of gendarmerie were stationed at every corner. Troops which arrived from Shkodër to protect the government were quickly drafted by the rebels. Disaffected officers distributed ammunition to the gendarmerie and to the soldiers on whom they thought they could depend.

Meanwhile, Zogu received messages from different parts of the country to the effect that any attempted coup would be resisted. The greater number of younger army officers informed the Minister of War that they would not obey the orders of their superiors if these involved rebellion against the established government. Much more tangible support came from the government troops and Zogu's own tribesmen who protected the Parliament House and the residence of the Prime Minister. Everyone waited for the first shot to be fired.[32]

Zogu was left with three options: he could resign and leave the field to the clique; he could compromise so as to preserve the status quo, play for time and little by little move against the opposition, or he could use those forces of the government faithful to him and his own personal followers and crush the movement and hang the conspirators. The first option was out of character for Zogu. He naturally leaned towards the third alternative since the use of force had so often proved effective in the past.

The Prime Minister would have adopted the third option were it not for a series of considerations, including the fact that it would have required Zogu to set up a semi-dictatorship until the next Parliament could meet since his cabinet ministers and at least two of the four Regents would oppose him. He was not yet confident enough to take such a step.

He was also clever enough to realize that foreign money in loans and investments, so badly needed in Albania, would not be forthcoming if politically chaotic conditions continued indefinitely. Rude violations of the Constitution had to be kept to a minimum if his policies were to retain any domestic, and, more importantly, foreign credibility. It probably made no little impression upon Zogu that the British Minister, who had supported him so staunchly in the past, recommended the second alternative.

There was of course another consideration, one which undoubtedly was paramount in his decision to adopt the second alternative. Zogu had dangerously underestimated the clique, thinking by the end of 1923 that he could simply push them aside without fear of serious consequences. He quickly became aware of the fact that they were not only determined but were also liberally supplied with funds. The clique had effectively permeated the administration and more importantly, the army. They were able to raise a considerable number of troops at short notice. In the final analysis, then, Zogu could not be sure that he would prevail, if he chose the military option.

The clique too, was initially reluctant to compromise because they felt themselves in a militarily superior position. They were finally persuaded to do so, however, when the Ministers of Great Britain, the United States, Yugoslavia and Italy let it be widely known that if Zogu was overthrown, the new revolutionary government would not be recognized even if a certain specious legality were given to it by the fact that members of the previous cabinet and two of the Regents lent it their support.

The attitude of the foreign representatives saved the situation. Once again Zogu had been rescued by a movement which had been initiated by the British representative. All parties were now agreed that a compromise had become necessary. The gendarmerie patrols were withdrawn and the immediate danger of civil war was averted.[33]

The compromise which was eventually worked out was a most curious one and perhaps typically Albanian in its inefficiency. Zogu was to retain his position as Prime Minister but the office of Minister of the Interior was to be rotated on a weekly basis, each member of the cabinet assuming the post for seven days. The natural result of this was that the entire tenure of each successive Minister of the Interior was spent in dismissing officials appointed by his immediate predecessor. This apparently was the only compromise acceptable to all parties involved, each believing that after the elections all opposition could easily be crushed. Both parties immediately set to work rigging the elections. A rash of political violence, including numerous assassinations, resulted.[34]

The elections, which took place at the end of November, were inconclusive with none of the major groups receiving a clear majority. Zogu did, however, increase his support, coming away with an absolute personal party of fifty in the reconstituted House of 102. The rest of the seats were distributed between Noli's democratic followers, the clique, the Christians, the conservative Beys and many with no particular allegiance. Zogu had overestimated his personal influence and the ability of his agents to undermine clique support, particularly in the south. Without an absolute majority, Zogu was unable to organize a new government. New political alliances became necessary. The time was right to finally win over the conservative Moslem Beys.[35]

Using his connection with Shevket Verlaci, Zogu was eventually able to attract most of the Beys, a political accomplishment of some magnitude considering that the Beys were anything but unified. Since the defeat of the various Vrioni governments, the Beys had been unable to construct a defensive, let alone a positive, organization. By 1923 they had reached such a point of disintegration that many were willing to support Zogu in the hopes of holding onto their privileges. Few had any illusions about Zogu and those who eventually came to support him did so reluctantly and with a good deal of mistrust. Nevertheless, the adherents of Vrioni, the supporters of Verlaci and a loose collection of Beys known as the Berat group, finally convinced many of the reticent Beys that Zogu was their last hope.[36]

Although the support of the Beys gave Zogu a composite majority, he was still unable to form a government. His old cabinet carried on provisionally during this period but a rapid breakdown of order was taking place. The gendarmerie, and many units of the army, no longer obeyed the orders of Zogu's government because they were still controlled by the rebel elements of the clique and because the economic situation had deteriorated to the point where they were no longer being paid. Zogu was desperate; he realized that he could not remain in office and yet he was reluctant to disperse the carefully constructed coalition which he controlled.

In the midst of this political chaos, on February 24, Zogu narrowly escaped death at the hands of an assassin as he was walking up the steps of the Parliament building. Beqir Walter, a member of the Union of Young Albanians, an organization formed by Avni Rystem the assassin of Esad Pasha and lieutenant of Fan Noli, shot Zogu three times. The Prime Minister, wounded in the hand, the thigh and the middle abdomen, staggered into Parliament with his gun in hand and managed to reach the government bench. He was immediately surrounded by his supporters who quickly procured a doctor, although Zogu at first did not want to see him because he did not know him.

The scene in Parliament was understandably tense, most of the deputies seemed to recognize the danger of an open gunfight since everyone present was armed. The President of the Parliament, Eshref Frasheri, and his staff, had crowded into the corner of the hall while shooting continued in the forehall between Walter and the followers of Zogu. Walter, who had locked himself in the bathroom, commenced singing patriotic songs as he shot through the doors. After the assailant had finally been subdued, Vrioni gave a short speech to calm the situation and Zogu from his bench announced in a loud voice, "gentlemen, this is not the first time this sort of thing has happened, I ask my friends to leave it alone and deal with it afterwards."[37] Vrioni and Zogu had possibly prevented wholesale carnage within the Assembly hall. The Prime Minister was willing to wait for his revenge.

Zogu was taken home under heavy guard. His wounds were apparently less serious than had originally been feared and did not prevent him from receiving guests at his home. During the weeks following the attempted assassination, he was visited by hundreds of well-wishers. He even took the opportunity to interview his assailant, who wisely decided to explain the various details of the attempt, seriously implicating Avni Rystem. Walter apparently told Zogu what he wanted to hear for his life was spared and he eventually took advantage of the late 1924 political turmoil to flee the country, not returning until 1939.[38]

The attempt on Zogu's life resulted in a number of significant political developments, including the crystalization of two distinct groups in the assembly. The opposition party, whose nucleus was Fan Noli and other exponents of Westernization through democratic means, was now joined by all personalities and factions opposed to Zogu. This group included Bishop Noli's co-religionists, former Progressives offended at not being represented in the government, army officers, conservative Sunni and liberal Bektashi Moslems, as well as many of the Roman Catholics.[39] Zogu's forces, meanwhile, were augmented by ex-Esad Pasha adherents who naturally had reasons for opposing Avni Rystem.

The attempt forced Zogu to leave the public limelight for a number of reasons, firstly by Albanian custom, he could not leave his house until the outrage had been avenged, and of course, secondly because his wounds prevented him from taking an active part as he might have wished. Most importantly, the attack convinced Zogu that his government was no longer tenable. On February 25, 1923, after one year and two months in office, Zogu resigned as Prime Minister.

The political struggle which ensued raged largely around the person of Zogu as his partisans and opponents were equally determined to insist on his inclusion or exclusion respectively. A number of combinations were suggested including an attempt to build a government around Iljas Bey Vrioni.

All of these attempts failed until finally, at the beginning of March, a compromise worked out chiefly by Zogu, was agreed upon. The Regents were persuaded to appoint Shevket Bey Verlaci, Zogu's prospective father-in-law, as Prime Minister. Verlaci, who had neither the experience nor the desire to accept the post, reluctantly did so only after Zogu agreed to support him by his presence in Parliament and by his counsel when needed. Zogu became the power behind the government, much to the eventual dismay of the opposition.[40]

The new government was unstable from the very beginning, and Verlaci had difficulty filling the cabinet positions. Those positions which could be filled were unfortunately accepted by politicians like Myfid Bey Libohova who did little to win the support of the powerful elements within the country. Libohova, who became Minister of Justice, apparently possessed little or no qualifications for the post to which he was appointed. His inclusion contributed considerably to the instability of the Verlaci government.[41]

The weakness of the government and its inability to deal with rapidly deteriorating conditions did little to increase its general popularity. Discontent both in the south, where the agrarian reforms still remained a dead letter and in the north where irredentism and the failure of the government to make progress towards improvement of conditions among the famine striken population, became even more serious. The opposition blamed the government for these conditions and successfully recruited adherents to their cause.

Zogu's role during this period, and his activity in pursuance of power, constituted the final straw which turned economic and political discontent into armed revolt. The former Prime Minister turned to methods with which he felt comfortable, including intrigue and violence. His position had degenerated to the point where he felt he was left with no other option. His plan was direct and simple, he would create a situation which required that the government declare a state of emergency in Albania and he would use the emergency powers of the government and the instability which would result, to do away with his major opponents.

On April 6, two American tourists, Mr. G. B. deLong and Mr. R. L. Coleman, were ambushed and shot while driving along the Tirana-Shkodër road, some twenty-five miles from Tirana. This was a very serious occurrence since under Albanian custom foreigners and guests enjoyed the protection of the besa.

Although they were probably shot by mistake in a blood feud related crime, it was never fully determined who was responsible. The government naturally accused the opposition of attempting to discredit it in the eyes of foreign and domestic observers. Bishop Noli and his party saw the murders as an attempt on the part of Zogu to demonstrate that only he could insure order in Albania. Indeed, Zogu was the first to benefit from this unfortunate episode. Soon after the ambush, the government declared a state of emergency.

Within a month, one of Zogu's major opponents had been assassinated. On May 5, 1924, Avni Rystem, who had become a deputy to the Constituent Assembly, was shot by a former follower of Esad Pasha who had become one of Zogu's minions.

Rystem had been active in organizing a group known as the Bashkimi Club at Vlorë and elsewhere. The club was an association of young students dedicated to the removal by murder of anyone who was considered an enemy of Albania. He had also become one of the principal leaders of Bishop Noli's Democratic Party.

This time there was no question as to the responsibility since Rystem had been implicated in the attempt on Zogu. The desired result of the assassination was not achieved, however, since Noli and the Democrats successfully turned the incident against Zogu and proclaimed Rystem as a national hero and a martyr. The coffin was transported to Vlorë where it was buried in a prominent downtown square to be marked with a large monument.

Noli and his followers felt they now had enough support and ammunition against Zogu to move on the government. It was clear that Zogu had become the power behind the throne and that they would never be able to gain power as long as he remained in the country. The Democrats felt that because the Verlaci government had shown itself to be not only weak but dictatorial and oppressive, they could easily win the support of much of the population.

The Democrats and their various followers withdrew from the assembly declaring that they would not meet in Tirana because it was too close to the territory controlled by Zogu and that no opposition deputy was safe in its general vicinity. Noli demanded that Zogu and certain of his followers leave the country.

Legally, the government was crippled, since the President of the Constituent Assembly could no longer produce a quorum. The government sent Foreign Minister Vrioni to treat with the opposition but before he could persuade Noli to accept a compromise, trouble in the north convinced the Democrats that open revolt could succeed. Noli's associate, Luigj Gurakuqi, had drawn up a manifesto signed by the northern Albanian deputies and Colonel Rexhep Shala, a northern chieftain commanding Albanian troops in the north, invited the assembly to meet in Shkodër. The government immediately dismissed Shala but he ignored them and declared martial law in his area. He then invited Zogu's perennial opponents, Elez Jusuf and Bajram Curri, to join him in taking up arms against the government, a request to which the two leaders willingly agreed.

In the south, Colonel Kiafzezi, Noli's military adviser, followed suit and declared martial law throughout his region. The Colonel was quickly joined by Shevket Korca, the gendarmerie commander, who mobilized his troops in the Vlorë and Berat areas.[42]

The government declared general mobilization on June 1, but found itself without much support. Verlaci took the opportunity to quickly resign. A new government under Vrioni made further attempts to come to some sort of compromise and sent Myfid Bey Libohova to Shkodër to negotiate. The insurgents, aware of their strength, simply took Myfid Bey prisoner and began their march on Tirana.

Since the government had almost no support by this time, very little fighting actually occurred. More and more army units defected to the opposition, after seeing that the Vrioni government was doomed to defeat. By June 9, the Council of Regency was non-existent, the Catholic member having resigned, the Orthodox member having retuned to Koritza and the two Moslem members having fled to Italy. The Prime Minister, the Ministers of War and Interior as well as the chiefs of police and many high ranking gendarmerie officials, also fled to Italy in a rather undignified manner, which caused the worst impression among all classes of Albanians.[43] Feelings ran so high against this group that when they disembarked in Bari they had to be protected by Italian police from hostile crowds of Albanians who held them responsible for the miserable conditions existing in Albania.

Once again, Zogu was the last to remain behind, hoping to recreate the conditions which had allowed him to come to power in 1922. The situation had changed, however, the insurgents had closed in upon Tirana with 7,000 troops, and it was too late to call for help from the foreign legations. On the afternoon of June 9, Zogu called the citizens of Tirana together to ask for support, but it soon became clear that they would not die for Zogu. In the early hours of the morning of June 10, he withdrew to the mountains with some 600 supporters. After light fighting with the forces of Curri and Jusuf, Zogu was obliged to retire into Yugoslavia, bringing to a rather ignominious end his first few years of active political life in Albania.

Zogu's accomplishments during this period were rather meager, primarily because the problems he faced were almost insurmountable. Nevertheless, Zogu had at least taken steps to deal with some of these difficulties. He had continued Delvina's process of developing some form of educational system to tackle the astonishing 90 percent illiteracy rate which existed. Zogu recognized the agrarian problem as paramount and took a few minor steps which might have given the peasants hope, if nothing else. He had directed the Parliament to dispense with the title of "Bey," and the expulsion of landlords from their property of tenants who continued to fulfill their normal obligations was declared illegal. Although these measures were for the most part unenforced, they did at least indicate that the government under Zogu had some understanding of the problems facing Albania.

Zogu must be credited with making some contributions to the general stability in Albania. Although the blood feuds had by no means disappeared, their number was reduced, primarily because Zogu had successfully disarmed a large section of the population. Law and order, a concept which had been absent for over five centuries was gaining a foothold even in the mountainous regions, an area which even the might of the Turkish Empire at its high point could not completely control. A small step towards unity had been taken.

On the other hand, serious difficulties naturally remained. The country was still seriously disunited, few people thought of themselves first as Albanians. There had been no economic reform, the budget was still basically in a state of shambles with huge deficits which the treasury could never hope to pay. Soldiers and civil servants remained without pay for months, while the northern tribes were so heavily hit by famine that they were forced to eat grass.

The administration was overburdened with officials who had little or nothing to do but to oversee the massive corruption which had continued from Turkish times. The governments had been intolerant, oppressive and violent, and were accused and were most likely guilty of numerous assassinations and attempted assassinations of citizens and foreigners. It was still very difficult to convince a skeptical Europe that the Albanian state would be able to survive these difficulties.

Clearly, some drastic measures were in order. Zogu had learned some lessons. He had learned that political stability was impossible without a measure of economic stability and fiscal sanity. More importantly, Zogu had learned that although it might be possible to eventually turn Albania into a Western state, the Western political model had been a miserable failure. Parliamentary democracy required an enlightened, reasonably well off populace, willing and able to participate in the political process.

In Albania the time was certainly not right for such a government. While Zogu was unwilling to give up the idea of some sort of Western political structure for Albania, a more authoritarian version was called for while the long process of laying the groundwork for popular participation was begun. As he matured politially he was able to more effectively draw on his varied experiences and hammer out a viable synthesis of these ideas, in order to create a system better suited for Albania. Although others had not yet learned this lesson, Zogu would not again make the same mistake.

CHAPTER FOUR

THE FAILURE OF FAN NOLI AND
THE MAKING OF THE REPUBLIC

For the next six months, Albania was dominated by the motley coalition which had formed to defeat Zogu. Tribal tradition had allowed those in opposition to the young Mati chief to unite for the quick overthrow of the government, but because of their vastly different political ideas, unity for a constructive program was unlikely. The new government started out under a cloud and was soon beset by insurmountable problems.

Bishop Fan S. Noli, Albania's next Prime Minister, had not yet lost faith in parliamentary democracy for the small Balkan state, his background would not allow it. Born in 1882 in an Albanian village in eastern Thrace, Noli was educated at a Greek elementary school and in a Greek gymnasium. As a young man he taught Greek in Egypt, eventually becoming acquainted with enlightened Albanian merchants who introduced him to the Albanian national movement. He was soon persuaded to travel to the United States to organize the large illiterate Albanian minority around the Boston area. He quickly became their leader and first bishop, after establishing the Albanian autocephelous Orthodox Church in America in 1908. Noli continued his education in the United States, eventually graduating from Harvard University. When post-war Albania established its first government in 1920, the American-Albanian community was allowed to send one delegate and, not surprisingly, Bishop Noli was chosen.[1]

Noli returned to Albania imbued with American democratic ideas, hoping to uproot the old order with its corruption, backwardness and exploitation. He was generally considered a man of principle and patriotism but politically he was somewhat out of touch, unable to work well in the strange political structure of Albania. He had been removed from it for too long, and he no longer really understood it.

His first involvement in Albanian politics, therefore, left something of a mixed impression. Representing Albania during the League of Nations debate concerning his country's adherence to that body, Noli acquitted himself with a good deal of honor. His role as Foreign Minister in the Ypi government was somewhat less distinguished, particularly since he sent in his resignation from Rome.[2]

By 1922 Noli, for personal and political reasons, realized that he could not work with Zogu and that if he hoped to achieve his goals of Westernization and modernization for Albania, Zogu would have to be removed from the scene. The bishop subsequently associated himself with elements opposed to Zogu and eventually accepted their conclusion that Zogu had to be removed by force.

His first involvement in revolutionary activity occurred in the summer of 1923 when he came in contact with an Albanian committee founded in Vienna by the ex-Regent Aqif Pasha. The group, which claimed to represent Albanian nationalists, also included Hasan Prishtina, Zia Dibra who acted as military adviser, and Irfan Bey, who served as an economic expert. Before long Noli was counted as their chief agent in Albania.

The committee's primay aim was to overthrow the government of Zogu and do away with what they saw as the Yugoslav influence in his administration. Once in power, the group hoped to obtain national unity by appointing a foreign ruler, possibly Prince Wied, as monarch. To secure Albania's position abroad, the group planned to ally with the Little Entente, although this seemed to conflict with their anti-Yugoslav bias.[3]

The committee claimed the support of thirty deputies in Parliament but was not strong enough to move against Zogu without further support To gain this needed backing the group appealed to Albanian emigres in America and Turkey, from which they actually received large sums of money. The committee also managed to recruit many Albanian students in Vienna, while Hasan Bey successfully woed many of the mountaineers. The call for revolt finally came in August 1923 but was at first badly received. Noli and his associates were forced to wait until July 1924 before Zogu's tactics had alienated and frightened enough Albanians to insure the success of a rebellion.[4]

True to his principles, as soon as Noli had entered Tirana and set up a new government, he promulgated an ambitious program which would have created a complete modern Western state. His program indicated the depths of his liberalism as well as the extent of his naivete. It included among other points: 1) the general disarmament of the population without exception; 3) to exalt the authority of the state over any personal and extra-legal power; 4) to uproot feudalism, free the people and establish democracy definitely in Albania; 5) to introduce radical reform in all branches of the administration, both in civil and military; 9) to balance the budget by radical economies; 11) to ameliorate the condition of the farmers so as to insure their economic independence; 12) to facilitate the introduction of foreign capital, protect and organize the wealth of the country; and 18) to organize the department of education on modern and practical lines so that the schools produce capable citizens, good patriots and able workers.[5]

Noli's program would have made any Western democrat proud, however, the Prime Minister lacked the two crucial elements without which no one could have carried such a list of reforms through: financial backing and domestic support. Recognizing the need for money, Noli immediately turned to the League of Nations despite the fact that Albania had been turned down under Zogu. Not only did the League reject Noli's overtures, but almost all of its members refused to recognize the new government.

Belgrade refused recognition because of the support given to Noli by Kosovo irredentists and because it was generally believed that the new Prime Minister was a tool of the Italians. The Yugoslavs were also in the process of dealing with Zogu who had in the meantime take up residence in the Hotel Bristol in Belgrade. France refused to recognize the new government because Paris usually followed Belgrade's lead with regard to Albania.

Probably most damaging in terms of international and indigenous prestige was the refusal of the British to recognize Noli. Officially, London would not extend recognition because Noli refused to regulate his position constitutionally by summoning the Assembly and proclaiming a general amnesty.[6] The primary reason, however, seems to have initially revolved around the question of petroleum concessions. One of Zoġu's last acts had been to give the British company, Anglo-Persian Oil, a virtual monopoly on all further concessions.

The British feared for their concessions, considering that Noli permitted what London saw as anti-foreign chauvinism to take hold in the country. It had also not escaped their attention that Noli maintained rather close ties with the Albanian-American group "Vatra" which apparently had been persuaded to represent the interests of the Standard Oil Company. Noli was also at something of a disadvantage where the British were concerned because of Sir Harry Eyres' close relationship with Zogu. Eyres had openly supported Zogu and the Vrioni government against the insurgents.[7]

Noli had no choice but to turn to Italy, his last hope for financial support. As early as the end of June, Noli had told an Italian journalist that Albania's financial crisis could only be solved by a foreign loan and that this loan could only be procured with the support and effective concurrance of Rome.[8]

This remark was followed by discussions between Mussolini and the Albanian Minister in Rome. The Italians were asked for a 100 million lire loan. The Duce was rather cool because he had recently concluded a non-intervention agreement with Belgrade so that he might be free to deal with the Matteotti crisis, which had essentially paralyzed his regime since the beginning of June. Without a clear willingness to reciprocate on the part of the Albanians, the Duce would have nothing to do with the new government. Since one of Noli's primary goals was to secure the independence of Albania by eliminating foreign penetration and foreign meddling in Albanian affairs, the Prime Minister refused to offer anything in return. The negotiations, not surprisingly, were entirely unsuccessful.[9]

Noli's failure to procure a foreign loan made his already difficult domestic situation even worse. The rather motley band of followers who came to power with him had nothing but their shared hatred and envy of Zogu in common. Once their common goal had been achieved, the coalition naturally fragmented, making it more and more difficult for Noli to achieve a consensus of opinion even within his own government. General as well as specific conflicts were quick to appear.

Noli was a confirmed republican but most of the nationalists including Jusuf, Curri and Gurakuqi, were in favor of a constitutional monarchy.

Many still professed loyalty to Prince Wied. In terms of domestic issues, most of those who had originally supported Noli were conservative. The Prime Minister's programs were much too radical to command the support of either his government or the general population. His agrarian proposals had alienated conservative Moslem landlords and then, because he was unable to raise the money to carry them out, he alienated the peasantry. Continuing economic hardship turned people against his government as it had turned the people against the previous government.

Bishop Noli's inexperience drove him to compound his mistakes. He constituted a political court which passed death sentences upon Zogu, Verlaci and Vrioni and nationalized their property, a move which provoked further trouble. Noli failed to legalize his regime by elections, leaving a bad impression upon those enlightened elements who supported Noli's Western reforms.

As the situation rapidly deteriorated, more and more of his original supporters disassociated themselves from his government. As its base of support dwindled, the supposedly democratic regime became increasingly more oppressive.[10] The Prime Minister quickly lost what little control he had as central authority disintegrated.

With Noli struggling for survival, Zogu, who had named himself the representative of the Vrioni government, was free to organize in order to facilitate his return. His entrance into Yugoslavia had been prepared by his brother-in-law Ceno Bey, who was one of the few Albanians living in Kosovo who had a good working relationship with Belgrade. Zogu was welcomed despite his reputation for intrigue, because Belgrade appreciated his position on irredentism, because Noli's connection with Italy was suspect and because Belgrade was in a position to extend its influence in Albania as its major rival Italy was crippled by internal problems.

Zogu was rather lavish with his promises of concessions and deals, since he really did not have much to lose. He readily promised the territory around St. Naoum and Vermoshe, areas which had been in dispute since the delineation of Albania's frontiers in 1913.[11] The Yugoslav government apparently accepted, since they eventually rendered Zogu invaluable assistance in his return to power. Belgrade clearly hoped that he would behave as Esad Pasha had and not become its tool.

Zogu was aware of Belgrade's designs so he branched out looking for support in other quarters as well. Like Noli, he looked to Italy and at least received a sympathetic ear, since Mussolini had been informed that Zogu could be bought. Zogu had actually asked for personal aid from Italy as early as the end of May, as the storm clouds were beginning to gather. Zogu promised to satisfy all outstanding Italian concessions and even offered to put up a three million lire note which he had received from the Italian Railroads for the lease of some forest areas in Mati as collateral. Mussolini eventually refused, however, as soon as the Italian Minister in Albania, Durazzo, advised him that Noli was destined to win. Durazzo also warned the Duce about Zogu's rumored ties with Belgrade.[12]

In August Zogu sent his secretary, Jak Koci, to Rome with another deal to procure financial support. Through the intercession of two Italian businessmen, Gildo and Carlo Pugni, and A. Lessona, a fascist deputy associated with Italian interests in Albania, Zogu offered Mussolini a naval base and extensive concessions in exchange for two million lire.[13]

Mussolini was naturally interested, seeing a chance to rectify the mistake of Giolitti. The murder of the Socialist deputy Mattiotti, however, still restricted his movements to the extent that he was loath to give up what he thought to be a solid deal with Nincic, the Yugoslav Foreign Minister. The Duce tactically turned Zogu down when he asked him to repeat his offer in writing, something which Zogu naturally refused to do.

The fact that he had in the meantime been successful elsewhere, confirmed Zogu in his decision to turn down the Italians. The Anglo-Persian Oil Company decided that they could work with Zogu. Although Zogu had already agreed to an extensive concession for this British company, as with other concessions he was still able to use it as a bargaining lever because the deal had not yet been ratified. Anglo-Persian agreed to give Zogu fifty million dinars, half of which was paid immediately, the other half to be paid once Zogu regained power and saw to the ratification of the concession.[14] With the financial support of Anglo-Persian and the military support of Belgrade, Zogu was in a position to challenge Noli.[15]

Zogu used his resources well. While Belgrade newspapers announced that he had gone to Paris, and Foreign Minister Nincic maintained that his whereabouts unknown but that he was last heard of in Switzerland, Zogu had secretly remained in Belgrade.[16] On December 4, 1924, Ceno Bey left Belgrade with a good deal of money in order to pay off chiefs in the Dibër district while Zogu travelled to Prizren to organize his military forces.

Zogu's main army eventually consisted of 1,000 regular Yugolsav troops, 1,000 reservists drawn mostly from the Albanian regions and wearing their native costumes, and 500 Mati men who had fled Albania with their chief. Zogu was also able to hire 800 of General Wrangel's men, commanded by forty White Russian officers. Belgrade provided sixteen uniformed officers, two batteries of mountain artillery, ten heavy and twenty light machine guns with gunners. Belgrade also included a plentiful supply of ammunition as well as military motor transport units to convey troops and supplies to Zogu's forward bases.[17] Zogu had only to wait for the appropriate moment to launch his invasion.

Noli's actions in late 1924 did much to hasten the approach of that moment. The bishop had been requested, by the Soviet representative in Rome, to grant recognition to the Soviet government. Noli hesitated but then decided to defer the matter until 1925. In spite of the provisional refusal of the Albanian government to accept a mission, a certain Krakovetski, with a large staff, appeared in Tirana in late 1924. The government refused to receive him and the secretary-general of the Ministry for Foreign Affairs persuaded him to withdraw.[18]

This event had serious repercussions, both inside and outside of the country. In spite of its subsequent departure, it was felt that the Prime Minister favored the introduction of the mission and that he was a partisan of the Soviets. There were even those who felt Noli was a paid agent. Although these charges were most probably untrue, the incident did a great deal to further damage Noli's popularity, considering how sensitive Albanians were to any outside interference.

Unrest, meanwhile, had once again manifested itself in open revolt. In the middle of November a movement in the army, directed at the overthrow of the government, was uncovered. Various officers, primarily in the area of Primeti, had come to an agreement with the agents of Zogu to join him in opposing the government and the remainder of the clique. Although the clique and Noli had not been a good terms since June, the common fear of Zogu caused both parties to sink their differences.[19] The clique went so far as to give up their own plans to overthrow the government which they had been working on since August.[20] Despite this last minute unity, the government was beyond salvaging.

In early December 1924, Zogu decided that the time was right. The international situation was favorable, Belgrade was ready. In October,

N. Pasic has again become Prime Minister and was in search of a foreign policy success to curtail the growing popularity of S. Radic and the Croatian Peasant Party. Italy was still clinging to the Nincic Agreements and therefore turned Noli down yet again when the Albanian Prime Minister visited Rome in October, returning from another unsuccessful appeal to the League for aid. Mussolini even went so far as to renew the nonintervention agreement with Nincic in December, despite the widely reported stories of Belgrade's complicity in Zogu's preparations.

The fall of the MacDonald government in London and the construction of the second Baldwin-Chamberlain cabinet did much to further convince Zogu and Belgrade that the time was right, since Chamberlain had previously expressed understanding for Italian penetration into Albania.[21] Zogu had to move before Mussolini changed his mind.

Internally the time had definitely come as well, since Noli had finally announced, in November, that elections for yet another Constituent Assembly were to be held soon. Zogu could not afford to allow Noli to turn his hitherto unconstitutional regime into one that might eventually gain the international recognition of more than just Greece.

Zogu worked out a careful plan, hoping to take advantage of the element of surprise. Attacking in December would insure that Noli would be caught off guard, since Zogu was generally expected to launch his invasion in the spring.

An end of the year invasion did, however, present a series of unique difficulties, stemming primarily from the disadvantageous weather conditions. The winter had been particuarly harsh, with extremely cold temperatures and heavy snowfalls which ruined many of the mule tracks which were to be used in crossing the border and in descending down into the central and southern plains.[22] The risk of bogging down in the mountains, as the Serbian army had done in 1915, obviously existed but Zogu ultimately reasoned that Noli would face similar obstacles. Zogu even enjoyed a few advantages in this regard, since communications on the Albanian side of the frontier were much more difficult than across the border. Zogu's Mati tribesmen were also familiar with the terrain.

A far more serious problem which concerned both Zogu and Belgrade was the internal and foreign impression Yugoslav guns on Albanian soil would make. Extensive precautions were taken to mask the complicity of Belgrade. Yugoslav soldiers were to wear native Albanian costumes and their military operations were to be confined to the initial phase of the invasion. They were instructed not to advance too far beyond the border. Belgrade hoped that this limited involvement would lend credibility to their official denials, while Zogu hoped to dispel rumors widely circulated by the Noli administration that he was a tool of Belgrade. The task was obviously a difficult one, since hiding an army is no mean feat and was therefore not always successful, especially with regard to the extremely conservative and xenophobic northern tribal chieftains.

Extensive efforts were made to buy off the major chieftains. Although many of the minor leaders eventually consented, the major prizes eluded Zogu. For some time before the invasion Zogu had been in communication with Elez Jusuf, the paramount chief of Dibra, and had asked him for his support. Zogu intially had good reason to expect this support, since Jusuf was a sworn opponent of the clique and had heartily espoused Zogu's cause when the attempted coup in November 1923 made it clear that Zogu was opposed to that organization. Although he had finally been convinced by Noli to lend minimal assistance in ousting Zogu in June, he quickly adopted an attitude of benevolent neutrality and rejected the advances of the government.

Not long before the invasion, however, Noli sent Zia Bey Dibra to Jusuf for the purpose of convincing him to remain loyal to Tirana. Dibra was able to do this by playing on the age-old fear of the Yugoslavs, explaining that Zogu was little more than a Yugoslav agent. As is usual in these cases, a good deal of money accompanied the explanation. Consequently, Zogu's advances were turned down and Jusuf even refused the proposal that he remain at home while events took their course. Instead, Jusuf took up arms and joined the government troops at Peshkopi.[23]

Despite efforts to downplay the connection, Zogu's Yugoslav alliance caused considerable apprehension in Albania.[24] Zogu was certainly aware of this but saw Yugoslav military support as indispensible and was therefore willing to face the consequences.

The military plan arranged for simultaneous attacks by seven different parties covering the entire Albanian-Yugoslav and Albanian-Greek borders. Hasan Bushati, starting from Podgorica, was to fain a movement in the direction of Shkodër and hold the government forces there; Ceno Bey was to march from Prizren; Major Ghelardi, an Austrian in Albanian pay, and one of the officers who Pasic assured the British Ambassador was interned and under military surveillance, was to descend into the Drin Valley; Zogu himself was to advance from Dibër and march northwards to Peshkopi, while further to the south Selahedin Bloshmi was to start from Struga and move on Elbasan.

These five columns were to be joined by Koco Kotta, a minister in Vrioni's government, and Myfid Bey Libohova who had been allowed to organize forces on Greek territory, in Florina and Janina respectively. The Greek government, although they had recognized Noli, assumed presumably that Zogu would be easier to deal with. From their bases in Greece, Kotta was to attack Korcë while Myfid Bey was to occupy Gjirokastër and Sarandë.[25]

The simultaneous attack was to take place on the 17th of December and because no system of communication existed, the sound of firing distantly across the hills was to be the signal for action. An astute use of rumor, concealed at one point and advertised at another, had convinced Noli's government that the main attack would be in the north and northeast. The Prime Minister therefore based the bulk of his first line troops at Shkodër, making it almost impossible to deal with attacks from the center and south. Noli was generally unprepared.

Of the seven columns, the first four in order were completely successful. Ceno Bey, who for some unexplained reason attacked on the 14th, met the main government forces under Bajram Curri. The old chieftain fought for five or six days but soon gave way, since by then most of his men had either gone home or defected to his opponent. Curri himself retreated into his own hills with a number of his supporters and was not molested for some time.

Zogu, upon hearing the guns to the north, although his preparations were not yet complete, immediately dispatched Ghelardi with a force of 800, including 100 Russians with four machine guns and two mountain cannons. The Austrian was to make his way along the line of hills which flank the Drin Valley, until he reached a point from which he could join in the attack on Peshkopi, the only garrison which the government was able to strengthen after the beginning of hostilities.[26]

The main force under Zogu crossed the border from Dibër, and by the early morning of the 17th had surrounded Peshkopi, which fell that afternoon. Elez Jusuf was severely wounded in the fighting and was carried to his home, while his kinsmen were barely restrained from killing Ali Riza

Topalli, the government commander, for his share in convincing the old warrior to oppose Zogu. Elez's son-in-law, Murad Kolosh, took over leadership of the tribe and joined Zogu with 900 men.

From Peshkopi one wing of Zogu's force under Ghelardi and Hasan Bushati forded the Drin and advanced across the hills into Mati. They quickly dispatched what little resistance stood in their way.[27]

The three other columns which had intended to subdue the south, ran into some difficulties, stemming primarily from Zogu's unpopularity in that region. Bloshmi, instead of marching on Elbasan and gaining adherents along the way, fell out with the chiefs and headmen in the neighborhood of the frontier and made no progress. Myfid Libohova did little more than raid a customs-house on the border, after which he immediately returned to Greece. Kotta had considerable difficulty in his advance on Korcë. He could do little more than enter Albania and wait for the moment when news of Zogu's success would render him universally welcome.[28]

Although Zogu was unable to facilitate a general insurrection because his action was not always supported and because his Belgrade connection created a bad impression even among his own partisans, he was able to attract support from northern tribesmen as he advanced. Recognizing his popularity problems, he gave orders to his men to simply disarm, feed and send home government troops that surrendered. He tried to avoid bloodshed as much as was practically possible, ordering that except when circumstances made slaughter imperative, his troops were to fire above the heads of their opponents.

These tactics proved quite successful. Zogu's seeming circumspection and the six month experience of what was generally looked upon as a Tosk government, finally brought armed men from most villages and hamlets of the hills to his side. By the time he reached Tirana, Zogu had 8,000 mountaineers at his back.[29]

The final defense of Tirana was more farcical than serious. On the evening of the 23rd a few men of Mati climbed the mountain behind Tirana and fired a few shots in the direction of the well-situated garrison where Major Shevket Korca, Commander-in-Chief of the government forces, had his headquarters. The Commander-in-Chief declared that all was lost and fled into Tirana with thirty officers, leaving his troops under the command of noncommissioned officers who fled shortly thereafter, without informing their men. The soldiers, with no one left to lead them, simply drifted away leaving excellent defensive positions. That same night, Korca fled with some of his troops to Durrës, so overcome by panic that on the road he pistolled soldiers who were not retreating fast enough for him.[30]

The government, which had avowed its intent to defend itself to the last, did not present itself in a much better light. Despite the serious situation, Noli remained confident, informing his secretary not half an hour before he left that the situation was under control and that he would sleep calmly after two or three anxious and wakeful nights. Within hours, Noli and the rest of his government had hired sailing boats to take them to Vlorë, where they asserted their intention to make a last stand among southerners.

All of this came to nothing. As soon as Italian steamers reached Vlorë the government embarked and continued its flight to Brindisi. Noli was accompanied by approximately 500 persons, including Gurakuqi, the Minister of Finance and Rexhep Shala, the Minister of the Interior, who had abandoned their supporters in Shkodër and had caught a steamer at Shëngjin to join their colleagues. Although they were already unpopular, the nature of their flight and the fact that they took with them the treasury consisting of approximately forty thousand pounds, left an extremely negative impression on the people and made it even easier for Zogu to subdue the country.[31]

On December 24, 1924, Zogu entered Tirana with his army and declared the day "legality day." He quickly proclaimed himself dictator and commander-in-chief and instituted martial law until a regular government could be set up. His two priorities at this point were the subjugation of the rest of the country and the consolidation of his position, and more importantly, the soothing of international ruffles caused by the invasion. He had learned from his own experience that with the military support of a neighboring country, Albania could easily be taken. Zogu was, of course, aware of the connection between Noli and the Italians and was rather disconcerted to learn that the fallen Prime Minister and his government had gathered in Rome. The possibility of an Italian invasion was clearly on his mind.[32]

Zogu was right to fear the Italians, for they viewed events in Albania with the utmost concern. Rome was disconcerted by the rapidity and completeness of Zogu's success. The Italians feared that the Yugoslavs might endeavor to profit unduly by the change in order to secure a preponderant position in Albania. Officials at the Italian Foreign Ministry were also convinced by the Italian Minister in Albania, the Marchese Durazzo, that Zogu must have agreed to some conditions in order to receive such extensive support from Belgrade.

Mussolini, personally, was a good deal disturbed by Zogu's victory, and felt himself obliged by an earlier statement holding Belgrade to their agreement. He had pledged prompt action in the event that Belgrade departed from that agreement. The Duce's position was made even more difficult by several opposition newspapers, notably the *Mondo,* which made capital out of Italian abstention from interference, and alleged a neglect of Italian interests and a free hand given to Belgrade.[33]

On December 24, Mussolini called together a council of state, including the Ministers of War, Marine, Finance and Interior, as well as certain generals commanding Italian forces on the Adriatic coast. He suggested to his group that Italy's respone should be a protest to the League of Nations and a demand for an Italian mandate over Albania. Everyone present, with the exception of Mussolini himself, was opposed to the idea. The consensus of opinion, shared by foreign policy officials, was that Albania was a hornet's nest and that Italy should stay out of it. The suggestion was subsequently dropped and Mussolini was forced to wait and see how the situation developed.[34]

Zogu in the meantime had done everything in his power to assure the Italians that he was not the tool of Belgrade. One of his first acts upon entering Tirana was to send a cordial greeting to the Marchese Durazzo, expressing regret that the Italian press should have lent any credence to reports suggesting that his forces had contained non-Albanian elements. Zogu's claim was rather curious, since at the same time Russian officers were clammering to be paid at the Yugoslav ministry in Tirana. Zogu further told the Marchese that he (Zogu) was the defender of the integrity and independence of Albania and that he hoped his country could remain on the best terms with neighboring states. He then gave the most categorical and formal assurances that no conditions of any kind had been imposed upon him, and that he had made no arrangement of any sort with Prime Minister Pasic.[35]

Because of his commanding firepower, Zogu was able to quickly consolidate his political position within the country. Hoping to dispel the widely accepted idea that he was a tool of Yugoslavia, Zogu circulated to all of his prefects a bogus message from Mussolini containing good wishes for the independence and prosperity of Albania. Although this message was promptly contradicted by the Italian government, which added that it did not recognize the new government, Zogu benefited nevertheless, since more people became aware of the original message than became aware of the denial.

In terms of more direct action to quickly consolidate his position, Zogu swiftly and effectively used terror to forestall any prolonged resistance. Although his troops behaved well in Tirana, where no outrages were reported, he allowed his men in Shkodër and Vlorë, the centers of Noli's support, to behave badly for a few days before they were disbanded.

Many of the leaders of the Noli government, including Zia Dibra and the old fighter Bajram Curri, were hunted down and killed. Zogu particularly wanted Dibra, who was reported shot while attempting to escape, because of his involvement in most revolutions and uprisings in 1922, 1923 and 1924. Another prominent leader, Lef Nosi, was also shot. Zogu's assassins even reached overseas to assassinate Luigj Gurakuqi in a cafe in Bari. His removal was useful to Zogu because Gurakuqi had been a primary organizer of the revolution and because his influence in the north was still rather significant.[36]

These ruthless methods removed many of the more formidable opponents of Zogu's rule. He was now in a position to construct the type of government which he believed would best suit his own, and Albania's purposes. The clique had, for the most part, fled with Noli's government leaving Zogu a free hand to deal with the south. Zogu was also relieved of most of the officers within the army, since approximately 300 of them fled with Noli.

This was certainly no great loss since their numbers were far in excess of requirements, leaving them with little to do but spend their time in political intrigue. They had been basically parasitical and a danger to the state. Zogu purged the remaining ranks of those who had participated in the revolution but had not fled. Many minor leaders of the opposition were sent into exile and the rest Zogu either persecuted or attempted to silence through fear of persecution. The vacant positions in the army, gendarmerie and the administration were immediately filled with supporters.[37]

Zogu took advantage of the momentary dirth of opposition to construct an autocratic centralized government, being careful to follow constitutional methods whenever convenient. Iljas Bey Vrioni returned to Tirana on January 3, to resume his duties. Neither his ignominious flight nor the impression that it had created seemed to bother him very much, but his nerves were shaken by copious alcohol abuse so when it was suggested that a strong hand might be needed at the helm, he quickly resigned.

The Regent Xhafer Ypi, who had been a supporter of Zogu's for some time, asked the self-proclaimed dictator to assume the post of Prime Minister and construct a cabinet. Zogu, ever loyal to those who stood by him in adversity, appointed his military commanders to the chief ministries. Myfid Bey Libohova became the Minister of Finance and eventually Minister of Foreign Affairs. Ceno Bey became Minister of the Interior, while Koco Kotta was rewarded with the Ministry of Public Works.

Aware that he needed to legitimize his position as quickly as possible, Zogu immediately called for the reconvening of the Constituent Assembly which had been elected in late 1923, naturally without many of those who had opposed him. Sixty-four of the original 103 deputies made their way back to Tirana at the end of January 1925, and all but two of them were persuaded to construct a republic and elect Zogu as its first president.

The constitution to accompany this change, which was quickly adopted in March, outwardly looked very much like the American version and included a bi-cameral system with an eighteen member Senate and a fifty-seven member Assembly. The Senate, whose members served for six year terms, was to consist of twelve elected and six appointed members. It was to serve as a high court at the discretion of the President and its approval was required on all measures passed by the Assembly. The Assembly served as the principal law-making body and was elected on the basis of electors who were controlled by local authorities.

The most significant change from the Statutes of Lushnjë concerned the increased powers of the executive. The President, who was elected for seven years, acted both as chief of state and head of the government. He completely controlled the cabinet, which he appointed and dismissed at will, and the Senate, of which he appointed six members, the rest being elected by the Assembly. The President commanded the armed forces, naming and dismissing all senior officers. He controlled the administration in that he was solely responsible for the appointment of all officials. The

President had the sole right to initiate changes in the constitution and he alone could propose laws concerning budgetary increases and transfers. He controlled the judiciary branch by appointing and dismissing judges at will.

Finally, Zogu was given considerable control over the Assembly. He received an unrestricted veto over the laws it passed and was able to dissolve the Assembly and call for fresh elections at any time. The Senate was also constructed basically to watch the procedures of the Assembly. The President could use the Senate to block the Assembly if he did not desire to become personally involved with an issue.

The ultimate control over the Assembly, of course, was through the electoral process. At the time of the first elections, while it did not appear that any violence or intimidation was exercised, there is no doubt that the electorate fully expected such pressure to be used at any sign of opposition. Consequently, only a small number of people took the trouble to vote and the returns, with few exceptions showed a clear victory for Zogu.[37]

The Constituent Assembly further obliged Zogu by initiating a number of projects and laws which the new President considered indispensible to the continuance of internal tranquility and, of course, his own regime. In his first proclamation as President, Zogu outlined a program for the complete reorganization of the military forces in Albania, which under the previous system had become a hotbed for politicians. The army had clearly proven itself to be a danger to the internal order of the country and no shield against foreign aggression.

The scheme developed by Zogu and two foreign advisers hired for the purpose, Colonel Mirach, an Austrian and Colonel Stirling, an Englishman, called for the complete disappearance of the 5,000-man army and its replacement with a 3,000 man militia to man the eighty frontier posts. Zogu, of course, planned to retain 2,000 of his own volunteers who would watch the militia.

The President was clearly interested in doing away with the role of the military in politics, primarily because the last time the military took an active role it was in oppositionn to him. The plan was presented, then, in terms of the necessities of internal order and the economy. Not surprisingly, the scheme gained wide support from everyone except the officer corps.[38]

Zogu's internal control was further enhanced by the establishment of a decree law instituting fresh measures for the suppression of treasonable propaganda. Provisions were made for the imprisonment of persons against whom evidence sufficient to satisfy the courts could not be found. The decision rested with a commission to be formed in each prefecture and to consist of the prefect, the gendarmerie commander and the public prosecutor. The decision required cabinet approval. Once taken, the suspect could be imprisoned for periods ranging from two months to one year.[39] This law, by overriding the ordinary process of justice, clearly gave Zogu greater power than the constitution would allow.

The censorship which these new laws imposed, however, was rather haphazard. Fortunately for the small intelligentsia, the new regime lacked ideological commitment, was not the monopoly of one party and did not use efficient means. This leniency can be further explained by the lack of sophistication of the old school and by the fact that many of the young men who served as censors were in secret sympathy with the ideas expressed by the university trained writers. Consequently, there was some freedom of thought expressed in the press and books, except when Zogu himself was personally attacked.[40] In such cases, and when communist oriented material was in question, Zogu never hesitated to ruthlessly crush his opponents.

In a further attempt to insure internal control, Zogu declared Tirana the new capital. The central Albanian town was close to Mati, which afforded Zogu a sense of security since his loyal tribesmen were close at hand. Previous governments had been unable to make this move because of strong opposition from Shkodër and Vlorë. Since the Christians had fallen into disrepute because of their complicity in the 1924 revolution, Zogu was able to confirm Tirana without much opposition.

The new capital was actually little more than an enlarged Moslem village, boasting only 12,000 inhabitants in 1925, and consisted primarily of a bazaar used for hanging offenders of the peace, four mosques, several barracks and a number of legations. Tirana gave the appearance of a gold rush town in the late 19th century American West, with its saloons, gambling casinos and ever present guns and gunbelts. A rickity Ford progressing slowly along the muddly unpaved unlite streets was the only sign of the twentieth century.[41]

The buildings of the town were rather unostentatious. Most of them consisted of old shanties interspersed with an occasional small villa, belonging to some Moslem worthy, many of which were in such a state of disrepair as to give the visitor "the impression that the whole town had been recently under shell-fire."[42] Two such unassuming buildings, dating back to Turkish times, became the presidential office building and Zogu's residence. Opposite these two buildings was a more substantial house occupied by the President's four sisters and mother, who became a close personal advisor.

Once Tirana was confirmed as the capital, plans were made for various public buildings including a Parliament and a number of hotels, primarily for foreign visitors. Construction progressed rather slowly, however, and in the meantime Tirana offered little in the way of Western social amenities, much to the distress of the one hundred members of the diplomatic world.[43]

Zogu had constructed a government more akin to his own plans and more in step with the realities of the Albanian political system. He had brought to an end the Western oriented democracy which had failed to create the basis for stable internal development but he had shied away from his ultimate goal, the crown of Albania. Although he had often spoken of what he would do if ever he found himself in a position to assume absolute power, once the moment arrived, fears of what the attitude of Europe might be, led him to draw back and be content with a qualified authority.[44]

That he was in a position to assume complete control cannot be doubted. His enemies had been vanquished and were either dead or in exile; his armies were in control of the entire country. Furthermore, many Albanians were willing to accept a more autocratic, even a monarchical regime. When the northern tribes came to Tirana to pay their allegiance and collect their peace money, many of them openly proclaimed Zogu as king, undoubtedly being unaware of what a president really was.

Although Zogu would have gladly accepted the dignity of a crown in 1925, his inability to understand European politics, because of his lack of education and experience, convinced him to set up what eventually became a republican transition period with the trappings of monarchy.[45] The President, with his white uniform and gold epulets, was convinced that with this strange combination he had successfully created the basis for stability. Events would soon prove him wrong.

CHAPTER FIVE

THE STRUGGLE FOR ECONOMIC STABILITY, THE PRESIDENT TURNS TO ITALY

While political chaos dominated the Albanian scene, the economy deteriorated further. With the construction of the presidency, Zogu believed he had finally provided himself with a political structure which he could control. This allowed him once again, to concentrate his energies on the appalling financial conditions of the country. Long before 1925, Zogu had already concluded that Albania would never become economically viable without extensive foreign assistance. Both Zogu and Noli had appealed to the League of Nations without success. Without political stability the League would not risk a loan, and without a loan political stability would never be achieved. The President was left with no other option but to turn to a foreign power, one which was willing to extend aid recognizing that the chance of economic gain really did not exist.

The choice was rather clear: Zogu was forced to turn to the Italians for a number of reasons. Politically, the Albanian leader was indebted to Belgrade and although he eventually paid his debt in 1926 by ceding disputed territory around the monastery of Sveti Naoum, he refused to accord them influence in his government because he feared their intentions. As with the leaders of most small states, the President seemed to feel more comfortable dealing with larger states more physically removed.

Zogu's distrust of Belgrade was strengthened by the Yugoslav readiness to intervene in Albanian politics to bring Zogu himself back to power.[1]

The idea undoubtedly also occurred to him that if ever he found it necessary to pursue an irredentist policy it would by necessity be directed against Yugoslavia, which still included almost half of all Albanian-speaking people.

Italy, on the other hand, was a leading state and shared no borders with Albania. An alliance with Rome would not be as unpopular because most Albanians had little contact with the Italians and were, therefore, not as threatened by them. Zogu also realized that he could always fall back upon the legend, which became more fantastic with age, that if matters ever reached crisis proportions, the Albanians could easily expel Italy as they had done in 1920.[2]

Economically the Italians were also the logical choice. Italy was already Albania's main trading partner and had a need for Albanian goods. Greece and Yugoslavia, the two Balkan nations interested in Albania, produced basically the same agricultural products and therefore had little need for Albanian goods. Nor were they in a position to undertake the type of unsound investments which financial cooperation with Albania required.

The only other interest shown came from Great Britain and the United States, but this was primarily of a private humanitarian nature and amounted to very little. In the final analysis, then, Italy was the only country solid enough and with enough strategic interest to be willing to underwrite and support the chaotic Albanian economy.

Italian interest had significant historical precedents, including classical contacts and more recently, the establishment of the large, still existent, Albanian colonies in the last third of the 15th century, following the defeat of Skanderbeg. Active Italian concern was resparked after unification by Premier F. Crispi, an Italian of Albanian descent, who recognized Albania's strategic position with regard to the Adriatic. His natural interest in matters Albanian and in the extension of Italian prestige was further fueled by Italian naval specialists who informed him that Italy had no suitable base for naval operations on its Adriatic coast. Crispi, and his admirals, eyed Vlorë with considerable interest.[3]

While the Premier eventually opted for status quo politics because of Austrian interests, he did move quickly on the cultural and economic plains to establish an Italian presence. Crispi's aims were pursued with such fervor that a prominent Italo-Albanian lawyer was driven to proclaim that "the Italians with their mania to found schools, new consulates and

new commercial agencies in Albania, regarded this land as an Italian province.."[4]

Italian interests in Albania were finally officially recognized in 1887
when the Triple Alliance fell due for renewal. A separate Austro-Hungar-
ian-Italian treaty bound the two signatory powers to preserve the status
quo as long as possible, but in the event that the status quo could no
longer be upheld, no action would be taken without consultation. It was
agreed that should any occupation of Turkish territory become necessary, it could only be occupied "based upon the principle of reciprocal
compensation for every advantage, territorial or other."[5]

This agreement was reconfirmed at Monza in 1896 when each power
stated that it had no intention of occupying Albania and yet would not
allow any other power to occupy it. The two powers also agreed that if
Turkey lost Macedonia, they would constitute Albania as a privileged province within the framework of the Ottoman Empire, or would raise Albania
to the status of an independent principality.[6]

The two powers continued to support the integrity of Albanian territory, not out of altruism but because they feared the consequences of any
other solution. Neither could afford a strong power situated on the shores
of the Adriatic. For these same reasons, both powers supported the independence of Albania during the Balkan wars and in case this proved impossible, in May 1913, drew up a secret agreement dividing it among themselves. Albania was to be partitioned into two zones and occupied. Although these plans were never carried out, they are significant in that
they demonstrate how easily Italy was willing to abandon the principle
of an independent Albania, despite its earlier pronouncements.[7]

Italy's role during World War I lends credence to the argument that
its first priority was security, which was often perceived as being synony-
mous with expansion into the Balkans through Albania. When the war
broke out in August, 1914, Italy remained neutral, arguing that its Triple
Alliance obligations did not require it to participate because the Central
Powers had not been attacked. Although a non-belligerent, Italy occupied
Sazan and Vlorë in October 1914, without incurring the wrath of either
side because all major powers courted Rome. Its eventual entrance on the
side of the Allies concluded a period of rather cyncial bargaining, leading
to the secret Treaty of London. In exchange for a military contribution
against Austria, Italy was pledged extensive territories in Albania, although

Rome was required to agree to an eventual division of the rest of Albania between Montenegro, Serbia and Greece.[8]

At the Paris Peace Conference, Italian territorial demands with regard to Albania grew once it became clear that Rome would be denied many of the additional areas promised in 1915. The Italian Foreign Minister, Baron Sonnino, decided to pin his hopes on Albania, (partially because most of the country was Italian occupied) and demanded Vlorë, Sazan and a protectorate over the rest of Albania, with no compensation for other powers. To further secure its position, Rome signed the Tittoni-Venizelos agreements in July 1919, which called for the division of Albania between Greece and Italy in the event that Albania was unable to reestablish its independence.

The Italians had gone too far, incurring the displeasure of the participants of the Peace Conference and the hostility of the Albanians. As a result, they came away from Paris empty-handed. The Italian attempt at direct occupation came to an abrupt end in 1920 when internal problems, and stiff Albanian resistance, forced them to evacuate all of Albania with the exception of Sazan, which they were allowed to keep after recognizing the independence of Albania.

Despite the fact that the Italians were responsible for considerable progress in the areas which they had administered up until 1920, as a rule Albanians would rather be governed badly by their own then be governed well by foreigners. The Italians did leave with a certain amount of dignity, however, and their general image was enhanced by their actions, particularly in light of the fact that portions of Albania were still occupied by Yugoslav and Greek troops.

Italy's Albanian disaster was further mitigated in November 1921, when the Conference of Ambassadors reaffirmed the 1913 Albanian boundaries, with a few changes favorable to Albania, and acknowledged Rome's prominent interests as follows:

> Recognizing that the violation of these frontiers or of the independence of Albania might constitute a danger for the strategic safety of Italy (the British Empire, France, Italy and Japan) have agreed as follows:
> 1. If Albania should at any time find it impossible to maintain intact her territorial integrity, she shall be free to address a request to the Council of the League of Nations for foreign assistance.

2. The governments of the British Empire, France, Italy and Japan
decide that, in the above-mentioned event, they will instruct their
representatives on the Council of the League of Nations to recom-
mend that the restoration of the territorial frontiers of Albania
should be entrusted to Italy.[9]

Although this agreement gave Italy a virtual protectorate over Albania,
Rome was unable to take advantage of its predominate position until well
into 1925. Albania was loath to recognize Italy's predominance and even
those who under other circumstances might have welcomed Italian aid,
saw the declaration of the Conference as a threat to Albanian integrity.
Italian internal political conditions, however, remained the most significant element explaining Italian reluctance to move, despite its mandate
from the Conference.

This rather benign attitude towards Albania continued even after Mussolini came to power, despite his bold assertions about the reestablishment of Italian prestige abroad. In his first years, the Duce was forced
to act with some circumspection in his dealings with the various political
forces which viewed his rise to power with anxiety. Prominent among
this group was the foreign policy establishment, directed by Senator
Contarini and Count Sforza. Although most elements in the foreign ministry welcomed Italian expansion, Mussolini's tactics, as demonstrated
by his behavior during the Corfu crisis, lacked the sophistication with
which they were accustomed.

Mussolini was further delayed in implementing an expansionistic foreign policy by what came to be called the Matteotti Affair, which shook
the fascist regime to its very roots. Because his government was heavily
implicated in the murder of the Socialist deputy Matteotti, Mussolini
feared not only a hostile domestic reaction but international ostracism by
respectable Europe.

Although the Duce did encounter serious domestic opposition, foreign
condemnation came primarily from the Soviet Union and Czechoslovakia,
states which had little effect on Mussolini. The rest of Europe eventually
followed the lead of British Conservatives who showed warm support for
the Duce. Austin Chamberlain, the British Foreign Secretary, and Eric
Drummond, the British delegate to the League, did a great deal to not only
help Mussolini weather the crisis, but their support left him free to return
to a belligerent foreign policy.[10]

By the beginning of 1925, Mussolini had recovered from the domestic crisis and was ready to begin a new phase of Italian penetration into the Balkans. Zogu was more than willing to participate in this process. The Albanian President had not always been so willing to extend a hand to the Italians, indeed, his personal relationship with Rome had been somewhat erratic. Zogu had been distrusted by the Italians since his entrance into Albanian politics, primarily because he had always been opposed to their interests. During the war he fought with the Austrians against Italy, indeed, Italy was the only country which never benefited from his services.

After the war, he had taken a leading role in opposing the Italian puppet government in Durrës and in driving the Italian forces out of Albania in 1920. Zogu had always been considered to be pro-Belgrade because of his consistent opposition to the cry of irredentism while the irredentists, like Hasan Prishtina, received considerable financial support from Rome. Until the beginning of 1924, all pro-Italian elements in Albania, including Noli and Gurakuqi, had been opponents of Zogu.

At the beginning of January 1924, all of this changed and Zogu and the Italians found that they could work together after all. Zogu, was, at that point, in serious domestic trouble and he required a great deal of money to hold off the forces of the opposition. Fearing the proximity of Belgrade, Zogu turned to Italy and offered to grant signficant concessions in return for financial aid. On January 20 a secret Italian-Albanian Shipping and Trade Pact was initialed, giving Italy a favored nation status in Albania. Further, Albania undertook to bar all other nations and non-Italian companies from setting up monopolies or purchasing concessions to the detriment of Italian interests. The shipping agreements included stipulations exempting Italian vessels from transit taxes and provided for arrangements concerning passenger traffic and fishing rights. The pact was followed one month later by an agreement regulating exchange or workers, colonization and business concerns of Italian and Albanian citizens in one another's countries.[11]

In return for these extensive advantages, Zogu received a note for three million lire from the Italian Railroads, the same note which he had hoped to use for collateral on a further loan just before he was forced to flee Albania. The money was supposedly paid for forest acreage in the Mati country but the land in question was unsaleable and impractical for exploitation without the sale of other properties around it. A deal had been made with the other proprietors but Zogu allowed it to lapse after he had been paid for his land. No one seemed terribly concerned since the money had clearly been paid for the pact and not the useless land.[12]

This rapproachement between the two previously opposed parties was postponed as a result of a number of intervening factors. Zogu held up ratification of the agreements not only in the hope of extorting more money from Italians but also because the newly signed friendship pact between Rome and Belgrade had begun to cause considerable misgivings in Tirana. It the two adversaries stopped their feuding what was to stop them from dividing Albania into spheres of interest?

Mussolini finally decided to break his contacts with Zogu after the Italian minister, Durazzo, advised him that Noli would eventually be successful in his power struggle with Zogu. The Matteotti crisis, which began on June 10, 1924, confirmed him in this decision.[13] The Duce turned down all further requests for aid during 1924, leaving the conduct of Italian foreign policy to Contarini and the moderates until March 1925.

It was in January 1925, that Zogu made his first appeal for aid as President of the newly formed Albanian Republic. Zogu informed Durazzo that he planned to give Italian interests, particularly Italian commercial interests, a special position in Albania.[14] Mussolini was initially reluctant, despite his regained freedom in foreign affairs, because of the prevailing rumor that Zogu planned to allow British and Yugoslav officers to organize the Albanian gendarmerie forces and that he hoped to appoint one of the leaders of the irregulars who had fought the Italians at Vlorë in 1920, as foreign minister. When Zogu dropped Belgrade from his plans and retained the Italophile Myfid Libohova as Foreign Minister, Mussolini began to recognize the possibilities. The Duce would not move, however, without "prompt and tangible evidence of goodwill," a device which he had used before and would use again.[15]

Zogu chose that particular moment to repay his debt to the Anglo-Persian Oil Company by satisfying their concession requests, claiming that British pressure was responsible for the move. Mussolini, who decided that the time had come to pursue a more aggressive policy in Albania, promptly complained to Chamberlain.

Although the Britsh Foreign Secretary would have preferred to oblige Mussolini, hoping to civilize him through tolerance of his foreign policy, he could not move against Anglo-Persian which had already invested large sums in direct payments to Zogu. Through direct negotiations, Italy and England finally came to an agreement on March 10, which confirmed the Anglo-Persian concession of 250,000 hectares and created a new concession for the Italian National Railroads and its counterpart the Azienda Italiano Petroli Albania of 80,000 hectares. On the same day, the Albanian government ratified the Italian trade pact of January 1924.[16]

While the negotiations for the various oil concessions were still in progress, talks began in Italy for the formation of an Albanian bank, a suggestion which Zogu had put forward in the hopes of mulifying Italian displeasure over the benefits acquired by Anglo-Persian Oil. Zogu commissioned the Libohova brothers, Myfid, the Minister of Foreign Affairs and Finance, and Ekrem, the Albanian Minister in Rome, to negotiate for Albania. The Duce appointed A. Lessona in Rome and Ugo Sola, the young dynamic former legation secretary in Belgrade who replaced Durazzo, a diplomat of the old school, to bargain for the Italians.

Zogu, whose passion for intrigue and Oriental dealing had not diminished since his time in Constantinople, opened direct negotiations with a group representing the English Midland Bank in the hope of driving a harder bargain with the Italians. The Midland group offered to found a bank with capital of 500 thousand pounds guaranteed by Albanian customs and monopolies. Once the agreement was signed, Zogu was to receive an immediate 100,000 pound advance, money which the President badly needed to pay his armies. Myfid told Sola about this offer near the end of February and from that point on, the primary question as to which financial group would eventually set up the bank revolved around the amount each was willing to pay in bribes.

Myfid was able to convince the Italians to offer a larger bribe, which included one million gold francs for Zogu, to be given immediately, followed by an advance on the loan of one million. For himself, Myfid was to receive one million gold francs plus 2 percent of the loan which the Italians offered to the Albanians. Myfid's brother Ekrem was allowed to spend the one million advance in Rome for what were called pressing state needs. These needs included a parade uniform for Zogu, two coastal patrol boats which after one trip were sold as scrap iron for a tenth of the original cost, and a mass of old cartridges which were eventually found to be worthless.[17]

Having been amply compensated, Myfid signed the agreements, Zogu was initially hesitant but also eventually approved the convention. Myfid had been sure to remove the most damaging passages of the text and the President, being something of an economic novice, was unable to tell the difference. Zogu's approval can also be at least partially blamed on his fear of a negative Italian reaction if he refused. The President, in addition, suffered from illness and overwork during the final stages of the negotiations. Had he been able to fully appreciate the terms of the agreement, he would certainly have rejected it.

This economic convention was so unfavorable to Albania that it virtually sounded the death-knell for any further economic independence. The two-part agreement included the establishment of the National Bank of Issue and Credit to be set up by Il Credito Italiano. The National Bank, with its headquarters in Rome, was to be governed by a board of five members, three Italians and two Albanians with Mario Alberti, the chairman of the Credito Italiano, serving as president.

Although Albania was to control 51 percent of the initial capital, of the 12.5 million gold francs it eventually had to settle for about 20 percent due to the inability and unwillingness of the Albanians to subscribe to the bank. Italy naturally took the opportunity to buy up the controlling interest of 320,000 (53 percent) shares, leaving the Albanians with only 150,000 shares. The remaining shares were divided between Yugoslavia (50,000), Switzerland (50,000) and Belgium (25,000).[18]

The new bank had the exclusive power to issue currency and acted as the treasury for the Albanian government, which meant that Albanian gold reserves were transferred to Rome. The first coins produced by the new bank ominously portrayed things to come. Since Albania had little to say in the design of the coins, Italian engravers produced twenty franc coins bearing the head of Skanderbeg on one side and the lion of St. Mark on the other. The coins were withdrawn only after strong protests from Albania.[19]

The directors of the bank were also trusted with all phases of the award of contracts for public works, which naturally resulted in the introduction of a myriad of Italian firms into Albania. The entire enterprise turned out to be such a success that after only eighteen months of operation the bank was able to distribute a dividend of 5 percent on the ordinary share, 5 percent to the board of directors and a bonus 10 percent to the personnel.[20]

Although the second part of the agreement was not as profitable for the Italians, it effectively tied Albania to Italy economically for the rest of the interwar period. This was done by means of a fifty million gold franc loan which the Italian government granted Albania through an organization created for the purpose, called Societa per lo Svilippo Economico dell' Albania or SVEA. Although interest on the large loan was originally set at 7.5 percent, through various subsidiary fees the actual rate was closer to 11.5 percent. The Albanian government, then, assumed a debt of 70.5 million gold francs, which was deposited in Italian banks while the functions of SVEA were determined by negotiations.[21]

The loan was to be guaranteed by Albanian customs and state monopolies up to 8.5 million gold francs a year. Although the Italian government was aware that Albania was in no position to repay this massive loan, it was eager to extend it for political reasons. Italian motives were clearly stated by the president of SVEA, Vincenzo Lojacono, who advised his stockholders that,

> due to the special character of our company, springing from and living in the orbit of a happy and much vaster political conception of the relations between Italy and Albania, our attainments unfold themselves in a sphere so superior and so foreign to the internal results of a balance sheet that it is a legitimate wish on your part to prefer to hear what our activities have contributed to the development of a program of Italo-Albanian collaboration.[22]

The directors of SVEA insured that the money served its proper political nature by reserving the right to determine how it was to be spent. The following chart indicates the initial plan for its use and how it was eventually spent (in gold francs).

	Estimated Expenditures	Actual Expenditures
Road Building	14,800,000	15,272,604
Bridges	11,265,000	8,771,857
Railroads (Durrës-Tirana)	2,300,000	3,025,755
Harbor Work	8,880,000	7,935,727
Public Buildings	6,735,000	9,613,737

Agriculture and Land Reclamation	5,000,000	1,613,737
Posts and Telegraphs	485,000	---
Surveys	535,000	954,683
Totals	50,000,000	47,188,100[23]

On the surface these figures seem to indicate that the Italians might have done some good with their money, but on closer examination it becomes clear that Albanian priorities were rarely considered. The roads were constructed not according to the needs of Albanian transportation and communications. As with the bridges, they were built for Italian military purposes, primarily in the direction of the Greek and Yugoslav borders. The port of Durrës was expanded to the extent that once it was completed, it was able to handle ships larger than the biggest commercial carriers. The buildings, which could have been useful, were generally of the non-essential type, including a palace for Zogu in Tirana and the reconstruction of Zogu's castle in Mati. Albania's pressing needs, including drainage and canalization and the development of indigenous industry, were generally ignored.[24] Despite the serious defects inherent in the agreements, Zogu, who had little understanding of finances, did receive the money he needed to insure his continued survival.

The various agreements produced a strong negative reaction in Belgrade, considering the commitments Zogu had made to Pasic while in exile. The Yugoslavs had been so generous with their aid primarily because Zogu had gone so far as to agree to a personal and customs union once returned to office. Belgrade was now aware that Zogu would not be their puppet. The Yugoslav government, therefore, came to the conclusion that the best solution to their problem was to come to some direct agreement with the Italians.

In pursuance of this policy, King Alexander suggested to the Italians that it might be prudent to simply divide Albania.[25] Mussolini refused to accept this proposal because he now felt himself to be in a position where he could exclude other powers from influence in Albania. By the summer of 1925, after having removed the influence of the moderates in decisions considering Albanian policy, Mussolini was ready for a political agreement. Zogu was receptive because by alienating Yugoslavia he had lost his quartermaster and was therefore in desperate need of more money and military equipment.

Despite the fact that both parties welcomed the negotiations, once the form of these agreements became the topic of conversations, serious disagreements resulted. Mussolini mistakenly believed that Zogu would sign most anything. Although his approval of the financial agreement betrayed his weakness when it came to economics, the President was no neophite with regard to politics and the military.

In June 1925, the Duce had sent Lessona to Zogu with three pacts and had optimistically expected their prompt acceptance. Zogu was offered a guarantee pact which would have put Albania under Italian protection and would have required Zogu to officially recognize Italian prerogatives as defined by the Conference of Ambassadors decision of 1921. Further, Zogu was offered an open convention which would have required Albania to grant Italy more concessions, and prevented Albania from contracting political agreements with other states without first consulting Rome. The third proposal consisted of a secret military alliance.[26]

Zogu needed Italian protection and Italian money but was not interested in a formal public treaty, fearing both an adverse internal and foreign reaction. Through concerted effort, he was able to sabotage the first two proposals, promising to consider them in good time. He eventually signed the third, but only after he had been paid six million lire and had been threatened with an Italian naval demonstration.[27]

On August 23 through 26, 1925, Zogu accepted the secret military agreement in an exchange of letters, without reference to either house of the legislature. The extremely far-reaching provisions included four major points. In the first three articles Italy agreed to protect Albania in time of war and the Albanians, in the event of an armed conflict with a neighboring power, agreed to place their military under Italian command. Point four required that if Italy was attacked by a Balkan state, Albania would declare war on that state. Point five bound Italy in the event of territorial changes in the Balkans to guarantee that Albanian speaking areas would be incorporated into Albania. In articles six and seven both Italy and Albania agreed to refrain from concluding public or secret treaties without first consulting the other party, and both countries further agreed that the pact would remain secret until both agreed to publish it.[28]

In this first round of agreements dealing with some form of political connection, Zogu very clearly bested the Italians. The President had extracted a guarantee against the much feared possibility of Yugoslav military intervention and was even in a position to drag Italy into a war with the hope of detaching the Kosovo Albanians. Furthermore, Zogu could blackmail Mussolini with the publication of the pact.

Zogu had also been promised that Italy would make no agreement regarding Albania with a foreign power without his knowledge. If the Duce actually kept this pledge, the ever present fear of a Rome-Belgrade agreement dividing Albania, would have been defused. For all these commitments, Italy received the dubious benefit of the Albanian army in time of war.

But Zogu was only able to hold on to his advantage for a limited time. Throughout the remainder of 1925 and into the early months of 1926, Italy was preoccupied with the construction of a Balkan Locarno Pact which required the adherence of Belgrade. Mussolini temporarily broke off negotiations with Zogu on the pretext that the Albanian President had made an agreement with Yugoslavia. The Duce soon failed in his endeavor and so decided to resume his offensive against Albania's independence, hoping to tie Zogu irrevocably to Italy.

At the beginning of February 1926, Sola was replaced at the Italian ministry in Tirana by the competent and unscrupulous Baron Pompeo Aliosi.[29] This appointment foreshadowed a new aggressive phase in Italian foreign policy toward Albania, a period which was initiated in April when the Baron demanded that Zogu openly recognize Italian rights in Albania based on the 1921 Conference decision. Aliosi also demanded that the Albanian army and gendarmerie be placed under Italian instruction, that the government accept the control of Italy in matters of finance and national economy and that Zogu place the whole of Albania under the protection of Italy.

The Italian Minister hoped to force Zogu to acquiese by threatening to institute the guarantee mechanism built into the SVEA loans, in other words, Aliosi raised the prospect of the confiscation of Albanian customs revenues. Aliosi, a direct and clever diplomat, also offered Zogu a series of personal bribes which included a yacht, a meeting between the President and Mussolini, weapons and instructors for two Italian divisions, six speedboats for the navy and Italian support for the constitution of an Albanian monarchy, complete with the hand of a member of the House of Savoy.[30]

Although the offer was tempting, the price was too high. Zogu could not afford to officially acknowledge the Conference of Ambassadors decision without fear of internal unrest which could serve as a ready pretext for Italian military intervention. The President was also unwilling to allow the Italians exclusive control of all of his armed forces, which he still considered the only protection against another enforced stay at a hotel in Belgrade.

Zogu resorted to the time-honored Albanian tradition of stalling, while he attempted to secure his position against the Italians in other quarters. The President approach Foreign Minister Nincic with a proposal for a Tirana-Belgrade friendship pact but was turned down since the Yugoslavs at that point did not wish to alienate Rome.[31] As a last hope, Zogu turned to the new British Minister, Edmond O'Reilly, who had replaced Eyres at the beginning of 1926.

O'Reilly, very much in the tradition of Harry Eyres, who in some circles had been credited with having become so influential as to dominate Albanian domestic and foreign policy until 1926, had assumed an active role in Albanian affairs. He was convinced, as Eyres had been, that Italian penetration into Albania constituted a threat to British interests and Albanian independence.

Soon after assuming his post, O'Reilly had begun negotiating for an Anglo-American loan for Albania. Although his efforts were unsuccessful, he did come to Zogu's immediate assistance after being informed about the Italian ultimatum. O'Reilly advised Zogu to turn down Aliosi's proposals while he appealed to London.[32]

Mussolini, having been informed about Zogu's moves, made one last attempt to force Zogu to accept the proposals before foreign, particularly British, reaction made itself felt. Continuing Aliosi's carrot and stick policy, the Duce threatened to take advantage of unrest in northern Albania. At the same time he offered Zogu a fifteen million gold franc bribe.[33]

The Duce's efforts came too late, however, since Chamberlain was quick to react to the new Italian attempt to dominate Albania. Although the Foreign Secretary had in the past been tolerant of Mussolini's rather erratic foreign policy moves, he felt the timing was wrong and advised the Duce to back down.[34] Chamberlain further demonstrated his displeasure by dispatching a British cruiser, which had been visiting Dalmatian harbors, to Durrës and a few days later it was announced that Zogu was to receive the French Grand Order of the Legion of Honor.[35]

Mussolini was left with little choice but to momentarily cease his efforts to subjugate Zogu. His first move was to attempt to blame the entire incident on Aliosi by suggesting that the Minister had overstepped his instructions.[36] The Duce was aware that he could not continue his desired Albanian policy without coming to some arrangement with the British. In the middle of June, then, Mussolini broke off negotiations with Zogu to deal directly with Chamberlain.

The Duce, through his ambassador in London, Pietro Tomasi della Torretta, bitterly complained to Chamberlain about O'Reilly and noted that the problem could only be cleared up by a recognition of Italian interests in Albania. Chamberlain ignored Mussolini's implicit demand for a free hand in Albania but did grant the Duce a number of concessions, including the recall of O'Reilly to London for consultation and his eventual transfer at the end of July.

More significantly, Chamberlain informed the Italians that in the future, when matters concerning a conflict of interest in Albania arose, the Foreign Secretary would deal directly with Rome. Chamberlain stated finally that he had grown tired of Zogu's constant appeals to London and that the Albanian President had, therefore, been informed that in the future "if he had complaints about the behavior of the Italians, he should complain directly to Rome."[37]

The Duce was naturally encouraged by this positive response from the British, but he was not satisfied. He wanted personal assurances from Chamberlain. The opportunity for such a final clarification presented itself at the end of September 1926 when Chamberlain and his family sailed to Livorno for a personal meeting with Mussolini. The Duce hoped to gain some form of British approval for his Albanian policy, while Chamberlain hoped to clear up a delicate situation which had developed as a result of Baron Aliosi's proud boast that O'Reilly had been recalled because of the wishes of the Italian government.[38] Both parties came away from Livorno basically satisfied.

Although the only record of the conversation between the two comes from notes taken by Mussolini, which Chamberlain later called incomplete, a number of significant points do stand out. The Duce admitted that Baron Aliosi had been indiscreet concerning the recall of O'Reilly.

For his part Chamberlain made it clear that Great Britain was interested in Albania exclusively from an economic point of view and he reiterated that even with regard to the British oil concessions, he would rather deal with Rome than with Tirana. Although the evidence suggests that the Foreign Secretary did not openly given the Duce a free hand in Albania, it is clear from his attitude and his general statements regarding Albania that Mussolini could and, indeed, did interpret the Foreign Secretary's position as not being opposed to Italian activity in Albania.[39]

The Duce was understandably pleased with the course of the talks and the general behavior of Chamberlain, so much so that he commented that "Chamberlain e nel suo intimo, piuttosta un simpatizzante per il Fascismo."[40] Mussolini was undoubtedly correct in his assumption. As Chamberlain's yacht left Livorno, both his wife and his son, wearing the fascist insignias presented to them by the Duce, gave Mussolini the fascist salute.[41]

Mussolini now believed that Great Britain would allow him to consolidate his position in Albania. The Duce's conclusion was reasonable when seen in the light the new British Minister's suggestion to Zogu that he come to an agreement with the Italians.[42] The new Minister, William Seeds, characterized the new British policy as "disinterestedness and tacit recognition of Italian claims."[43]

Zogu was certainly not oblivious to these developments and it soon became clear to him that he could no longer play the British off against the Italians, a severe blow to his foreign policy. Being a realist, the President recognized that his only remaining option was to reopen negotiations with the Italians. Zogu also found himself facing yet another financial crisis which became all the more serious because of the rumors of substantial unrest in the north which Mussolini could easily use to his advantage. The Italians were naturally mistrustful of Zogu after their experiences in the summer so Aliosi travelled to Rome to work out a proposal for Zogu. On October 11, 1926, the Italian Minister presented the President with the first Italian offer.

Following his usual line, Zogu stalled after the initial proposal in order to wear the Italians down and possibily extract more money from them. Zogu's initial demand was for three million gold lire, a figure which was quickly raised to five. In the meantime, Zogu had instructed Foreign Minister Vrioni, the new Albanian Minister in Rome and Zogu's brother-in-law, Xhemil Bey Dino, the former Minister in London, Mehmet Konitza, and Myfid Libohova, all rather staunch Italophiles, to cooperate with Aliosi and work out an Albanian counter proposal. On November 3, the Italian Minister was officially presented with the so-called friendship and security pact which, when compared to the Italian version, actually gave Rome more advantages.[44]

The Baron was delighted, but Zogu was not finished with him. On November 10, Aliosi was informed that for another five million lire Zogu would have the pact ratified immediately. Mussolini reacted angrily to this new demand for money but was eventually persuaded to agree to pay the ten million if everyone's "tips" were included and if Zogu agreed to sign an open convention along with the political pact. Zogu took this opportunity to try and withdraw from the pact altogether, claiming that internal and foreign complications prevented him from signing.

It was clear to Aliosi that Zogu would in the end be forced to sign, precisely because of the threatened internal insurrection, the severe financial crisis and the fact that Albania was diplomatically isolated. Because he feared that Zogu would demand more money and more control over the SVEA loan, he suggested to Mussolini that he drop the open convention plan and return to the original proposal. Aliosi had learned since his unfortunate experience during the summer, that dealing with Zogu required a great deal of tact and patience.

The Italian Minister's task was made considerably easier by the outbreak of the expected northern revolt on November 20, 1926. The revolt, which will be dealt with later in this volume, constituted the most serious threat to Zogu's regime since the creation of the Republic. It began among the northern Catholic tribesmen, where foreign influence remained a significant factor.

Zogu, who was aware that the Italians were still supporting Albanian elements hostile to him who had fled his invasion in 1924, found himself in a difficult position. He needed immediate financing to mobilize and equip his bands. On November 22, Aliosi was able to assure Mussolini that conclusion of the pact was imminent but that Zogu wanted money immediately. On his Minister's advice, the Duce dropped his demand for an open convention, agreed to pay Zogu five million lire and deposit an additional 200 thousand gold francs into the Albanian National Bank.[45]

Zogu, aware of the gravity of tying himself to Italy politically, attempted once again to deal, despite the increasing seriousness of the revolt in the north. When the Italians, who had finally lost all remaining patience, threatened to send a fleet, the President realized that the long game was finally up. On November 27, diplomatically isolated and threatened from within, Zogu was forced to place himself under the dreaded protection of Mussolini. After a final stormy two-hour session, the pact was signed by Vrioni for the Albanians and by Aliosi for the Italians.

The provisions of the Pact of Friendship and Security, which was to last for five years, contained the following significant articles:

> Art. 1 Italy and Albania recognize that any disturbance directed against the political, judicial and territorial status quo of Albania is opposed to their reciprocal political interest.
>
> Art. 2 To safeguard the above-mentioned interest, the High Contrasting Parties undertake to give their mutual support and cordial collaboration. They likewise undertake not to conclude with other powers political or military agreements prejudical to the interests of the other Party as defined in the present Pact.[46]

On December 5, an exchange of notes between Vrioni and Aliosi cleared up a question which seemed to have been omitted from the pact. The Italian Minister assured the Albanians that collaboration could only be interpreted as collaboration resulting from proposals made by one of the parties and voluntarily accepted by the other. It seemed that in some Albanian circles, doubt existed as to whether Italy had obtained the right to intervene in Albania whenever it pleased, or only when asked to do so by the government.[47]

Many enlightened Albanians were not satisfied by Italian assurances Despite this opposition, Aliosi was able to secure its ratification by December 9. As usual, a combination of threats, this time a revolt in the south, and bribes, about five million lire distributed to the deputies, helped secure this prompt action.

Zogu had given more than he had planned and received less than he had hoped. In monetary matters, however, the President did extremely well. Although no exact figures as to the final amount are to be found, both Yugoslav and German sources mention up to twenty million lire as payment. Zogu was to have received fourteen or fifteen million for his personal use while his brother-in-law Dino very likely received approximately

three million. The remaining money was divided among the various middle-
men whom Zogu had commissioned to draw up the Albanian text of the
treaty.[48]

Zogu, of course, also hoped to receive a certain amount of security
from the treaty, particularly since Italy had committed itself to the protection of the political status quo, i.e., Zogu's regime. Like the secret military treaty, it also left the door open for Zogu to drag Italy into a war
with Belgrade, since the President could readily maintain that Yugoslavia
was giving aid to his political opponents, thereby threatening the political
status quo.

Zogu had, however, lost more than he had gained and finally received
a good deal less than had been offered to him in the summer. He did not
receive the desired support for constituting Albania as a monarchy, an
idea which he increasingly favored as he came to the realization that the
republican structure did not offer him the political control for which he
had hoped. Although the Republic was a definite improvement over the
Principality, it was clear to Zogu that a monarchy would provide a greater
degree of stability.

In exchange for the money and the protection he himself received as
a result of the pact, Zogu had signed away any foreign policy independence he might have had. Although it is true that as a small impoverished
state, Albania's foreign policy options were always very small; once the
pact was signed they were restricted even further. Zogu had agreed to conclude no military or political pacts with other powers. Italy had essentially
replaced the four power guarantee which Albania had been given in 1921
by the Conference of Ambassadors. Mussolini believed that he had finally
achieved a de facto protectorate over Albania.[49]

Despite their apparent victory, the Italians could at no time rest easy
and assume their subjugation of Zogu was complete, for as soon as the
pact was signed Zogu began devising schemes to undermine it. The President had signed in a moment of extreme need but once the crisis had
been overcome, he was ready again to do combat with the Italians. As the
German Minister, Rudolf von Kardoff, noted at the time,

> nach orientalischer Denkweise hat er sich darauf verlassen dass die
> Suppe nicht so heiss, wie sie gekocht, gegessen werde und sich Ge-
> legenheiten finden würden, den Kopf aus der italienischen Schlinge
> zu ziehen.[50]

CHAPTER SIX

THE STRUGGLE FOR POLITICAL STABILITY, ATTEMPTS AT WESTERNIZATION

Deteriorating internal conditions had made Zogu's hasty signature on what came to be called the Pact of Tirana necessary. Before the President was forced once again to turn and face this growing internal opposition, he was able to make some progress transforming Albania into a modern state.

The increased power which he had relegated to himself allowed him to make changes beneficial not only to the continued retention of his authority but also for the good of the country. Apart from economics, Albania's major problem during Zogu's presidency remained the basic lawlessness in the northern highlands. Although some progress had already been made regarding the carrying of guns in the years preceding 1925, truly effective steps could not be taken until the central government was sure of a relatively secure power base in order to withstand the inevitable resistance to such measures.

Zogu tackled the problem of brigandage and blood feud warfare through a number of methods, including the creation of a reasonably effective gendarmerie. Before the President addressed himself to this problem, the gendarmerie had become more of a plague on the people than a means for protection. Because pay was so minimal and usually in arrears, the gendarmerie in remote outposts generally lived off the land.

Bands of them remained in mountain outposts for months at a time and openly worked with criminals. The officers were always in a position

101

to make more money than the men, so promotion depended upon nepotism and political connections.[1]

Zogu moved quickly to remedy the situation by appointing Colonel W. F. Stirling as Inspector-General of the Albanian gendarmerie. Stirling, who had been with T. E. Lawrence in Arabia, had come to Albania as early as 1923 when he was appointed as an adviser to the Minister of the Interior. The colonel was allowed to appoint nine army officers to serve with him as assistant inspectors.

This first attempt to police the gendarmerie ended in failure, however, when disputes arose among the British contingent, culminating in the dismissal of several of Stirling's officers. The colonel also found that he could not advise the Minister of the Interior while at the same time tackle the herculian task of reorganizing the police forces. Accordingly, in August 1926, Stirling resigned his position with the gendarmerie and was succeeded, much to the chagrin of the Italians, by another British officer, General Sir Jocelyn Percy.

Percy, who was to remain Inspector-General until 1938, was to a large degree responsible for Zogu's success in decreasing random violence. His charge was anything but simple, and it required years to cut his way through the age-old Albanian traditions of corruption, petty intrigue and favoritism. Percy had difficulty procuring the required and promised financing for the planned reorganization. Not the least of the general's problems revolved around Zogu himself, who used the gendarmerie as a means to enrich himself and to pay his loyal supporters.[2]

To illustrate Percy's difficulties, in 1927 four young officers in charge of large districts were frequently denounced by the Inspector-General for notoriously using their positions to smuggle on a large scale and for the perpetration of other serious irregularities. One of the officers was responsible for a considerable force which existed only on paper, for which he systematically drew pay from the treasury. Although Zogu repeatedly promised to act, nothing was done because the President, desperately in need of money at that time, was using these young officers to fill his own coffers. The money to pay the phantom troops together with three-quarters of the booty derived from smuggling went directly to Zogu.[3]

Despite these obstacles, Percy was able to instill a basic respect for law and slowly reorganized the gendarmerie so that it would no longer be feared by the people. He eventually convinced Zogu to allow him to control the officers and also to directly supervise four battalions. The Inspector-General further demanded and received the right to report to the President personally, since many of the other high government officials got in the way of his reforms and disfigured them for their own purposes.[4]

To complement the reformed police force, Zogu instituted a new Civil Code, which called for civil marriage and divorce. By so doing, the President hoped to end the shooting of faithless wives, a custom which was still generally accepted in Albania at the time.

In defending his program, Zogu cited a specific incident. "There is a case here in Tirana now," the President noted, (where)

> the wife of a Roman Catholic left him and spent a week with another man: the priest rescued her and induced the reluctant husband to take her back. She has now run off again, with the priest in pursuit, but if the worthy man brings her back a second time the husband will certainly shoot her. And then I shall have to tell my gendarmes, judges and executioners to get to work. Now divorce would stop all that.[5]

As with all other reforms, the Civil Code too resulted in considerable domestic and foreign opposition. The Vatican objected strenuously to the new law and refused to sign a Concordat with Albania while divorce was sanctioned. The Italian Minister naturally urged the President to meet the Pope's wishes, pointing out that domestic reaction among the Catholics in the north might result in the organization of a opposition party. Zogu simply replied that he did not allow opposition parties in Albania and informed the Archbishop of Shkodër that he would not tolerate the protests of the church and that "any priest whose enthusiasm ran away with him beyond proper bounds would soon be provided with a tree with adequate strength to support his weight."[6]

Although there were problems, Zogu was able to make some progress. The blood-feud killings were further reduced during his presidency as Albanians were forced to surrender their weapons. The President eventually convinced the average Albanian that unless he had political connections of some sort, killing would be treated as murder.

Brigandage diminished to the point where long strung-out caravans passed and repassed along the roads with little fear of attack by armed bands. As a result, trade figures became much more favorable throughout the country.[7]

Other progress was made as well. Building was undertaken at an increased pace, although in many cases priorities were somewhat awry with ministry buildings and palaces taking precedent over schools and hospitals. The government made an effort to collect taxes and recruits even in the north where such activity would have been considered impossible a few years earlier.

The President pledged himself to continue along these lines and eventually put roads at the top of the list of Albania's needs. It was imperative to link the outlying districts near the frontiers with the plains in order to open communications between the mountains and the outside world. Roads of course, facilitated not only trade but also made it possible for the government to further extend its direct control.

Zogu also put much stock in the development of national education, hoping to eventually create a body of honest efficient administrators. The President also drew up plans for the systematic drainage of swamps in order to combat the endemic malaria, which sapped the strength of the country, and to produce more agricultural land. From 1925 industry grew as well, because of active encouragement from the government, with heavy emphasis on agricultural industries such as the manufacture of woolen goods.[8]

Considering the circumstances under which Zogu was forced to function during his presidency, his accomplishments were quite remarkable. His failures were, however, equally as striking and when added to continued foreign intrigue and the reviving indigenous political rivalry, the contributed to widespread unrest and frequent insurrection which eventually drove Zogu closer to the Italians. At the top of the list of his failures were his inept appointments to high government positions.

Zogu frequently complained that it seemed to be his fate to be served either by fools or by knaves. "If intelligent and energetic they are rogues," he lamented, "if honest they are incompetent or idle."[9] Granted that he had a limited pool to choose from, nevertheless, Zogu himself was ultimately to blame for the sorry group of officials with which Albania was saddled. Indeed, it was his first appointments which caused him the most trouble and initiated the long series of rebellions which plagued the presidential regime.

Zogu, remaining faithful to one of his most dangerous faults, continued to appoint officials and advisers based upon past service rather than ability, character and continued loyalty. Upon becoming President, Zogu's cabinet looked very much like his last one as Prime Minister. Myfid Libohova became Minister of Finance and Foreign Affairs, Ceno Kryeziu became Minister of the Interior, Koco Kotta became Minister of Public Works and Petro Poga was appointed Minister of Justice. The two remaining ministires, war and public instruction, were suppressed in the interests of economy. Zogu installed Eshref Frasheri as President of the Senate, and retained his faithful Mati protector, Abdurrahman Mati, nicknamed "Krossi" the hairless, as his chief personal adviser.

Of this distressing group of associates, Myfid was undoubtedly the most notorious. His political career began in 1909 when he served as a deputy in the Turkish Parliament when he first showed his corruptibility by accepting a subsidy from the Greek government. In late 1918, he served as one of the members of the provisional government under Turhan Pasha which worked in collaboration with the Italian army of occupation. He was very active and among the most pro-Italian elements in the government, becoming one of the two signators of a secret agreement with Italy which provided for the establishment of an Italian mandate over Albania.[10]

Myfid, trying to live down his connection with the Italians, remained politically inactive until he was appointed Minister of Justice in Shevket Verlaci's government in March 1924, and remained in that position after the government was reformed under Iljas Vrioni. Having committed himself to Zogu, he fled Noli's forces and played a rather undistinguished role in the invasion which brought Zogu back to power. As a reward for his steadfast loyalty, the President appointed him Minister of Finance and temporary Minister of Foreign Affairs. In this capacity he was entrusted with negotiating the bank concessions with the Italians in April 1925. Myfid took this opportunity to sell his country into economic dependence.[11]

His disgraceful private life and his notorious official actions convinced the Albanian Parliament to demand that his conduct be investigated by a Parliamentary Court of Enquiry. The court discovered that the original of the document containing the penal clauses of the bank concession and the loan convention had disappeared, and that an annex to the convention rejected by the cabinet had nevertheless been signed by Myfid and was claimed as being in force by the concessionaries, with the result that Albania had lost much of the bank capital secured to the country under the convention. The court also found that considerable sums of money deposited at the Ministry of Finance as subscription for the capital had been diverted to other uses. Myfid was completely unable to account for much of the money.[12]

The Minister of Finance was clearly guilty of peculation and corruption and the court formally charged him with high treason. The charge was eventually not pressed, however, due to the support Myfid received from the landowning class of central Abania, which was very largely Italophile like Myfid. The Minister undoubtedly also distributed some of the embezzled money among the deputies and judges responsible for the case.[13] The only inconvenience which Myfid suffered was the loss of his lucrative offices.

Libohova was succeeded as Minister of Foreign Affairs by Hysejn Vrioni, a nonentity with no ability as a diplomat. He was a man of weak character and lasted in his post until 1927 only because he usually took refuge behind his government and would discuss nothing without reference back to his superiors.

At the beginning of 1927 he was succeeded by his brother, Iljas Vrioni, who after serving as Zogu's puppet Prime Minister in 1924, was rewarded with ministerships in London and Paris. A few weeks after his arrival in Tirana, Vrioni had a breakdown resulting from overindulgence in alcohol and cocaine so he left for Paris to convalesce, where he was able to return to his chief interest, the pleasures of the tables.[14]

Vrioni returned to Tirana a few months later, somewhat recovered, and was rewarded for his trials with an additional ministry. Still subject to relapses, he took frequent convalescing visits to Paris and on one of his return trips shared a compartment with an American who maintained that Vrioni's intense nervousness was betrayed in his every move. Although normally in a state of intoxication, the Minister never failed to see that the big revolver he carried was always handy. He carried it in his hip pocket during the day and upon retiring placed it under his pillow.[15]

This nervousness apparently stayed with him, for back in Tirana in his usual alcoholic frenzy he was often seen screaming in the night for help while waving pistols wildly in the air, hardly the sort of behavior designed to inspire confidence in Albanian officials.[16] The Minister brought discredit on Zogu both at home and abroad.

The sinister figure of Abdurrahman Krossi, Zogu's closest advisor, did a great deal to further undermine the President's political position. Krossi had been a close confident of Zogu's father and after Xhemal Pasha's death, he took the young chieftain under his protection. While Zogu was in Constantinople, Krossi introduced him into the circle of the Albanian palace guards where he learned a great deal about the successful use of Oriental intrigue. Upon Zogu's return to Albania, Krossi was instrumental in helping his mother secure Zogu's position against his older brother.

Krossi remained constantly by Zogu's side and once the young chieftain had achieved power, he became one of the only people in which Zogu was willing to confide. This proximity to the seat of power naturally aroused the indignation of those who aspired to the same position but were unable to achieve it. Krossi took full advantage of his position, becoming involved in most every shady deal in the country. Naturally, he amassed a considerable fortune in the process.[17]

The old retainer eventually achieved a position where he could control access to Zogu and thereby not only keep the President in the dark about what was occurring in the country, but also keep even the highest members of the government in ignorance of what transpired in the presidential palace. His special function was to act as go-between in Zogu's dealings with the clan chieftains. Since the President continued to believe that his internal position depended on the attitude of these chiefs, Zogu valued Krossi very highly.

Because of his power, Krossi was feared by cabinet ministers and ordinary peasant alike and eventually gained the reputation of an Albanian Rasputin. Whoever was able to secure his support could misbehave with impunity, while those who opposed him found themselves faced with the wrath of Krossi, who later became known as "the knife in the King's hand."[18]

Although the above-mentioned associates did Zogu considerable damage, they remained loyal at least for the most part. Eshref Frasheri and Ceno, on the other hand, not only discredited Zogu but plotted to overthrow him in the bargain. Eshref, the President of the Senate and one-time clique leader, had always avoided open opposition to Zogu and the President of the Republic reasoned therefore that it might be worth reconciling Eshref because of his powerful family connections in the south. Within six months of his appointment in early 1925, however, it became known that he was the chief conspirator in a plot being planned in Korcë to revive the clique and overthrow the President.

Frasheri, who tentatively enlisted Myfid Libohova in his plans, atttempted to rouse his followers by playing on the sentiments of the reactionary Moslem element which was suspicious of the President's marked freedom from any religious or ethnic faction and generally distrusted his outwardly Western ways. Zogu, however, was warned in time, partly through the testimony of Myfid who almost immediately turned informer to help himself out of his own troubles.

The President quickly sent a force of mountaineers to Korcë before the plot could come to a head. Because there was little hard evidence, Myfid's testimony not withstanding, Zogu hesitated to openly move against Frasheri. The only public action which the President took involved the removal of a number of Tosk officers who had been implicated in the plot.

Details of the conspiracy, however, soon became widely known and were even the subject of press comments. Frasheri asked for the suppression of a newspaper which had accused him of being part of the revolt.[19] Zogu refused to move against the paper, undoubtedly sensing a way to be rid of Frasheri without incurring the emnity of his followers. Zogu offered Frasheri an open judicial inquiry so that he might be vindicated. The President of the Senate realized that such an enquiry would be controlled by Zogu. Even if it were not, it would still have found him guilty of complicity. Frasheri saw no alternative but to resign.

Before the dust had been able to settle, a much more serious attempted coup was discovered involving Zogu's brother-in-law, the Minister of the Interior Ceno Bey. Ceno had been a great help to Zogu during his stay in Belgrade and was instrumental in negotiating the agreement with Yugoslavia which enabled the President to return to Albania. Zogu had appointed his brother-in-law Minister of the Interior since Ceno was generally believed to be energetic and devoted to the President.

Ceno turned out to be extremely energetic but did badly when it came to devotion. It soon became increasingly clear that Ceno was not following Zogu's direction in terms of policy and that he was involved in a good deal of corruption. Ceno's chief weaknesses included his tremendous ambition and overweening confidence in himself. He listened greedily to flatters who told him that he was the only possible successor to Zogu.[20]

Ceno was finally convinced to join a plot initiated by prominent men in the armed forces and among the exiles in Greece, Italy and particularly in Yugoslavia where Ceno found most of his support since he himself was a native of Yugoslav Kosovo.

Again Zogu became aware of the plot before it could mature and confronted Ceno after he had returned from one of his many trips to Belgrade. The Minister made no attempt to conceal his complicity. Because of friendship, family ties and the wish to avoid a scandal, Zogu took no action other than to demand his resignation and exile him to Paris.[21] The President was apparently shaken by such blatant disloyalty so close to the palace and therefore diligently attempted to repress information about the attempted coup.

Although Zogu's position within Albania was considerably restored by the removal of some of these unhealthy elements, he was not spared the trials of perpetual assassination attempts, coups and insurrections. During the last few months of 1925, Zogu, his adherents and his regime were assaulted from all sides.

At the end of August, Dion Bushati, an Albanian tax official, attempted to assassinate Kal Mijedu, the Vice President of the Albanian Assembly, while he was vacationing in Bosnia. Near the end of September an unknown assailant tossed a bomb at Zogu's villa, injuring no one.[22] At the beginning of November a plot was discovered, supposedly engineered by Fan Noli, with the purpose of overthrowing Zogu and placing Prince Omar Farouk, son of the late Abdul Mejid on the Albanian throne. The plot came to nothing because of a few guards who betrayed the entire plan to the President.[23]

The next year, 1926, began with the arrest of Kemal Bey Vrioni, one of the great landowners of Berat province, on the charge of conspiracy against the government. Vrioni was implicated in various letters which the government had intercepted.[24] Although this minor matter was despatched rather quickly, before the year was out, Zogu was faced with the most serious insurrection since he was forced to leave the country in 1924.

Rumors began as early as February that various emigre groups were plotting to foment a large insurrection during 1926. The former Regent Sotir Peci, a perpetual foe of Zogu's along with others in southern Italy were coordinating an uprising with Macedonian committees to overthrow Zogu.

The Albanian exiles in Italy were in the process of making preparations for an armed descent on the Albanian coast and were collecting a force for that purpose in Bari and Brindisi. At the same time, Hasan Prishtina, Mustafa Kruja, Rexheb Shala and the Italian revolutionary Gabriele D'Annunzio were reported organizing at Zara. Similar agitation was reported in Greece at about the same time.[25]

The conspirators played on the discontent which perpetually existed among various levels of Albanian society. The more well-to-do Moslems in the south resented their political eclipse and remained apprehensive about Zogu's more liberal programs. Among the common people there was a certain amount of agitation against the drafting of labor for work on the roads and the continuing state of poverty in which they were forced to exist, a condition which all the money which Italy was pouring into Albania through SVEA did little or nothing to alleviate.

Emigre propaganda and local conditions are important in themselves in terms of causes for unrest but as with modern non-developed states, these considerations rarely lead to insurrections. Arms and ammunition were needed for an attempt against the government and in a poor country like Albania these material necessities could only be procured from a foreign sources.

It had long been the policy of both Rome and Belgrade to subsidize the northern tribes of Albania and the exiles in the event that their foreign policy interests required the overthrow of the Albanian government.[26] As with most Albanians, however, payment of large sums of money by foreigners rarely purchased undying loyalty. The tribes acted primarily in their own interest. That the spark, direction and course of the November 1926 uprising came from the Albanians themselves is demonstrated by the fact that neither Rome nor Belgrade wished to see Zogu fall at that time.

The Italians successfully used the revolt once it started, however, in order to pressure Zogu into signing the Pact of Tirana. The insurrection not only threatened his security but also put a significant strain on his finances, forcing him to turn to Italy.

The insurgents were interested in much more; they wanted the downfall of Zogu, something which the Italians would never have condoned considering the time and energy they had already expended. Furthermore, Italy was on the verge of successfully completing negotiations which would allow them extensive control. Belgrade had a much clearer reason for not supporting the insurrection in November. They found it in their interest to avoid giving Italy any excuse to intervene. Nevertheless, it was money from Rome and Belgrade, paid to emigre groups and indigenous Albanians which made the revolt possible, whether they intended so or not.

On November 20, 1926, the long planned revolt finally broke out among the Geg Catholic tribesmen who along with all their other grievances still resented the attempt at disarming mountaineers and Zogu's moves to stop brigandage. This activity still provided the only means of livelihood for many of the men in this depressed area.

The insurgents, led by Don Loro Tzoka, advanced on Shkodër driving five companies of government troops before them. They advanced within eight kilometers of the city before they were stopped by government reinforcements from Shkodër. Zogu moved quickly, transferring large bodies of troops from central to northern Albania until he was able to concentrate 10,000 troops and several batteries of mountain guns against the insurgents. The Geg chieftains could not compete against Zogu's overwhelming firepower. By December 2 the insurrection had been crushed and the insurgents driven into the hills.[27]

Despite the fact that the revolt had ended so quickly, Zogu was aware of how serious it had been and realized that had he hesitated, it might have been successful. He therefore acted just as quickly in punishing those guilty of complicity. He sent his Minister of the Interior, Musa Juka, the successor to Ceno Bey, to deal with the insurgents. Juka conducted swift, severe and effective reprisals. He burned a number of villages and constituted a special political court which engaged in large-scale hanging and imprisonment, even sentencing a number of Catholic priests to death.

Although the two priests who were so sentenced had led insurrectionary bands with their crosses held high as standards, Zogu was prevented from hanging them due to representations on their behalf from Rome and Belgrade. The President was put in a rather awkward position, for if he reprieved the priests who had openly confessed their guilt he would have been attacked by the Moslems who remembered that some years before he had hanged several Moslem ecclesiastics for complicity in a revolt. He would also have been accused of being a slave to foreign pressure. When the British Minister added his voice in support of amnesty Zogu lamented, "But I do so much want to hang them as they deserve."[28]

The problem was finally solved by use of Zogu's odd system of checks and balances. The President eventually bowed to foreign pressure and commuted the sentences of the priests who had proudly confessed to having participated in the revolution. In order to satisfy the domestic demand that he hang a priest he brought forth one whom few knew had been arrested and quickly hanged him. This action prompted the American Minister to comment that unlike the personification of Western justice which is a goddess with eyes blindfolded holding a scale and dealing impartially with those brought before her, Albanian justice is a Mohammedan lady who now and then peeps through her veil to see what or whom she had on her scales before adjusting the balances.[29]

Juka and his associates might have gone too far in their persecution, not realizing that if unduly harassed northern tribesmen had a tendency to come back at one with renewed vigor rather than be cowed into submission. The peaceful inhabitants of Shkodër looked upon the complaints of the mountaineers with sympathy since they too continued to see Zogu's rule as central Albanian dominance of the north. The economic grievances which had been instrumental in bringing the late 1926 revolt about were of course still in existence. As a result, by the spring of 1927, rumors of new unrest became more and more evident and the President was naturally concerned since mountaineers need little incentive to take up arms in the spring.

Zogu reacted to these unhappy circumstances by employing various means including of course the customary repression and political assassination, but first he made an effort to peacefully do away with the major grievances. Although Zogu had always preferred force to conciliation, he was shrewd enough to realize when alternative means were necessary to pacify the people.

The President was also aware that although he would undoubtedly be able to crush another revolt from the north, the perpetually depleted treasury could not sustain a full mobilization so close on the heels of the last one. Zogu, then, decided that the time was right for some form of conciliation. His first gesture was to do away with the government officials most implicated in the overzealous repression which had followed the 1926 revolt.

In Machiavellian form, Zogu dismissed his Minister of the Interior Musa Juka in February 19127. This was undoubtedly a wise move since Juka, following in the footsteps of his predecessor, had become extremely un-popular with various elements of Albanian society. Because Juka was also the Minister of Public Works, he was held responsible for recruiting citizens to donate their time for the construction of roads, a program which had become a major grievance. Juka's too sudden wealth and the rumors that he had been in the pay of Rome and Belgrade made him a mark for public distrust and hatred. Within government circles he was feared because of his power and his closeness to the President.[30]

Although Juka's dismissal did much to relieve tension in the north, Zogu felt that more significant gestures were required to defuse the situa-tion entirely. He decided that a personal visit, surrounded with consid-erable pomp, would help convince the citizens of Shkodër and the north-erners in general that they were no longer out of favor. The President made certain, however, that the visit was not misunderstood as weakness. He arrived in the middle of August in an armored car accompanied by a strong contingent of troops which was billeted on the population.[31] Zogu's implied threat was quite clear.

The President was received by a large crowd and was presented with a golden key and the traditional salt and bread. On a hill above the city the letters "AZ" were written. A massive parade of a primarily military character took place which included about 1,600 troops accompanied by a "reserve battalion" of Malissori with rifles. A group of sports clubs brought up the rear with one contingent carrying a sign which read, "Ah-med Zogu, the Prince of Shkodër."[32]

To further impress the people, Zogu brought with him the entire government along with the diplomatic corps for whom the President gave his first official dinner. Although Zogu was somewhat embarrassed by his lack of French and the novelty of the occasion, he apparently bore himself with great dignity.[33]

The trip was considered a personal success for Zogu. While few Catholic priests, with the exception of the Archbishop of Shkodër and the papal delegate took part, Zogu had been able to win back most of the tribal chieftains with guns, honors, money and food. Their particpation in his military parade was their way of acknowledging that a bargain had been struck. As a last gesture just before he left Shkodër at the beginning of September, Zogu announced that seventy-four people in prison as a result of the November uprising, including fifteen with life sentences, were to be amnestied. Zogu thereby emptied the jails of the remaining participants of the revolt.[34]

The President was not, of course, naive enough to believe that all of his problems since establishing the Republic would be taken care of with parades and threats. Those who would not be won over with positions, money or fear had to be dealt with by more traditional means. Zogu became even more convinced that traditional means were necessary after the assassination of his brother-in-law Ceno Bey in the Cafe Passage in Prague in October 1927.

Although Zogu had had serious trouble with Ceno, he was apparently genuinely cose to his brother-in-law and recognized his value as a liaison to Belgrade. Because of these connections, Ceno was appointed Albanian Minister to Belgrade after living in Paris as a private citizen for one year.

In October 1927 Ceno was also appointed Minister at Prague and had travelled to the Czech capital to officially present his credentials. Although he had been warned of a possible attempt on his life, he apparently paid no heed and was subsequently shot to death by Alcibiades Bebi, a student from Elbasan who claimed that Ceno was about to sell Albania to the Yugoslavs.[35]

Bebi's motives and backers were never firmly discovered since he was assassinated in a Prague courtroom on the first day of his trial. The assassin, one Aziya Vuciterna, was the personal servant of Gani Bey, the brother of Ceno, and had been given money by Gani to accompany him on the first day of testimony.

The examination of Bebi had just begun and the defendant admitted that he had killed Ceno in obedience to the orders of a secret political committee of which he was a member and that he would have been killed himself if he had not carried out his instructions. Before he could further explain this statement, Vuciterna sprang forward from the back of the courtroom and fired several revolver shots from a new Belgian weapon. Bebi was killed instantly.[36]

Vuciterna later maintained that he had acted on impulse and that he had not come to the courtroom with the intention of killing Bebi. He further argued that he had become so enraged at the defendant's insolent and provocative behavior during his examination in court that he completely lost his self-control. He did not remember having a revolver in his hand or firing it. Gani Bey, who had procured a card of admission to the trial for Vuciterna, of course denied that he had any knowledge of the plan and professed to be horrified by the deed.

Vuciterna's assertions can be discounted since Bebi's examination in court was conducted in Italian. Vuciterna did not speak Italian and so could not possibly have followed what was being said. The fact that the gun was loaded with dum-dum bullets lends further credence to the argument that Bebi had been the victim of a premeditated attack.[37] Whether Vuciterna acted out of revenge following the tradition of the blood feud or whether he killed Bebi to prevent him from making damaging disclosures was never determined. Indeed, no clear motives for either murder were ever established, leaving room for endless rumors and opinions.

The Greek Charge d'Affaires and the Rumanian Minister in Tirana were convinced that Zogu himself had been responsible for the murder of his brother-in-law because Zogu supposedly hated and feared Ceno as his most powerful rival.[38] It is certainly clear that Ceno had wanted to put himself in Zogu's position but the same could of course have been said about any self-respecting Albanian politician. Ceno actually had less of a chance of succeeding Zogu than most because of his unpopularity in Albania which resulted from his close contact with the Yugoslavs. Ceno lacked any real internal power base and therefore presented little or no threat to Zogu.

Had Ceno been a threat and had Zogu wanted him eliminated, the President could certainly have had him killed in Tirana and avoided all the adverse publicity which his assassination in Prague engendered. Zogu had always been sensitive to foreign reports concerning the violent nature of Albanians, realizing that such reports discouraged financial investments on the part of foreign firms. In Tirana the deed could have been done quietly and quickly as for example with the pro-Yugoslav Senator Jusuf Bey Dibra whom Zogu had assassinated only a few months before. In this case, as in so many others, the ensuing investigations quietly faded away.[39]

The only remaining interested party, the only one who would benefit from Ceno's death was Mussolini. Rome had on numerous occasions attempted to have Ceno divested of his political influence. The Italian supported opposition in 1924 had demanded his dismissal. When the interests of Rome and Belgrade came to a head in 1927 over the activities of a Yugoslav agent in Albania, Ceno very vocally supported Belgrade, much to the chagrin of the Italians. Although Ceno was temporarily relieved of

his position as a result, once the crisis had passed Zogu reappointed him
to his old post over strenuous Italian objections. Ceno continued his pro-
Yugoslav activity and worked to develop closer Belgrade-Tirana relations,
the possibility of which offered Zogu an alternative to Italian domination.

Italy's connection with Bebi also appeared to be more than simply cir-
cumstantial. Bebi had studied in Italy and at one point even mentioned
that the well-known Albanian expert, Professor Baldacci of Bologna, had
suggested that he do away with Ceno because of the latter's connection
with Belgrade.[40] Bebi had also been connected with pro-Italian anti-Zog
elements outside of Albania including Mustafa Kruja and with pro-Italian
elements within Albania including Shevket Bey Verlaci.

Zogu was apparently considerably depressed by the assassination and
became extremely suspicious as a result. The President convinced himself that he had been the original target of the plan and seemed to accept
the idea that Bebi had conspired with emigre groups who enjoyed Italian
support. Once his grief had subsided somewhat, he struck out against
his opponents, seeming to concentrate on those with general pro-Italian
sympathies. Recognizing that the time had come for direct action, his
first target was his prospective father-in-law, Shevket Bey Verlaci.

In early December an entire infantry unit opened fire on Shevket Bey
as he was getting out of his car in Tirana. Although bullets went through
his clothing he escaped injury. Two of his servants were killed. Even
though the attempted assassination took place under the eyes of the
police, the investigation which followed turned up nothing except the
fact that one of those involved had previously been in the service of
Ceno Bey. After the attempt, Shevket Bey was placed under special
Italian protection.[41]

The most generally accepted explanation implicates Zogu. The President had for some time been attempting to withdraw from his arranged
marriage with Verlaci's daughter, a move which had been favored by
Ceno Bey since Ceno feared the increase of Italian influence if such a
match succeeded.

Zogu and his relatives were of course aware that Ceno's assassin was
a native of Elbasan where Shevket was the uncrowned king. Since the
breaking of an engagement resulted in a blood feud regardless, Zogu
undoubteldy reasoned that if he struck first a number of problems would
be taken care of simultaneously. The marriage problem would be solved,

the President would receive satisfaction for the death of Ceno Bey and the primary Italian replacement candidate would be removed. Once they heard that Shevket had survived the attempt, panic gripped Zogu's family and supporters. Several relations, including Xhemil Dino, left the country for unknown destinations.[42]

Undaunted by this setback, the President continued his campaign to finally rid himself of his most troublesome opponents. Less than two months later, a certain Ibrahim Lica from Krujë was arrested in Vienna after it came to the attention of the Austrian police that he had travelled to the Austrian capital for the purpose of murdering Hasan Bey Prishtina, the longtime anti-Zog pro-Italian emigre leader.

Lica, whose brother had been among Zog's supporters during the 1924 invasion, confessed after strenuous police examination that he had been approached by Gani Bey who took him to meet Zogu whereupon both Zogu and Gani encouraged him to kill Hasan Bey for a considerable sum of money.

According to Lica, he changed his mind, threw his revolver away and informed the Albanian consulate in Vienna that he no longer intended to carry out his charge.[43] No charges were brought against Lica but he was escorted out of the country in March, travelling to Belgrade. Zogu's government was somewhat exasperated by the confession.

Zogu did not have long to wait for Prishtina's reaction as the continuing series of attacks and counterattacks resumed in July 1928 when an Albanian merchant and two Bulgarians were arrested for plotting to kill the President in Durrës. At the same time, six or seven others were arrested in another plot in Korcë.

According to official Albanian sources, the first plot was organized at Trieste in 1926 when Theodor Vulkanoff and Denko Abagjiff, members of the Communist Committee of the Balkan Federation met with an agent of the Federation named Zankoff and Hasan Bey Prishtina to draw up details of the plan. Upon Zogu's assassination, Prishtina, with the help of emigres in Yugoslavia, was to advance on Tirana and seize the administration of the country.

While the plot was originally to have been carried out in 1927, the conspirators found it impossible to keep to their timetable because of the closing of the frontiers following a Belgrade-Tirana incident to be explained later in this volume. The action was postponed until the summer of 1928 when the President was expected once again to make his annual holiday in Durrës at his seaside villa. The plan called for the placing of bombs, which were to be exploded by electric current from a distance, in the sewer at the corner of the Durrës public garden. They were to be detonated as the President's car passed on its way to the baths from the villa or on its return.[44]

The trial of the accused was badly handled by the government and caused a good deal of unrest among the general population since all were eventually sentenced to death despite the inability on the part of the prosecution to come up with evidence solid enough to convict the three. Numerous appeals were made on behalf of the condemned men and word was finally passed out by the government that the death sentences would not be carried out. All of the President's Ministers, with the exception of K. Kotta, the Minister of the Interior, were convinced that the men would not be hanged.[45]

Much to the surprise of the people of Tirana, on the morning of July 12, fifty gendarmes led the three men out to the marketplace where three tripods had been set in place, two in front of the Parliament building and another some distance away. The three men were hanged.

To make matters worse, the hanging of one of the Bulgarians, a man named Georgieff, was a blundering atrocity. His giant frame brought the tripod down with a crash when the box was pulled out from under his feet and he was allowed to drop. He had to be put back up and it was forty-five minutes from the time he was first hanged until he was pronounced dead. He died finally with both feet on the ground. Although the depression on public mind was far more noticeable than ever before on the occasion of the execution, this did not prevent the usual mad scramble for slices of the rope, always in demand after a hanging as good luck charms.[46]

Concurrent proceedings were conducted for the seven arrested in late June in Korcë for having received letters from Albanian emigres including Mustafa Kruja, the much feared pro-Italian exile living in Zara. These letters apparently called for the assassination of the President on his proposed triumphal tour of southern Albania in July or August. Two spots had been selected for the attack, one by Lake Ohrid not far from the Yugoslav frontier and the other on the stretch of road between Korcë and Leskovik. As the trial progressed it became clear that Kruja was not involved nor were those who had been arrested. The political court still considered the letters from the emigres to be authentic, however, and so sentenced eight Albanian refugees living in Vienna to death in absentia.[47]

Zogu was now seeing plots around every corner and it seemed that Albanian officials were taking advantage of the President's increasing paranoia to denounce their rivals in the hope that they might assume the positions of the compromised bureaucrats. Such plans did not always succeed, however, as evidenced by the alleged Kavajë plot which surfaced in July.

Originally, ten residents of Kavajë, near Durrës, one of them a close friend of Shevket Bey Verlaci, were arrested and charged with visiting the local mosque under the pretense of praying while actually plotting to murder the President during his projected summer vacation in Durrës. The accused plotters, however, proved to the satisfaction of the court that they were in fact loyal supporters of the President. In these cases Albanian justice requires that false witnesses be condemned to the same punishment as would have been meted out to those they falsely accused. Two of the accusers were subsequently sentenced to death.[48]

Although in the Kavajë case Zogu might have overreacted somewhat, in most cases his fears were justified. The President saw plots around every corner because there were a good many people bent on doing away with him. His progress to power was punctuated by assassinations which because they were political rather than personal killings removed them from the operation of the besa. Blood feuds thus initiated could not be cancelled by any interpositions. One can reasonably estimate that by 1928 Zogu had as many as 600 such blood feuds on his hands, more than a few with extremely important families. The lengthy list of his victims included six clan chieftains of Mirditë, numerous priests, and many prominent politicians like Rystem and Ali Tabaku, a judge of instruction whose report on the death of the American tourists accused Zogu of responsibility. Tabaku was poisoned while in prison.

In addition, Zogu was clearly responsible for many abortive attempts, including those against Prishtina (who was finally assassinated in Salonika in 1933), Shavket Bey, and the wounding of Brindisi in Shevket Korca, former general in command of the gendarmerie.[49]

With every unsuccessful revolt the refugee committees scattered throughout Europe grew in size. Their main function of course was either to kill the President or overthrow his regime. The largest of these groups, the

"Bashkimi Kombëtar" and the Independent Association of Albanian Refugees were headquartered in Vienna and included many ex-ministers and ex-deputies. Also prominent was "Kanara," Fan Noli's group which was reportedly subsidized by Moscow, and the National Albanian Organization, centered in Belgrade, whose opposition was strictly personal, presenting programs identical to Zogu's own.[50] These groups continued to operate because they could always rely on the financial support of some foreign power, primarily Italy and Yugoslavia, which found it in their interest to subsidize possible replacements for Zogu.

The President, as a result, became ever more security conscious. He spent more of his time shut away in his palace working in his overheated office chain-smoking cigarettes, a daily routine which was adversely affecting his heath. His meals were prepared by his mother who occupied the villa across from the palace and were delivered to Zogu's office in a locked container by an armed guard.

When receiving visitors the President would sit behind his desk carefully eyeing his guest, watching for any unexpected movement in which case Zogu's hand would stray toward a handkerchief laying on top of his desk covering a revolver. The President and most of his cabinet ministers carried revolvers at all times and were rather quick on the draw.[51]

On those rare occasions when he did leave his house there were a number of set procedures which he followed. He generally left the palace only in the company of his mother since it is contrary to Albanian blood feud practice to jeopardize the safety of women. When he was with her, he felt reasonably safe from attack. When Zogu appeared unattended, on a short horseback ride for example, it was unannounced, at a fast gallop and he was guarded by a detachment of cavalry. The American Minister once commented how the atmosphere at the palace very much resembled the closing Tzarist days in St. Petersburg when Nicholas II took his only outings in similar fashion.[52]

When on his way to an official function or on a longer trip, Zogu never travelled without a large contingent of troops made up exclusively of his own loyal Mati tribesmen. His travel plans were always kept secret as long as possible and abruptly changed. On this way to Parliament two roads would be cleared of people, doors and windows were locked and the streets were lined with nothing but troops, police and agents. If there were any trees along the route, they would be shorn of their branches so that no would-be assassin could hide in the foliage. Zogu frequently arrived before the announed time requiring all those who wished to attend to be there well in advance.[53]

To further minimize the risk, Zogu took few long trips with the exception of his summer excursions to his residence in Durrës to escape the heat of Tirana. His one major trip during the presidency was to Shkodër in 1927 where security was extremely tight. The road from Tirana to Shkodër was carefully patrolled by units of the gendarmerie and the military. Zogu rode quickly in an armoured car which protected him from bullets and bombs.

The President was so pleased by the outcome of the expedition that he made plans for a triumphal tour of Korcë, Gjirokastër and the other southern Albanian cities during the summer of 1928. This trip, however, was eventually cancelled because of the numerous threats against his life which were discovered.[54]

During 1928 he even cancelled his yearly trip to Durrës spending the hot summer as his own prisoner in his heavily guarded palace, relying on his associates to keep him advised about developments in the country. When he resumed his trips to Durrës the next year, he did so with a larger contingent of troops. Usually, more than 600 troops were encamped near the summer residence. A few hundred yards from Zogu's cottages, which were built over the water, a small ship with watchers on board rode at anchor. In the even of a successful attack by land, Zogu could retreat by water.[55]

As concerns for his personal safety mounted, Zogu was forced to move closer to Italy. It soon became clear that the first pact had not been sufficient to insure Zogu's longevity, ironically the obverse had occurred. The pact had helped bring an anti-Italian, anti-Zogu ministry to power in Belgrade, thereby increasing Zogu's security problems. Nincic who had been the Foreign Minister in Belgrade prior to the first pact, resigned in December 1926 declaring that the pact had destroyed the basis on which he had built his foreign policy.[56]

The new Yugoslav government accepted the viewpoint expressed by most Belgrade newspapers that the pact could be considered the first link in the chain of Italian encirclement.[57] This deterioration of relations between Italy and Yugoslavia is best characterized by the Belgrade-Tirana crisis of the summer of 1927.

In May a certain Vuk Gjuraskovic was arrested in Tirana and in his possession was found some low-level material concerning Italian military
activity in Albania. The Yugoslav government reacted strongly to this
arrest, sending an insulting note demanding his immediate release and an
apology. When Zogu refused, Belgrade broke diplomatic relations.

The Albanian President was left with no alternative but to turn to
the Italians for support. Italy recognized that this crisis could end Zogu's
attempts to include the Yugoslavs in the pact, one of the many schemes
Zogu had come up with to emasculate the agreement. Rome was more
than happy to assume the role of peacemaker. With the support of England and France, a compromise was finally worked out calling for the re-
writing of the Belgrade note along with the release of Gjuraskovic.

The significance of the hardening in Albanian-Yugoslav relations was
obvious. The Italians had been trying since November 1926 to further
ensnare Zogu but had been unsuccessful. The President had vigorously
rejected a long list of Italian proposals drawn up by Aliosi which included
a push for control of shipping and more importantly, an attempt to slowly
enlarge and subsequently dominate the Albanian military.[58]

Zogu's freedom of action in rejecting Italian demands was slowly beginning to fade away. He needed more personal security, internally and ex-
ternally. With Ceno Bey dead and Belgrade seemingly committed to a
position of hostility, Zogu found that he could no longer use the Yugoslavs as a counterweight as he had earlier used the British. In von Kardoff's
appropriate words, Zogu understood "dass die Hand die nich abgehagt
werden kann, zu küssen ist."[59]

Zogu changed his tactics somewhat this time, relying less on his usual
obstructionism and more on direct serious negotiations, a policy shift
which eventually netted the President a good deal more in return. Italy
too had softened its approach somewhat, realizing that its entire Balkan
policy had essentially been reduced to Albania. Rome no longer felt it
was prudent to resort ot the tactics of Baron Aliosi who had damaged
Italian interests by ruffling Albanian sensibilities. In Ugo Sola, who replaced the Baron, Rome procured a tactful and intelligent representative
who could be relied upon to avoid needless difficulties.[60]

Despite this new attitude on the part of both sides, the negotiations
were still slow and arduous. The Italians wanted an extension of the
first pact with increased control of the military. Zogu basically wanted

more security from his enemies at home and abroad, something which he hoped to procure through guarantees, more financial assistance and the construction of a monarchy. With the conclusion of the second Tirana pact, which was eventually signed in November 1927, both sides achieved their goals.

Outwardly it seemed that little had changed since the new defense pact did little more than restate and formalize the most important points of the first Tirana pact. The Italians were even careful to make it sound more bilateral than the first pact. The text seemed perfectly innocuous with the most important article reading:

> Art. 3 . . . In the event one of the two Parties being threatened by a war not provoked but it, the other Party shall use all means at its disposal not only to prevent hostility but also to secure just satisfaction to the threatened Party.

> Art. 4 When all efforts at conciliation have failed each of the high Contracting Parties undertakes to throw in its lot with the other, and to put at the disposal of its ally the military, financial and other resources at its disposal if such aid is requested by the threatened Party.[61]

The serious element in this new series of agreements was contained not in the text of the pact but in the exchange of letters afterwards and the subsequent increase of Italian military activity in Albania. Although Zogu assured the British Minister, William Seeds, that he could make the pact useless, the Italians, through this and subsidiary agreements effectively did away with any remaining independence which the Albanian military might have had.[62]

They had not always been as concerned about the army. Immediately after the founding of the Republic, the Italians seemed to have expressed little interest in the Albanian military. This lack of concern probably stems from Zogu's ambitious program to reform the army which the President, with the help of Colonels Mirach and Stirling, laid out soon after the fall of Tirana. The 5,000 man army was to be replaced by a 3,000 man militia. The scheme never got off the ground.

Officially the original plan for a 3,000 man militia came into force in March 1925 but by early June, owing to apprehensions of a possible attack from Yugoslavia, nine more companies were recruited. Three of these companies were disbanded at the end of August after repeated and urgent representations from Colonel Mirach. At the same time, however, steps were taken to form an additional three shock companies which were to be on a basis different from that of the rest of the troops, since they were to receive the extra pay of the gendarmerie.

Apart from these increases, the nine companies of gendarmerie originally provided for was increased to ten in order to gave a guard company for the President and in June this was increased to twelve companies because of the threatened attack. By the end of 1925 then, there were about 8,000 men under arms which was approximately 1,000 more than there had been at the time Zogu set out his new program.[63]

The Albanian military increased every year thereafter consuming 45.7 percent of the national budget in the fiscal year (March-April) 1926-1927, while in 1927-1928 the figure jumped to 48.03 percent, almost one-half the entire year's expenditures.[64] The problems caused by such a large army were rather substantial. Apart from the intolerable financial burden, it naturally aroused serious misgivings among Albania's neighbors.

Zogu defended his military expenditures by maintaining that they were necessary to uphold internal order and protect the frontiers. The President argued that he needed a disciplined force since he was loath to rely too heavily on irregulars, a contradiction of earlier statements. He complained that untrained mountaineers inevitably utterly devastated the districts through which they marched and in which they fought.

Zogu's distrust of all but his own tribesmen was basically supported by most foreign officers in Albania. The British gendarmerie officers complained that discipline was nonexistent and that the mountaineers' skill with a rifle and even their courage was not what romantically inclined writers had proclaimed to the world. The British proudly boasted that with a few companies of Ghurkas they could sweep the whole of the north.[65]

There were most likely more pressing reasons for the maintenance of such a large army, including pressure exerted by the vested interests in the old army and the political groups associated with it. Zogu had not yet acquired the power base necessary to completely ignore indigenous pressure groups.

The Italians saw the growing army as a positive development and undoubtedly exerted considerable pressure to insure its continued growth.

Rome recognized an opportunity to enhance its influence by becoming the quartermaster and the trainer of the enlarged force. The Italians were determined to gain control of Zogu's motley army.

Although some inroads were made previous to November 1927, the second Tirana pact and its subsidiary agreements made control possible. Italian supplies and advisors streamed into Albania. In 1927 alone, the Albanian government purchased some 20,000 rifles, forty mountain guns, 120 machine guns and other supplies.[66]

Mirach, who was eventually promoted to brigadier-general and appointed Chief of Staff, reported to the British Minister, on the authorization of the President that by the beginning of 1928 the army had grown to over 11,000 men and officers. He noted that this rapid growth occurred against his advice and mostly behind his back by consultations between the President and the Italian military attache, General Pariani.[67]

The Chief of Staff went on to report that approximately fifty Italian officers, paid by the Italian government, were serving in the Albanian army. Apart from staff and headquarters in Tirana, Italian officers were attached to, or in some cases practically commanded, units on the following scale: one to each battalion, two to every three batteries, one to each engineer group. In addition, Italian officers served in every medical, veterinary and transport unit.[68]

Zogu was willing to live with this situation provided he received what he considered paramount for survival in return. In exchange for the second Pact of Tirana and the corresponding increases in Italian military influence, Zogu required a number of assurances. The President's first demand concerned Italian involvement with Albanian emigre groups.

Mussolini had remained in close contact with these groups, first supporting Noli and then after it became clear that Noli lacked support within Albania, shifting Italian involvement to other groups. Over the protests of Zogu, Mussolini even allowed an Albanian emigre meeting to take place in Trieste in February 1927. In April the Italian Ambassador in Vienna opened direct negotiations with Hasan Bey Prishtina who tried to convince Rome that it was in everyone's interest to do away with Zogu.

Although the Italians were not at that point ready to act on Prishtina's suggestion, Mussolini wanted control of these organizations and in that interest agreed to pay Prishtina fifty thousand lire a month. Italian connections with one of Zogu's most dangerous rivals, Mustafa Kruja, had been longstanding and continued throughout this period.[69] Zogu naturally protested strongly, particularly when it became clear that Prishtina had been planning to assassinate him for some time.

Zogu also hoped to extract some concessions concerning the SVEA loan and the interest due which, not surprisingly, Albania had been completely unable to pay. Zogu suggested that the Italians grant Albania a moratorium and the conversion of the lire at his disposal into gold since it had appreciated following the revaluation of the lire.[70]

The one point most dear to Zogu's heart, however, and something which had slipped through his hands on previous occasions was a throne. The President desired this change not only to satisfy his own increasing ambition but also to do away with the remaining remnants of Western democracy which had been found to be not only cumbersome but dangerous. To complete the picture, Zogu also hoped that he could convince the Italians to allow him to marry a member of the House of Savoy.

In principle, the Italians agreed to these conditions with Sola drawing up a three-point proposal in September 1927 which included an Italo-Albanian defensive alliance, the creation of an Albanian kingdom and the recruitment of a suitable wife for Zogu.[71]

When all of the details had been worked out, Zogu received basically everything for which he had asked. Mussolini promised to withdraw support from the emigre groups and broke contact with Prishtina. With regard to SVEA, Mussolini allowed the conversion of the money Albania still possessed and authorized negotiations which eventually ended in the establishment of a moratorium in March 1928.

The Italians also agreed to allow Zogu to assume the throne, although they stipulated that he could not do so for one year in order to dispel the inevitable rumors that the President's price for the pact had been the throne.[73] The Italians were also hoping to dispense with all possible problems which could arise with the pact before they supported Zogu in his monarchial dreams.

The President had to do without the Savoy marriage since Boris of Bulgaria had begun to court the Savoy Princess Giovanna. It is doubtful that Mussolini even brought the matter up with Victor Emmanuel since the King would certainly have turned the suggestion down. Victor Emmanuel considered Zogu to be little more than a better bandit.[74] Regardless of the failed marriage plans, Zogu had received his final reward.

CHAPTER SEVEN

ZOG I, MBRET TË SHQUIPTARVET

The concept of monarchial power was certainly nothing new to the Albanians, indeed the construction of the Monarchy in 1928 was more of a return to a familiar system than an innovation. The example of Skanderbeg and the 500 years of Ottoman domination did much to firmly establish the principle. The idea was further ingrained in 1913 when the powers instituted a principality as the first 20th century independent Albanian government under the unfortunate Prince William of Wied. Zogu recognized this element of historical continuity attached to monarchy in Albania and was more than ready to return to it since it was something which he had at least considered for quite some time.

It is of course the habit of biographers, once an event had taken place, to search the past for evidence which demonstrates that the event was inevitable. Despite the risks, it is interesting to note how the concept of monarchy or at least despotic power seems to have intrigued Zogu from an early age. The clearest historical examples for Zogu's shift from a republic to a monarchy can be found in the careers of Julius Caesar and Napoleon, both of whom he greatly admired. In an interview given shortly after he accepted the dignity of the crown, Zogu maintained that since his visit to Rome immediately after the war on his way back to Albania, he had considered Ceasar to be the greatest incarnation of a political man. Zogu explained how he would sit amidst the ruins of the Forum and dream of the glories of ancient times and about the possibility of bringing them back. The river Tiber divulged its secrets to him during his long walks from Hadrian's castle to the Molle bridge.[1]

Zogu's fascination with monarchy predates his experiences in Rome, however, and stems from his studies first in Constantinople as a youth and then as a guest of the Austro-Hungarian Monarchy in Vienna during the war. While at the Galata Serail Lyceum in Constantinople Zogu did more than concentrate on conventional education. Because of his close contact with the Sultan's Albanian guards, he was able to observe the inner functions of an Eastern despotic government, an experience which was to have no small impact on the structuring of his own court. It was also in Constantinople that the young Zogu developed a love for the live and times of Napoleon Bonaparte, apparently even hoping to pattern his own life after that of the great French leader.[2]

Soon after his return to Mati, Zogu was presented with another example of monarchial government, this time in Albania itself. Although the reign of Prince William was more useful in describing how not to construct and run a monarchy, Zogu was astute enough to realize that the basic political theory might be appropriate although the method in which it was implemented in this particular case was not. Zogu withdrew his support from Wied as soon as he realized that the Prince's position was hopeless. The young chieftain came away with a desire to replace Wied as Prince rather than help him stabilize his position.[3]

Zogu's stay in Vienna further contributed to his ever growing desire to set up a monarchy with himself on the throne. Zogu maintained that while in Vienna he not only spent a great deal of time studying Western culture and political organization but also had the opportunity to establish a personal relationship with both Emperor Franz-Josef and Emperor Karl.[4] Queen Geraldine insists that the old Emperor Franz-Josef personally decorated the young Albanian.[5]

While little evidence exists for either of these claims, Zogu could not have been unaffected by the pomp and ceremony surrounding the imperial House of Austria, even during the war. Faik Konitza, in his book *Albania, the Rock Garden of Europe,* suggests in fact that Karl's coronation might have been decisive in Zogu's eventual decision to see himself crowned as monarch.[6] Although it is unclear exactly when Zogu came to the initial decision to actively seek the throne, once he entered the mainstream of Albanian politics after the war, it soon became obvious to most of those around him that he was interested in more than just limited authority.[7]

Zogu's moves toward his goal during his early period of political activity were often rather slow and cautious as a result of prudence on the one hand and fear on the other. Few had as clear a picture of the Albanian mentality as Zogu had, recognizing the natural conservatism and suspicion of rapid radical changes. Domestically he was astutely aware of how far and how quickly he could move.

Because of his incomplete education, however, he never had a sufficient grasp of European politics to accurately judge what influence Europe might have on internal Albanian politics. Out of ignorance, he feared Europe's reaction. This fear led him to delay his planned change until he could rely upon the unqualified support of at least one European power.

While he waited he never missed an opportunity to lay the groundwork or sound out those who would be affected by the change. In 1924 while he was in exile in Belgrade, Zogu maintains that he questioned King Alexander about such an eventuality and received a favorable reply.[8]

Soon after he reentered Albania with the help of the Yugoslavs he decided not to continue within the Belgrade sphere of influence. This decision forced him not only to find a new economic and political protector but also to find another power to support his monarchial dreams. The campaign to extract sympathy from the Italisn for the change as well as to ready Albanian public opinion began in earnest when Zogu triumphantly returned to Tirana in late 1924.

The republican transition period which Zogu constructed in 1925 reflected both his common sense in dealing with internal policy and his fear of foreign powers. Domestically, because he controlled most of Albania's power in 1925, Zogu could easily have declared himself king and could probably have constructed a viable state. But because the country had just experienced a left-wing revolution, Zogu did not want to give the Albanians the impression that he was an unregenerated conservative working in his own interests rather than in the interests of the country.[9]

In an effort to attract Albania's rather limited number of talented administrators, many of whom had served in Noli's regime, Zogu hoped to create a government which might serve to sink some of the political and tribal differences which had brought on the revolution. He hoped thereby to unite the politically aware elements of Albanian society behind him.

Zogu's fear of an adverse foreign reaction did much to confirm the decision to wait on the monarchy in 1925. But Zogu had no intention of squandering his new found power position and so took the opportunity to create a government which was as close to a monarchy as possible. The royal bearing which he had learned from Abdul Hamid's guards was supplemented by all manne of royal trappings from his white uniform and gold spurs down to the wide dissemination of his likeness on stamps and official buildings. His name and initials appeared everywhere, including on the side of a mountain above Skhodër.[10] (After he became king "I" was added to the letters "AZ.")

Like those who had attempted to gain the throne before him, including the 18th century Albanian warrior Ali Pasha and Zogu's unfortunate uncle Esad Pasha, Zogu took pains to tie himself as closely as possible to the memory of Skanderbeg whose praises were still being spread through story and song.

All three maintained that they were attempting to rebuild the national monarchy which Skanderbeg had initially constructed. Medieval Albanian history was rewritten to include a connection by marriage between Skanderbeg's sister and one of Zogu's ancestors.[11] Much was made of the similarities between Zogu and the Albanian hero. Both rose from relative obscurity in the Mati country to become rulers of all Albania in a very short time at a very young age. To further ingrain the connection, Zogu adopted the helmet of Skenderbeg as the symbol of the nation, with "AZ" superimposed.[12]

Opponents were quick to point out that the similarities were and would always remain superficial, arguing that Skanderbeg was motivated by neither ambition nor hunger for power but rather by the fulfillment of Albania's national dreams and the fight for Christianity. It was further argued that his rise to power was accomplished not through force and violence but because of the crusading spirit which his cause inspired. His cause remained credible because his pockets remained empty. Zogu, on the other hand, was characterized as one who by using his power indiscriminately had forced his will upon the Albanian people. If he had ever had noble motives, opponents argued, they had long since disappeared under the overwhelming desire to proclaim himself king.[13]

Objections of this sort worried Zogu very little, however, since he was in control of the resources of the country. He commanded the propaganda machine run by local officials. Since the vast majority of Albanians were still illiterate, the actions of emigre intellectuals who constituted the only vocal open opposition, was of little consequence. They could do nothing more than rail against Zogu in the foreign press, something which had little effect on Zogu's plans. Of much greater concern to the President was the strong support of Italy, support which Rome seemed willing to give for a price.

Zogu's elevation to the throne had become the subject of negotiations as early as 1926 when Baron Aloisi hoped to persuade the President to sign the first Pact of Tirana by holding out the crown and the possibility of an Italian princess as a reward.[14] Although Zogu would have been happy to accept, Aloisi required acknowledgement of the 1921 Conference of Ambassadors decision as a provision of the agreement. Zogu was unwilling to became an Italian puppet. The agreement which Zogu signed in November of that year made no mention of the crown; the prize had slipped through his hands.

But is was not long before the President received another chance. Since Mussolini was not satisfied with the original Pact of Tirana, he suggested a new agreement. Recognizing that he would need to trade something, Mussolini with the help of Sola, drew up a three point proposal in July which was to include, apart from a defensive treaty and increased Italian military involvement, the construction of a monarchy for Albania with an Italian princess thrown in for good measure.[15]

Sola first presented this proposal to Zogu in early September and then did not see him again for close to two weeks possibly because the President was somewhat surprised by the suggestion.[16] The extra two weeks also gave Zogu time to formulate more monetary demands, a consideration which undoubtedly came as no surprise to Sola when the negotiations resumed. Sola was clearly ready for these new demands and informed the President that Italy had no intention of directly financing the Albanian budget but that Italy would supply the Albanians with military and financial experts, a suggestion which Zogu did not particularly welcome.

Nevertheless, Zogu tentatively accepted the proposals, subject to bargaining.[17] He saw a chance to be rid of the 1925 secret military treaty, and deal with the problem of the emigre groups. In addition, he was determined not to allow the opportunity for Italian support of the monarcy to slip through his fingers again. He was willing to pay the price: a new pact and further Italian involvement.

As with other Albanian-Italian agreements, Zogu immediately tried to undermine the new pact. This process began as early as December 1927 with a series of pointedly anti-Italian actions. The attempted assassination of the Italophile Shevket Bey on December 13 was the first step and was followed immediately by a sharp article in the semi-official *Telegraph*. the only paper in Albania which could actually be called a paper, warning Italy not to treat Albania as a colony.[18] The author of the article concluded by suggesting that the goal of the new pact would be fulfilled only when both parties to the agreement understood that Albania could never be an area for Italian expansion.[19]

The Italians naturally enough were unhappy with this sort of activity but it is safe to say that they had expected it. Having delayed the proclamation of Albania as a kingdom, Italy had the leverage to do something about Zogu's moves. The President found himself in a position where he was forced either to back down or face the possibility of losing Italian support for his long sought after constitutional change. The Albanian government was prevailed upon to close the *Telegraph*, giving as a reason that it had hindered relations with friendly and allied countries.[20]

At the beginning of 1928, with Italian support in his pocket, Zogu decided that the time had come for the next step, to sound out other European powers. He went first to the British, indicating the continued influence which London enjoyed in Albania despite the fact that many Albanians felt that their country had deliberately been handed over to the stewardship of Italy.[21]

In February Foreign Minister Vrioni travelled to London for a personal interview with Austin Chamberlain. Vrioni, who personally opposed Zogu's plans arguing that the time was not right for such a change, hoped that the British would express some form of displeasure in order that he might use this against Zogu.[22] Recognizing Vrioni's game, however, Chamberlain merely replied that it was not the custom of His Majesty's Government to assume responsibility for giving advice in regard to internal affairs of an independent nation.[23]

Privately the British had numerous concerns and were left unconvinced by Zogu's explanation. The President argued that a monarchy was necessary for Albania because the republican form of government did not give the sense of security that was indispensible to a young country just emerging from disorder. What Albania chiefly needed and had been lacking in the past was a stable government which would encourage the people to set to work and build up the state on a firm foundation. Only the crown, which would be a permanent authority and would rise superior to the conflicts of personal interests and political groups, could present the idea of continuity and create the general stability which Albania needed.[24]

London was skeptical about Zogu's panacea argument concerning continuity and stability, being aware of the fact that the tribes in the north had been since time immemorial the dominant factor in the settlement of Albania's internal disputes. Although they had all signified their allegiance to his person, this was as far as they were likely to go. They had made no commitments to support a successor to Zogu. The Mati tribe was a comparatively small one, overshadowed by the powerful Mirditë tribe and half a dozen others. It was Zogu's own merit and achievement which had rallied these tribes to him, a feat which few Albanians would be able to duplicate.[25]

The British were unconvinced that a monarchy would solve the problems of internal stability, particularly since Zogu was unmarried. Since the attempt on Verlaci's life, he was no longer even engaged. His natural male heir was Esad Bey Kryeziu, the four year old son of the late Ceno Bey, whom Zogu had made a full general by executive order.[26] Esad Bey was no real asset to Zogu, however, since the Italians would never have allowed anyone related to Ceno Bey to come to power since this might easily lead to a resurgence of Yugoslav fortunes in Albania.

The British were also concerned that the monarchy and the resulting succession problem would cause nothing but trouble abroad. As General Percy delicately put it to Zogu during an interview in August, 1928; Zogu was surrounded by "three young ladies, Miss Yugoslavia, Miss Greece and Miss Italy" and an ill-conceived matrimonial venture could only lead to serious problems.[27]

Zogu hoped to assuage Percy's fears by insisting that he had no intention whatsoever of seeking a consort in one of the neighboring countries, something which he had of course unsuccessfully attempted. For Percy's sake, however, Zogu was willing to overlook the small matter of the Italian princess. A friend's embrace, he added, when the friend becomes over intimate, is prone to become a hug and a hug may mean broken bones. He assured Percy that he had no intention of having Albania's ribs broken.[28]

Finally, the British were concerned about the reaction of Zogu's immediate neighbors to the change in general, fears which the President insisted were groundless. Zogu explained to Sir Robert Hodgson, the British Minister, that he was convinced that the Italians would welcome the change. He added that the Greeks with whose government relations were generally quite good except for a few local disputes, were fully sympathetic to the change. The Greek Charge d'Affaires had volunteered the assurance that immediate recognition would be accorded to the new regime.[29] From the rest of Europe Zogu received answers of "benevolent disinterest."[30]

This left only the Yugoslavs and despite Zogu's earlier assertion that Alexander had announced in 1924 that he was favorable to seeing Albania become a monarchy, relations between the two countries during 1927 and 1928 were not the best. Belgrade was still unhappy about what they considered to be Zogu's betrayal in 1925, the Vuk Gjuraskovic crisis of the summer of 1927 was still fresh and of course the two pacts of Tirana had left a lingering aftertaste. To add to this hostile atmosphere, the Albanians treated the Yugoslavs at their legation in Tirana rather badly, surrounding the place with secret police agents and imposing an unofficial boycott by Albanian officials.[31]

Although this negative situation had been relieved somewhat in April 1928 with the arrival of a new Yugoslav Minister, M. Mihailovic, who abandoned the general Yugoslav attitude of sulky resentment for hopeful resignation, Zogu nevertheless was reluctant to consult the Yugoslavs about the change. The British Minister argued that since the Yugoslavs were passing through a crisis they must be consulted, otherwise they would naturally conclude that Italy and Albania were profiting by the disarray in Belgrade to draw up some devil's bargain to their detriment.[32]

Zogu finally assured the British that the Yugoslavs would be informed but was able to find reasonable excuses to delay. M. Mihailovic had left Albania at the beginning of August without paying a farewell visit to Zogu. Since the Albanian Minister in Belgrade had just been replaced, Zogu decided to wait until his replacement, Raouf Rico, who was still in Ankara, arrived in Belgrade. Since Rico intended to travel through Durrës, his arrival in Yugoslavia was considerably delayed.

Recognizing that Zogu had decided to allow the Yugoslavs to wait, London and Paris took it upon themselves to inform Belgrade of the impending change and asked them to declare that they had no objections to the change. The Yugoslav government refused, stating that it would await developments.[33] So it stood with the Yugoslavs until near the end of August.

Zogu recognized of course that extensive final internal preparations, at least in terms of the government, were also necessary. He came to this conclusion less as a result of apprehension concerning popular Albanian rejection but because he hoped to convince his opponents of the unanimity of his people.

His first move in this direction was his acceptance in December 1927 of the title "Savior of the Nation." Zogu's gesture was seen as somewhat ironic both by enlightened Albanians and foreigners considering the continued internal difficulties as well as the tightening Italian stranglehold.[34]

Next, Zogu decided that the unquestioning support of the cabinet was necessary. Although it is unlikely that any of the members of the government would have openly opposed the President, thereby jeopardizing their positions and possibly their lives, since the dismissal and reorganization of the government could be done with ease, Zogu decided to take no chances. A cabinet crisis was manufactured in May to faciliate the change. A quarrel between the Minister of the Interior and the Minister of Public Works over the question of road taxes and the corvee system, which eventually degenerated into an exchange of personal recriminations, resulted in the resignation of the entire cabinet. Within twenty-four hours a new cabinet was formed which was quickly christened the "Marionette Cabinet" because its members appeared to be merely a collection of tools in the President's hands.[35]

The new cabinet was not taken seriously, particularly with the appointment of a hodja as Minister of Public Works. British Charge d'Affaires Jordan noted that his appointment created much amusement and quipped that speculation was rife as to whether his experience in directing pious Moslems over the narrow and stony path that leads to the land of houris would assist him in having the equally narrow but more difficult road between Durrës and Tirana repaired without delay.[36] The cabinet changes convinced all but a few that Zogu was preparing to declare himself king.

With the government solidly behind him, the next step was to receive a mandate from a seemingly representative institution. Zogu, who was forever concerned with superficial legality, took great pains to insure that

the change be constitutionally correct. Since Parliament was not empowered to alter the republican constitution, the President convinced its members in June to pass an organic law providing for their own dissolution
and the election at an early date of a special Constituent Assembly which
could revise the constitution. Zogu felt that a unanimous decision on
the part of this Assembly might aid in convining those who were skeptical about the level of popular enthusiasm for monarchy.

Albanian electoral politics under the Republic were basically a sham
and generally much less lively than they had been under the Principality.
Zogu had left nothing to chance. As a result, however, the populace did
not look upon the Parliament as an instrument of government; for them
a deputy was only an important man to whom the President had granted
a high salary. The masses knew well that the deputies voted only as they
were told. People were generally uninterested and participated in the process only when the local gendarmes ordered them to do so. This active
aid from the police and the army basically insured the outcome but
required a considerable expenditure on the part of the government. Zogu,
then, was left wit the familiar problem of finances and as usual only one
source to which to turn.

The Italians were willing to give Zogu enough money to successfully
manipuate voting for the Constituent Assembly but not without their
usual fee. Indeed, in this instance they realized that they were in a position to demand more considering how determined Zogu was not to jeopardize the crown.

Sola was concerned about the legality of agreements made between
Italy and Albania once the change had taken place and so demanded two
notes of Zogu, one substantiating all previous agreements. The second
letter was to go a good deal further; it was to remain secret and in it Zogu
was to assure Mussolini that Albania would do nothing against Italian
interests as well as personally put himself under the protection of Italy
and the Duce. At the same time Italy was to guarantee Zogu that if the
Yugoslav state was destroyed, Albania would receive Kosovo.[37]

Zogu quickly agreed to these stipulations, realizing that the secret
letter would be basically worthless to the Italians since both the duties
and claims of Albania were included and since the publication of the
letter could only occur on the case of war with Yugoslavia. Mussolini too
saw the flaw and suggested that the secret note be divided into two letters.

The letter containing Zogu's commitment was to be published while the letter containing Albania's territorial claims was to remain secret.

Sola was aware that despite his hunger for the throne, Zogu would never consent to such an agreement. After explaining this to the Duce, a compromise was arrived at in which the first letter was to remain secret at least temporarily while the second was to remain secret indefinately. Mussolini was pleased with the compromise since, as he told Sola on August 9, he saw it as a formal acceptance that the new throne was founded in the shadow of the Italian flag.[38]

Well aware of their advantageous position, the Italians also took the opportunity to push through further subsidiary military agreements. Although the Italians already possessed considerable control over the Albanian army as a result of the second Pact of Tirana and its attached agreements, Mussolini and Sola were not satisfied. Sola set down clear mutual obligations for both war and peace which included a restatement of the provision that in case of war the Albanian and Italian units would be united under Italian command. The Albanians were also asked to agree to exclude all other foreign powers from the organization of the army, which was expected to be able to mobilize, incredibly enough, 60,000 men by the end of five years time. The Italians agreed to finance only part of the costs thereby leaving the door open for further Italo-Albanian agreements.

The status of the growing number of Italian officers in Albania was further clarified. A special General Staff made up entirely of Italian officers was to be organized to personally advise Zogu. This group was to have no connection with the Albanian high command. Furthermore, unlike all other foreign officers serving in Albania in one capacity or another, the Italians were not required to become Albanian citizens, wear Albanian uniforms or even adhere to Albanian law.

The agreement was signed by Sola and General Pariani for the Italians and Vrioni and General Aranitas, who soon replaced General Mirach, for the Albanians. Mussolini hoped that these extra-territorial agreements, somewhat reminiscent of European agreements with the last Manchus in the 19th century, would finally turn Albania into a complete protectorate.[39]

Zogu was not particularly happy with these concessions but he had come too far and he had no intention of threatening his own crown at the last minute. He finally agreed to the new military provisions and the two letters, neither of which was published even after the Italian annexation of Albania. In exchange for these considerations, Zogu received ten million lire paid through the Italian state Railroads, five million of which was received on June 18 and five million of which was received on September 5 after he had signed the agreements.[40]

With the money he received from Rome, Zogu conducted what a German newspaper termed a typically Balkan election.[41] First a few dozen possible opposition candidates were arrested and general political meetings banned. By virtue of the indirect nature of the election process, in the end only about 1,200 people members of the electoral college actually voted. Although the deputies were to have been selected by the people, their election was little more than a formality in which no election box actually played a role. While some were local men of weight and standing, others were elected from districts which they may have never seen. It is not surprising therefore, that when the Constituent Assembly finally met to amend the fundamental law, not a single member was returned whose vote was not safe for Zogu.[42]

Having assured a successful election, Zogu and most of his advisors assumed that their job was done, intending simply to wave the crown in the face of the populace after the meeting of the Constituent Assembly on August 25. Foreign Minister Vrioni, who despite his many faults understood something of public relations, felt it was necessary for the country and the world in general to be officially informed of these plans. For this purpose Vrioni summoned K. A. Chekrezi, the publisher of the *Telegraph* and convinced him to write an article which was to be not so much a straight news article but instead something in the way of a news editorial to prepare the public mind for eventualities.[43]

Chekrezi initially agreed but by the next day had become nervous enough to try and reach the President. Vrioni had by this time convinced the council, along with the President, of the necessity of such a course of action. Chekrezi thereupon sent a despatch to the Associated Press Bureau at Vienna saying that the purpose to create a kingdom had been officially revealed. On August 5 he published an article in the Tirana *Telegraph* concluding that, the republican form of government has proved to be, after a three year test, incompatible with the essential political needs of the country, the internal and foreign state of which is so as to be in need of a government with greater and more recognized authority.[44]

Italian newspapers quickly picked up Chekrezi's lead in pointing out the necessity of the change. The *Popolo d'Italia* maintained that,

by the constitutional change Albania reaffirms her independence, exalts the attainment of internal pacification, consolidates the central power and pays tribute to the firmness and faith of a man who had secured for his people the benefits of internal peace. Ahmed Zogu's greatest merit has been to have freed the country from the machinations of Pan-Serbism and to have prevented it from becoming a Yugoslav province. Moreover, the republican form of government is not suited to Albania's mentality, social institutions and history.[45]

The *Tribuna* joined the chorus stating that,

Italy looks upon a permanent Albanian monarchy as an efficient guarantee for the national and organic consolidation of her friend and ally and also as a guarantee for peace in the Balkans and in Europe.[46]

Zogu decided eventually to go one step further than simply informing the populace; he hoped to give the impression that they had even been asked for their direct approval. The President felt this last gesture was necessary because he had guaranteed Hodgson that " . . . while the change is most desirable I of course will not take the step without consulting the people of Albania."[47] In order to make it seem like they were indeed consulted, the Italian money not spent on the election was used for the purpose of "spontaneous demonstrations" on the part of the populous which by the end of August had reached feverish proportions.

The Assembly was inundated by telegrams stimulating it to the suppression of a form of government alien to the traditions of the Albanian people. The British Minister reported that these numerous telegrams were obtained from villagers detained in the local centers until they had set their mark to petitions clamouring for a king.[48]

Similar tactics were apparently used to secure the assent of the Catholic chiefs of the north, who were not enthralled with the idea of a Moslem king. The chiefs were invited to Shkodër and held for a few days almost as prisoners after which they were asked to attach their thumb marks to vaguely explained documents. These documents, of course, turned out to be petitions asking the President to become king. The chiefs were well paid for their trouble.[49]

The President exhibited deep satisfaction over the outcome of the propaganda drive although few foreigners were convinced that the people had been consulted. As the American Minister noted, "any seasoned observer of Albanian affairs must know at once that the people of the country, if consulted, never have any knowledge of having been approached."[50]

Having dealt with the immediate domestic considerations to his own satisfaction, Zogu felt in August that one last move to assure the international situation was necessary. Zogu was still concerned about the Yugoslavs since their reaction was still unknown. Having failed to win them over, the President decided that because Belgrade was still in the midst of internal political problems, he could with impunity simply let them know that his actions were none of their business. Zogu turned again to Mr. Chekrezi and the Tirana *Telegraph* to convey this idea to Belgrade.

Mr. Chekrezi was prevailed upon by the government to set up the straw man of foreign opposition in one of the issues of his paper and then to quickly knock it down. He dutifully wrote that the question was not entirely a domestic one and that as a result consideration may have to given to the question from the standpoint of foreign relations. In a succeeding issue Mr. Chekrezi published a letter, written by himself and signed "Justus," which declared that the proposed change was not the concern of any foreign government but a purely domestic question to be settled by the Albanians themselves in their own way.[51]

Having achieved this minor demonstration of independence and not wanting to put the British off any longer, Zogu finally summoned the Yugoslav Charge d'Affaires M. Kasidolac and informed him of the proposed change. Zogu cited the same arguments he had used with the British including the assertion that the people of Albania were obstinate in their desire to make him king. Further, the President gave Kasidolac a solemn assurance that the new government would take an independent line which was likely to be quite different from that which its predecessor had taken. Kadidolac, in keeping with the new Yugoslav attitude of resignation, gave the stereotyped reply that it was a matter which, as far as he could see, concerned Albania alone.[52] Zogu was satisfied that all that could be done had been done.

On the morning of August 25 the Constituent Assembly met. The opening session was attended by the fifty-seven delegates, the members of the government, the heads of most of the missions and a few spectators. The proceedings on this first day were purely formal and included the taking of an oath and a message from the President of the Assembly, P. Evangjeli. After appointing two commissions, one for the conduct of current affairs and the other to formulate the amendments to the constitutional law, the Assembly adjourned without anything being said about a change in the form of government.[53]

Zogu was clearly showing considerable caution and went so far as to absent himself from the first session. So that no one completely forgot the purpose of the proceedings, however, he saw to it that Tirana remained beflagged during the duration of the Assembly and that "spontaneous" demonstrations continued to occur at regular intervals.

On August 30 the committee organized to deal with constitutional law notified the President of the Assembly that they had unanimously decided that morning to establish a monarchial regime in Albania and proclaim the country a democratic monarchy. "The illustrious crown of the historical Albanian throne," runs the resolution, "is offered to the Savior of the Nation under the title of Zog I King of the Albanians." The commission further begged the Assembly to urgently approve this resolution.[54]

On September 1, 1928 at 9 o'clock in the morning the Constituent Assembly unanimously adopted two resolutions: to modify the text of the constitution to provide that Albania become a monarchial state with a hereditary ruler; and to offer the crown to President Ahmed Zogu in accordance with the will of the nation.[55] At 10 o'clock the President of the Assembly, with a delegation of eighteen members waited upon Ahmed Bey and informed him that "the Constituent Assembly invested with full powers by the Albanian people in today's majestic and historical setting, bowed before the spiritual will of the nation . . . " and decided to offer him the crown.[56] Zogu signified his acceptance and it was announced that a short ceremony would take place at five o'clock at the Parliament building.

True to his cautious habits, Zogu had carefully arranged security for the short trip from his residence to the Parliament building. As usual two roads had been cleared and lined with troops while trees had been shorn of their branches to prevent assassination attempts.

Zogu arrived in the House twenty minutes or more before the advertized time dressed in a field-marshal's uniform, traversed the hall rapidly followed by his personal retinue and mounted the platform. The officers of state, ministers and other functionaries grouped themselves around him. The members of the diplomatic body were present at the ceremony except the Rumanian Minister who had taken the hour of the invitation too literally. All the diplomats gathered wore morning dress except for the Italian Minister and his staff who, having arrived with pomp and circumstance in eight automobiles, wore uniforms, a distinction which undoubtedly did not go unnoticed by the assemblage.

Zogu, in a low and apparently nervous voice, swore on the Bible and the Koran to,

> maintain the national unity, the independence of the State and its territorial integrity, to observe the constitutional law and act strictly in accordance with the legislation in force, having always in mind the good of the people.[57]

In a short speech which followed he assured the Assembly of his intention to use his utmost energy for the uplifting of the country. "The world has understood that, if the sons of the eagle are left in peace they can build a state." In the realm of foreign affairs, "Albania will be a peaceful factor in the Balkans," while "the relations which exist today between Albania and her neighboring friendly States will, it is to be hoped, be strengthened yet more." Zogu did not fail to mention his particularly cordial relationship with the Italians noting that,

> the Italians will encourage the Albanian people, on occasion with an iron hand that does not shake, to achieve the high ideals which nature has preordained.

"Gentlemen, may we come forth with honor in the eyes of history."[58]

The ceremony came to an end several minutes before it had been scheduled to begin. Under cover of the burst of applause which followed, the now King Zog hurried from the hall, the members of his suite running into one another in an effort to keep up with their master. The new King quickly returned to his residence amidst the ringing of bells by hodjas on minarets. Later in the day he reviewed units of the Albanian military as well as representatives of his people from his balcony. To further emphasize his gratitude to the Italians, groups of Albanian youths were sent to break out in ovations for Mussolini and the King of Italy in front of the Italian Hotel Continental.[59]

A three-day public holiday was decreed by the Assembly during which "spontaneous" demonstrations were to abound. The municipalities were in charge of the arrangements and took very seriously the duty of insuring the semblance of universal rejoicing over an event which only excited the enthusiasm of the few. Tirana and Durrës blazed with fireworks. An Italian band played music for hours in the central square of Durrës while units of the Albanian navy, despite numerous technical problems, entertained crowds with maneuvers in the bay.

Every hovel obeyed orders and had its garland of green prominently displayed while the demonstrations continued. As the three-day period wore on the organization of these outbursts became more and more obvious while claims of spontaneity became more and more ridiculous. Few details had been missed with elaborate regulations governing every minute of their duration.

The official instructions were explicit. In Tirana all houses were required to be closed from a fixed hour and all were to be decorated with flags, "among them one large size with the eagle."

> The whole population of the capital, without any exception of class or calling, must take part. . . . No Albanian man or woman shall sit during the demonstrations in a coffeehouse, shop, restaurant or street; all must accompany the population in their manifestations.

At one moment the people were required to clap their hands and at another hail the Savior of the Nation, all of which was to be interspersed by hearty cries of "Long live Zog, King of the Albanians." These popular demonstrations were to be headed by groups of eighty women and twenty girls "dressed in national costumes or in new fashionable clothes."[60]

Although everything went well domestically, the initial foreign reaction with the exception of the Italians, was somewhat negative, not because of the change to a monarchy but because Zog had chosen to call himself "King of the Albanians" rather than "King of Albania." While at first glance the difference seems somewhat trivial, when seen in the context of Balkan politics it certainly was not.

The Yugoslavs, who possessed a large Albanian minority in Kosovo, interpreted this as a signal for a future irredentist campaign against their state. Supporters of the title, on the other hand, maintained that Zog was simply following in the tradition of Balkan monarchs who all used a similar form for their titles. In Greece the monarch was called "King of the Hellenes," in Bulgaria "Czar of the Bulgarians" and in Yugoslavia "King of the Serbs, Croats and Slovenes."[61]

The title which had originally been proposed in January was "King of Albania" and indeed it was this version which was used during the first days of the demonstrations. A number of explanations have been put forward to account for why the title was changed. The Italian Minister in Albania came up with one senario in which it was he, Sola, and the Italians who initially suggested the title "King of Albania" to correspond with "King of Italy," after being asked by Zogu which title he should assume.

Near the end of August Zogu had come to Sola and asked him what attitude his government would take if the title "King of the Albanians" was used. Sola replied that his government would not change its mind over so small an issue and further noted that the new title was actually in perfect harmony with the situation. The designation "King of Albania" was more reminiscent of older days when kings asserted their divine right to rule and called themselves "King of . . . by the grace of God." Such a title, Sola argued, would have been ill adapted to the democratic monarchy being formed in Albania.

Sola further maintained that Zogu and the Albanians were originally perfectly happy with the first choice but had abruptly changed their minds once they had been threatened. What had apparently done the harm was the action of the Yugoslav Charge d'Affaires who had alluded to the question of the title in the course of his interview with the President. His allusion had been taken to imply a menace and that had been enough. The Albanians had immediately done what they were dared to do.[62]

This argument seems plausible except for one point crucial to the entire senario, no evidence exists to support the allegation that the Yugoslav Charge d'Affaires M. Kasidolac even alluded to the question of the title. In fact, Kasidolac claimed that he purposely refrained from doing so, knowing that the British Minister had already done so and his remarks therefore could easily have been misconstrued. He did mention the subject to Vrioni but only to ask what decision had been made.

A more likely senario goes as follows: when the question first became a topic of debate in December 1927, Vironi assured Chamberlain that "King of Albania" would be used. Zogu was satisifed and directed that this title be used during the demonstrations calling for a change of regime. As late as August 24 the President reiterated this position to the British Minister.

At this point, however, forces within Albania that were either too strong for him or which he did not care to antagonize began to spread the rumor that Zogu, once he became king, would restore to Albania the frontiers to which it was ethnically entitled. This suggestion evoked a good deal of enthusiasm, appealing particularly to the chauvinistic instincts of the ever important northern tribes who had up until this time been rather lukewarm in their support of a monarchy.

This enthusiasm was further inflamed by the rumor, begun apparently by a misinformed article published in an Albanian newspaper in Bari, suggesting that the Yugoslavs had signified their objection to the title "King of the Albanians." This was enough to induce an exuberant Assembly to decided that it should be used.

Zogu was in a rather difficult position. The British, whose opinions he still considered to be the most impartial, had strongly advised against it. His own Foreign Minister, Iljas Bey Vrioni, fought tooth and nail against it and was confident enough to assure the French Charge d'Affaires as late as August 28 that the objectionable title would not be used. Yet the Assembly, much to the embarrassment of Vrioni who had not expected that his counsel on such a matter would be discounted, chose the belligerent title. Zogu, who was actually attracted to the title but recognized the difficulties, could hardly refuse without jeopardizing his popularity in circles which were all too important to him.

The President believed that the title might even help him with those who opposed the Monarchy. At the very least it would restrict the influence which people like Prishtina still enjoyed in Kosovo.[63] In the end Zogu, claiming that he had "fallen into a nest of monarchists," took the line of least resistance and asked the Italians whether he could reply upon them should he adopt the objectionable title.[64]

Rome made it clear that he could count on them since they were aware that they could only benefit from such a development. The title would cause recognition problems for Zogu thereby tying him closer to the Italians. That Rome not only supported the move but actively encouraged it is evidenced by the fact that in the debate in the Assembly which decided the question, the orators who spoke most vehemently in favor of the objectionable title were Shevket Verlaci who had always had pronounced Italian sympathies, Alizoti, a discredited ex-minister of finance who was universally believed to be a paid Italian agent and Dibra, the head of the family by that name whose former large estates were mainly in Yugoslav territory. The Italian position can probably best be illustrated by a comment made by an Italian colonel sitting next to General Percy at a banquet of 250 officers who said, "I like the title 'King of the Albanians,' it sounds aggressive."[65]

Ultimately the question of the title caused a good deal less trouble than most everyone had expected. The Yugoslavs made it clear that some mark of displeasure should be shown but were also very anxious not to be the last to recognize the new situation.[66] After exchanging notes with the Italians, Belgrade extended recognition to the Monarchy. It was generally believed by the diplomatic community that the Yugoslavs remained hostile and accorded early recognition only so as not to play into the hands of the Italians.[67]

Rome, of course, had been the first to extend recognition, indeed, the speed with which it did so convinced many that it had a good deal more to do with the whole process than it was willing to admit. The new king exchanged a series of telegrams with Victor Emmanuel and Mussolini. The Duce, in expression good wishes stated that,

> I am happy to assure Your Majesty that Italy will continue in the future to pursue her policy of constant friendship towards Your Majesty and Your Government who are both doing in every field such noble and effective work for the progress of the Albanian nation.[68]

Sola, in a letter to Zogu, explained the official attitude of the Italian government making certain that the King kept in mind the reason for Italy's enthusiastic support.

> The Royal Italian Government considers the establishment of the monarchical regime in Albania as a happy event which while further strengthening the bonds existing between the two countries, will ensure the continuity of their foreign policy as laid down in the Treaty of Alliance. Italy will therefore always remain faithful to that intimate entente whose brilliant results in general policy it has pleased your Excellency to emphasize. I can assure you that the Italian Government will never fail to consult the Albanian Government in every matter that may affect our common interests and to act in agreement with it in all questions pertaining to the situation in the Balkans.[69]

This chorus of praise was continued in most of Italy's government-controlled newspapers with the semi-official *Giornale d'Italia* leading the way. "Instead of the alleged tendency of people toward republicanism and the left," maintained the editor,

> Albania has shown that the traditional value of state and government and the instincts of a nation are stronger than ever. Italy welcomes this fresh evidence of vitality and cannot but express her satisfaction at the political consolidation of Albania which is an element of order in the troubled sea of Balkan politics.[70]

The *Impero* published a similar editorial expressing its satisfaction with the fact that Albania should give

> an example of internal discipline at the very moment when Yugoslavia is disturbing the tranquillity of European Chancelleries.... Italy hails Ahmed Zogu's proclamation as King as marking the opening of an era of fecund tranquillity in the Balkans and as representing a check to Albania's restless neighbors who have everything to gain from a turbulent political life.[71]

The fact that the British and French did not recognize the change with the same alacrity disturbed many Albanians, particularly since Yugoslavia accorded recognition before London and Paris. The British decided to delay recognition because of the title, and the French, whose policy towards Albania at this point generally fell in line with London, decided to follow suit.[72] Their joint recognition finally came on September 21.

The primary effect of this delay was to convince many Albanians that Great Britain did not necessarily support all of Italy's actions in Albania. Zog was displeased and the esteem with which the British were held in official circles in Albania suffered to a certain extent. Zog, from this point on, consulted the Britsh Minister a good deal less often than he had previously.

The only serious recognition problem was caused by Mustafa Kemal Ataturk's government in Ankara which refused to recognize the regime at all. Zog maintained that this occurred because Kemal did not want to see Turkish tutelage overthrown and because of a dispute over some land which belonged to an Albanian who had married the daughter of Abdul Hamid.[73] While Zog had confiscated some land belonging to the Sultan, the effective cause of the difficulty dealt first with a general antipathy which Kemal harbored for Zog. The Turkish leader was exasperated with Zog's betrayal of the republican form of government and was particularly incensed by the appearance in one or two British and French papers of reports attributing to him the intention of following King Zog's lead. Hodgson suggested that another reason might have been that Turkey probably had some military agreement with Albania that Zog had repudiated.[74]

The problems with Turkey were not entirely unwelcome to Zog since he felt he no longer needed to impress the Moslems by maintaining close ties with Kemal. It was now more important to divorce Albania from Turkey and more importantly from negative Turkish influence. Zog had already taken numerous steps in this direction including the issuance of secret orders stopping the importation of Turkish newspapers into Albania.[75]

In a more open example of this trend the new King dropped the Arabic Turkish "Ahmed" as well as the "u" from "Zogu" in order to strengthen his image as a national Albanian King. Zog allowed relations with Turkey to deteriorate to the point of breaking relations, a situation which was not corrected until November 1931. Despite the advice of both the British and the Italians, Zog saw his strained relations with Turkey as an opportunity to make a relatively strong statement concerning the direction he hoped the Monarchy would pursue. Although a combination would eventually result, Zog was determined to become more a European king than a sultan.

Apart from Ankara, opposition did come from several other foreign quarters but these posed less of a problem for Zog since they had much less influence than did the Turks. The unfortunate Prince William of Wied took the opportunity to remind the world that he had never actually abdicated the throne of Albania.

The Times of London reported that Wied not only claimed the throne but also maintained that the majority of Albanians still supported him. Since a free and uninfluenced referendum was at that time impossible, the Prince felt his immediate return was out of the question. He did, however, declare that he was free from personal ambition and that, thinking only of the welfare of the people, he would avoid external and internal political difficulties by awaiting the proper moment to return.[76]

Wied later stated in the *Pesti Naplo* in Budapest that many of his followers in Albania were working diligently for his return and that he had the support of many influential statemen who also lobbied on his behalf. He had a plan for Albania, the Prince maintained, and would carry it out as soon as he regained the throne.[77]

The Italio-Albanian paper *Gazeta Shqipetare* reported that the Prince would not only protest against the construction of a monarchy under Zog but had actually planned a revolution. The uprising was to have been financed and carried out by the anti-Italian Albanian emigres in Vienna. These rumors were discounted by most informed sources and since nothing ever became of these threats, it is safe to assume that they simply did not exist.[78] Wied did not protest to any of the governments involved in the 1912 decision of the Conference of Ambassadors nor can any connection between the Prince and the Albanian emigre groups in Vienna be found.

Albanian emigres protested on their own behalf, calling for intervention by the League of Nations and the Great Powers. On September 1 the Central Committee of the Albanian Republican Organization, a makeshift group of emigres in Belgrade, warned all European chancellories that the party would use weapons to prevent the ascension of Zog to the throne. The next day *The Times* of London received an exchange telegram dispatched from Tirana stating that republican leaders in Albania had issued a manifesto demanding foreign intervention against what they termed "the tyranny of the new King of Albania, Ahmed Zogli." Failing this, they threatened to start a revolution.[79]

Among the large Albanian community in the United States, the declaration of the monarchy was met primarily with apathy. The only vocal opposition came from Fan Noli and his newspaper *The Republic,* published in Boston. Noli called the change to monarchy "a farce prepared at Rome" as well as "an odious crime against the Albanian people and the Balkanic people in general." He added that the change was made under a terrorist regime with fascist protection, against the wishes of the Albanian population. Albania, he said, was thereby transformed into an Italian colony on a military Italian basis against neighboring Balkan states.[80]

In a more practical vain, the Bishop complained that the Albanian economy was already in serious trouble and that the further expense of the trappings of monarchy would only add to the critical financial state in which the country found itself. With the Monarchy, Noli maintained, the reactionary landowning elements would grow stronger and would continue to keep the peasants in slavery, darkness and poverty.[81]

The Bishop's assessment of internal opposition was somewhat inaccurate. In Albania during the time of Zog, where life was difficult and survival from day to day consumed most of the energies of most of the people, the change actually aroused little emotion except among those who were directly affected.

Zog for example was very much aware of the worth of a reliable officer corps. To gain their support for the Monarchy he granted each new officer a step in rank, a raise in pay as well as a new dazzling uniform, all of which increased their collective social prominence. Although this bribe did not necessarily make them reliable, it at least succeeded in convincing them to acquiesce to the change.[82]

On the other hand, many of the Bey class landowners saw Zog's attempt to construct a European type monarchy as a serious threat to their privileged position under the old Turkish social system which Albania had inherited. Many of them, believing that their time was rapidly coming to an end, began looking for a market for their large land holdings. Several of the most prominent managed to sell their property, investing their money in Italy, Austria and Corfu.[83]

Among the common people, those not directly involved, the reaction when it could be discerned, was not surprising. Either they did not react at all because it really did not affect them or, as the British Minister suggested, they were cyncially indifferent.

In general, then, both domestically and in foreign quarters the change was met with varying degrees of disinterest. In Albania only those directly involved, the very small percentage who felt they had something to gain or to lose by the change, reacted at all. The majority of the population, the townspeople and peasants, demonstrated approval when they were required to do so but showed little unrehearsed excitement, probably because they expected the Monarchy to be much the same as the Republic.

Similar motivating factors shaped the reaction of Europe and the Balkans. Italy, the only country to anticipate advantages from the change, welcomed it. Others, including the Yugoslavs were either mildly hostile or indifferent. This mild reaction on the part of most foreign powers resulted from a number of factors, including the significant decrease in economic interest exhibited by the West since the race for petroleum in 1924-1925. The Americans lost interest rapidly, particularly after the Italians and the British found very little oil. The Yugoslav copper mine at Puka, which had initially caused much trouble, was given up for similar reasons.[84] Although political interest in Albania certainly did not decline, after the Tirana pact of 1927 Italy did seem to have Albania wrapped up and this helped to dampen negative reaction to the Monarchy.

Zog had finally accomplished his long sought after goal of turning himself into a king, and he had been able to do it with a minimum of trouble. He had proved himself strong enough to put through a project over the heads of an apathetic people and wise enough to wait for a moment when the internal situation was propitious and no complications with neighbors were likely to ensue. He must be given credit for the change itself as it was basically a wise move.

Certainly an Albanian republic was an anomally whereas a monarchy with its pomp and ceremony could be understood by people who were accustomed through the ages to owe allegiance to a chieftain or a pasha. Despite British misgivings, the argument that a throne conveys the idea of permanence and continuity and that these attributes are particularly desirable in the government of a country which had been torn by internal feuds and external jealousy as had Albania cannot be ruled out. While it is true that tribal allegiance to Zog was strictly personal, the creation of the Monarchy allowed the King time to either change the attitude of the chieftains or decrease their influence. Zog gained in prestige within his own land by the assumption of the Royal title and eventhough the change resulted in a few smiles in Europe, which had seen so many thrones totter and fall, this is of little consequence. General stability was one step closer.

CHAPTER EIGHT

THE FIRST YEARS OF THE MONARCHY

During the first years of the Republic, Zog had been able to substantially decrease random violence as well as make some preliminary general internal progress. Much was left to be done and during the first years of the Monarchy the new King was determined to reinforce this positive trend, hoping to successfully deal with the endemic political violence while simultaneously continuing the process of constructing a modern independent state. Albania's difficulties under the Monarchy remained extreme and in some cases more were created, but still Zog achieved some success, which resulted in the beginning of a much needed period of tranquillity. A number of significant factors explain how the King was able to achieve such an unusual state of affairs, the most important being the complete destruction of political life in Albania.

Under the constitution of the Republic, Zog had assumed wide but by no means absolute power, holding back basically because of his fear of foreign reaction. By 1928, however, Zog had become considerably more aware of general European attitudes towards internal political trends in Albania. The realization that Europe was, for the most part, unconcerned about domestic politics in Albania convinced Zog that his early circumspection had been misplaced. As a result he instructed the Constituent Assembly, which continued to meet after the declaration of the Monarchy, to draw up a constitution which left all of the power, not just part of it, in the hands of the chief executive. The Constituent Assembly, which automatically turned itself into the Parliament, obligingly complied.

Although it seemed outwardly democratic, the new constitution promulgated in December of 1928 gave the King unrestricted legislative, judicial and executive powers. Significant changes in the lawmaking procedures insured Zog's dominance. The bicameral Parliament of the Republic was reduced to a simple Assembly, primarily because the Senate had registered a certain amount of opposition to the construction of the Monarchy.[1]

The King clearly found a small number of politicians more easily controlled. In keeping with this idea, the number of deputies was kept to fifty-six. A census showed an increase in the population which would have automatically raised its membership to sixty-seven. At the King's request, however, a law was enacted whereby the returns of the last election were so proportioned so as to not require the election of more deputies.[2]

The election process continued to insure that only such candidates who were of certain loyalty, or appointed by local officials, stood a chance of victory. The fact that the head of the commune, or local government, was an official appointee made it possible for him to secure the election to the body of second electors only those who could be relied upon to elect to Parliament the slate prepared in Tirana.

Since no political parties were legal, no other candidates ever stood for election. Moreover, one hundred gold francs had to be paid to the municipality by every would-be candidate before his name was listed. Few could afford to pay the heavy fee without the help of the government. As with the constitution of the Republic, a candidate could stand for any prefecture irrespective of the place of his actual residence.

No candidacies were announced for the position of any officer of the Parliament without first being designated by the King in advance. Zog fixed the agenda for the Parliament, had the sole right to introduce bills and could dismiss the Parliament at will. Parliament, which was otherwise elected for a period of four years, as a result sat very rarely and when it did sit, it occupied itself in voluminous debates on smaller legislation to which the King was indifferent. From time to time a communication was sent to them, rubber-stamped by the appropriate cabinet minister but emanating from the King, directing specific legislation, and this was at once carried out. In November 1933, for example, while the Assembly argued a proposed pension measure affecting government employees, a

Royal memorandum was laid before it by the Prime Minister which after ordering a campaign of intensive planting directed as follows: "You are instructed to provide for the purchase and storing for export, of the wheat crop of the coming year." The required bill was immediately passed and the Assembly returned to its petty pension measure. No political issues of importance, then, were decided by the elections or by the Parliament.[3]

The uncooperative Senate was replaced by a Council of State which was composed of ten members and two deputy members chosen by the King from a list presented to him by a commission of the Prime Minister, the President of the Chamber and the Minister of Justice. The duties of this new purely consultive body included the preparation of codes, the writing of all bills for the King and the examination of concessions and conventions.[4]

Zog's judicial powers were significantly augmented by the new constitution. Under the presidency he had been able to control the judiciary branch only through appointments. Now, judicial decisions were pronounced and executed in his name, a change which completely did away with what little independence the courts might once have had. Zog's Royal court and his trusted supporters were allowed considerable license under the law and generally could count on the King's direct intervention on their behalf if they were ever obviously guilty of some indiscretion.[5]

The primary source of his power, of course, came by virtue of his executive prerogatives. While he gave up his position as head of the government as unbefitting of his new Royal station, he was careful to remain in complete control. Although the Prime Minister, nominal head of a cabinet of seven, was charged by the King with the formation of a government., the King of course made his own selections for the cabinet posts. Invariably, once a government was chosen and appeared before the Parliament for the customary vote of confidence, it was unanimously approved.

Nominally, the Parliament was empowered to summon any minister for questioning or to depose the entire cabinet, but in practice any such summons required the advance approval of the King. As usual, the King retained the power to appoint and dismiss cabinet ministers at will. Similarly, no appointments or dismissals of higher municipal officers were sanctioned without his order or consent.

Zog's domestic control was further enhanced by strict codes which effectively emasculated any internal opposition. For the handful of

Albanians who had the advantage of a foreign education and had not been coopted by the regime, censorship became somewhat stricter than it had been under the presidency.

Albanian intellectuals were constrained to silence by the rigid Penal Law for Political Offences. Although rarely employed, this law prohibited propaganda of any kind against the regime, against the King and against the constitution, with the penalty of life imprisonment or death prescribed for,

> those who organize or participate in secret and anti-national committees whose design is to disturb the existing order or to change the form of the regime established by the National Assembly.[6]

All of these political offenses were to be tried by an extraordinary court whose judges were chosen by the King's Ministers of Justice and Interior. The new law made it a crime even to have knowledge, gained in any manner, of the existence of these offenses.

A close censorship, which concerned itself even with postal correspondence was introduced to complement the law against political offenses. The two small newspapers, which constituted Albania's press, were censored by the Ministry of Foreign Affairs although due to loose enforcement the occasional article critical of the government, was published. The only place in which criticism of the King and his policies could be publicly expressed on a regular basis was in the press of other countries.

As a result of these numerous precautions, criticism of the regime and the King was made very difficult and public opinion, if such a thing existed, could have no voice. Agitation for improvement in the monarchial form of government was rare and political violence decreased.

Zog had simply refused to share his domestic political power with anyone, internally or abroad. His prerogatives with regard to foreign affairs, however, were somewhat more limited, owing to the ever increasing role of the Italians. According to the constitution he had the power to direct foreign policy and was authorized to conclude pacts of friendship, alliances and other treaties with foreign states. He was also supreme commander of all Albanian armed forces and had the power to appoint all officers of the rank of company commander and above. These officers, as well as the rest of the army, swore personal allegiance to the King.

Despite these superficially wide-ranging powers, Zog was under rather tight control when it come to foreign policy because of the series of pacts he had felt it necessary to sign. Recognizing this fact, he took the opportunity presented by the new constitution to divest himself legally of his warmaking powers, realizing that by virtue of the Tirana Pacts he really did not have them anyway. He insisted that the Constituent Assembly insert a clause curtailing the Royal prerogative to involve the country in hostilities. As a result, Albania could not be called on to lend military aid to a foreign country, nor could it invoke the assistance of a foreign country, unless the King and Parliament were in accord.

This was done partially to protect his successors in case they turned out to be weaker than he and more prone to misue their powers. More importantly, Zog was able to weaken the Treaty of Alliance by this move. Although the Parliament was of course completely compliant to Zog's will, this constitutional insertion gave the King a loophole in case the Italians demanded something which he was loath to give. Zog could henceforth blame his lack of alacrity on the intransigence of Parliament.[7]

Zog had worked hard to give the appearance of Western political forms but it is difficult to break the habit of centuries and to abrupty separate oneself from one's heritage. Moreover, Zog had learned from past political experience that attempting to institute a Western political system in Albania without the proper adjustment was a dangerous proposition. As a result, an Oriental-Western Monarchy was created, encompassing all the problems which such a basically unnatural union might entail.

Although he wore Western uniforms and suits, Zog continued to rule in the classic Oriental fashion. In many ways his court was a miniature version of what he had seen in Constantinople as a youth and included the intrigue and suspense which one might expect to find surrounding an Oriental potentate. Zog, through his treatment of subordinates, reinforced and even extended this atmosphere. The King made a point of playing people and different interests off against each other.

Zog ran a personal dictatorship in which he was the only route to success for the political climbers around him. To find loyal supporters he had a set method which included thorough inquiries about an individual's movements, family and friends. Zog would then hire the person in question and shortly thereafter fire the same individual in order to make it clear how absolutely dependent he was on the King. If an official struck up a friendship he was either moved or sacked. He was constantly watched and was made fully aware that there was always a rival in the background ready to denounce him.[8] The King even acquired the unfortunate habit of having his subordinates fight with one another in order to demonstrate his own power.[9]

While this structure of government might have suited the Albanian environment quite well, it did generate special problems. Many of Zog's personal failings became significantly more serious during the early years of the Monarchy and he even exhibited some new ones. Several observers complained that once he had reached his goal, complacency set in and he lost the gift of energy which had characterized his earlier years. He seemed to cling to methods of government which had served him well in the past but were no longer adequate to meet a changed situation.

Under the new conditions, Zog's well developed craftiness in many cases proved to be more of a handicap than as asset. Because of his inability to confide in others and his jealousy of power, he had pushed through a new political system which made him constitutionally unable to delegate authority in most cases. The entire weight of the administration, therefore, rested on his shoulders, a burden which he often found too heavy, having neither the constructive ability nor the knowledge required to deal with every situation.[10] As a result, he lost some of his resolve and power of decision making which had been so indispensible in his earlier years. At the worst of times he began to resemble a small-size, indolent, Oriental potentate surrounded by a group of hangers-on who lived upon him and whom he was unable to shake off.

Under these circumstances it is not surprising that other aspects of Albania's Oriental heritage remained. The most signficant manifestations of these resilient elements included the unrelenting corruption among Albanian officials as well as a considerable degree of Royal extravagance, at least in the early stages of the Monarchy.

The average Albanian citizen was no less honest than any other Balkan citizen but once he assumed the burden of office, most Albanians of Zog's period believed that they had been invested with a license to rob the treasury. It is important to realize, however, that few of these officials actually felt they were doing damage to Albania primarily because the practice of corruption was so widely accepted. The question of social conscience rarely came into play.[11]

In some cases corruption was even economically understandable. The gendarmerie, chronically underpaid or not paid at all, often had little choice but to live off the land. Even cabinet ministers, who were expected to live and behave as their European counterparts, were paid a mere thirty pounds a month and were not provided with pensions. Since Albania was a poor country and could not afford to pay generous salaries to its civil servants, they considered it natural to reward themselves on the side.[12]

Although some cases could at least be understood, there was also much excessive corruption which damaged the Monarchy with regard to public relations. Zog's personal assistant, A. Krossi, used his political position to further line his already bulging pockets. By December 1928 Krossi was drawing pay for 200 soldiers, at the rate of 10,000 gold francs a month and it is doubtful that any of the money found its way back to Zog.[13] Krossi became rich and lived well, a clear sign to fellow Albanians that he was dishonest for there were few opportunities to become wealthy legitimately.

Although Zog's personal behavior in no way rivaled Krossi's, the King was not beyond criticism when it came to finances. Approximately 9 percent of the state revenues went to the King in the form of salary and allowances, a sum which worked out to about 3½ million gold francs a year.[14]

In many respects Zog was basically frugal. He resisted the temptation of an expensive coronation and refused to create an Albanian nobility other than his immediate family. He did show some inconsistency here, however, in that he seemed to delight in throwing himself extravagant birthday parties.

While national celebrations admittedly serve a purpose in terms of national unity, Zog's birthdays in 1929 and 1930 seemed to have outstripped the bounds of reasonable policy. On October 8, 1929, an impressive parade was held in Tirana. Included were cabinet ministers in national costumes wearing large revolvers in high gold belts. Costumed princesses and the ladies of Tirana society marched next to troops in khaki green accompanied by tanks. Various elements of the "Youth Movement" inspired by fascism's organization of the youth in Italy also played a large role. In addition, five thousand boys between the ages of fifteen and twenty, members of the Enti Kombetar or Premilitaires under the instruction and control of Colonel Selahedin Bloshmi, an active army officer, marched passed the King wearing uniforms and white skull-caps carrying carbines with bayonets.[15]

The festivities also included a long program of honors and song. The first event was the presentation by the King of colors to the various units of the Enti Kombetar, representing the principal towns of the kingdom. It was noticed that one flag presented bore the name "Kosovo" and another "Dibra," both districts within the frontiers of Yugoslavia. Zog did not shy from trotting out irredentism to appeal to those who still had questions about the monarchy or still harbored hoped of reuniting with their brothers in Yugoslavia.

Next, the second or junior group of the Enti Kombetar, comprised of boys between the ages of eight and fifteen organized and administered by the Ministry of Public Information made an appearance. Together with school girls uniformed in red shirts, they marched past the King singing the national anthem and a lauditory song to Zog.

Tirana in the meantime, had been profusely decorated for the occasion. The streets were festooned with colored electric lights, the trees and telephone poles were wrapped in laurel and the flag was displayed everywhere. The entire show, which incidentally was filmed by Fox Movietone News, the first sound pictures in Albania, cost the government more than one million gold francs, a considerable sum to be spent out of a revenue liberally estimated at thirty million gold francs a year. The Foreign Minister remarked hopefully at the time that this was to be "the first and last big parade."[16]

The Foreign Minister was not to have his way for in 1930 the entire spectacle was reproduced. Tirana was again decorated with the usual array of flags, laurel bushes and electric signs reading "Long Live Zog I." The celebration of 1930 was even extended to include an Italian aircraft demonstration and an "artistic week." To honor the King and demonstrate his continued support while at the same time remind him of Italian military might, Mussolini sent fifty-seven airplanes, including bombers, transports and pursuit planes, from Rome under the command of General Valle, Chief of Staff of the Air Forces. The general was received by the King and a dinner was given to honor the commander and officers of the squadron. Much to the King's disappointment, this part of the festivities seemed to arouse little enthusiasm among the people.[17]

In an effort to lend credence to the argument that Albania was becoming, in part, a Western Monarchy, Zog had ordered the founding of dramatic and chorale societies and took the opportunity presented by his birthday to show them off to the world. Theatrical presentations were organized and given by the Enti Kombetar under the direction of Rexhep Yella, the prefect of Tirana.

The Choral Society of Korcë and the Philodramatic Societies of Shkodër, Elbasan, Bilishtë and Durrës were brought to Tirana and gave performances at the National Theater in the presence of the High Patroness of the Arts, Her Royal Highness Princess Ruhije, a sister of the King. The high point of the week was the performance by the Philodramatic Society of Shkodër of *Uncle Tom's Cabin* in five acts, much to the amusement of the American Minister and his staff.[18] Undoubtedly sensing that these celebrations were not serving their original purpose and being concerned about the rising costs, Zog conducted further celebrations in a considerably more modest fashion.

Priorities in the allocation of funds for building projects left much to be desired and constituted another manifestation of Royal extravagance. The renowned British philanthropist and Albanologist Mary Durham expressed concern during the early years of the Monarchy regarding the money which Zog borrowed from the Italians and then spent unwisely, complaining to the Albanian Minister in Washington, Faik Konitza,that,

> I am anxious about the state of Albania. I do not like the immense debt to Italy. The Italians are not able to be trusted and I do not see what can prevent them from seizing an Albanian port as payment if they think fit. To my mind it would have been far better to do without palaces and public buildings and to have avoided a big public debt.[19]

The Italians, of course, were content to see that part of their money which was not spent on their own projects, squandered on ostentatious buildings because if Albania ever succeeded in becoming a viable state economically, Italy's role would clearly become considerably less significant. Rather than building needed roads and bridges to bring the country closer together, Zog, despite his publically state priorities, built large government buildings, broad boulevards in Tirana and planned to construct a large palace in a fine position a few miles from Tirana. Although the palace was never finished and Zog continued to live in the same unpretentious villa he had occupied as President, many of the government buildings saw completion, considerably changing the face of Tirana.

Before long Tirana began to visually represent the paradoxes of Zog's Monarchy. While the old malaria-ridden section of town remained basically unchanged, large streets like the Boulevard Zog and the Boulevard Mussolini were haphazardly constructed throughout the city. These new streets were eventually lined with ministerial buildings of modern design which lacked nothing when it came to interior technical wonders. To complete this picture of paradox, none of the roads in Tirana were paved, resulting in large clouds of dust wandering between the new buildings giving a ghost town impression.[20]

When seen in a Western context, little of the preceding would be called overtly extravagant but when considered in light of the chronically critical Albanian economy, the corruption, the celebrations and the poor building priorities take on added significance.

On the surface, as with the presidency, Albania's economy during the first few years of the Monarchy looked rather healthy. In certain respects Albania even looked to be in a prosperous state. In 1928 Zog began spending some of the Italian loan money which benefited thousands directly and indirectly. Owing to the influx of Italians, house rents and food prices went up considerably. As a result, thousands of Albanians found work while countless others found means of gleaning a small part of the money being put into circulation.[21] Furthermore, due to a series of changes in the agreements between Albania and Italy, the SVEA loans, which at the outset were a harsh imposition on the Albanians, were eventually developed into a monument of Italian philanthropy.

As we have seen, in 1927 Zog had asked the Italians for a moratorium on the annual payment of interest from the 1925 loans, as part of his demands in exchange for the Treaty of Alliance, or second Tirana Pact. The Italians were willing to acquiesce, being cognizant of the benefits they could expect from the pact and also recognizing that such a delay would only spread the payments out further, thereby tying Albania to Italy economically for an even longer period.

With the negotiations almost complete, Zog suddenly realized that what he was about to sign entailed an eventual payment by the Tirana government of interest on the postponed annuities. However natural such a stipulation might be in a business sense, Zog complained bitterly to the Italians that it was new to him and that he had been deceived. He refused to accept the arrangments which would have required the Albanian government to eventually pay annuities on the scale of some eight million rather than 5½ million.[22]

The Italian Minister, Sola, flew to Rome with a personal letter to Mussolini from Zog detailing Albanian objections to the terms of the moratorium. The Duce accepted Zog's point of view and issued the necessary orders that no interest should be chargeable to the Albanian government on the annuities affected by the moratorium. Apparently, the Italian financial officials whose duty it was to make the fine manly gestures of the Duce fit in as far as possible with the more sordid demands of business then endeavored to obtain some compensation in other directions.

These further attempts were checked with the assistance of Mussolini. The final agreement basically read as follows:

> The Albanian government will as hitherto continue to make no payment until the year 1930, when they will pay 1 million gold francs. In 1931 they will pay 2 million. In 1932 the regular interest and amortisation scheme as provided by the original contract will come into force, but the Albanian government will, in addition have to repay, during the six years of 1932-1938, the six annuities of which payment had been postponed by the moratorium.[23]

Zog was delighted with the new agreements since the net result was highly beneficial for the Albanians. In November of 1925 the Albanian government had received fifty million gold francs loged to their credit for which they had been receiving interest at the rate of 6 7/8 percent. They had not paid and now would not have to pay a penny in interest until 1930, nor would their delay in beginning such payments cost them anything. Meanwhile, the Italian government had been and would continue to steadily pay 7½ percent per annum to the Italian shareholders of the loan. This refurbished SVEA loan was not only a far cry from the original settlement which Myfid Bey had contracted but it had actually turned into an excellent business proposition, at least as long as the prospect of repayment remained in the distant future.

When asked whether the payment of doubled annuities between 1932 and 1937 (about eleven million gold francs per annum, i.e., about one-third of the 1928 revenue) would be a heavy burden, Zog mentioned that he counted on putting aside 1½ million to two million gold francs annually out of the state revenues which would form a sinking fund to meet that eventuality.[24] Zog's figures, as usual, proved to be astoundingly optimistic when seen in the light of the remainder of the Albanian economy.

Despite these few optimistic notes, Albania's total economic picture had if anything taken a turn for the worse since the early 1920s. The unhealthy structure naturally continued to produce desperate results. The government revenue sources had changed very little and Tirana continued to relie heavily on archaic tax systems and tariffs. In excess of 28 percent of the state revenue was collected from the agricultural segment of Albanian society, 76 percent of which was paid by the poorest peasants. These taxes were made up primarily of old Turkish revenues including the animal tax and the tenth which required the peasants to sit on their produce until the government collectors came and collected their share.

Approximately 59 percent of state revenues were still received from tariffs which accordingly were not set up to encourage business but simply to net the government as much money as possible. The tremendous duties on food which this system entailed failed to increase domestic production. The net result was that life for the simple people was made more difficult.[25]

These basic unresolved problems helped to produce figures very similar to those listed for the early 1920s. As usual the revenue intake was always overestimated and the old Turkish method of beginning each financial year with "O," without figuring in the previous years debts, distorted the figures so as to make them look more favorable.

As a result, sources quoted by a League Memorandum made it clear that the budgets for 1925-1931 closed with a deficit of three million gold francs each year, owing to over-optimistic estimates of expenditures, and the amounts being covered by the collection of arrears and payments out of current receipts.[26]

Nevertheless, as with the official budget figures for the early 1920s, those of the late 1920s and early 1930s seemed to be reasonable on the surface as demonstrated by the following:

	receipts	expenditures
1928-29	28,700,000	28,200,000
1929-30	31,800,000	31,800,000
1930-31	31,385,000	31,385,000
1931-32	29,097,000	31,933,000[27]

As we have seen, the money was obtained in a way so as to prevent the economic growth of the country. The money was spent in the same manner, with most of it, generally between 45% and 50% going to the military and the gendarmerie.[28] Major expenditures for 1929-30 were distributed chiefly as follows: Army 45.5%, Ministry of the Interior 7.3%, Ministry of Finance 7.3%, Ministry of National Economy 5.7%, Ministry of Justice 3.9%, Directorate of Posts and Telegraphs 3.7% and the Ministry of Public Works 3.5%.[29]

The expenditures for the few years immediately following showed the same trend as evidenced by the official figures.

Expenditures (in 100 GFrs)

	1930-31	1931-32
Army and Gendarmerie	5,407	5,423
Ministry of Public Works	1,359	1,129
Ministry of the Interior	1,415	1,538
Ministry of Justice	1,269	1,266
Health	593	524
Ministry of Foreign Affairs	800	806
Ministry of Posts and Telegraphs	1,339	1,189
Ministry of National Economy	1,147	1,000
Ministry of Public Instruction	3,534	3,167[30]

Again, as in the early 1920s, the most serious economic problem revolved around the adverse balance and the basic structure of Albania's foreign trade.

Albanian Foreign Trade 1928-1932
(in million of GFrs)

	imports	exports	deficit
1928	32.3	14.9	17.4
1929	38.6	14.7	23.9
1930	33.3	12.4	20.9
1931	29.5	7.5	22.0
1932	22.8	4.5	18.3[31]

The Italians, not surprisingly, remained in control of the lion's share of Albanian foreign trade as the following chart suggests.

Italy's Share of Albanian Forign Trade 1928-1932

	exports	imports
1928	61.4%	48.4%
1930	59.7%	50.2%
1932	62.7%	39.1%[32]

Italy had achieved and was able to maintain this position because it was Albania's natural trading partner and because it successfully used pressure on the Albanian government to block other nations from assuming too large a role in Albanian trade. As a result, Albania often signed concessions which were extremely disadvantageous to its national economy. A prime example gave the Italian organization known as A.G.I.P. (Agenzia Generale Italiana Petrolio) the sole right to import petroleum products into Albania, beginning in July 1929.

Not only was the agreement itself a disaster but the circumstances under which it was signed indicate a certain fiscal irresponsibility on the part of Zog's government. The negotiations were erratic, first plagued by seemingly interminable delays and then eventually rushed through in such a hurry that possible competition had no time to prepare their offers. During the six weeks of the talks no provisions were made to supply Albania with gasoline, with the result that the entire transportation system, including mails, was held up. When supplies were at last received they were inadequate and were allowed to fall into the hands of a few speculators who made outrageous profits from them.

For the sum of 1.8 million gold francs per annum over a three-year period, Zog put into the hands of a foreign organization, which possessed no oil of its own, the power to paralyze at any moment the entire movement of the country. There were still no railroads in Albania so motor traffic was the universal means of transport. Whoever possessed the petroleum monopoly could control communications at will. Furthermore, the agreement robbed Albanian firms which earned a living from the importation and sale of oil products, of the source of their livelihood.[33]

The problem here was the matter of priorities. Zog, who was perenially in financial need, could only rarely resist the prospect of immediate monetary gratification. The Italians who were fully aware of this weakness, took every opportunity to tighten their economic stranglehold over Albania. Small wonder that Albania's foreign trade situation remained so basically unhealthy.

Despite his failings, Zog was not totally unaware of this and the other serious problems which faced Albania. As he mentioned to Mr. E. Ashmead-Bartlett of the *Daily Telegraph* of London in a special interview given in October 1928, Albania was confronted with a maze of difficulties. Zog noted that,

> We are centuries behind the rest of Europe in civilization. The people can neither read nor write; there are few written laws which are obeyed, and blood feuds are still prevalent in many parts of the country. It is my determination to civilize my people and make them as far as is possible adopt Western habits and customs.[34]

Here we see the other side of Zog's nature, that of the Western reformer King creating a modern civilized state.

In his initial speech to the first Parliament of the Monarchy Zog made it clear that he recognized Albania's major problems and promised to deal with them directly. The King pledged to continue the reorganization of Albanian justice through the introduction of new law codes and extensive administrative reform on every level.

In order to facilitate the process of civilization, Zog promised to introduce extensive social reforms. Arguing that the various occupation forces of the past had imposed unsuitable customs on the Albanians, the King was determined to remove those which he deemed to be morally and materially harmful to Albania.

In matters of economics he planned to create the necessary environment for extensive agricultural, industrial and commercial expansion. He promised a long overdue agrarian reform program and active state involvement in the encouragement of industry. To further alleviate Albania's serious economic difficulties, the King pledged to create a special commission to root out favoritism, incompetence and general corruption amongst the administration.

Finally, Zog was determined to direct the attention of the state to the construction of an efficient educational system as well as the institution of health care facilities. He ordered that the municipalities be empowered to deal with canalization, water supply, road making and electrical power, to assist in the abovementioned endeavors.[35]

Privately, however, Zog suffered no illusions concerning how rapidly Albania could be changed. As he commented to his Minister in London, Albania had to reverse a 1000-year trend of no development. He concluded that such well-trenched inactivity could not be changed overnight.[36] The process of transforming Albania required time, energy and money even after those responsible for bringing about significant change acquainted themselves with reasonable procedures to pursue such an end.

The first years of the Monarchy witnessed the introduction of many badly needed reforms, as Zog attempted to live up to his carefully cultivated image of a progressive Western ruler. To complement the Civil Code, patterned after the Napoleonic model, which had been introduced in early 1928, Zog added a Penal Code based upon the Italian model which finally supplemented the old Ottoman Law, and a Commercial Code based upon Italian and French examples.

In the field of education, the government was faced with a towering problem. The disappearance of the "schools of influence" which had existed in Turkish days left no foundation on which to build a national system of education. The only effective educational institutions in 1928 were run by religious organizations, or by foreigners. No facilities for higher education existed at all.

In the north Jesuits and Franciscans ran a number of schools which enjoyed good standing and filled to a certain extent, the local need. The

Americans supported a technical school and two agricultural colleges which they staffed and financed. From the technical point of view the Italians were the most helpful, for they created four arts and crafts schools in different localities to train mechanics and artisans.[37]

In southern Albania the position was less discouraging than in the north. An educational system dating back many hundreds of years was still in existence. The schools were good, the teachers fully qualified and the standard of education relatively high. Whether Greek propaganda as was asserted by many nationalists, took the form of subsidies distributed secretly for the upkeep of these schools, or whether their prosperity was the result of public spirited endeavors of the local population, there existed in southern Albania a state of well-being from the educational point of view which was unknown in other parts of the country.[38]

In order to establish educational facilities in the rest of the country, Zog launched an ambitious reform program aimed at introducing a network of primary schools throughout Albania, with boarding schools for children who lived at distances too great to permit them attending day schools. He also hoped to reform the system of selecting students for scholarships to study abroad, which had operated more on favoritism than on the basis of individual promise.

Some progress was actually made and by 1930 there were 580 primary schools and thirteen secondary schools staffed by 1,000 teachers serving 33,000 people.[39] But the quality of education was poor and the original project had called for many more schools to be opened. The chief problem included a lack of financing and a complete dearth of teachers posessing even rudimentary qualifications.

The government in 1929 allotted 3.5 million gold francs for their ambitious project. In 1930 this totally inadequate sum fell to 3.1 million. As a result, ordinary teachers received only five napoleons a month with no prospects of promotion since they possessed nothing but a primary education themselves. The secondary schools could produce a maximum of thirty male and fifteen female teachers a year. The pay in these schools, ranging from eight to twenty napoleons a month, was inadequate to attract the right type of teachers.[40] Furthermore, the selection process for scholarships abroad continued to be based upon favoritism.

Significant changes in the administration were inacted as Zog attempted to centralize the country. In the early 1930s local administrations were reorganized to facilitate the greater control which Zog sought. The haphazard remnants of the old Turkish system were replaced by the following:

1. Ten prefectures or provinces, each governed by a prefect responsible to the Minister of the Interior.

2. Subprefectures, each governed by a subprefect responsible to the prefect and the Minister of the Interior.

3. Municipalities, or seat of prefectures, each governed by an appointed mayor responsible to the Minister of the Interior.

4. Communes governed by a council whose head was responsible both to the prefect and the Minister of the Interior.[41]

It was hoped that these 300 communes, each containing 3,000 inhabitants, apart from facilitating centralization, might serve to further reduce the vendetta. The communal officials were given the task of inquiring into disputes immediately, before they had time to develop.[42]

Zog had been struggling for years to create a strong national consciousness among this fellow countrymen, recognizing that this was a prerequisite to modernism. A major obstacle was the cultural influence exercized by the Orthodox Church, the Moslems having separated themselves from any outside control in 1923. Since 20 percent of his citizens were still members of the Orthodox Church, the King concluded that it was unacceptable that so many should continue to declare loyalty to an extra national organization, i.e., the Ecumenical Patriarchate in Istanbul. Accordingly, Zog worked to construct an autocephalous Albanian Orthodox Church.

The first step in this direction had been taken as early as 1921 by Fan Noli who had already played a leading role in the formation of the Orthodox Church among the Albanian emigres in the United States. He and a few associates, undeterred by the fact that the mass of the Orthodox faithful seemed to be out of sympathy with their aims, proceeded to open a violent campaign in favor of religious independence. They received the support of successive Albanian governments who could not but look favorably upon a movement whose organizers preached liberation from alien control.

In September 1922 the Congress of Berat was called by the government to deal with the question. The Congress, made up of various delegates chosen in no organized fashion, declared the Albanian Orthodox Church to be autocephalous, ruled that Albanian instead of Greek should be used for liturgical purposes and constructed a council headed by Vassili Marco, one of Noli's aides, to control the church and appoint bishops to an Albanian Synod. The Congress also appealed to the Patriarch to legalize the projected severance.[43]

The decisions of Berat remained largely inoperative, however, because of the lack of a hierarchy. Albania did not have a single bishop after the war. The mission sent to Istanbul to discuss matters with the Patriarch failed to convince the Phanar to recognize the autocephalous character of the new church.

Zog, as President in 1926, had reopened these negotiations but by 1928 the position of the church remained what it had been in 1921. Having decided that the Patriarch was nothing more than an instrument of Greek propaganda and was dragging matters on in the hope of being able to impose upon the new church restrictions which would secure the supremacy of Greek influence, Zog decided to take the situation into his own hands.

In February 1929, a meeting took place in Zog's villa for the purpose of creating a Synod. The only bishops available through whom Zog could achieve his ends, were unfortunately of questionable character. Bishop Vissar, described by Istanbul as an Albanian adventurer with a reputation for moral degeneracy, educated and ordained in Greece and consecrated at Cattara by two Russian bishops, became the first head of the church. He was assisted in the organization of a council by Bishop Victor, a Serb by birth and citizenship who was for some time in charge of the small Serbian colony at Shkodër and who was consecrated bishop in Belgrade in 1923 by the Serbian Patriarch. Upon returning to Shkodër, Victor began acting in an episcopal capacity, illegally in the eyes of the Phanar since he was technically part of the Serbian Church which had no jurisdiction over Albanian territory.[44]

Zog prevailed upon these two prelates to consecrate three uneducated country priests in order to fill the remaining seats on the five-man Synod. Istanbul immediately excommunicated all but the Serbian bishop hoping that Belgrade would independently condemn Bishop Victor. Istanbul sent Mgr. Chrysanthos to Belgrade to attempt to convince Patriarch Dimitrije to condemn Bishop Victor, but to no avail.

Thus the autocephalous Church was established with a certain semblance of legality. But the solution brought little immediate tranquility in

its train because the new Synod was distrusted by the rank and file of the
Orthodox. Incidents which revealed hostility to it led to petty acts of
persecution on the part of the authorities. Zog, although he professed
contentment, was fully aware of the blemishes and continued to search
for a solution.[45]

The rift between the Albanians and Istanbul remained unresolved until
1937 when Zog relieved Vissar of his duties, apparently because the latter
had continued living a scandalous life. Zog found a certain Bishop Kissi,
who had been a bishop before the war but was without a see, to replace
Vissar.[46] As a result of Kissi's appointment and because the other bishops were also replaced by more acceptable candidates, the Patriarch
finally, on April 13, 1937, recognized the Albanian Orthodox Church
as autocephalous. Zog had accomplished his goal.

To alleviate the miserable economic conditions, the King came up with
a number of schemes including another plan to reduce the massive military
expenditures. In 1930 he let it be known that he intended to implement
a plan which would reduce the size of the army. The strength of the infantry would be reduced from nine battalions or approximately 6,000
officers and men to six battalions. During 1932 he hoped to further
reduce this number to three battalions. Similarly, the period of service
was to be reduced from eighteen months in 1930 to twelve months in
1931 and six months thereafter. Following the completion of their service the men would pass into the reserves and as reservists would be
required to attend drills twice a week. The men in the militia would
continue to drill twice a week.[47]

Zog also planned cuts in artillery effectives and the introduction of
cavalry units. The artillery complements of 180 men per battery were
to be reduced by one-half. In order to make the organization somewhat
more effective, considering Albania's terrain, the King decided to introduce mounted troops. Since the maintenance of such a force was too
expensive for the government to deal with on its own, Zog decided to
create something in the nature of an English yeomanry organization
where the recruits would supply their own horses and serve for only three
months as an incentive.[48]

Zog argued that these suggestions would create a more efficient, even
larger and yet less expensive military force which would be perfectly
adequate for defensive purposes. The new organization would include,

then, six battalions of each class, militia, regular army and reserves, raising the 1930 total infantry strength to eighteen battalions. The King projected the savings to be close to three million gold francs a year, a reduction of approximately one-fifth of the army budget.[49]

The most significant and far-reaching element of Zog's economic reform program and, indeed, of the entire reform effort in general was the Land Reform scheme which was proposed in 1930. The King engaged the Italian agrarian expert, Professor Lorenzoni, to study the problem of Albanian agriculture and suggest a possible remedy.[50] The professor completed his task in early 1930 and presented his findings to the King in the form of an agrarian reform proposal which Zog pushed through Parliament in April.

The plan was to remove a significant portion of the land from the few families who controlled it. Under the provisions of the proposal, the estate owner was permitted to keep forty hectares of land for himself and five hectares of cultivated land and ten hectares of pasture land for his wife and each child. One-third of the remainder was to be sold to the tenants who were to pay twenty gold francs per hectare in ten annual installments to the agricultural bank which was to be created for the purpose. The estate owners could keep the other two-thirds for fifteen years if it was modernized, otherwise it too was subject to sale to the tenants under the same conditions. If the owner leased this land he was required to share with the tenants the cost of irrigation and other development. Finally, the owners were to be paid in shares of the State Agricultural Bank.[51]

The volume of reform and legislation, then, was quite considerable, unfortunately much of it either remained on paper or failed completely. The chief reason for this was that the Albanians and even Zog himself were too closely wedded to century-old traditions to allow for the rapid assimilation of foreign ideas. As with political forms, legislation borrowed from Switzerland, Italy, France and Germany and rapidly introduced failed to harmonize with the psychology of a people which had derived its ideas and attitudes towards life from an old association with Turkey.

Not only was the administrative machinery still too primitive to enforce these many reforms but the principles upon which the modern changes were based were alien to the people. The functionaries which Zog had to cope with were still subject to the limitations imposed upon them by the Turkish entourage which had surrounded them in their early days. The passage of time and possibly even the disappearance of Zog's generation was required before significant progress was possible. The King would nevertheless continue to experiment.

Not surprisingly, then, Zog's new codes did not work as well as they might have. When the codes got in his way, the King simply passed special laws to circumvent them, hardly the attitude which would inspire public confidence in the new idea of rule by law. Education, as we have seen, remained in a primitive state. The proposed army reforms were delayed and the serious economic position of Albania deteriorated further.

The most far-reaching reform program proved to be the biggest failure. The operation of Zog's progressive land reform program was described by a contemporary observer as follows:

> It seems, however, that too long a time has elaspsed between moot-ing this reform, passing the law and putting it into execution. The other day government officials went down to Fier in Myzeqe to ex-propriate certain lands, and found that the owner had so sub-divided it among the various members of his numerous family by antedated deeds of sale and gift that there was nothing left to expropriate. The same thing happened near Tirana also. At Elsaban, too, a certain youthful Bey received early information that grazing lands were to be exempt from expropriations, then evicted his tenants at almost a moments notice, burned their houses, and turned down to grass all the land they had formerly cultivated.[52]

From the time the program was instituted in May 1930 until May 1938 only 4,698 hectares or 11,600 acres of state land, was affected. Compared to the total of 130,000 acres of state land and 255,000 acres of private property in Albania, the land affected was rather insignificant. The State Agricultural Bank which was to handle these transactions was not set up until 1937. In many cases the bill further discouraged maximum effort by the tenants on land which did not belong to them while landowners were reluctant to make further investments or generally modernize prop-erties of which they might be deprived. In practice, then, the reform bill remained more of a warning to the Beys and something of a sop to the few liberals.[53]

But just the fact that Zog was moving in the direction of reform was significant and made it clear that he had abdicated his position as head of the conservative group of landowners which he had led during the period until 1924. While these regressive elements were still advocating the continuance of feudal tenure and violently opposed social and economic reform, Zog at least stood for change. Given enough time and continued tranquillity, the chances for success seemed good.

Zog was rewarded for curtailing political violence and moving towards reform by a good deal of genuine popularity. His personal ability and patriotism were rarely questioned. While general dissatisfaction continued, it was laid upon his counsellors and Prime Minister, very much in the tradition of Louis XVI and Nicholas II.

Opposition to the government of Koco Kotta, Zog's first Prime Minister under the Monarchy, became more and more pronounced both in Albania and abroad. The *Dielli,* the major Albanian paper published in the United States, suggested that Prime Minister Kotta and his colleagues had the brains and imagination of Stamboul barbers and were accused of betraying their country into Italian and or Greek hands.[54] The British Minister seemed to concur, maintaining that Kotta's only virtue consisted of his truculent disposition which rendered him unsusceptible to outside influence and counted for patriotism among this adherents.[55] The opposition to Kotta eventually became so shrill that Zog finally replaced him in April 1930 with his old supporter Pandeli Evangjeli, producing a sigh of relief throughout the country.[56]

The people did complain that Zog seemed too removed. While political violence had dropped, the caution which it produced in Zog remained. There was a general desire that the King should come among his people and be their King in person and not by proxy. The people objected to being ruled indirectly, particuarly through such mediums as Krossi who so closely protected Zog that even the populace of the capital were allowed to see him only on the rarest occasions, and the country-folk never.

A prominent Albanian in the south mentioned to one of the British officers in the gendarmerie:

Why does not the King come to see us? If he is afraid to come, tell him that I will stand under a tree with a noose around my neck during the whole time he is in this district, and if a hair on his head is touched he may have me hanged on the spot.[57]

The King might have heeded this advice for the problems relating to his seclusion soon renewed internal political fears and produced extensive international complications.

CHAPTER NINE

THE CRISES OF 1931

In 1931 the King found himself faced with a number of rather serious crises, both health related and diplomatic. Rumors about Zog's health became particularly numerous during the first weeks of 1931 although stories of this nature had circulated on occasion since Ahmed Bey assumed the title of President in 1925.

As early as May of that year, reports surfaced that Zog's doctors had ordered him to Durrës for a change of air and a good deal of rest. The German Minister reported that rumors suggested that the President was a very sick man, even near death, although no one seemed to have a clear idea exactly from what the supposedly ailing President was ailing.[1] The Germans maintained that he was being treated for *eiternden angina,* although their information could not be substantiated.[2]

Queen Geraldine asserts that all of Zog's heath problems stemmed from an attempt made by the government in Belgrade to have him poisoned while he was preparing for his return to Tirana in 1924. The Queen further maintains that as a result of this poisoning, the King developed a bleeding ulcer which was eventually further complicated by cancer.[3]

Although Zog did suffer from acute bleeding ulcers during his later years and eventually died from cancer, it is unlikely that either condition developed as a result of poisoning. The poison senario becomes even less plausible when considered in a political sense. Prime Minister Pasic had gone to a great deal of trouble to assure Zog's success against Noli, therefore, he had no reason to do away with him. Although Queen Geraldine's explanation for the method in which Zog contracted these diseases is questionable, then, the argument that the King was suffering from an ulcer condition even as early as 1925 seems highly likely.

Rumors began to circulate anew in late 1928 and early 1929 after it became known that the King had asked two Viennese physicians, Doctors Bauer and Holzknecht, to come to Tirana and examine him. Although it is doubtful that their report was ever officially released, a Viennese newspaper and the German Minister in Tirana both reported that Zog was suffering from some sort of stomach ailment stemming from lack of exercise, overwork (Zog had a habit of working long hours) and heavy nicotine use. It was further reported that the doctors warned Zog about his unhealthy lifestyle and suggested fresh air and less work. They apparently did not consider the situation to be serious, however, and expected the King to recover soon.[4]

When two more specialists from Vienna were summoned under a cloud of secrecy near the end of 1930, rumors once again began to circulate widely. Because no mention was made in the official press either with regard to Zog's illness or to the visit of the Austrian physicians, speculation was even more imaginative than it had been in the past. Reports, which the American Minister felt emanated from Yugoslav sources, had the King dying of tuberculosis, gall bladder problems, syphilis, cancer of the throat, cancer of the stomach and so forth.[5]

Even people close to the King were kept in the dark, thereby also falling victim to the varied rumors. Dr. Terenzio Tocci, Zog's former Secretary General, told the American Minister that,

> The King is on the verge of death. A. Krossi, his foster father, has not left the palace for three days and nights. Local physicians are attending the King. The Austrian specialists who examined him more than a year ago said the first complication of the disease would kill the King. He is now in bed with bronchitis.[6]

Although Tocci's version of the situation was misinformed, Zog had indeed been critically ill during December of 1930. He had been attacked by violent pains causing hours of agony and the loss of some thirteen pounds. Mehmed Konitza, a prominent Albanian official and much more reliable source, gives this account of a meeting with Zog during this trying period:

I dined with the King on Tuesday evening December 16 (1930). He complained of an acute pain in the abdomen. He took only a cup of bouillon. Suddenly he became very pale and I feared that he was fainting. I felt his forehead and his pulse. I advised him to go to bed and send for his physician. . . . The King has been suffering from some intestinal trouble for about two years. He seems very weak and I am afraid that if the specialists operate on him he would not survive it. While he was not seriously ill during the past year, I believe his mode of life was such as to weaken his system and an operation would prove fatal.[7]

By the time the second group of doctors arrived at the end of 1930, however, they found Zog already convalescent. After a thorough examination, palace rumor had it that the two doctors diagnosed his ailment once again as due to intestinal trouble, to overwork and lack of exercise. Zog himself seemed to prefer this version of the rumors since he later explained to General Percy, with the assistance of a pencil diagram, that he had a kink in the large intestines.[8] The two specialists, it was reported, prescribed a special diet and shorter hours of work for him, after which they returned to Vienna.

The rumors persisted however with Tocci confidently informing the American Minister that,

The specialists have returned (to Vienna) but no matter what you may hear about the King's improved health, I can assure you that Zog is done for. It is a matter of weeks, not of months. One should not be encouraged by his seeming recovery. This is the way with tubercular patients. Zog will pass away soon. He is afflicted with an acute form of tuberculosis and cancer of the throat besides. Zog is very fond of the pleasures of the flesh and he will not follow the doctor's orders if they interfere with his pleasures. . . . He cannot restrain himself.[9]

But Minister Bernstein noted that on the very day when the King was supposed to have been on the verge of death, he spent the afternoon with him and Zog appeared to be enjoying excellent health. On another occasion when reports from Belgrade described the rapidly approaching end of the King and a hurried call from members of Parliament to his bedside, Zog took a three-hour ride on horseback.

Although the improvement in his health had been maintained, Zog nevertheless took the advice of the Viennese specialists. He decided, near the end of January 1931, to travel to Vienna to undergo x-rays which the doctors had been unable to perform in Tirana because some particular medicine could not be procured.

The decision to leave must have been a difficult one for Zog considering that he rarely left the security of his palace even for short domestic trips. Few ruling Balkan politicians could afford the luxury of leaving the country without risking some form of political upheaval. Once Zog had made up his mind, however, the various attractions of Vienna including the memories of his pleasant years spent there during the war convinced him to reject the Italian proposal to go to Rome instead for security reasons.

Recognizing that there was a certain amount of danger involved, Zog took steps to insure that all went well. Consistent with his general approach to security, Zog told no one but his immediate entourage that he was even considering such a trip. Not until the eve of his departure did he summon a delegation of deputies headed by the President of the Parliament, K. Kotta, to issue his final instructions. Officially, Zog expressed the hope that during his absence Parliament would cooperate with the government in harmony. Apparently, however, he took the opportunity, using rather vigorous language, to tell the deputies that he expected them to behave and cautioned them against starting any trouble.

Security precautions of a more substantial nature were also taken. Three battalions were stationed in Tirana in the event of political disturbances. A few days before his departure, the King appointed new prefects in those prefectures where signs of unrest had occurred.[10]

On January 26, before he had originally intended to leave, Zog travelled to Durrës in the company of four of his six sisters, the Council of Ministers, the President of the Parliament and a number of prominent Albanians. Before the population of the town had any idea of what had transpired, the Italian cruiser *Quartro* appeared at Durrës harbor and spirited the Royal party away.

Apart from the King, the party consisted of Abdurrahman Krossi, Zog's personal physician, Dr. J. Basho, Major Topallaj and Captain Chupi who served as bodyguards, Minister of Court Ekrem Libohova and Sotir Martini, an aide. Colonel Sereggi, the King's adjutant, had gone to Vienna a week before to make all the necessary preparations there.

The first official announcement given to the press mentioned neither the purpose of the King's trip abroad nor his destination. It was only the next day that the morning paper announced that the King had left for Vienna for a visit and a medical examination.

The question of security for the King in Vienna was clearly a pressing one, considering the multitude of Albanian political refugees unfriendly to Zog who resided there. The Albanian government attempted to make certain that the Austrians were well prepared for the King's arrival. On January 21 the Court Minister informed the newly arrived Austrian Minister in Albania, Herr Günther, in the strictest secrecy that Zog intended to travel to Vienna in the near future, incognito, for medical purposes. Libohova also suggested at this time that if the Austrians required time to install the necessary security precautions, the King would be willing to postpone his visit for a few months.

Günther thereupon assured Libohova that his government would indeed do everything possible to insure Zog's safety and made a few suggestions which he felt might help with regard to security. Günther mentioned that protection would be less difficult if Zog avoided the larger hotels and stayed instead in private quarters or a sanitorium. He further suggested that Zog leave the train in Wiener Neustadt and continue his journey by car. Libohova, who obviously knew Zog very well, correctly assumed that the King's pride would not allow him to take these precautions.[11]

On their own initiative to further insure Zog's safety, the Austrian police took various steps against the leading figures among the Albanian emigres in Vienna who were known to be hostile to the King. On February 11 the police detained Lazar and Luigi Shantago, two prominent anti-Zog Albanians, in Mödling, removed their passports, forbade them to go anywhere near Vienna while Zog was there and required them to report to the police three times a day.

The rest of the members of the Albanian community were also invited to appear and were informed that they must respect the right of sanctuary. The emigres declared that they would not take a hostile attitude towards the King, primarily because they were so thankful to the Austrian government for allowing them to stay.[12]

Much to the chagrin of the security agents assigned to protect the King in Vienna, Zog, who was normally extremely careful, seemed unconcerned about the dangers that were present. Upon his arrival in the Austrian capital, Zog and his party checked into the Hotel Imperial on the Ring, one of the most conspicuous hotels in Vienna. To make matters worse, Zog developed the habit of not informing anyone when he was leaving or where he was going.

The primary reason for his odd behavior on Zog's part turned out to be two Austrian ladies, the Baroness Franciska de Janko and the Baroness Maria de Janko, sisters who were staying at the Hotel Regina. According to the *Stunde,* a Vienna newspaper and Dr. Terenzio Tocci, Zog was on intimate terms with the younger of the two.[13]

In a sensational headline story which other Viennese newspapers termed an unnecessary invasion of Zog's private life, the *Stunde* published a detailed report of Zog's relationship with the young Austrian who, the paper claimed, was actually the daughter of a gardener and had merely "acquired" the title of "Baroness." According to the paper, Zog frequently went to see her, bought her expensive furs and had the two sisters sit in the next box whenever he went to the opera or the theater.[14]

Zog's behavior was all the more unusual considering the numerous rumors about an assassination attempt to be made against him. Near the end of January, the Yugoslav Minister in Albania, Nastasijevic, notified the Albanian government that his government had learned of a plot against King Zog's life in Vienna and had asked the Albanian government to communicate this information to the King. At the same time, the German Minister in Tirana sent a telegram to the Foreign Ministry in Berlin requesting that the Austrian government be made aware of the fact that the King's life was in danger.[15]

Despite Zog's numerous indiscretions, the first weeks of his extended stay were uneventful. The King's medical business was taken care of rather quickly. While the original doctors that Zog visited in Vienna encouraged him to have an operation, because of his fear of coming under the knife, the King searched until he was able to find a doctor who could assure him that surgery was unnecessary. He soon found what he was looking for in Dr. Franz Chwostek, who decided that an operation was unnecessary as long as the King modified his lifestyle somewhat.[16]

Vienna papers announced that the King was suffering from a form of nicotine poisoning brought on by excessive smoking and overwork, allaying the fears of some but never all of those who felt Zog was soon to die. On February 13, Colonel Libohova informed the American military attache, Major James Collins, that the King had greatly benefited from the medical treatment received in Vienna and that he would return to Albania within the next ten days.[17] Meanwhile, Zog took advantage of his stay to re-acquaint himself with Viennese culture.

On the night of February 20 the King and several members of his suite attended the performance of "Pagliaacci" at the Vienna Opera House on the Ring. A few minutes before the end of the performance Zog and his party left the Opera House by the side door leading out to the Operngasse where two automobilies were waiting for them. The King got into the first car as did Colonel Libohova. Major Topollaj was just about to enter the King's automobile and the Counselor of the Albanian legation with the remainder of the party were getting into the second car when two young Albanians dressed in evening clothes opened fire from behind stone columns.

As the first shot was fired, the detective sitting in the front seat of the King's car jumped out of the car and rushed at the assassins. Zog was on the point of leaving the car and Major Topollaj was leaning forward to help him to his feet when the second shot was fired. This bullet struck the Major and a regular fusillade ensued. Major Topollaj, who appears to have covered the King with his body was hit again twice, this time in the base of the skull. He died instantly, sadly adding credence to the add-age that serving as an officer with the entourage of King Zog was like being a night-watchman in a powder factory when lightening is striking all around.

The King, who drew his pistol tucked inside his tuxedo, returned the fire of his assailants, as did Colonel Libohova and the chauffeur. Twenty or more shots were fired with the only other casualty being Colonel Libohova who was shot in the leg, with another bullet passing through his hat. The King was untouched. After a running fight with the detectives guarding the King, the two assailants were caught and arrested. The King in the meantime returned to the Opera House, where according to the not always credible Terenzio Tocci, Zog became hysterical swinging his revolver around and swearing excitedly in German.[18]

The two assassins, Ndok Gjeloshi and Aziz Cami, were both Albanian emigres and former officers in the Albanian gendarmerie. Gjeloshi, thirty-seven, a Catholic from Shkodër was originally a lay-brother of the Franciscans before he became involved in politics. Before World War I he fought for Prince Wied and during the war he became an Austrian officer. He claimed to belong to the Albanian Nationalist party and was always anti-Zog. Under Bishop Noli's government he had become a captain in the border guards and with Zog's return to power fled to Yugoslavia where he lived until 1929 when he came to Vienna. While in Yugoslavia he had become a member of the Bashkimi Kombëtar group, an Albanian exile organization closely tied to the Yugoslav government.[19]

Aziz Cami, the second assassin also thirty-seven, was a Moslem from southern Albania and had also been an officer in the Austrian army and in the border guards. He had been a member of an anti-Catholic group in Albania which had initially supported Zog. Somewhat later, however, Cami joined the party in opposition to Zog and because of his support for Noli was forced to flee to Italy and then Vienna after the political troubles of 1924. Cami also apparently spent some time in Belgrade where he was arrested because of his close connection with Noli, a fact which also caused him considerable trouble among the Albanian refugees in Vienna where the story had circulated that Cami was supported by the Bolsheviks.[20]

Following their arrest, both declared that they had hoped to kill the King because he had betrayed the Albanian people and had ruined the country. Gjeloshi originally maintained that he had just happened by the Opera that night and saw the King's car and decided to wait for him. He further maintained that not only was his action unpremediated but that he had acted independently of Aziz Cami.

Gjeloshi stuck to this less than credible story even after Cami admitted that on the afternoon of the 19th he and Gjeloshi had met at the Operncafe to plan the attack and when on the 20th they saw the King's car, they went home to get their guns. Both of the assailants maintained that they supported themselves in Vienna on what friends sent them from Albania but the Austrian police soon discovered that the two were receiving money from others in the Albanian community in Austria and from the Yugoslav government.[21]

The trial of the two, which began near the end of September, took place in Ried in Upper Austria rather than in Vienna for reasons of security. Lawyers for the two accused informed the police that they had received information indicating that Zog had sent a number of supporters to Vienna in order to take revenge on Gjeloshi and Cami, reminiscent of the murder of Bebi, the assassin of Ceno Bey in Prague in 1927. The Albanian Consul in Vienna likewise expressed concern about the life of Court Minister Libohova who was also scheduled to appear at the trial.

Taking all of these warnings and fears into consideration, the Austrians finally decided to hold the trial in Ried, away from the immigrant community in Vienna. Ried was apparently also chosen because the prison was directly adjoining the courtroom making it unnecessary to expose the two defendants to possible attacks outside the building.[22]

Due undoubtedly to tight Austrian security, the trial was short and uneventful and was chiefly directed towards establishing the course of events on the night of February 20. Both accused admitted their intentio of murdering the King. Cami changed the story that he had originally told the police and stated that he had not acted on a well-laid plan but rather that his action was due to sudden impulse.

This assertion was belied, however, by the fact that the Austrian police in their search of the dwellings of various Albanian emigres found regular timetables indicating that the Bashkimi Kombëtar had set up a "Zog watch" at various hotels including the Kursalon, the Grand Hotel, the Hotel Bristol and the Park Hotel.[23]

There was initially some question as to who was responsible for the death of Major Topallaj, with the Yugoslav Minister in Tirana stating that medical evidence established that Zog himself had accidentally shot the Major. During the course of the trial, however, Austrian medical examiners positively determined that the bullet which killed the Major came from Gjeloshi's gun. Both defendants denied having intentions of assassinating Major Topollaj but neither of them expressed any regret at his death.[24]

The trial ended on October 2 with Gjeloshi being convicted of the murder of Major Topollaj and the attempted murder of King Zog for which he was sentenced to seven years hard labor. Cami was convicted of attempted murder of the King, complicity in the murder of his adjutant and inflicting grievous bodily harm on his Minister of Court for which he was sentenced to three years hard labor. The president of the court added that the previous good behavior of the prisoners in Vienna as well as the fact that the offense was committed "for no mean motive" was taken into consideration at the time of the sentencing.[25]

While the trial itself was concluded without any serious problems, the international implications of the event were not so promptly dealt with. The Italians immediately cried Yugoslav involvement and indeed the case against Belgrade at least on the surface seemed quite strong. Yugoslav money and aid seemed to crop up in too many embarrassing places.

The Austrian police discovered, and the right-wing Viennese press particularly the *Reichpost* and the *Freiheit* spread over their front pages, that the assailants were on Belgrade's payroll. Both the assassins received monthly sums of money from a certain Angelin Suma, another Albanian emigre in Vienna who was a member of the central committee of the Bashkimi Kombëtar. Angelin Suma, along with other members of the Albanian emigre community, had direct contacts with the Yugoslav Embassy in Vienna, were often seen in the company of Embassy officials and indeed once they came under strict police surveillance, were even observed taking money from Yugoslav officials.

One of Suma's associates, a certain Don Loro Caka, who was taken in for questioning by the police on March 11, was, upon his release, contacted by a member of the Yugoslav delegation who set up a meeting between Caka and Marian Ujcic of the Yugoslav Ministry of the Interior. After his meeting with Ujcic, Caka was again arrested and found to be in possession of 1800 lire, a sum which he apparently was being paid monthly by the Yugoslavs.[26]

To complicate matters further, the Austrian police soon discovered that the two assailants were in possession of permanent diplomatic passports issued by the Yugoslav government, a charge which Belgrade continued to deny. During the trial, the prosecution expressed some surprise that the prisoners were being defended by such eminent and expensive lawyers as Dr. Pressburger and Dr. Frischauer. There was much thinly veiling insinuation regarding the source of the funds for the fees since Gjeloshi stated during the trial that his total income was in the neighborhood of ten pounds a month. The Austrian Ministry for Foreign Affairs was convined that these fees were paid by the Yugoslav government, an opinion shared by the Italians and many Albanians.[27]

The evidence became even more damning when it was learned that a large group of Albanian emigres in Yugoslavia were positioned on the border waiting to attack Albania once word reached them that the King had been assassinated. Gani Bey Kryeziu, the brother of Ceno Bey, who had frequently been mentioned in connection with attempts to overthrow Zog in the past, had apparently organized several hundred Albanians on the frontier, many of whom belonged to his own retainer and some being the followers of other leaders who had temporarily set their differences aside. Gani, who was in possession of two heavy guns and a number of machine guns, hoped to use the chaos which would undoubtedly have followed Zog's death to overthrow the Tirana government.

When the Austrians found connections in confiscated emigre correspondence between the assassins, Gani Bey, and the Yugoslavs, the Italian press and diplomatic corps accused the Belgrade government of instigating both events. The Italian Minister in Tirana, even before the evidence was discovered, openly informed the American Minister that,

> Yugoslavia has acted more than strangely in this affair. . . . If the King had been assassinated last night, Gani Bey would have crossed the Yugoslav frontier and would have entered Albania this morning. Yugoslavia must have known of the attempt on Zog and of the activities of Gani Bey in organizing armed forces against the Zog government.

The Minister continued:

> We have definite information that Gani Bey Kryeziu was not only permitted but urged to organize the other Albanian emigres in Djakova. In fact he was helped by the frontier authorities. . . . The Yugoslavs have recently published glowing descriptions of his home and life in Djakova, saying that he belonged to a more distinguished Albanian family than Zog of the tribe of Mati. In other words, he was being groomed for leadership while Zog was away in Vienna where he was to be assassinated.[28]

Zog himself, in a very uncharacteristic remark during an interview with the *Neue Freie Presse* in Vienna, supported these suggestions. The King commented that,

> the history of centuries had sufficiently proved that the Albanians will tolerate no foreign yoke. We therefore require of our neighbors

that they respect the sovereign rights and integrity of our country. The organization of bands on our frontier disturbs order and weakens our finances, thereby hindering the consolidation of Albania and endangering peace. Such activities obviously make mere empty phrases of the most hopeful assurances.[29]

The King's statement was considered unfortunate by the entire diplomatic community with the exception of the Italians, particuarly since it came directly on the heels of a statement made by King Alexander in which he declared to a Reuter correspondent that no one was more interested in the independence, the integrity, the well-being and the progress of the Albanian nation than the Yugoslavs. Zog's slip would eventually cost him dearly.

Although Alexander's statement may have been a bit over-dramatic, numerous considerations lend credence to the Yugoslav claims of innocence. The policy of paying emigres, although undoubtedly a bad one and particularly embarrassing to Yugoslavia in this case, is something that was generally accepted among European nations. Prime Minister Pandeli Evangjeli said of this point that,

> I do not believe that Yugoslavia was involved in the attempt on our King's life in Vienna, although I know that Angelin Suma and many other Albanian political refugees, as well as Gani Kryeziu, receive money from the Yugoslavs. They admit it themselves and so does Yugoslavia.

Asked what these men were being paid for, the Prime Minister shrugged his shoulders, smiled and said, "Yugoslavia pays them merely as political refugees."[30]

The Italian Minister in Tirana, in a less heated moment, admitted that,

> I have discussed this matter with Nastasijevic (Yugoslav Minister in Tirana) and have told him that I understand perfectly well why Yugoslavia is keeping and subsidizing some of the Albanian emigres. . . .I realize the value of these Albanians to Yugoslavia in the event of the war with Italy. Yugoslavia has in them valuable allies. Yugoslavia can use them for intelligence work. They can also use them

> when they desire to stir up trouble in Albania. I don't say that
> Yugoslavia is wrong in subsidizing and keeping them for these pur-
> poses. I suppose it we were in Yugoslavia's place, we should do the
> same. (Which, of course, they had been doing for some time.) . . .
> But when anything happens, when these emigres are involved in a
> plot against King Zog, when we know that these emigres are being
> paid by Yugoslavia, it is but natural that we suspect Yugoslavia.[31]

Considerations against Gani Bey can, of course, be seen in the same
light. Gani, who in an interview with the Zagreb paper *Novosti,* naturally
denied all allegations, maintaining that he, being a good host, could not
help it if some of his guests turn out to be revolutionaries. Nevertheless,
it was clear that he had spent time in Belgrade shortly before the attempt
on Zog and that he was receiving money from that government. While in
the Yugoslav capital he was reportedly even received by Prime Minister
General Zivkovic.[32] Nevertheless, this is no indication that Belgrade was
pinning all of its hopes on him, particularly since Gani was often described
as a nonentity with few retainers who would receive no help once he crossed the frontier.

Despite Yugoslav assurances to the contrary, Gani was undoubtedly
making preparations. It is doubtful that Yugoslav authorities had enough
direct control over border regions to make such categorical statements.
Even if no standing force existed, Gani's retainers, who worked in the
fields, could in the space of a few hours be assembled and on the move.
It must be emphasized that this in itself is not unusual considering that
we are dealing with a region inhabited by tribes whose pastime from
time immemorial had been foraying one another and whose abstinence
from indulging in this occupation was due not so much to a sudden conversion to the ways of peace but to an arbitrarily imposed barrier in the
shape of the Albano-Yugoslav frontier.

In the final analysis, the fundamental question with regard to Yugoslav complicity must come down to whether Belgrade stood to gain by
having King Zog removed. The answer to this must be no, in fact, Yugoslavia would only lose with Zog's disappearance. The removal of Zog
would undoubtedly have been the prelude to a state of turmoil in Albania.
As a result, the Pact of Tirana would have come into operation with a very
probable sequel: the landing of Italian troops in order to maintain the

"political status quo." Had Yugoslavia been responsible for the attempted assassination and the encouragement of Gani Bey, it would have been directly working for just the end that its entire Albanian policy had been trying to avoid.

Despite the fact that the attack seems to have been planned and carried out by the emigres on their own behalf, King Zog, nevertheless, continued to believe that the Yugoslav government was responsible for both actions, maintaining that the military and not the politicians were responsible for Yugoslav policy. Zog did not have a high opinion of General Zivkovic and considered him completely capable of pursuing a policy which damaged Yugoslav interests.

The Albanian emigres in Austria and Yugoslavia were not the only ones making plans as a result of Zog's hurried departure, his extended absence and the attempted assassination. Before his cruiser was even out of sight, many political elements in Albania, believing that the King would never return, began jockeying for position in post-Zog Albania. The idea that Zog's regime would survive him seemed to occur to no one, not even some of the top figures in Zog's government.

General Aranitas, the Commander of the Albanian army, for example, ordered an airplane prepared for himself to carry him out of the country at the first sign of revolt.[33] In the north the tribes started to hold talks and initiated a movement which was to supplant Zog's administration. Rumors circulated that as soon as the King was out of the way Mark Gjonmarkaj, the Mirditë leader, would march on Tirana. He was said to be able to put together in excess of ten thousand men, mostly Catholics but with the help of the Moslem Dibra and Kosovo tribes.

The planned move seems to have been arranged down to the smallest detail. Mark, who lacked money and ammunition, apparently made a political deal with Muharrem Bajraktari, the Commander of the gendarmerie who was to open the government stores of munitions as soon as Zog was dead, and was to become Mark's adjutant for his trouble. Although Mark had been contacted both by the Italians and the Yugoslavs, he committed himself to neither. The Mirditë leader would most likely have set up some sort of a council of regency until he had time to arrange a new government, of what type no one was willing to speculate.[34]

Mark and his confederates went so far as to approach the British Minister, Robert Hodgson, and asked him to don the mantle at one time worn by Sir Harry Eyres and act as a counsellor to the leaders of the movement. Hodgson, who explained that times had changed since Eyres' day, refused the invitation not wanting to be accused of sanctioning the tribal warfare which would have inevitably followed.[35]

The supporters of a republican form of government organized a loose association in the hopes of forestalling a foreign takeover or political anarchy in the event of Zog's death. This group, many of whom were later arrested and sentenced to death, had planned, if Zog died, to seize the government quickly, force the Parliament to recognize the new government, declare Albania a republic again and then dissolve the Parliament. The probable result of this move would have been the return of the various emigre leaders who had fled the country since Zog's advent to power. Fan Noli, the Italophiles Hasan Prishtina and Mustafa Kruja and the Serbophiles of the Bashkimi Kombëtar might have been expected to put in an appearance in the hope of profiting from the turmoil. Their conflicting organizations would have undoubtedly led to prolonged disorders.

The Italians, too, moved quickly in order to secure their investment. They seemed initially to not have foreseen the contingency of the King's death and did not have a solid candidate to replace him. They lost no time, once the general rush had started, in attempting to remedy this oversight, making themselves look rather foolish in the process. The Italian Minister di Soranga scurried off to the north in the hope of discovering which Italian candidate would encounter the least resistance.

In an interview with Mgr. Lazar Mjeda, the Catholic archbishop of Albania, the Italian Minister commented that Italy was greatly concerned over the welfare of Albania and that his government would be happy to help the Albanians in choosing a successor to King Zog. He stated that if the Albanians wanted the Prince of Wied, Mussolini would render the greatest assistance by diplomatically arranging his return. The Minister suggested the Duca d'Aosta if the Prince of Wied was unacceptable. The archbishop politely and diplomatically replied that he would be happy to assist in a choice as noble as the Duca but that the Church in Albania had creased to interfere in political affairs.[36]

So as to cover all of their bases, the Italians also sent the Counsellor of the legation, Quaroni, to test the various waters of Albania. Quaroni was assigned to contact the various nothern tribes in the hope of gaining their acquiescence for an Italian supported successor. The Counsellor was also seen in Elbasan conferring with Shevket Verlaci, Zog's old rival and still a candidate to succeed the King.

These obvious Italian moves caused considerable concern among Albanian politicians and did a great deal to lend credence to prevailing rumors that the Italians were preparing to actually take Albania. A member of the Council of State informed the American Minister that General Roberto Pariani, Commander of the military department of the Court and Mussolini's personal friend and representative in Albania, was at work on a plan to have the government of Evangjeli superseded by a council of regents composed of a Moslem, a Catholic and an Orthodox acceptable to the Italians.[37]

Albanian exiles in Greece, too, made preparations so as not to be caught unaware in the event of Zog's demise. Reports reached the Albanian government that a certain Koco Tassi, an Albanian refugee in Janina, was stirring up trouble by enlisting other Albanian refugees to cross the Greek frontier for the purpose of conducting a revolt against the Zog government. The Greek Charge, Kollas, was asked to inquire of his government whether there was any truth to these reports. Kollas called on the Prime Minister a few days later to assure him that Koco Tassi had been removed to the interior of Greece and that Athens would not permit any unfriendly actions organized on its territory against Albania.

Aware of much of this agitation, Zog's advisors would have preferred that he return much sooner, but it was not until March 11 that Zog left Vienna by special train paid for by the Italian government. Before his departure, the King graciously received Deputy Police President Herr Brandl to thank him for the efficiency of the inspectors who had been assigned to protect him, six of whom accompanied Zog to the Austrian border. On his way back the King stopped in Venice for approximately one week and then on March 20 returned to Durrës on the Italian light cruiser *Quartro*.

Upon his arrival in Durrës he was met by his mother, his six sisters, members of the government and a crowd of officials of various grades. The welcome was rather disorderly and the King immediately stepped into his car and started to Tirana. Zog looked considerably fatigued, adding fuel to the continuing rumors that his health problems were really more serious than anyone in Vienna was willing to admit. These recurring rumors worried the Italians who in vain offered Zog's doctors large sums of money for information concerning his health.

The Minister of the Interior, Musa Juka, who had been the leading figure in the government during Zog's absence, staged a series of spontaneous demonstrations in Durrës and Tirana to welcome the King home. The trip to Tirana was uneventful, due at least in part to the two battalions of infantry who were concealed next to the gendarmerie patrols all along the road. Once in Tirana, however, the King decided to forego security for a short period and showed himself in the grounds of the palace. He also reviewed several thousand pre-military training youths who had gathered to do him honor.

The festivities continued throughout the next day. The Minister of the Interior had hoped to close the celebrations with a very elaborate and expensive reception, but Zog, who had already spent some 300,000 gold francs on his trip (the entire education budget for the year was only 367,171 gold francs), opted instead for a simple and informal reception.[38]

Upon his return, the King discovered that despite the rumors and plans, and despite the fact that criticism of the regime had become open and widespread, tranquillity had prevailed from one end of the country to the other while he was gone. Minister of the Interior Juka, who had acted basically as a dictator, had made preparations to deal drastically with any attempt at an uprising or with large organized manifestations of dissatisfaction with Zog's government, preparations which the Minister found it unnecessary to implement.

Indeed, the only organized demonstrations during Zog's absence were in sympathy for the King. Once it was announced that the King's health problems were not serious, Juka ordered deputations to come to Tirana from various parts of the country for the purpose of expressing to the Queen Mother their sympathy for the King's illness and their hopes for his speedy recovery and return to Albania. In accordance with Musa Juka's instructions, prayers were offered in all churches and mosques for the King's health. Expressions of joy were ordered on the occasion of the reassuring news that the King was in perfect health again.[39]

Juka was given a further opportunity to perfect his public relations technique following the attempt on the King's life. A great show of national rejoicing was staged to celebrate Zog's survival. Bands played for days in various towns, school children paraded, services of thanksgiving were again held, the troops of the Tirana garrison marched past the Queen Mother and every house was hung with bunting.

Although the demonstrations were anything but spontaneous, there was a genuine feeling of relief at the King's escape. This relief was undoubtedly based upon the realization that the country owed such tranquillity that it enjoyed to Zog, and that had the assassins hit their mark, Albania would certainly have been plunged into a state of chaos unmatched since the end of World War I.

Zog's personal contribution to tranquillity in Albania was only one of the important lessons which political observers derived from the experiences of early 1931. Dangers became more evident, including how narrow the base was on which the King's authority rested. Plans to replace him began to be formulated while the King was still within sight of Albania. As the search for a successor reached feverish proportions it also became clear to objective observers that the gulf which separated the King from most of his subjects in intelligence, political acumen and in ability to deal with opposing forces was fixed by his Royal title. While this did not prevent the King from continually making serious mistakes, nevertheless, from the personality of Zog, there was a sheer drop to a level of crass mediocrity. In the event of the King's death a successor would have to be chosen from this pool of mediocrity.

Assuming that there would be no interference from beyond the Kingdom's frontiers, an assumption quite unimaginable, it would have been difficult to believe that the body politic or an assembly of representatives would have elevated so far above themselves one of their own number. Without a leader, opposing Albanian factions, from Korcë, from Vlorë, from Shkodër and the fighting tribes of the north would certainly have introduced a period of confusion. Law and order would have disappeared with the King.

The experiences of early 1931 also reemphasized the importance of Albania with regard to Adriatic politics. The Czech Foreign Minister, Edward Benes remarked in late 1931 that,

> the two most dangerous political points in Europe are Albania and the Polish Corridor. If King Zog . . . should die suddenly, or if something should happen to him, the Italians will intervene in Albania by force of arms. This Italian action will be followed immediately by a Yugoslav counter-action. The Yugoslav Foreign Minister Marinkovic recently made this declaration to the Italian Foreign Minister Grandi in Geneva.[40]

A possible solution was suggested by Robert Hodgson who stated "there is but one way of securing the independence of Albania and preventing war here and that is by neutralizing Albania, by making her the Belgium of the Balkans."[41] The idea was probably a good one, unfortunately Zog, by his discourteous retort to King Alexander, had come down definitely on the Italian side in the dispute. By supporting Rome's accusations against Belgrade, the King had weakened his powers to resist Italian encroachment, a further step away from the desired neutralization of Albania. The Italians were not long in attempting to exploit their newfound advantage.

CHAPTER TEN

FOREIGN AFFAIRS,
THE STRUGGLE WITH ROME

The harried King did not have much of a respite after his experiences in Vienna before the Italians, who were of course aware that Zog had made something of a diplomatic blunder, attempted to press their advantage. The pill as usual needed to be sugar coated which, not surprisingly, took the form of an extremely generous loan package. Once again, the Albanian government was unable to reject the plan due to desperate economic conditions which seemed perennial.

Albanians were of course accustomed to hardship and generally accepted it with resignation. The year 1931 tested their stoic qualities to the utmost. The torrential rains of winter invaded the ploughing season and ceased in time for only one in the place of the usual three or four turnings of the soil to be accomplished before the grain had to be sowed. Then the rain held off for six months. Five-sixths of all the crops in the country were lost. The government found it necessary to import 30,000 tons of maize, a commodity which in normal years served as the second largest export product.[1]

Russian dumping ruined the market for Albanian butter in Greece and Turkey while high tariffs imposed on foreign cheeses by the United States destroyed the market for Albanian cheeses. A number of other sources of income gave up at the same time, including that earned as a result of immigrant remittances, the export of foreign currency and the SVEA loan.

The last two sources of money supply had come to an end. The accumulation of foreign gold and silver left in Albania during the war years had, by 1931, almost entirely found its way abroad again. The income from the SVEA loan, which had provided work for many Albanians, had by this time been all but exhausted. The immigrant remittances had by 1931 been drastically reduced as the effects of the worldwide depression began leaving their mark.

The Italians, although they too were in serious financial straits, could not let such an opportunity slip and by April 1931 rumors began to circulate in Tirana that another plan for financial assistance was in the offing. Two versions were presented, one expounded by the Italian Minister, the Marchese di Soranga who had replaced Sola at the beginning of the year, and the other by General Pariani.

The Italian Minister spoke of comparatively small amounts of money which were to be given in order to meet Albania's pressing needs, either in the shape of annual installments or in a lump sum. The Marchese insisted that no political conditions would be demanded as a price and that no part of the sum placed at the disposal of the Albanian government would be used for military purposes. The general, on the other hand, spoke of an annual sum of ten million gold francs which would essentially be Italy's contribution towards the cost of maintaining the Albanian armed forces. Pariani added that the subsidy would be conditional upon Albania undertaking to continue to spend some fifteen million gold francs annually on her armaments and agreeing to allow Italy the right to control expenditure. In essence, then, Pariani's version would have amounted to the conversion of the Albanian army into a mercenary force in Italian pay.[2]

As events progressed it became clear that General Pariani's estimate of the new proposals was more accurate, suggesting a rather important shift in the relationship between the legation and the military mission. Prior to the appointment of the Marchese di Soranga, it was the legation and the Foreign Ministry which made policy with regard to Albania, policy which at least most of the time pursued a moderate to reasoned line of action prone to conciliate rather than to force the pace.

As the details of the loan agreement became known, it became clear that a change had occurred. Italy, or more specifically, Mussolini, was now opting for a more forward policy which demanded results and was impatient of obstacles, a policy shift which probably came about at least partially as a result of Zog's unfortunate comment concerning King Alexander.

The 1931 loan agreement, concluded in the summer, dispensed with the thin veils which had characterized many earlier Italo-Albanian financial agreements. Rather than establish another organization like SVEA to loan the money, this time the Italian government did it directly, government to government, despite Zog's initial desire that the loan take the shape of a private transaction between himself and Rome. The terms of the agreement can be summarized as follows:

1. The Italian government concedes to the Albanian government over a period of ten years, without interest, a sum not to exceed ten million gold francs annually for economic and cultural purposes and for remedying the deficit in the Albanian budget with the proviso that the amount of the annual payments shall be decreased in proportion to such increase in revenue or decrease in expenditure as may follow from improvement in the financial condition of Albania.

2. The sums so advanced shall be repayable when the financial conditions in Albania permit, but not before the Albanian revenue reaches the figure of fifty million francs.

3. The duty of allocating the sums advanced shall be vested in a mixed commission of four persons, two Italians and two Albanians, to be appointed by the Albanian government. The decisions of the commission are to be by a majority of votes.[3]

The loan, of course, seemed very much like a free gift. It carried no interest and no repayment was scheduled until the annual Albanian budget reached fifty million gold francs, something which could not be expected in the foreseeable future considering that the 1931 budget was approximately thirty million gold francs.

The Italians had their own price, however, which as usual constituted a further encroachment on Albania's sovereignty. Reportedly, Zog was required to request the services of a number of technical experts approved by the Italian government, whose advice was not to be restricted solely to economics. The list included one at the Ministry of Finance, four at the Ministry of National Economy, one at the Ministry of Education and two at the Ministry of Public Works.[4] Italy further made it clear that the annual payments were to depend on the continuation of full and sincere technical and political collaboration between the two governments, suggesting that as soon as the cooperation stopped so would the flow of money.

Before the loan agreement had even been signed, just such an eventuality was already in the making. The Pact of Tirana, which was due to expire in November 1931, rapidly developed into a bone of contention which eventually plugged up the free flow of Italian gold since Zog decided early in the year that it was in the best interest of his country and his own political future to deny the Italians the extension of their pact.

The primary motivation for this dangerously defiant move was a continuing upsurge of anti-Italian feeling in Albania due to Rome's ever increasing influence. By 1930 there were two thousand Italians employed in Albania paid by the Italian government. A substantial number of these Italians served in the Albanian army where there was approximately one Italian officer for every six regular Albanian officers.

This rather conspicuous presence did much to reinvigorate the usual xenophobia which all Albanians, irrespective of social origin or religion, seemed to possess. Growing anti-Italian feelings became evident among all segments of Albanian society, including members of the lower classes, the peasants and soldiers, members of the upper classes, the landowners and members of Zog's political bureaucracy. Clearly, the Italians were less than popular.

For various reasons, feelings towards the Italians ran basically from dull antipathy to wholesale detestation. The sensitive pride of the mountaineers refused to countenance any foreign involvement in their affairs, which led them to view the Italians as a threat. The peasants directed their xenophobia against the Italians because they were the largest group of foreigners in Albania. The British, whose presence was obvious only in the gendarmerie, received basically the same treatment although to a lesser degree. They were less feared primarily because there was less of them.

The landowning classes, although they too suffered from xenophobia, had other reasons to dislike the Italian influence. While nationalism often played a minor role, the Italian support for land reform was probably a more important reason. The landowners feared that if Zog fell too far under the wing of the Italians, the reforms which had been worked out by Rome and accepted by Zog but never implemented, might be carried out.[6] Their economic domination and indeed their very way of life would of course have been threatened.

Of the members of Zog's political bureaucracy who were opposed to the Italians, probably a substantial majority were motivated by considerations similar to those of the landowners. Zog's personal rule and the heritage of corruption left by the Ottomans combined to make penury not only an acceptable method of running the government but necessary for survival. Italy was seen as a threat to this whole system basically because Italian officials, who by 1931 permeated most ministries, had assumed positions of power which theoretically at least allowed them to interfere with corrupt practices. This of course is not to imply that they actually did move to stop corruption, but Albanian officials were aware that they had the power to intervene if they so chose. The Italians naturally used bribes liberally but most Albanian officials were not considered important enough to warrant bribing. Italian money remained in the hands of the few.

Popular hostility by itself would have been of little consequence but it soon began to manifest itself into direct action. In June of 1930 an Italian officer of engineers, Lieutenant Chesti, ws murdered near Sirocca by one Islam Sole, a solider in one of the frontier battalions. The attack was clearly premeditated as it was soon learned that Sole had made himself familiar with Chesti's movements and had primed himself with alcohol before taking up his position on the road leading to Chesti's home. As the lieutenant cycled by, Sole emptied the contents of his magazine into his back and fled to Yugoslavia.[7]

Although the motive for the crime was never absolutely established, the available evidence suggests that Chesti was murdered merely because he was an Italian. There was apparently no connection whatsoever between Chesti and Sole, ruling out the possibility of a personal grudge. The behavior of the Albanian authorities lends more credence to the argument that simple anti-Italian feelings produced the attack.

The government was originally noisy in its demand that the Yugoslavs hand over Sole under the terms of the extradition treaty, but seemed to lose all enthusiasm when it became known that Belgrade would make no difficulty about acceding to the request.[8] The prospect of having to try the man before an Albanian court was clearly not a welcome one, suggesting that the government had some idea as to why the incident has occurred.

Another serious episode involved the Albanian Foreign Minister Raouf Bey Fitso, who soon after his retirement in late 1930 saw fit to give an interview to the Tirana correspondent of a newspaper issued by the Albanian colony in Rumania. The ex-minister, who was often prone to let the intensity of his feelings run away with his discretion, took the journalist into his confidence and enlarged upon the insufferable arrogance of the Italians, the dishonesty of their contractors and the lessons that one day or another the Albanians would administer to them.[9]

The Italian Minister in Tirana was, of course, provoked and demanded an explanation from Fitso who blandly denied having said a single word against Italy. Not satisfied with this disclaimer, Sola instructed Fitso to send a communique to the press which Sola himself had written. In it Fitso maintained that the observations attributed to him were "the product of a diseased imagination"; their author "a vulgar and malevolent liar." Fitso extolled the altruism of the Italians in Albania "dedicated to the well-being of their ally a labor devoted and loyal, even at the cost of their own lives" and announced that "every word directed against Italian citizens can be nothing but a manifestation of ingratitude and imbecility."[10]

Neither of the participants emerged from the altercation with credit. Fitso was guilty of an act of gross indiscretion which his ignominious retreat failed to cover up. Sola merely succeeded in making the Albanians more suspicious than ever of the motives underlying Italian generosity. Signor Sola, who had been in Albania for four years, was recalled shortly after this incident and replaced by the Marchese Lupi di Soranga.

A third episode which occurred at Shkodër within a month of the Fitso fiasco further conveyed the message of animosity to Italy, and in this instance the Catholic community was involved. The church of the "Madre dei Boni Consigli," which was destroyed by the Turks, had contained an ikon of the Virgin. According to legend, the ikon took to itself wings and flew across the Adriatic to Genozzano where it was preserved in a church. In the early 1920s a movement was set afoot among Shkodër Catholics to rebuild the old church and a committee was formed to take charge of operations. Funds were difficult to come by and the work went slowly. Finally, in despair, the archbishop and the parish priest asked the

Italian Consul for aid. The Consul offered ten thousand gold francs but asked that a tablet be set in the church recording that the completion of the work of restoration had been rendered possible thanks to the aid given by the Italian government.

The church committee had apparently not been consulted about these arrangements and a storm of popular indignation broke out as soon as news of the deal got out. The true facts were ignored or purposely distorted and the rumor spread that the archbishop had sold the church for ten thousand francs to the Italians who intended to place a bust of Mussolini on the high altar in the place formerly occupied by the ikon of the Virgin.

The outburst was only quelled after the archbishop returned to the money to the Italians. An elaborate project which included the bringing over by airplane of a replica of the Genozzano ikon, blessed by the Pope, to be installed by Cardinal Vannutelli had to be abandoned as well.[11]

The Albanians, in their desperation to liberate themselves from their dependence on Italy, seized upon any means to replace Italian interests. In late 1930 a notorious international crook of American nationality, a certain John Dekay also known as Mordecai who had published an anti-Ally newspaper in Geneva during the first world war, convinced the Albanian Consul in Vienna, Saracci, that he was a wealthy financier given to philanthropy.

With a recommendation from Saracci, Dekay in due course arrived in Tirana accompanied by a private secretary and presented himself as the representative of a powerful syndicate which had entrusted to him the mission of negotiating with the Albanian government concessions for the execution of public works. He rapidly won the sympathies of the Albanians by presenting the Red Cross with a bad check for four thousand pounds and by declaring his readiness to liberate them at once from their financial obligations to the Italians.

Despite numerous warnings from the American Minister, Dekay captured all hearts, particuarly that of Mehdi Bey Frasheri, the Minister of Public Works, who fell completely under his spell. Dekay was even received by King Zog and presented with the Order of Skanderbeg. After a few days in Tirana he departed for Durrës armed with an option granted to his syndicate by the Albanian government for the execution of a long list of public works. His departure from Albania in a state of collapse after a long debauch in a Durrës restaurant coincided with the receipt by the Albanian government of information to the effect that John Dekay was a complete fraud.[12]

The anti-Italian feeling, then, was all pervasive and although Zog's political position was never actually threatened as a result of the anti-Italian activity, he could not afford to completely ignore public opinion trends indefinitely. Nor did he particuarly want to since the Italians, who had a great deal to learn about Albanian psychology, inadvertently added more reasons why Zog needed to make some offiicial move against Rome.

In August 1931 it came to the attention of the King that the Italians had struck upon a new method to instill a warlike spirit into fresh, somewhat unenthusiastic army recruits. They began to openly encourage the specter of irredentism. Zog had made up his mind early on in his political career that Kosovo was lost to Albania and he had expended a good deal of energy suppressing the old Kosovo Committee and its militant irredentist leaders. This is not to say that he never used irredentism in small doses for his own purposes but, nevertheless, he could not afford to allow the idea to spread too widely.

Although the Italian legation was probably innocent in this instance, the military mission was not. Because the mission was in the process of creating an army, undoubtedly an extremely difficult task in Albania, the proper mentality was needed. Holding up Yugoslavia as the enemy of every proper Albanian was one of the simplest ways in which such a mentality could be achieved. That it happened to serve the needs of Italian foreign policy was also, of course, a factor.

Various specific incidents occurred. An Italian instructor named Antico, who was employed in the training of Albanian youths at Kukës, was reported by the British gendarmerie inspector for impressing upon his pupils that the future of Albania lay in the recovery of Kosovo and that Italy, their only friend, was there to help them fulfill their national aspirations. The Yugoslav Minister on several occasions informed the British Minister of cases where Albanians had been approached by the Italian military mission and urged to undertake subversive acts against Yugoslavia on the frontier and over the border. In several instances the Yugoslav Minister accompanied his accusations with enough details to convince the British Minister that they essentially represented the facts.[13]

Everything pointed to the need for some sort of a stand against the Italians. Zog chose as his issue the question of renewing the Pact of Tirana, scheduled to expire in November of 1931. The King was not oblivious to the dangers involved here particularly since it was this agreement which gave the Italians the right to intervene in internal Albanian affairs. Zog moved very carefully, assuming that Rome would put up a fight. In his usual Balkan manner, he allowed his underlings to broach the subject initially so if a hasty retreat was required, it would be their heads on the block and not his own.

In January 1931 Prime Minister Evangjeli informed the British Minister, who had asked him about the pact, that relations between Albania and Italy were governed by the 1927 Treaty of Alliance and, therefore, the pact had become unnecessary and the Albanian government had no intention of prolonging it.[14] Indeed, from the Albanian point of view, the pact had become rather irksome.

When it was originally concluded, Albania was in a state of turmoil and Zog needed the security of an Italian guarantee for his own position. By 1931, however, the situation had changed considerably and Zog had been able to stabilize the regime and bring about a degree of tranquillity Under these new conditions, the provisions of the pact dealing with internal stability constituted little more than a humiliating admission of weakness.

The Italian Ministry of Foreign Affairs wanted it renewed, although it could easily be argued that they had little or nothing to gain from its renewal. It was clear that the Albanians had no intention of renewing willingly, therefore, the Italians could achieve their goal only by force thereby outraging national sentiment. It was also by no means inconceivable that Albania, based upon the pact, could still drag Italy into an awkward situation requiring it either to honor the pact and risk war or refuse at the cost of sacrificing the whole position Italy had so laboriously constructed. Finally, it must have occurred to the Italians that renewal of the pact would have been interpreted as little more than a piece of gratuitous provocation in Belgrade.

The Italian government apparently needed a document to produce at home to critics of its Albanian policy. The renewal would be used as evidence that in return for the considerable financial subsidies, the government had again obtained a contract which made the head of the Albanian state dependent on Italy.

The first Italian move to renew the pact took the form of attempts on the part of the Italian Minister in Tirana, who personally professed only a detached interest in the matter, to broach the subject during the negotiations for the 1931 loan. Each time the King waved it aside for discussion at a more opportune moment. Zog maintained his sphinx-like attitude, always leaving himself an escape route when questioned directly. In August, for example, he told the British Minister that renewal depended upon the attitude of Albania's neighbors, although he admitted that they had been behaving well in the recent past. The King commented that he was still concerned, however, about the possibility of Belgrade driving a crowd of Kosovar emigrants across the border which Tirana could not feed.[15] His waiting game gave him an easy exit in case Italian pressure became overwhelming.

As November approached, the Italians discovered that they had essentially been outmaneuvered by Zog. Their own situation had become a difficult one. The public purpose of their endeavors in Albania was, of course, to endow the small faction-ridden land with the attributes of strength and independence. It would have been impossible to convince the world at large that in forcing upon Albania a guarantee which the Albanian government considered objectionable, Rome was pursuing the lofty aims it had set out for itself.

The Italians managed to dig themselves an even deeper hole by suggesting that their only interest in renewing the pact stemmed from their anxiety that its lapse would weaken Zog's position among his own people. They clearly made it difficult for themselves to reopen the question publicly once the King had declared that the had the internal situation well in hand and had no further need of the Italian guarantee.

A few days before expiration, Mussolini turned to Pariani in a final effort to convince Zog to renew. After a stormy session Pariani, exasperated, declared that he would have nothing more to do with Albania and asked the King to accept his resignation. Although matters were smoothed over and Pariani received the Order of the Besa, the highest decoration which Albania could confer, Italy had broken a lance with Zog and lost. Zog finally informed the Italian legation that the pact had lapsed and that he had no intention of renewing it. The King concluded that Italo-Albanian relations would henceforth be governed only by the Alliance of 1927, which had successfully been presented as an agreement between equals.

Zog's victory was applauded by Albanian nationalists and did a good deal to raise their estimation of his ability and his patriotism. The price of this renewed popularity, however, was an on-again, off-again crisis in Italo-Albanian relations which lasted until 1936. The Italians had no intention of allowing Zog to make political hay at their expense. He had made Rome look rather foolish both at home and abroad, for which he would have to pay.

The obvious weapon was economic and the first victim of the new period of hostility was the loan which had been concluded just a few months earlier. The mixed commission which had been appointed to dispense funds was given only a few minor sums before the money stopped completely. The Italian action was a rude shock since ten million gold francs was a considerable sum to a tiny nation living just above the starvation line with its finances continually in a state of crisis.

The Italians proceeded to lay the rest of their cards on the table. Soon after the loan money dried up, a representative from SVEA appeared in Tirana and clamored for the payment of the amount due under contract only in the following January. The representative went so far as to suggest that since the Albanian customs revenue was pledged to cover the loan, SVEA, in order to help out, might furnish Italian employees who would assist the Albanian government in the collection of dues.[16]

The King could not do without the money and he could not give in to the Italians so he resorted to Balkan political intrigue. In late December 1931 he summoned one of his former ministers of finance, Fejzi Alizoti, a well-known tool of the Italians. Alizoti was asked to prepare a new budget, slimming it from thirty-one million gold francs to twenty-one million with the primary cuts to hit the military and the King's civil list, both of which were to be reduced by almost 50 percent. The army was to be particularly singled out, losing five million gold francs from its yearly budget, as well as 160 officers.[17]

When Alizoti asked why the King had not changed his cabinet with the preparation of the new budget, he was told that the cabinet was useless and that a complete change would soon come. Alizoti himself was to be the new Minister of Finance. To make the rouse even more credible, Zog instructed Mr. Kareco, the Minister of Finance, to give Alizoti all the help and information he required in connection with the preparation of the next budget.[18]

Because of Alizoti's past activities, the King was convinced that the information which the former minister had been given, would be secretly transmitted to the Italians. This is, of course, precisely what Zog had in mind, to let Rome know, through means other than a direct statement to the Italian Minister, that Albania was determined to reduce the size of the army, which the Italians had so painstakingly built. Zog, who was generally aware of his limitations, saw this as the most reasonable move in his attempt to restart the flow of Italian funds.

Although the Italians refused to inform the Albanians until February whether normal financial relations would be resumed, they did finally come around. The King was told in a note that the continuance of aid for military and economic purposes could be counted upon provided that the Italians retained some control over the expenditures. Rome also asked for a number of concessions including the extension of the Italian Petroleum Agency concession as well as permission for an Italian electrical company to operate in Durrës. Zog quickly agreed to these provisions and just as quickly scrapped the projected lean budget for the year 1932-1933.

The King's little victory would have been complete had it not been for Italian intransigence regarding the SVEA loan. Maintaining the farce that SVEA was a private company, Rome informed Zog that it would do what it could to bring about an alleviation in the conditions of the SVEA loan and suggested direct conversations on the subject between debtors and creditors. The Italian Minister accompanied the promise given in the note with the assurance that a moratorium would be conceded for another year, during which it was expected that the two sides would come to some sort of an agreement.[19]

The King was disappointed since he had hoped for some concrete proposition rather than another year's delay, a simple postponement of the evil day of reckoning. Albania had been unable to make the eight million gold franc payment of 1932 and nothing indicated that it could even consider producing the sixteen million gold franc payment which was to become due in 1933.

Italy finally began to use the loan for its original purpose of political pressure and, therefore, had no intention of allowing Zog to escape with an easy settlement. The King could not have been surprised by these moves for although he might not have been fully cognizant of the economic implications of the loan, the political aspects had not escaped him. The political aspects of any issue directly involving his own or Albania's interest, rarely did.

Despite this realization, Zog hoped to soften the Italians by the use of the only level of pressure he could bring to bear, namely some form of international, particularly British, indignation. The King was careful to cultivate the image of a small nation exploited by a more powerful neighbor.

He complained to the British Minister that the Albanians had been promised again and again that they would never be asked to repay the loan, which was, of course, perfectly true. In their rush to obtain his signature in 1925, the Italians had made it very clear that he could accept these obligations with complete tranquillity inasmuch as he would never be pressed to meet them.

Ugo Sola, in speaking with the British Minister, had always treated the loan lightly, suggesting that Rome had no thought of enforcing its terms and was prepared to accord moratorium after moratorium indefinitely. Indeed, Foreign Minister Dino Grande had given similar assurances as late as 1931.[20] The Italians had weakened their position by this loose talk and Zog was prepared to take full advantage of it.

Zog further argued that the Italians were perfectly aware that Albania was thoroughly unable to meet even a fraction of its obligations to SVEA adding that there really was no moral obligation to do so, since the money had been spent largely on Italian strategic objectives and much of it had gone into the pockets of Italian contractors.[21]

Rome was quick to join the verbal barrage standing firm on the point that SVEA was a private organization and that, therefore, its first duty was to its stockholders. Armando Koch, the Italian Minister in 1932, maintained that he and SVEA realized that Albania was in no position to meet its obligations although he himself did not consider them to be too onerous. Koch maintained that Albania could at least meet some of the payments and the very fact that Tirana had not done so lent credence to the argument that Zog was acting in bad faith. Under terms of the agreement SVEA could, if it wished, seize the Albanians by the throat and take their customs, but Italy, Signor Koch argued, had no intention of doing anything of the kind.[22] Zog was not reassured.

In accordance with the February 1932 note, two delegates from SVEA arrived during the summer for the purpose of comparing notes with the Albanians to come up with an agreement as to the amount for which Zog was prepared to admit liability. After discovering that the two sets of figures differed substantially, they left Albania to consult their superiors.

In November they were to return and collect at least a part of what the Albanian government was liable for, but Koch, who was holding his own negotiations with Zog, apparently instructed them to wait. The King held out for some time against the idea of Albania making any payment at all.

Early in 1933, after having come to the conclusion that at least some gesture was necessary to placate the Italians, Zog finally presented a proposal for repayment. Albania, the King declared, would consent to pay one million gold francs a year for fifteen years with annual increments at the rate of four percent on each year payment (i.e., in the first year 1,040,000 francs, in the second year 1,080,000 francs, in the third year 1,120,000 francs and so on). From the sixteenth year onwards Albania would pay at the rate of 2.5 million annually, until the total sum of fifty million was wiped out.[23]

Zog sent a memorandum to the Italian legation and asked that Koch forward the proposal to Rome to obtain the signatures from SVEA. Albania would then insert the amount of the first payment into the budget. Koch, whose general attitude towards the situation was rather inflexible, refused to do so inasmuch as it constituted a unilateral modification of a bilateral agreement and, as such, could not be regarded as a basis for negotiation. Thus ended Zog's only serious attempt to repay the SVEA loan.

By this time, however, the negotiations regarding a repayment structure for the loan had become less important in the light of several more serious differences which further soured relations between the two states. Italy had on more than one occasion attempted to draw Albania into a customs union. Zog had always refused these advances, recognizing that Albanian independence would have essentially come to an end with such an agreement. The Albanian government had little outside the seven or eight million gold francs it received from its customs to defray the cost of administration. The union with Italy would have automatically put an end to this source of revenue inasmuch as it was derived from Italian goods imported into Albania. Italy, geneally, was responsible for approximately 60 percent of Albania's imports. With the union Albania would have become a closed preserve for Italian manufactures and the government would have been forced to turn to the Italians to finance every facet of administration. Albania would have been reduced to a tributary state.[24]

In December of 1932 rumors of renewed Italian pressure to construct a union began to circulate. The chain of events remains somewhat obscure not only because the versions emanating from Tirana and Rome were at variance but also because those supplied by Italians in authoritative positions contradicted one another. The Yugoslavs were among the first to spread the rumor, suggesting that Italy had threatened to withhold all financial aid to Albania unless the demand for a customs union was conceded.[25]

The Italian Minister in Tirana declared to the general public that no proposal for a union had been put forward by Italy but assured close friends that the Albanians had asked Italy to consent to a union and that Italy had refused. The head of the department interested in the Ministry of Foreign Affairs in Rome declared that no one had even mentioned a customs union adding, however, that were the proposal for a union to emanate from Albania, it would be carefully considered in Rome, but he thought that such a contingency was extremely improbable.[26]

The most likely version of what had actually transpired was presented by King Zog himself who admitted that he had been approached academically. Near the end of 1932 Ekrem Bey Libohova, the Minister of Court in Tirana, returned from a visit to Rome convinced of the benefits which a customs union with Italy held in store for Albania. Ekrem Bey attempted to convince the King that he had everything to gain by making a proposal for such a union. Zog appointed a committee of three persons to look into the matter and this group quickly came to the unanimous opinion that the union would spell the loss of independence for Albania. Ekrem Bey, a fervent Italophile who had most probably been primed in Rome, was essentially working as an emissary of the Italian Foreign Ministry. After the committee had submitted its report, Ekrem Bey, presumably to save his position, recanted.

The final result of this rather clumsy attempt on the part of the Italians to obtain a customs union was to further damage the already strained Italo-Albanian relations. The Albanians, who were slowly being affected by Zog's attempts to instill nationalism, saw this as another indication of Italian malevolence. The heavier their liabilities the more distrust they exhibited toward Rome.

Albanians were more firmly convinced that although the union had once more been avoided, Italy would try again, waiting only until the attention of Europe was distracted by other matters. The Tirana government became firmer in its resolve to resist Italian penetration. Zog announced that nothing would induce him to agree to a customs union. Before the dust had settled, however, an even more serious conflict developed dealing with the nationalization of the education system.

Zog's Minister of Public Instruction in 1932, Hil Mosi, a man strongly inbued with nationalism, had for some time pushed for the creation of a truly national educational system. He had long maintained that foreigners, particularly the Italians, were improperly using their positions as instructors in Albanian schools to politically and culturally influence their students. Mosi argued that in some instances the Italians went so far as to replace portraits of Albanian heroes with those of Victor Emmanuel and Mussolini.[27]

Mosi's complaints were not entirely unjustified, particularly since many of the foreign schools in Albania used languages other than Albanian for purposes of instruction. Albanians, whose language had been basically forbidden by the Turks for five centuries, were naturally sensitive in this regard.

Mosi's most persuasive argument and the one which probably won Zog over in the end was that the Italians were particularly active among their coreligionists in the north and had actually constructed more schools in the Shkodër area than were necessary. The King, eternally suspicious, assumed the Italians were making insidious advances to the entire Catholic north in an attempt to undermine his influence among the tribes and to replace it with their own.[28] Zog also saw the possibility of striking a blow for nationalism.

As Italo-Albanian relations began to seriously degenerate, Mosi was allowed to set some of his long cherished programs in motion. Owing to his exertions, a measure which marked a complete change in the attitude of the Albanian government was placed on the statute books. Prior to the change, parents had been free to bring up their children where and as they wished; foreign schools of all grades religious or lay, established and financed by organizations outside Albania, were not handicapped in any way. Grants from the Albanian treasury were freely given to permit young Albanians to obtain their education abroad.

The new legislation made it a penal offence, punishable by two to six months imprisonment, with a fine of five thousand to ten thousand francs, for parents to send their children to foreign elementary schools, whether in Albania or elsewhere. Further, with respect to government posts, students who had completed their secondary education in Albanian schools were given precedence over those who had studied in Balkan schools, while those who had studied in Western Europe and had failed to complete their course were disqualified from government positions until they had completed their studies in Albania. Lastly, to accept a scholarship from a foreign source and attend a foreign school for the purpose of a secondary education was made punishable by imprisonment and disqualification for government employment for a period of three years.[29]

Despite the adoption of these laws, little was apparently done during the last months of 1932 to implement them. At the end of December, however, Hil Mosi died and was replaced by Mirosh Ivanaj who turned out to be an even greater enthusiast for national education than his predecessor had been. He was also staunchly anti-clerical and felt that Catholic schools which owed allegiance to foreigners were intolerable. Zog agreed and decided in April 1933 that the time for implementation had arrived.

Ivanaj vigorously carried out his program. All private schools were ordered closed. Those affected included all foreign schools, but little effort was made to hide the fact that the Italians were the primary target. Seventeen Catholic schools belonging to Jesuits, Franciscans and Stigmatini, with 2,560 pupils were abruptly closed, twelve of these in Shkodër and the surrounding areas and the rest in Tirana. Eight small village schools, with an attendance of 160 in localities where there were no government schools shared the same fate as did also a Protestant school in Korcë and a music school in Tirana.

The four excellent Italian technical schools with 1,000 students, which the Italian government had set up in 1929 and supported financially, had Albanian directors appointed to take charge of them. The Italian Minister, however, summoned the teaching staff of these schools and sent them home, leaving a certain number on the spot with order to pack up the machinery and equipment to prepare for its transfer back to Italy.[30]

The American technical school in Tirana, the Kyrias Institute for girls, as well as the Kutzo-Vlak and Serbian minority schools, were also given Albanian directors but unlike the Italians they accepted them and were thereby allowed to remain in operation. The Greek schools in the south, where the government had already run into so much difficulty forcing the teachers to learn Albanian, were closed. Only the seminaries for the preparation of the clergy were allowed to remain open provided they abstained from anti-Albanian propaganda. But even here the government left the path to their suppression open by requiring that they be maintained by Albanian religious communities.[31]

Had the Albanian school system been somewhat stronger, the departure of the foreigners may not have had such a resounding impact. As it was, the entire system was thrown into chaos. To make matters worse, the Albanians refused to allow the foreign instructors to finish out the school year, which in most cases had about three months to run. With his meager resources the Minister of Public Instruction could not even hope to make up the loss. The best that could be done immediately was the procurement of 50,000 gold francs for a supply of school textbooks in the Albanian language.

Although the original motives might have been reasonable enough, the impulsive and uncompromising attitude of the Albanian officials did great harm to the educational system. Zog and his ministers had destroyed the prevailing system without the means or even the slightest hope of replacing it with another.

Foreign reaction was sharp. The Greek minority in southern Albania immediately took their case to the League of Nations, complaining that Albania was in violation of the rights of minorities agreement which it had signed in 1921. Tirana reacted by arresting many of the leading Greeks in the south thereby causing unrest as well as damaging Albanian-Greek relations. The Hague Court eventually ruled in favor of the Greeks, requiring the Albanian government to reverse its policies. Zog was a bit soured by the proceedings arguing that Yugoslavia gave the Albanians no schools whatsoever and even went to the length of denying that they were Albanians at all.[32] Zog's biggest problem, however, came from across the Adriatic.

The Italians had been pushed to the limit and did not wait long to strike back. The commission dispensing Italian loan money from the 1931 loan once again ceased its function. All financial assistance was suspended and Italian personnel, civil and military, were gradually withdrawn. The army ceased to receive anything in the way of arms and equipment.

General Pariani, head of the military mission was withdrawn in April to the regret of Zog and many Albanians who were particularly attached to him for a number of reasons. Not only was he an able officer who stood out as the only Italian to gain the respect and confidence of the Albanians, but his liberal use of government funds came as a welcome relief to military suppliers and chronically underpaid soldiers. More importantly, it was common knowledge that on frequent occasions when difficulties between the two governments appeared, he did his best to bring about a settlement favorable to the Albanians.

The general was replaced by Colonel Boloccio who was given a much less important role. While Pariani had been Chief of Staff, Boloccio merely became the military attache to the Italian legation under the control of Koch who was rarely as generous as Pariani. Zog, to show his displeasure, announced that he would in the future only attach Albanian officers to his personal staff.

The Italians had decided to wait for the economic hardships which would inevitably follow their withdrawal of funds to bring the Albanians around, meanwhile, watching the country slide into a state of chaos. As Koch picturesquely informed the King, he remained expectant at the open window. At the first sign that the Albanians intended to abandon their recalcitrance and become again the collaborators of Italy, he would fling himself from his window to their aid.[33]

This wait and see attitude was accompanied by a reevaluation of their foreign policy towards Albania. Few informed observers, including Italians, were willing to admit that Rome had thus far been successful in its Albanian policy. They had by 1932, by their own estimation, sunk no less than one billion lire into the country in the form of two loan agreements, military equipment, fortifications, payment of experts and non-profit organizations.[34]

In the very early period of Zog's presidency the money had certainly helped to create some political stability. Since then, however, apart from a few bridges and roads, some non-functional building in Tirana and the harbor at Durrës, Italy had little to show for it. To compound the irony, Rome's general approach had robbed them of the good will that one might reasonably have expected such an outlay of capital to engender.

The Italians seemed either unwilling or unable to break away from the erratic course their policy had followed since 1925, alternating between the hard unbending tactics of Baron Aloisi and Commander Koch and the vacillation and yielding policy pursued by the various ministers inbetween. The Italians continued to treat the Albanians as half-tamed creatures to be cajoled and/or petted rather than as allies whom they hoped to render strong and independent. Mussolini himself set the mood for this approach. He once inquired touchingly of Koch how the Albanians liked the little army Italy had bestowed upon them, whether they were rallying around the national flag, how the organization of their youth was progressing and so forth.[35]

The Albanians quite naturally approached this odd mixture of sentimentality, strategic interest and economics with a good deal of suspicion, suspecting nearly every move that the Italians made. The lack of trust was enhanced by the fact that Italy's economic policies had completely failed to construct a viable business structure. On the contrary, Albania, during the years it spent as an Italian protege had become steadily poorer. The country had gradually been drained of the not inconsiderable treasures buried in it in the shape of savings in gold coin which the peasants had accumulated from past times. Albanians could purchase nothing. Such national resources as the country possessed were still undeveloped. Its forests uncut, its agriculture backward and its plains, which reclaimed and fertilized might have been rendered highly productive, remained waterlogged and neglected.

In July of 1932 Mussolini fired Dino Grande as Foreign Minister. Grande lost his position primarily because he believed in the policy of conciliation, for which he had been implicitly criticized in the Grand Council. Mussolini himself assumed the portfolio and almost immediately brought about changes in Italy's relations with Albania. The Duce, not unaware of Italy's lack of progress with the Albanians, decided to try his hand at bringing Tirana around. Typical of many of his foreign policy initiatives in the 1930s, his first concrete attempt to deal with the small Balkan nation was impulsive and aggressive.

Koch had for some time predicted that if driven too far, Mussolini might permit himself an authoritative gesture to bring the Albanians around. On June 23, 1934, the Duce made his gesture in the form of the unannounced arrival of an Italian squadron of six cruisers and thirteen destroyers under the command of Vice-Admiral Cantu. The ships, failing to salue the Albanian flag, anchored off of Durrës. The Albanians naturally believed that this armed force was to be employed by Italy in order to compel them to come to terms. The government immediately began taking defensive measures including the dispatch of troops to Durrës. Local authorities removed all military stores and ammunition by truck to Tirana and even ordered the digging of trenches around the Durrës area in preparation to resist the attack.[36]

An hour or so after the squadron arrived, an Italian officer landed and called upon the prefect in the name of the Italian Commander-in-Chief. When asked to clarify his position, the officer explained to the prefect that his unceremonious arrival was to be attributed to the desire to avoid causing the Albanian government the expense and trouble of an official reception.

Once again official Italian explanations of the event are contradictory. The most often quoted version lays the blame on Signor Koch who was accused of overlooking the telegram announcing the proposed visit of the fleet until it was already in the harbor. The Ministry of Foreign Affairs in Rome, meanwhile, informed the Albanian Charge d'Affaires that Admiral Cantu had been guilty of an indiscretion in taking his squadron to Durrës without orders.[37]

The least convincing of the myriad of explanations was that of Signor Koch who suggested to the Minister of Foreign Affairs that on the occasion of a courtesy visit between allies, such formalities as the giving of notice beforehand could easily be dispensed with. This explanation is particularly ironic since Koch apparently presented the Albanian Foreign Minister Villa with a list of demands which would have acted as the precursor to the resumption of normal Italo-Albanian relations while the Italian navy threatened Durrës. The demands included the reopening of Italian private schools, the reintroduction of Italian advisers particuarly in the military and the immediate resumption of talks concerning the repayment of interest and principal on the various Italian loans.[38]

Zog knew why the ships had come and he was determined to stand against Italian pressure. Villa, under orders from the King, informed the Italian Minister that for the renewal of discussions an atmosphere of general serenity was necessary, something which the presence of Italian warships in Albanian waters certainly did not foster. On June 25 all but four of the ships were withdrawn with the remainder leaving five days later. Despite his new tactics, Mussolini had lost the first round and the

Albanians, though weakening, had not given in. Italy's ill-conceived exhibition of naval force produced two concrete results: first it intensified distrust of Italy throughout Albania and second it succeeded in rallying King Zog's subjects from one end of the country to the other.

By the summer of 1934 Zog was in desperate need of this support. His economies and alternative means of procuring financial aid had been inadequate. It was a matter of too little too late. Still, Zog had made some efforts to deal with the problem even if most of them remained little more than window dressing.

Beginning in 1933 Zog initiated well-meaning but rather ineffective cuts in the budget to meet the pressing situation. The King began by relinquishing 50 percent of his own civil list. Zog even went so far as to severely curtail the annual festivities in celebration of his birthday. Where the citizens of Tirana had become accustomed to rather extravagant events, the 1933 birthday was marked by celebrations of a quiet and less expensive nature. A salute of twenty-one guns was fired at eight in the morning followed by a small parade of trades people and children. The high point of the day was a bicycle race to Elbasan and back. Evening festivities were restricted to a moderate display of fireworks followed by a concert in which Albania's foremost singer, Mr. Kristoq Antoniu, was the principal attraction.[39]

Other methods to raise revenue included an attempt to recover outstanding arrears as well as to more effectively collect current taxes, a policy which was met with little enthusiasm on the part of the already hard pressed peasantry. Some villages, particularly those of the Molakastro area, let it be known that if the tax-collectors made another appearance it would go ill with them. By the end of 1933 the Mirditë tribesmen were once again reduced to eating grass. In the districts north of the Drin, heavy rains prevented the peasants from harvesting their maize while their stores of forage rotted from the same cause or were carried away by floods. The price of wheat, which early in the year had been down to thirty lek the quintal, had jumped to seventy lek and the people had no money with which to buy bread.[40] The general outlook was one of unrelenting gloom, hardly the ideal moment to increase tax collecting.

Zog finally saw the necessity to launch a long overdue attack on Albania's top-heavy administration. He hoped that by greatly reducing government expenditure in this area the most significant contribution to solving the crisis could be made. The King began by dismissing a large number of government employees, primarily those luckless individuals with no friends in high places to protect them. Only a powerful patron or a university degree could render a position secure.[41]

Those who survived Albania's version of the Saturday night massacre, many more than should have survived, were also persuaded to help out. Under article six of the 1933 budget law, all employees of the state receiving more than one hundred gold francs per month contributed one month's salary. Twelve percent was shorn off of all civil pensions, which had finally been instituted, and a similar percentage was deducted from the pay of all those officials, civil and military, whose salaries exceeded twenty gold francs a month. Additionally, all remaining personnel were relieved of one percent of their salary for the creation of a fund of 250,000 gold francs to temporarily help those government employees who had been let go as a result of the cuts.[42]

While all of these changes looked good on paper, few really made a significant difference, considering that by the end of 1933 salaries for government employees were roughly four to six months in arrears. Because these salaries were not being paid and because receipts dropped steadily during the years of the crisis, Zog was forced to continually cut the budget as the following chart shows (figures in gold francs).

1932-1933	31,588,395
1933-1934	23,832,293
1934-1935	18,888,192
1935-1936	18,035,746[43]

In terms of percentages, the department hardest hit by the reductions was the Ministry of Foreign Affairs which lost close to 50 percent of its funding in one year. As a result, the Administrative and Consular Department had to be suppressed entirely together with five consular posts. The rather haphazard method of carrying out these economies left the entirely useless legation in Washingtion, which cost 15 percent of the entire budget open, while offices in more important locals were closed.

Zog managed to actually save the most money by severely reducing the army and gendarmerie estimates. In the first year of the conflict the army lost 4.4 million gold francs. Each year the army estimates were

further reduced but because the general budget was also drastically reduced, it turned out that the army as late as 1936 still swallowed up more
than 50 percent of the income of the state.[44]

The crux of the army expense problem remained the corps of some
seven hundred officers which had been brought into existence with the
assistance of the Italians. Zog either felt he could not govern without them
or could not dismiss them lest they form a nucleus of opposition which
he would have been powerless to control. Much of the money spent in
this fashion still went as bribes to chieftains, a tradition which would be
the last to go under any circumstances.

The officers, then, were among the first to receive funds, even when
the members of Parliament remained without salaries. In order to continue, however, extraordinary measures had to be taken. Near the end of
1933 the last few thousand francs remaining in the fund set aside in 1931
for the construction of the agrarian bank to begin the agrarian reform was
distributed among the army officers.[45]

By the beginning of 1934 there was nothing left to be raided. Zog's
internal policies had been woefully inadequate to deal with the crisis,
everything had come to a stop. Public works in the making had been
abandoned and the personnel employed upon them dismissed. Contractors
were refused payment of money due to them for work already completed.
Because no one was paid, the merchant community could not dispose of
the stock on hand so they stopped buying from abroad.[46]

Retail dealers went bankrupt, being unable to collect old debts. Credit
dried up completely and those with capital refused to risk it in difficult
times. Had Albania been a more advanced economic community, a complete breakdown of internal organization would have resulted. The people,
however, were accustomed to poverty; they had seen it all before.

Having failed internally, the harried King looked for outside help. His
first impulse was to appeal once again to the League of Nations, suggesting to the British Minister in March 1933 that unless an agreement
with Italy was arrived at during April, he would be left with no alternative
but to go to Geneva. April came and went without an agreement, indicating that the King had either been bluffing, or that it had occurred to him
that the League would undoubtedly be of no help. Indeed, the League
would most likely have done little more than to encourage Zog to appeal
once more to the magnanimity of his creditors, exactly what he was hoping to avoid.[47]

This left only Western Europe and Albania's immediate neighbors. With the former, Zog had no success whatsoever. His appeals for a loan were turned down by the governments of Great Britain, France, Belgium and Holland. With Albania's immediate neighbors, Zog had considerably more luck, indeed, Albania's relations with the surrounding Balkan states achieved a level of surprising cordiality. Both Greece and Yugoslavia used the opportunity created by the altercation between Rome and Tirana in order to improve their economic relations with Albania.

Of the two, Yugoslavia went the furthest both economically and politically and began this new period of Balkan cooperation by signing a commercial agreement with Tirana in December 1933. Under the terms of the agreement, basically a supplement to the 1926 trade agreement which was not instituted until 1929, Yugoslavia agreed to import Albanian products worth 2.6 million gold francs a year, ranking her Albania's second most important trading partner. The agreement also included provisions for the opening of a number of Yugoslav banks in Albania to deal with the financial transactions connected with the exchange of commodities between the two countries.[48]

Relations between the two states were further improved by the May 1934 agreement which lessened the tension on the border. The agreement allowed the creation of a fifteen kilometer border zone enabling peasants on either side who had been cut off from their markets by the creation the frontiers, to ply their goods in their natural outlets. The new agreements also made provisions for the establishment of a regular bus line between the two countries for the purpose of encouraging tourism and better facilitating the exchange of goods.[49]

Unlike the Greeks, the Yugoslavs were eager to take advantage of the nadir in Italo-Albanian relations to improve their political position as well, and Zog, concerned with security, was not unreceptive. There were rumors, emanating from a generally reliably informed French journalist who had accompanied the French Foreign Minister, Louis Barthou, to Belgrade in the summer of 1934, that the trade agreement mentioned above also contained a secret addendum in the form of a military agreement by which Yugoslavia undertook to come to the aid of Tirana if Italy violated her sovereignty. Although no solid evidence has yet been presented to support this allegation, a verbal understanding of some sort may have been reached.[50]

Although their attitude had not always been so positive, the Yugoslavs hoped to draw Albania into the Balkan Alliance. Zog himself had taken the initiative here well before Yugoslav-Albanian relations took a turn for the better by sending a delegate to the meeting of the Council of the first Balkan Conference at Salonica in January of 1931. The King saw the conference first as an opportunity to demonstrate independence in foreign policy and second, as a forum to vent grievances concerning the treatment accorded to Albanian minorities in Greece and Yugoslavia. Zog's involvement was met with little enthusiasm either from the Italians, who were naturally unhappy with the King's little demonstration, or from the Yugoslavs because Albania had not yet broken with Italy.

Despite this cool reception, Albania became even more involved in April 1931 when a subcommittee on municipalities, formed by virtue of a resolution taken at the earlier meeting, came to Tirana. Included were representatives from Turkey, Bulgaria and Greece, the Yugoslavs failing to attend on the pretext that they had not had time to get a delegation together, and the Rumanians sending only their secretary to the legation as an observer. The entire affair seemed to have been a pleasant one and all the delegates seem to have gotten along with one another.

The Albanians were particularly charmed by M. Paraskevopulos, president of the Administrative Council of the Municipality of Athens, an Albanian on his mother's side, who won all hearts by his impromptu discourses in the Albanian language. That the meeting made little progress with regard to civic problems is neither important nor really surprising considering that Albania did not possess any municipalities except in embryo. Indeed, the published records of their proceedings gave no indication of their having at any time touched on municipal questions.[51]

The meeting in April seems to have gone off far too well for it immediately engendered opposition. The chief Albanian delegate Mehmet Bey Konitza, was severely criticized for not having attacked Albania's neighbors on the minorities question and for harboring Serbophile sympathies. Since the strongest attacks against Mehmet Bey came from the Albanian press which had the support of persons in the King's entourage, his fall and the withdrawal of Albania from the conference seemed imminent. Mehmet Bey weathered the storm, however, as a result of his abilities, with some unintentional help from the Yugoslavs who chose that particular moment to despatch a memorandum to the Albania committee taunting them with being an instrument in the hands of Italy.

Mehmet Bey used the opportunity presented by the second Balkan Conference at Istanbul in October 1931 to confound his critics by becoming an ardent debater in favor of the rights of minorities. Ironically, it was just at this point that Italo-Albanian tensions began to occur, resulting in a thaw of Yugoslav-Albanian relations. As soon as Belgrade became convinced that the difficulties were genuine, their attitude towards Albanian participation began to shift until by 1933 Yugoslavia had become one of the chief supporters of Albanian adherence to the planned Balkan Pact of 1934, which had developed as a result of the various conferences.

The remaining Balkan states were also generally in favor of Albania's adherence. The Turkish Minister in Tirana, Russen Esreff Bey, directly attempted to persuade Zog while Turkish diplomats in Paris hoped to win over the Albanian Minister there.[52] Even the Greeks eventually came around although they had been reticent while the school dispute remained unresolved. Once this had been dealt with Athens dropped its opposition but refused to become too vocal in its support, lest the Italians objected.

Albania's adherence to the pact would, however, have been a mixed blessing. On the one hand it would have been a way out for Zog, a way to decrease if not completely eliminate Italian influence. On the other hand, it is questionable whether Albania would have received the needed financial assistance from the Balkans. Albania was miserably poor and the Italians had unwittingly or wittingly ruined Albania's morale by the wastefulness of the methods which Rome had employed. Albania had been reduced to the condition of a mendicant on the dole and nothing had been done to encourage Tirana to stand on its own legs. Albania would have constituted a significant financial burden to any who took it under their wing.

It is doubtful that the Balkan states were qualified to assume the task of guardian. Rumania and Turkey were a long way off and Albania's welfare was of no immediate concern to them. Greece was too concerned about international complications to become too heavily involved. The Yugoslavs, despite their prolific promises concerning the rendering of economic aid, were in the midst of their own fiscal difficulties and the adoption of Albania into the Balkan family would have heaped considerable responsibilities on Belgrade, a situation about which Zog was well aware. As a result of these problems, the chances of Albania joining were never very good.

Zog's various attempts to extricate himself from the economic and political difficulties caused by the break, and particularly his flirtation with the Balkan Alliance, were naturally extremely unsettling to the Italians and encouraged them to redouble their efforts to force or cajol the King to return to the Roman camp.

Several months after Italy's unsuccessful attempt to bring the King around by the use of the fleet in June 1934, Koch asked the Albanian Foreign Minister if he was prepared to begin conversations with a view to settle the dispute. Xhafer Bey Villa replied that he was, whereupon Koch announced that as a condition before further discussions could begin, the Albanian government had to agree to reopen the Catholic demoninational schools. Xhafer Bey naturally refused, since such a concession would not only have again given the Italians the opportunity to do just what the Austrians had done in the past, to foster a Catholic minority and take in under their tutelage, but it would also have required Zog to do the one thing that he could never do, suffer humiliation in the eyes of his people. The conversations with Koch went no further.

At this point Mussolini used an Italian foreign policy tactic which had often been used before and would be used again; i.e., the employment of private intermediaries to conduct secret negotiations behind the backs of those representing official channels. Some time after the cessations of conversations with Koch a special messenger arrived with a memorandum for the King. It was signed by the President of the Italian Chamber of Deputies and two professors. It commenced by deploring the difference of opinion which had arisen between the Italian and Albanian peoples and went on to note that the writers, as friends of both peoples, were willing to act as mediators.

There followed an addendum to the effect that, in the view of the authors, the misunderstanding had come about as a result of the faulty handling of the relations between the two countries by the Foreign Ministries. Signor Mussolini had, it said, expressed his agreement with this pronouncement and had invited the King to come and see him in person, an invitation which Zog declined, stating that he would be pleased to see the Duce but only after some of the outstanding difficulties were solved.[53]

At about the same time an Italian by the name of Rocco asked that the King receive him in person. Rocco, an insurance broker in Durrës, was known to be a secret agent employed by Rome. Zog sent his aide-de-camp, Colonel Sereggi, to see Rocco and the colonel was handed a note from Baron Aliosi. The Baron maintained in his note that since conversations through official channels were liable to be interminable, more private methods should be used. Aloisi asked the King to send a representative to treat with him in secret. Unknown to even the Minister of Foreign Affairs, Zog sent Colonel Sereggi who returned to Albania in late August 1934 with proposals set forth by the Baron. These included:

1. Albania must for the future have no foreign policy of its own, but must take, on all questions a line identical with Italy.
2. It must consent to the Italians having a naval station at Durrës and an air base at Tirana. . . . The army and the gendarmerie must be amalgamated and their training be in Italian hands.
3. All foreign organizers must be dismissed.[54]

In exchange for these concessions the Italians were prepared to:

1. Bring influence to bear at the Vatican with the object of enabling an emissary, whom King Zog would send to Rome, to reach agreement in regard to the question of the denominational schools on terms acceptable to both sides.
2. Concede to Albania a moratorium of ten years on its obligations under the SVEA loan contract, while making a pretense of insisting on her discharging these.
3. Grant a loan of thirty to forty million gold francs for agricultural development in place of the 100 million franc loan which King Zog found the conditions objectionable.
4. Purchase Albanian produce on the same terms as were extended to Austria and Hungary.[55]

The Baron, indicative of his style of diplomacy, strongly urged the necessity of pushing on the discussions as rapidly as possible and wanted to send over a special envoy to conduct the negotiations. Zog, however, would not be pushed into such an agreement; in fact he had no intention of accepting it at all. The King was clever enough to realize that although the Italians had dropped their insistence that the denominational schools be opened immediately, Aloisi's package would have stripped Albania not only of its power to maneuver but of its independence as well. Zog decided to bide his time and wait, in the hope that Mussolini might soften his demands.

Zog's political intuition once more stood him in good stead for in 1935 Mussolini not only offered a series of proposals that were a good deal less onerous, but the Duce began the year by presenting Zog with the one gesture of conciliation always the closest to the Albanian King's heart, namely a cash gift. In December 1934 rumors began to circulate regarding the mysterious transfer of from between one and three million gold francs from Italy to Albania for unspecified purposes. Finally on January 23, 1935, an announcement appeared in the Albanian press to the effect that,

> the Italian government, in order to enable Albania to liquidate a part of the arrears resulting from expenditures in connection with past extraordinary budgets, have been so good as to place at the disposal of the Royal Albanian government spontaneously and as a mark of the warm friendship existing between the two states, a sum of three million gold francs.[56]

The official explanation invented by the Albanians to sooth their pride was that the gift represented a payment which they had a perfect right to demand. Italy in 1932-1933, instead of handing over ten million gold francs, being the years installment of the one hundred million loan, had only paid seven million. In making up the difference, Rome was only making good on past promises.

In actuality the gift was neither a legitimate payment nor spontaneous. Rather, it was an attempt on the part of Mussolini to direct the King away from the Yugoslavs who had just offered to loan Zog three million at reasonable interest. The Duce offered the money with the stipulation that Zog immediately cease negotiations for the Yugoslav loan.[57] The King, already beyond the end of his financial rope and never very enthusiastic or optimistic about the Yugoslav connection, decided to accept and with the money paid the salaries of state employees who had not been paid for at least six months.

In April 1935 the Italians, who had never really accepted the King's argument that the Albanian army needed to be reduced for financial

finally admitted that Albania was too poor to support a military establishment of any importance. This realization was seen as another indication
that the Italians might be softening their hard line position on Albania.
A few months later, in June, Rome presented a new set of proposals, this
time by way of the new Italian Minister, Indelli, who had replaced the
rather unsuccessful Koch in the autumn of 1934.

Zog was no longer called to relinquish the right to conduct his own
foreign policy, nor was he compelled to dismiss his foreign organizers.
Rome would expect that the King spend no more than five million gold
francs annually on armaments. In the matter of the Catholic schools, an
arrangement was suggested which though in substance would have constituted a departure from the principle of the government monopoly of
education, would at least have saved appearances. The seminaries in
Shkodër would be allowed to reopen and to receive and educate children
who were not intended for the priesthood while the Albanian goverment
would not be required to recognize the certificates issued by these institutions to their pupils. As for the Italian industrial schools which the
Albanians had closed, they too would be allowed to reopen with their
Italian technical staffs, though formally they would be classified as state
schools.

Another condition had to do with an Italian experimental farm near
Durrës for which an extension of territory was demanded with the proviso that the Agrarian Reform Law should not be put into operation
upon the extension and that the use of imported Italian labor be permitted. An additional area was to be placed at the disposal of the Italian
firm exploiting the Devoli oil fields. Finally, and this was the crucial
condition on which the entire proposition hinged, the Italians demanded
that the port of Durrës be put into their hands for a period of forty years
to be equipped and deepened so as to fit it to accommodate ocean-going
shipping.

The Italians were prepared to be generous in return. They were willing
to allow the matter of Albania's indebtedness to SVEA to stand for five
years during which time the Albanians would be expected to study a basis
for an ultimate settlement. Secondly, Rome would undertake to pay
each year an advance of two million gold francs on account for expected
royalties from oil production. Thirdly, they would make an annual grant,
for five years, of 3.5 million gold francs together with three million gold

francs with which to make good budget deficits. Lastly, the Italians agreed to place at the disposal of the Albanian government a lump sum of eight million gold francs representing the difference between the sum of the partly paid up annual installments on account of the one hundred million gold franc loan and the total amount they would have had to pay had the loan agreement continued in operation.[58]

Once again the King felt he could afford to wait on most of these proposals, particularly since many of them were unacceptable. If he had agreed, Albania would have been put in precisely the same state of financial dependence on Italy as followed the 1931 loan agreement. Italy could once again cut off the subsidy at any time, crippling the Albanian economy. The most serious concern in the new package, however, was the proposed Durrës harbor project. The harbor had a depth of 7.5 meters at the entrance and seven meters alongside the quay, which was more than sufficient for the coast shipping which used the port. Apart from an occasional tourist steamer which landed its passengers by boat, no ship of great size ever called at Durrës.[59] Nor was there the remotest prospect of trade increasing to the point where ocean-going vessels would want to use the port. Italy was clearly not thinking in terms of the needs of its merchant marine.

Rome was obviously in search of a naval base capable of accommodating ships of war. Since the withdrawal of General Pariani and the end of the military subsidies to Tirana, the Albanian army had deteriorated quite significantly. Italy's ability to control military affairs in Albania had declined concurrently. The suggestion for the port, then, was an attempt on the part of Rome to adjust to the changing situation by strengthening its position on the coast to make up for what it lost elsewhere.

Italian efforts were not completely fruitless this time, however, since Zog accepted their compromise dealing with both the denominational and technical schools, a move which constituted the first clear indication that a thaw in Italo-Albanian relations had finally set in, for it was this issue which had for so long kept the two sides apart. Zog could never have given in completely on this point without suffering a drastic loss in domestic prestige. The new Italian proposals essentially offered both sides the opportunity to gracefully withdraw, ruffling the feathers of only the most uncompromising nationalists.

Following the school settlement, a number of other events confirmed the fact that the former was more than just an isolated agreement. In October Zog made the important decision not to support sanctions against the Italians, an issue which the League of Nations had taken up in response to Mussolini's invasion of Ethiopia. After the move, the King took pains to declare his loyalty to the ideals of the League in an attempt to keep his feet in both camps while moving closer to Italy.

His declarations were in vain, however, for international reaction was all negative. Yugoslavia abruptly terminated conversations which were to lead to Albania's adherence to the Balkan Pact. But Zog's choice was rather clear since the League had been of little or no economic help and the Yugoslavs, despite their profuse promises, had done next to nothing. Instead of buying 2.5 million gold francs worth of Albanian goods annually, as they had proposed to do, they imported only 60,000 gold francs worth.[60] The export bank which they opened did nothing while their vague offers of assistance in the economic field remained completely unfulfilled.

Zog undoubtedly reasoned that Italy was in need of friends and would be well disposed to be more reasonable with regard to earlier demands if this gesture of friendship were made. It might also have occurred to the King that the Duce's aggressive imperialism could very easily be turned against Albania.

Whether out of fear or calculation, the rapprochement continued apace. Shortly following the decision on sanctions a Tirana newspaper, the *Arbenia,* was suspended for printing anti-Italian articles, something for which the editor would have been congratulated a year earlier. In response to a message of congratulations from Mussolini on the occasion of the 23rd anniversary of Albanian independence, Zog's new Prime Minister, Mehdi Bey Frasheri, sent an overly sentimental reply. The Prime Minister wrote that the Duce's words "fill our hearts with gratitude towards the noble Italian nation, our friend and ally, and towards the Fascist government."[61]

The editor of the newspaper *Besa* meanwhile commented that,

> King Zog himself in his message to the Chamber, the government in its declaration of policy, the Chamber in its reply, solemnly declare and reiterate that we shall be faithful and unswerving in relation of

our alliance with Italy. We have given a magnificent and chivalrous example at a moment of crisis, in the darkest and most disappointing hour for the Italian people, by holding out a hand to support it in its time of trial; by manfully standing by Italy as her friends and allies we associated ourselves with her sorrow. Our behavior is the most eloquent and incontrovertible proof that we stand by our pledged word to maintain our friendship with Fascist Italy in loyal collaboration with mutual solidarity.[62]

Despite its ring of unblushing insincerity, articles such as the one quoted above helped Mussolini, who too was in need of friends, decide to extend further gestures of reciprocation. The marriage of one of the King's sisters provided him with an ideal opportunity to do so.

In early January 1936 it was announced that the Princess Senije was to marry Prince Abid of Turkey, a law student in Paris and the youngest son of the late Sultan Abdul Hamid II. As it was an official wedding, the diplomatic corps was invited, the Albanians making certain to inform the Turkish Minister well in advance of his colleagues so that he could arrange for a decent absence from the festivities. The Turkish government was far from satisfied and suggested to the members of the Balkan Pact and the Little Entente that their Ministers should boycott the proceedings. Responding to the call, the Greek and Rumanian Ministers left Albania while the Yugoslav and Czech representatives declared that they were indisposed.[63]

The reasons for this action remain obscure. To think that Zog might have been involved in some Hamidian intrigue is somewhat far-fetched. Even if he was, the marriage of an Albanian princess to a junior and insignificant son of the most detested of Sultans could not possibly have served the lost cause of the House of Osman in Turkey. The idea that the King might have made Abid his heir is equally ridiculous. No choice would have been less popular in Albania even if the King could have gotten around the constitutional rule which precluded the succession of any person not of Albanian origin. Zog probably approved the marriage in order to associate his house with one of imperial standing and simply to take care of one of his sisters who according to the Almanach de Gotha was born in 1908, but who was believed to be considerably older.

Zog was incensed by the discourtesy shown him. The rather foolish demonstration basically finished the chances of Albania subscribing to the Balkan Pact. He demanded and was given satisfaction. The last of the Ministers involved was removed in August of 1936. The Italians in the meantime had staunchly supported the position of the King seeing an opportunity to put an end to the speculation concerning Albania's adherence to the Balkan Pact as well as to show Zog that he could still count on Rome. Italy was rewarded by a speech presented by the Vice-President of the Parliament as the newlyweds left for Bari. Italy, its fascism and its Duce were praised in language so ardent as to embarrass the Prime Minister and the Minister of Foreign Affairs.

The time for a full reconciliation had come. Zog's financial situation had never been more critical, the chiefs had not been paid for some time. The King's hopes for assistance from his immediate neighbors or from Western Europe had come to naught. He knew he would eventually be forced back into the Italian fold and the middle of 1936 at least appeared to be a good time for it. Italy was more conciliatory, at least outwardly, and was in need of some support, however small. Most importantly, Italy had seemingly given up some of its unacceptable demands.

In March 1936 a new comprehensive agreement was finally announced which addressed itself to virtually every outstanding problem existing between Albania and Italy. The 1931 loan was cancelled as of April 1933. The SVEA loan was dealt with in an exchange of notes by which the Italian government undertook to effect an arrangement under which Albania was to provide in her budget 250,000 gold francs a year for five years towards the service of the loan. The Italians maintained that these payments would not be insisted upon as long as Albania found itself in financial difficulties. The Albanian government, to whom Italy promised full support, was to negotiate within two years of the exchange of notes, a settlement with SVEA for the "complete systematisation of the burden resulting from the loan, having due regard to Albania's possibilities."[64]

In order to deal with Zog's tragic economic difficulties, the Italians agreed to make good deficits in the Albanian budget up to the end of the financial year 1934-1935 for which Italy would provide a sum of nine million gold francs including the three million advanced in 1935. Of the balance of six million, a sum of 3,200,000 was to be paid within two months of the entry into force of the agreement. The remainder was to be applied to the reconstitution of the projected agricultural bank over a three-year period. All of these payments were to be a free gift to the Albanian government.

Further, Italy agreed to lend to Albania a sum of ten million gold francs for agricultural development in five installments of two million, the first to be paid two months after the entry into force of the agreements, the rest at yearly intervals. The cost of the materials to be bought in Italy was to be deducted from the first installment and Albania undertook to devote not less than 500,000 gold francs out of each subsequent installment for the purchase of similar supplies in Italy. Zog was required to pay one percent interest on this loan and his government was to provide for a sinking fund by paying annuities of 275,900 gold francs for fifty years beginning in 1945-1946. The annuities were to be obtained from money paid to the Albanian government by a company formed by the Italian State Railroads to exploit oil in Albania.

Finally, Italy undertook to lend three million gold francs, with no interest, for the creation of a State Tobacco Monopoly in two equal payments, the first to be paid within two months of the entry into force of the agreements and the second a year later. The loan was to be repaid in fifteen annual installments of 200,000 gold francs secured on the assets of the monopoly, beginning in 1940-1941. The Albanian government agreed to rely exclusively on Italian financial and technical assistance in organizing the working the monopoly.

Although Zog and Frasheri fervently denied it and while the actual text in nowhere to be found, it is likely that the agreements also included secret military features of a comprehensive nature. The British contend that it is "fairly probable" that Italy gave the Albanians a secret subsidy of 3.5 million gold francs for military expenditures. Both Athens and Belgrade were convinced of the existence of such a stipulation and one Yugoslav historian, Z. Avramovski in his work *Italijanska ekonomska penetracija u Albaniju,* produced various provisions of the supposed agreement. The Albanian Minister of Finance at the time, Mr. Berati, in an interview given after the war, also argued that such a secret provision did in fact exist.[65]

In exchange for these financial considerations, the Albanians agreed to grant Italy a series of concessions including one dealing with the harbor at Durrës. Zog allowed Rome to form a corporation to finance the further development of the port. This organization, which was to remain in operation for fifteen years and was to be run by an Italian, obtained a loan of approximately four million gold francs from the Bank of Naples to conduct works "of a purely commercial character." The loan was to bear interest at one percent and was to be prepaid in twenty-five half-yearly installments to begin after the completion of the work. Zog also agreed to allow the Italian experimental farm further use of various tracts of land in the Durrës area.[66]

Zog did very well by these new agreements. The King's obstructiveness had its rewards for he had at last succeeded in extracting money from the Italians without committing himself to engagements which seriously encroached on Albanian sovereignty. Unlike the agreements of 1931, the new agreements contained no stipulations requiring Albania to merge its foreign policy with that of Italy and to accept Italian guidance in all technical matters. Nor were they as onerous as those presented by Baron Aloisi in 1934 requiring Albania to give up any notion of an independent foreign policy and dismiss all foreign organizers. Zog was also not required, as the 1935 proposals suggested, to allow Italian peasants to be settled on the Italian experimental farm or to lease the port of Durrës for forty years on a concession basis.

None of these earlier demands figures into the 1936 agreement. In general, the new relationship was to be based on a much more businesslike nature, with most of the loans carrying at least minimal interest and geared towards the creation of a healthy economy in Albania, something which the Italians had always been unwilling to do.

Naturally enough, the agreement was not free of blemishes. One obvious weakness was that the prospective payments were in the form of annuities extending over a five-year period, allowing the Duce, at any time that suited his convenience or on any pretext, to suspend payments as a means of bringing pressure to bear on the Albanians. Albania's position with regard to SVEA remained unsatisfactory. Although the Italians granted a virtual moratorium of five years, they did not abandon their rights and were still therefore in a position to use SVEA as a stick with which to beat the Albanians in the event of fresh quarrels.

The fifteen year Durrës harbor concession could but lead to serious problems with Albania's neighbors and certainly finished the remaining slim prospects that Zog might come to some agreement with the Balkan Pact, if indeed these hopes were not already dead. Clearly, every time Zog accepted economic aid from Rome and the Italian investment in Albania increased, his field of maneuver was narrowed.

While foreign reaction was generally hostile and suspicious, except for the British, domestic reaction was mixed. The unanimity with which the

Parliament voted in favor of the agreement, the enthusiasm with which it vibrated when the measure of the Duce's generosity was communicated to it meant nothing, considering that the deputies had been carefully primed beforehand by the President of the Parliament. Although this reaction was totally expected, the Italophiles within the body were of course pleased with the agreement, believing that Albania's only hope lay in close relations with Italy. Many of the remaining deputies, too, supported the new agreements because they saw pickings for themselves. Also generally in favor were the commercial interests who saw the possibility of resurrecting the Albanian economy by the influx of money and the revival of trade.[67]

Approval was by no means universal. No one who had disliked the Italians previously suddenly learned to appreciate them. Those elements which had been the most staunchly opposed to Italian penetration were again wary. The conservative Moslem landowners were concerned about the reconstruction of the agricultural bank, a necessary prerequisite for the long overdue introduction of some type of land reform to deal with the peasant problem.

Among the enlightened nationalist elements, few were in favor of the new agreements despite the fact that many were aware of Albania's financial condition. These people foresaw the reoccurrence of a familiar pattern, more money for the military, more reliance on Italy. Although not as much emphasis was put on the army as had been put on it in the past, the Albanian budgets of 1937 and 1938 to a certain extent justified the fears of the enlightened Albanians who felt that their country's independence was once again being threatened.

The reaction of the general population was, as usual, difficult to judge since they still had no clear means by which to make their feelings known. One can assume, however, that although they were somewhat in the dark about the implications of the agreements, they were passively hostile, based upon their general distrust of anything the Tirana government did and based upon the fact that dislike and distrust of Italy had always come instinctively to them.

CHAPTER ELEVEN

INTERNAL DEVELOPMENT,
"TOWARDS OCCIDENTAL CULTURE AND CIVILIZATION"

During the long hard years of the Italo-Albanian conflict Zog slowly moved ahead on his attempt to pull Albania out of the fifteenth century and force it into the twentieth. The King showed a good deal of determination here, considering the conservative nature of the Albanian peasantry and the economic hardship which the conflict with Italy and domestic corruption had caused. Zog's domestic policies during this period indicate the confidence which the King had in his own abilities to maintain tranquillity. For the most part, his confidence was not misplaced, as the years from 1932 to the late 1930s were remarkably quiet for a country accustomed to continual political upheaval. It would, however, have been too much to expect all elements of Albanian society to remain absolutely still during these critical years. The King was faced with a series of minor disturbances which were not always handled wisely.

The first of these unfortunate incidents was probably the least dangerous and yet was rather brutally repressed. In the summer of 1932 a bandit by the name of Idriz Iaso, wanted for a number of years for murder in a blood feud, was finally arrested. In order to save his own life, Iaso turned government informer disclosing the existence of a plot against the government involving a number of people whom he apparently had hoped to murder.

Within ten days over one hundred people found themselves in prison. This group included highly placed government officials, former officials, a judge, two doctors, two Moslem holymen, lawyers, teachers and business people all of whom were primarily from the south. Among those sought in connection with the supposed conspiracy were K. Chekrezi, the Vice-President of the Council of State and Kiamil Vlora, the director of the consulate division of the Foreign Ministry and son of Ismail Kemal Bey Vlora, the father of the modern Albanian state. While Chekrezi was eventually apprehended, Vlora fled the country to avoid arrest.[1]

Forty-nine were eventually brought to trial before the political court in Tirana where they were accused of forming a secret society which intended to overthrow Zog's regime in conjunction with political refugees supported by a foreign consulate in Vlorë. The prosecution argued that the Yugoslav Consul in Vlorë had promised this group 45,000 napoleons, 5,000 of which had supposedly been paid, in order to topple the regime. Once the government had been done away with, the group was to set up a dictatorial republic and liberally use terrorism to rid themselves of the remnants of Zog's followers. Krossi was apparently slated to be one of their first victims.[2]

Despite the fact that the prisoners behaved badly, vying with one another in expansiveness as to the culpability of their fellows, the government had a remarkably weak case and had blown the entire incident out of proportion. The court's case was weak basically because no such broad well-organized revolutionary plot ever existed.

They had arrested a group of Vlorë intellectuals who had, primarily out of patriotism, organized in December 1930 in the midst of rumors of Zog's imminent death in order to forestall an Italian takeover of Albania. When the King did not die, the unarmed loose organization simply went to earth in Vlorë but continued to maintain at least a certain vitality. It apparently was partially resurrected in 1932 for the purpose of organizing propaganda for the upcoming election. The group was so innocuous, however, that even the local gendarmerie was totally unaware of its existence until the advent of Idriz Iaso.

The group was not even directly opposed to the King, rather, they feared Italian penetration and were opposed to the old Turkish types like Krossi who had become known as the "Besa group" based upon their control of the newspaper *Besa* in Tirana. Although the conduct of the intellectuals was ill-advised, they had done nothing more serious than the dramatic move of swearing on the butt of a gun to save Albania from the

Italians and the Besa group. Even members of the government admitted in private that the conspiracy was of little importance and that the conspirators were guilty only of having made fools of themselves.

Popular opinion in Tirana was in favor either of clemency or discharge with a caution. It was public knowledge that even Major Bilol Nevica, the president of the Political Court, was against anything more than light sentences. Shock was the general reaction, therefore, when of the forty-nine, seven were condemned to death, twelve to 101 years imprisonment and fifteen to fifteen years imprisonment.

The King further compounded his blunders by waiting for many weeks before commuting the death sentences to life imprisonment.[3] The delay allowed the Italians, who were certain that the King would eventually make the concession, enough time to spread the story that Mussolini had intervened personally in order to secure a reprieve and that Zog had only granted it under pressure. The King had handled the entire situation miserably.

Zog himself, supported by his close associates and the Italians, was behind the ferocity of the sentences. Rome, at that point represented by Count Barbarich who was described as an indiscreet dilettante, favored the death sentences apparently based upon the anti-Italian character of the organization. Also in favor of death were Ekrem Libohova the Minister of the Court who was still in the pay of Rome, and of course, Krossi who saw any enlightened group as a threat to his political dominance. Zog's motives stemmed from the fact that many of the participants were members of the old clique, the group which had caused him so much trouble in the 1920s. The King believed that stern repression was necessary to prevent the birth of a new clique.[4] Zog hoped to nip any opposition in the bud as quickly as possible, fearing that political disenchantment might easily link up with the economic disenchantment which was growing as a result of the cessation of Italian loans.

Zog, ever suspicious, was not content to confine his retribution to what he thought was internal opposition. Accepting his own propaganda regarding the involvement of emigres, the King apparently saw to the removal of one of the last significant emigre leaders, Hasan Bey Prishtina. The old chieftain, who had been Prime Minister for two days in 1924, had remained a staunch irredentist and a confirmed enemy of Zog. The active animosity between Zog and Prishtina had resulted in a series of assassination attempts, with Prishtina even being implicated in the 1931 shootout in Vienna.[5]

In early 1933 a certain Hysejn Ibrahim Celo appeared in Vienna asking for the whereabouts of Prishtina, who supposedly owned him a great deal of money. Celo finally found the old man in Salonica and there shot him to death, bringing the game to a violent end. The assassin maintained that his action was motivated by a blood feud stemming from the execution of Celo's brother, for which Pristhina was supposedly responsible.

The Greek press initially reported that Prishtina was killed after Celo had asked him to plot against Zog and Hasan Bey had refused. Later newspaper stores had it that the old man was killed because he had plotted against Zog. It was freely suggested in Tirana, however, that Zog had personally sent Celo to shoot his old enemy Prishtina and this remains the most plausible of the various arguments.[6]

Zog's campaign of domestic and foreign terror had damaged his own position. By dealing with these problems as a serious crisis, the King had created the impression abroad that Albania was seething with revolution, something which, to his credit, was not true. It had been five years since a serious revolt had disturbed the Albanians.

Soon after the debacle of the Vlorë conspiracy, the unfortunate Zog was faced with another incident which further damaged his prestige. A series of revenue frauds dealing with tobacco prices were discovered. As usual, members of the Council of Ministers were immediately implicated. The King was reportedly furious but, once again, he remained loyal. The chief offenders went unpunished.

With all of these difficulties added to the economic crisis, the King was in need of something which might improve his flagging image. The general elections announced by Royal decree on August 28, 1932, gave him his opportunity. This was to be the first election of the Monarchy since the Constituent Assembly was elected. Since that Assembly had simply constituted itself into a Parliament, Albania's new electoral law had not yet been tested. Under the new structure all males eighteen years of age were entitled to vote as first electors for the second electors, of whom the number was fixed on the basis of one to every 250 people. The second electors returned the deputies.

The first elections began on September 9 and were completed within the statutory twenty-five days. The paper *Besa* proudly announced that some 90 percent of the electorate had participated in the election when in fact only about 10 percent, encouraged by the police and the gendarmerie, actually voted. The numbers were low as usual because most everyone assumed that the candidates for whom the electors would be permitted to cast their votes could not be other than those whom the local authorities regarded as suitable.

The second elections, however, witnessed an innovation. On November 2 it was announced that no list of government approved candidates would be presented. The order went out that the electorate should be at liberty to return whomever they pleased.[8]

Zog's rather novel decision came about as a result of a number of factors, not the least of which was the exasperation caused by the wrangling of his Ministers and members of his entourage as to who was to be included on the official list. Zog hoped, furthermore, that his magnanimity might mitigate some of the ill effects of the problems which he had caused. The King was also taking an important step towards his cherished goal of modernization.

Despite the innovation, the election was, as always, basically a farce. The short space of time between November 2, when the decision to hold free elections was made, and November 11, when the second elections were held, was insufficient to allow anything in the way of an electoral campaign to be organized. Of the fifty-eight deputies returned, therefore, only sixteen were new and all of the new members could be counted on to support the government. Even so, something important was done here, a principle was established. A definite step in the direction of free representation had been proclaimed.[9] Albania was not really ready to go much further in 1932.

With the new elections, the Council of Ministers tendered its resignation and Zog, in no great hurry, constructed a new government three months later. Few changes were made; Prime Minister Evangjeli and Minister of the Interior Juka continued to dominate. Evangjeli, of advancing years, (he clung tenaciously to an admitted seventy-three) was in ill health. His colleagues complained of his growing tendency to be secretive and that it was becoming more and more difficult to extort a decision from him. His forgetfulness was also beginning to impair his usefulness. Juka still possessed a strong if unscrupulous hand, an intimate knowledge, acquired by quite indefensible methods, of the inner life of the country, and the primary virtue of loyalty to his master.

Three Ministers in the new government had never held ministerial rank before. Xhafer Bey Villa, the new Foreign Minister, had good qualifications for his post. For some time he had been Secretary-General of the Ministry, then Minister in Belgrade and Minister in Athens. He was pleasant and affable and in normal times would have made a reasonable Foreign Minister. But the times were abnormal because of the problems with Italy and since he possessed neither the effrontery of Raouf Fitso nor the bland ignorance of Hysejn Bey Vrioni, his immediate predecessors, Villa found the task thrust upon him to be beyond his powers.[10]

Also new was the Minister of Public Works, Sander Saracci, who had served as the Secretary-General in the Ministry. Incorruptibility was apparently not his strongest virtue but since his department had little or no money owing to the stoppage of Italian financing, circumstances were not favorable to the indulgence of any weakness he may have had in this respect.[11] The other newcomer, Mirosh Ivanaj, the Minister of Public Instruction, who began his ministry with an attack on Catholic schools, has already been described.[12]

The new government, then, was composed basically of old hands who were ready to carry out Zog's orders to the letter. Their complete lack of independent initiative was made amply clear by the fact that long periods frequently went by without a cabinet meeting. In November 1933 Villa informed the Greek Minister that he had not seen the King from two weeks and that the cabinet had not met for three.[13]

Not surprisingly, the new government did little to discourage Zog's often reckless approach to administration. The campaign to nationalize education, which particularly hit the Grecophone villages in the south, resulted in some agitation throughout 1934, mitigated only by the fact that the prefect of Gjirokastër, the center of the affected area, was a capable and kindly official. His calming influence and the efforts of the Greek government to restrain bands of Greek volunteers poised on the border, prevented bloodshed. In the north a strike of school children resulted after the prefect of Shkodër, on his own initiative, placed a ban on religious teaching. The grievance was immediately removed and the strike, the most serious manifestation of unrest in the north during the period of the Italo-Albanian dispute, came to an abrupt end.

In late 1934 a rather comical incident occurred which because of over-reaction on the part of the government, was interpreted abroad as another Albanian revolution. The problem involved Muharrem Bajraktari, originally a Serbian officer whom Zog had recalled to Albanian in 1922 to assist in organizing the gendarmerie. Bajraktari joined Zog in exile in

Belgrade in 1924 and upon the overthrow of Noli was rewarded with the rank of major and the post of prefect. Because he used his post to extract money from the people in order to strengthen his own position among the northern chiefs, and because he was behaving basically like an independent pasha, Zog was forced to recall him to Tirana.

The King, ever loyal to supporters regardless of how harmful their presence was to his own position, appointed Muharrem to be Commandant of the Gendarmerie, leading General Percy, who was appalled by the corruption, to tender his resignation. Once again Muharrem was transferred, this time becoming Zog's personal adjutant. While in this position, in late 1934, Bajraktari was apparently responsible for some unspecified act of treachery which Zog chose to overlook.[14] Krossi and Juka, and the remainder of the Royal entourage, were not prepared to be quite as generous.

Soon afterwards, Bajraktari maintained that an officer in the Royal Guard attempted to murder him. Muharrem actually captured the supposed would-be assassin and turned him over to the King for punishment. Much to his dismay, Zog released the officer, explaining that no harm was meant. Muharrem immediately requested permission to take a leave and hurried off to Lumë, his original home.

Upon the death of his mother in October 1934, Zog called Muharrem back to Tirana. Bajraktari refused to obey, having become obsessed with the idea that a plot existed at the palace to assassinate him. The simple act of insubordination was eventually magnified into a revolution by Interior Minister Juka who had received questionable reports form his agents to the effect that Muharrem was conspiring with his neighbors in the mountains to organize a rising to overthrow the government.[15]

Not content with relying on the 150 gendarms in the area, Juka mobilized two battalions of infantry and despatched one of them to support the gendarms. Muharrem, on the approach of this army, did what might have been expected of him under the circumstances; he fled to Yugoslavia. The result of Juka's folly was, first the expense of mobilizing two battalions, and more seriously, an excuse for the sensational press abroad to report another revolution in Albania.[16]

Nineteen thirty-five brought probably the most serious threat to Zog's government during this period, and yet by the standard of the 1920s revolts, it was harmless. Seemingly unable to learn from mistakes, the government again seriously overreacted and Zog tried once more to make up for his indiscretion by granting political concessions. The rather pathetic uprising, later known as the Fier revolt, occurred in the middle of August and was led by Kosta Chekrezi, the Albanian journalist and politician who had been released in February 1935 for his part in the so-called Vlorë plot of 1932. Chekrezi was assisted by a certain Musa Kranja, a lieutenant of the gendarmerie who, in the absence of the regular commandant, was in charge of the gendarmerie post at Fier.

Kranja had let it be known in the surrounding villages on August 13 that all those liable for military service were to assemble in the market-place the following morning for an announcement. When the villagers had assembled, Chekrezi addressed them and stated that a revolutionary government was already in power in Tirana and that he had been sent to Fier as the representative of the new government. Kranja then made a speech inviting those present to give their adherence to the new regime. Approximately 150 people, including many refugees from Kosovo whom the Albanian government had settled on the land near Fier, decided to support the revolutionary government, including the fifteen gendarmes who were prepared to follow their officer.

At that point General Leon Ghelardi, third in the military hierarchy in Albania commanding the army group at Berat, happened to pass through Fier on a private visit to Pojan. Seeing an unusual assembly, the general stopped his car to make inquiries and he and his orderly were immediately set upon and shot.

Musa Kranja then left a handful of men in Fier and he and Chekrezi marched on Lushnjë with a force of 130. Upon their arrival, the local gendarmerie and the inhabitants decided to oppose their advance and an exchange of gunfire took place but without any casualties. The revolutionaries decided to return to Fier.

Meanwhile, news of what had occurred had reached Tirana and half a battalion of troops from the capital and one battalion from Elbasan were ordered to Lushnjë. On arrival they found that all was quiet and so went on to Fier which they reached on the morning of August 15. At the approach of the government troops, Chekrezi and Kranja, with two or three others, fled to the coast and embarked on an Italian fishing boat near the mouth of the Semeni River. A few of the insurgents fled into the hills but the majority surrendered to the troops without offering any resistance.[17] Had it not been for the death of General Ghilardi, the whole affair would have appeared rather ludicrous.

Zog was again taken by surprise and he struck out almost in panic. Juka was unleashed and more troops were hurried to the spot. Indiscriminate arrests, numbering one thousand or more, were made and a special military tribunal was immediately set up in Fier. What was expected of it was obvious from its composition. Of the three members, one was a former Turkish officer named Topoli, as ferocious as he was ignorant; another an ex-gendarmerie captain who had only emerged a short time before from the lunatic asylum at Vlorë. A reign of terror ensued, brutal and senseless; prisoners were tortured and most elementary safeguards for the dispensing of justice were ignored.[18] The Fier trials constituted the worst such episode in Zog's Albania.

A series of five trials were staged to deal with the 530 who were eventually brought before the court. The first group to appear included the gendarmes, some of whom were responsible for the death of General Ghilardi. Within a matter of hours, eleven gendarmes were sentenced to death and executed. Several of the boys among the eleven were apparently quite unaware that the operations they had taken part in had any revolutionary character, believing instead that they were acting under the orders of the government to suppress a seditious movement at Lushnjë. The court decided, however, that they mere fact that they had discharged their rifles against the Lushjnë force constituted evidence of their intention to act against the government.[19]

The other trials dealt with the civilian elements involved and produced another forty-two death sentences as well as 160 sentences of life imprisonment. Among those convicted were members of the major families of the area including Nuredin Bey Vlora, son of Abdul Hamid's last Grand Vizier, and members of the Dibra family. Almost no firsthand evidence was produced against any of these defendents, the court being satisfied with second or third-hand hearsay. Even the hearsay indicated only general discontent with the government and more particularly with certain individuals such as Musa Juka, Zhemal Aranitas and of course the ever-unpopular Krossi.

A number of persons were approached by the actual ringleaders of the Fier incident to know whether they would rise in revolt, and, although they did not join the movement, they failed to notify the authorities.

This inaction was sufficient to obtain their condemnation by the court. Others were condemned on the strength of their names appearing on lists at Fier of people who were expected to throw in their lot with the revolutionaries in the event of the movement spreading to their districts.[20]

Not content with just terrorizing the population in and around Fier, Zog decided in the beginning of October to stage a massive mobilization of Albania's armed forces, presumably in an attempt to intimidate the rest of the people of the country. The first reports from Belgrade mentioned the mobilization of some 40,000 which seems highly unlikely since Albania did not have that many reserves. Later estimates ranged from 1,500 the number which Zog himself presented, to 15,000, the figure suggested by the Commander of the Gendarmerie.[21] Whatever the final figure, Zog's move was most unusual, considering that he informed neither the cabinet nor the Chief of the General Staff. The episode did little more than put yet another burden on Albania's finances.

It was difficult for Zog to defend the rather extreme measures connected with the Fier revolt. The King eventually did what most leaders do when faced with internal difficulties, he blamed an international conspiracy. The newspaper *Besa* desperately but unsuccessfully attempted to connect those arrested with communism. Zog himself seemed convinced that the Italians were behind the uprising and indeed this belief probably helped to break down his resistance to signing a new pact with Rome. This view was logical and widely accepted in Tirana, and yet, beyond the fact that a boat was lying in an unusual place near the scene of the outbreak and that the insurgent leaders made their escape by its help, no known circumstances incriminated the Italians.[22]

Zog had overreacted. Whether or not the Italians were involved, the revolt was such a miserable failure that only minimal attention to it was warranted. Few Albanians supported it. The northern tribes remained loyal. The chief of the Mirditë, Mark Gjonmarkaj, and other leaders had immediately, upon hearing of the event, wired to the King expressing loyalty and placing armed men at his disposal.

Whatever differences of opinion and whatever discontent existed in the country, all Albanians remained very jealous of the independence of their country. Most realized that any serious internal disturbances would only provoke interference from outside. It was also still univerally recognized that Zog was the only individual capable of commanding the loyalty of the different elements of Albania. As a result, while he alone was in fact responsible for the government and its many shortcomings, discontent was still directed almost exclusively against the cabinet and not against the King.

As if he recognized that a temporary lapse in sanity had occurred, Zog began to make amends for his unfortunate actions. All but one of the forty-two had had been sentenced to death had their sentences commuted to 101 years imprisonment. As in the past, few of those condemned to 101 years served more than a few years. In fact, Zog reduced most of these sentences as early as December 1935.

The King's greatest concession, however, was the construction of a new, relatively liberal, government under Mehdi Bey Frasheri in the middle of October 1935. The appointment of Mehdi Bey as Prime Minister constituted a significant break from Albania's political past. Frasheri, who for years had been Albania's representative to the League of Nations, was an attractive figure with progressive ideas with regard to both domestic and foreign policy. He was a good speaker, well served by an extremely retentive memory and stood out as having received a thorough education in the Turkish schools. He was a historian of some merit, an erudite jurist and most significantly, his honesty was above suspicion.[23]

Mehdi Bey maintained none of the cabinet officers of Evangjeli's last government. The Besa group, including Juka, Dibra and Krossi, were finally excluded from significant positions. They were replaced by a group of youthful Ministers, who, though they had never held office before, brought with them solid educations and a healthy desire to dig the Albanian administration out of the hole it had fallen into and to endow it with order and efficiency. The new Minister of the Interior, Ethem Toto, was honest and poor while the new Foreign Minister, Fuad Aslani, was described as able and intelligent.[24] The new government was greeted with general relief and a good deal of popular sympathy.

The new cabinet's program, as presented to the Parliament on October 26, clearly indicated the direction in which it hoped to propel the country. In foreign affairs, Mehdi Bey realistically called for a closer relationship with Italy while at the same time declaring respect for the League of Nations as "the great international institution which confirmed our independence and our integrity after the Great War."[25]

With regard to internal affairs, the new government pledged to improve and consolidate the administration and develop art, culture, education and morality. Nepotism and corruption was to be rooted out and the independence of the judiciary protected. In matters of finance it would observe the Albanian adage, "not to stretch the legs beyond the quilt," and in regard to public works and the national economy it intended, while paying due heed to limitations imposed by the paucity of means available, to do what was possible in order to develop the road system, encourage and systematize production and organize agriculture. The crowning feature of the program was actually an omission: nothing was said about the country's armed forces.[26]

Considering the ambitious nature of the program, it is not surprising that the new government quickly made many enemies and ultimately scored few successes. In fact, the only major success for Mehdi Bey and his young colleagues was negotiating the 1936 financial agreements with Italy, for which they were unjustly criticized.

Serious problems soon developed between the liberal government and the old gang Parliament which contained many of the members of Evangjeli's last cabinet. In August the paper *Besa* published particulars of instructions calling for information regarding probable candidates at the next general election, which the government had addressed to local authorities in May. The paper was suppressed but its editors, Abdurrahman Dibra, the former Minister of Finance and another deputy, were protected from prosecution by parliamentary immunity. Toto, the Minister of the Interior, chose a shorter road to the truth. He sent for Dibra, put two revolvers on the table and declared that one or the other would not leave the room alive unless Dibra told him how he had acquired the instructions.

Dibra confirmed in writing a statement that he had received them from Krossi. The Minister took the paper to the King, who was also appealed to by a group of deputies headed by P. Evangjeli on the grounds that a member of the House had been outraged.[27] The King did nothing more than to pass the dispute off, a bad omen for Mehdi Bey and his government.

Within a few weeks another dispute surfaced, concerning an extra session of Parliament. The House had completed four sessions but not the four years of life for which it was elected in November 1932. The government held that a fifth session was basically unnecessary but the King accepted the majority view of a commision of jurists which had gathered to review the situation. Although Zog was still seemingly unwilling to dispense with his only liberal government, he was clearly not prepared to support them against his old school Parliament.

Mehdi Bey's time finally ran out in November when he and his government resigned after being handed an overwhelming vote of no confidence by Parliament. Of the members present, thirty-six voted against the government, three supported them and three abstained. The size of the adverse majority showed clearly that the King was behind the attack although Zog had at least applied a new method to an old game, since Frasheri's fall was the first time that a ministry had been overthrown by Parliament. Another democratic precedent had been established.

Several factors contributed to this important event, including Mehdi Bey's own shortcomings. Despite his long career as a Turkish official and an Albanian functionary, Mehdi Bey remained a somewhat indifferent administrator who had acquired a good deal of knowledge but not much wisdom. He lacked practicality and had a general tendency to wander off during talks into dissertations on subjects which had little or no connection with the matter at hand. Basically, he was a 19th century liberal trying to deal with a country struggling out of the Middle Ages.[28]

Ultimately, of course, Mehdi Bey fell because the King wished him to fall. Zog decided that it would be wise to replace Frasheri and his Anglophile colleagues with men who looked somewhat more kindly on Rome, in light of the far-reaching new agreements which had been signed with Italy. Koco Kotta, the old crony who headed the new government, being not only scrupulously loyal to Zog but also a great friend of the Italians, fit the mold very well.

On November 24 Zog told the new British Minister, Sir Andrew Ryan, that while he really preferred the progressive men of Mehdi Bey's cabinet, internal considerations had made it desirable to replace them with Ministers of greater experience, a euphemism, of course, for those who could successfully deal with Zog's odd political system and do what they were told. Zog clearly did not approve of the conflict that had occurred between the liberals and the old school and when it came time to choose between the two, the liberals did not stand a chance. Zog seemed to have decided that he himself could bring about the changes suggested by the liberals without actually retaining them in office, a step back in political reform but not necessarily a step backward in terms of social reform.

Musa Juka, who was thought to have filled the cup of past inequalities by his handling of the Fier uprising in 1935 and to have disappeared finally from political life, was resurrected much to the dismay of enlightened elements in Albania, to become the Minister of the Interior in the new government.[29] Since one of his specialities had always been the handling of elections, it was safe to assume that Zog had given up his earlier dabbling in electoral freedom and needed Juka to shape the upcoming election.

Juka could easily insure the return of a Parliament which would be compliant to the King's wishes no matter what policy direction was chosen. The elections in January saw Juka at his best. He was able to return all the Ministers and other old cronies who had been deputies in the past.[30]

By January 1937 it had also become clear that Zog was indeed determined to adopt many of the ideas presented by the liberals. On New Year's Eve 1936, the King gave one of his very rare parties at the Royal palace at Tirana, requiring all of his guests to attend in Western dress. In a speech he gave that evening, he declared that,

> we must make speedy and strong paces towards occidental culture and civilization. This is imposed upon us by history, by our geography and political positions and by the character of our Nation.[31]

Within a few weeks the King had come up with a concrete social and economic scheme in order to bring this about. In the social realm, Zog proposed the unveiling of Moslem women and the elimination of mixed Albanian and European costumes among the males. Also included in the King's program was instruction for the poor peasants by the presidents of the communes in the art of constructing rough wooden beds to discourage the peasants from sleeping on dirt floors which, the King was convinced, was responsible for much of the disease among the population.

Economically, Zog came up with another ambitious program, beginning with the establishment of a Commercial and Mortgage Bank with Albanian capital in order to provide loans at very low interest rates and on favorable terms. Zog argued that,

> I am not opposed to foreign capital, to the contrary, I am in favor of foreign capital provided it does not have political aspirations. During the past ten years many propositions have come to me for

the creation of a Commercial and Mortgage Bank with foreign capital, but every proposition had political aspirations behind it.

Nor was he satisfied with the Italian handling of the banking situation. "The so-called National Bank of Albania here makes loans at 13 or 14 percent interest and these for short term of from three to six months."[32] Zog wanted a completely independent institution which would be used to distribute government aid to the peasant farms for the purchase of modern farm tools to supplant the wooden plows still in use, to furnish seeds and plants to the peasantry and assist in selling their crops through the organization of cooperative societies.

Zog planned to encourage the construction of small industries for the manufacture of cheap woolen cloth, cement, and cheese and oil products. To this end the King had brought a German specialist to Albania at his own expense for the purpose of conducting an investigation of Albania's possibilities.

The King further proposed to create an agricultural school for small farmers in the Musakia plain, compromising 50,000 hectares of land. Zog explained,

> all young men whom I will recruit for military service and who own land will perform their service at this school so that when they return to their villages they will know how to cultivate the soil and plant their crops. In each commune I will create a small model farm where every farmer can see how it is done. The President of each commune will take a course in agriculture and will hear lectures on public sanitation. In this way I hope to improve the living conditions and the situation of the peasants.[33]

Zog had, of course, come up with innumerable programs and suggestions in the past, must of which, like the agrarian reform of 1931, had been quietly forgotten. In this instance, however, at least part of the program was almost immediately implemented. The King began with the social reforms which could be put into operation without a serious drain on the budget. In March a law was introduced and quickly passed by Parliament making it an offence punishable with a fine not exceeding 500 gold francs for any woman to conceal her face wholly or partially and imposing still more stringent penalties on those preventing or dissuading women from compliance with the law.

Zog and Juka, who were by trial and error finally learning some of the fine points of government, handled the entire situation extremely well. Rather than just charging blindly ahead, as they had done so often in the past, they carefully laid the groundwork for this potentially dangerous innovation.

First, the King sent three of his unmarried and unveiled Moslem sisters, the Princesses Myzejen, Ruhije and Maxhide, on a barnstorming tour of the extreme northern section of the country including Shkodër, the supposed center of the remnants of Moslem fanaticism in the country. The purpose of the visit was basically to give visible and convincing evidence of the feasibility and practicality of having all of the women of Albania uncover their faces, by revealing the charm of Zog's unveiled sisters.

The three Princesses, fully arrayed in very up-to-date Western European dress, with short, tight-fitting skirts and makeup, spent a week in Shkodër accompanied by Juka and Aranitas and other officials. The sisters visited schools, churches, religious shrines, hospitals, marketplaces, ruins and spent a good deal of time mingling with the people. Business in Shkodër came to a standstill. The Princesses, who up until this point had been virtual prisoners in the Royal palace with their public appearances being limited to a little horseback riding under heavy guard on the secluded roads near Tirana, were seen continually at parades, luncheons and dinners always in the company of photographers. The expedition was extremely successful.[34]

But the King wisely did more than just encourage popular enthusiasm. Zog was careful to enlist religious support for his move. A council of the Moslem community was called together to consider the change and it eventually approved a report presented by the head of the community in which he demonstrated that Islamic law did not require women to conceal their faces or their heads. He also proclaimed the need for the participation of women in all social activities.[35]

The new law was naturally met with some resistance, many Albanians being primarily concerned with the increased expenditure which the need for modern clothes would entail. There was rumor of possible opposition in Shkodër and of passive opposition in the shape of stay-at-home striking. Ultimately, no real opposition occurred anywhere, in fact, some elements of Albanian society welcomed the change with joy. The small group of Albanian gypsies, who had scandalized their fellow townswomen by displaying their features, found much to their delight, that they had been right all along.

Zog himself was responsible for the generally mild reaction, not only by carefully laying the groundwork but also by not pushing matters too far. He tolerated the very general practice of removing the veil and preserving the rest of the former dress, including the head covering intact. Even the showing of just a small portion of the face was tolerated by the authorities.

In May 1937 the King's forward progress was temporarily slowed by the last in the series of minor disturbances, reminding Zog that vigilance was still necessary. The small revolt, lasting only two days, began in Delvinë in southern Albania under the leadership of Ethem Toto, the Minister of the Interior in Frasheri's government. Toto, after Mehdi Bey's fall, was reemployed in the gendarmerie with the rank of major and was to go to Italy for additional training. In the meantime, he lived quietly in Delvinë awaiting his orders. Late in the afternoon of May 15, shots were heard at his house after which he and a few supporters occupied the office of the subprefect.

Toto made a speech, winning the adherence of some twenty-five people who immediately set upon a loyal officer and killed him. The ex-minister and his group thereupon marched on Gjirokastër where they took the authorities by surprise and proceeded to destroy the local records. Next, they released some 300 long-term prisoners, and quickly convinced these men to support the rebellion. The much enlarged group proceeded to march on Vlorë.

News of the uprising reached Tirana early on May 16, whereupon numerous officers were rushed to Vlorë. Two or three hundred gendarms were dispatched from the gendarmerie school at Borel and some 600 volunteers were sent from Krujë. In the meantime, local forces in Vlorë advanced along the road to Tepelenë and engaged and routed the rebels at a place called Ciafa Proci. Government forces were also moved from Korcë and a local Bektashi religious chief turned out 400 of his followers on his own initiative to support Tirana.

By the morning of the 17th the position was restored in the main centers which had been surprised by the rebels, who had by this point broken up into parties of stragglers. Toto, who was not at Ciafa Proci, had disappeared. A price was put on his head and he was eventually rounded up with four of five of his supporters. As is usual in these cases, Toto either committed suicide to avoid capture or was killed while trying to escape.[36] Toto had secured the support of some of the chiefs of warlike tribesmen who inhabited the surrounding mountains of his own district of origin but the tribesmen themselves did not rise. Without their support his project was doomed.

The affair might have been dangerous had Toto assured himself of serious support or had he been able to take Vlorë. As it was, because of the rapid and surprisingly restrained action of the government, the loyalty of the local gendarmerie, the support given Tirana by the Bektashis, the failure of the Kurvelesh tribesmen to move in any numbers, general discontent among the Orthodox population and the absence of any repercussion elsewhere in the country, the attempt at revolution proved to be as inept as that at Fier in 1935.

The Greek authorities did their best to close the frontier and no important number of rebels got anywhere near the Yugoslav border. Before long the government had rounded up practically all of the remaining rebels including the prisoners who had been liberated at Gjirokastër. Casualties do not appear to have been great on either side.[37]

Proving that he had learned from his unfortunate experience in 1935, the King used discretion and common sense in dealing with the insurgents. Zog publicly disclaimed any wish for arbitrary or vindictive action and to prove the sincerity of his sentiments, he constituted a political court which inspired confidence. Although the sentences were numerous, only four people were condemned to death, including Toto's brother Ismet, who was said to have urged Toto on, and three members of the gendarmerie. Four others, including one of the Kurvelesh leaders, were sentenced to 101 years imprisonment and 148 people, about half of them Gjirokastër prisoners, were sentenced to shorter terms. After some delay and apparent hesitation, Zog confirmed the death sentences and the four were finally executed on July 12.[38]

As usual, a series of explanations for why the revolt had occurred were presented. All manner of foreign influences were seen, including British, French, Greek, Italian, etc., depending upon the taste of the author. It was suggested that the unveiling of women had been a cause but this can

easily be dismissed since Toto had been in the forefront of the modern-
izers. The government, once again, contributed the revolt to communist
inspiration but as usual was completely unable to produce reliable evidence supporting this thesis. By the 1930s Communism was indeed gaining converts among the three or four thousand European trained intellectuals and cells were organized in Tirana, Shkodër, Korcë and elsewhere.
Since these groups remained disunited until 1941, however, their impact
on Zog's regime was minor.

Toto's actual motives were never fully discovered. He was a man of
considerable experience and apparent good sense but because of his
honesty had made enemies, including Juka who went out of his way
to harass Toto. Accordingly, the most plausible explanation for his hare-
brained and ill-prepared attempt is that it was the last gesture of an exasperated man. As far as those who followed him are concerned, the Gjirokastër prisoners were obviously drawn by freedom and spoils. Of the rest,
some acted out of personal loyalty to Toto while some participated presumably out of opposition to the regime. Others were reacting against
the renewed official tolerance of Italian penetration.

Despite the weakness of the revolt, Zog nevertheless concluded that
his regime could use some further stability and he was convinced that
one method to help produce this stability was to move ahead with the
projected reforms. Superficial changes were still the least painful so
these continued apace.

In the summer of 1937, a stricter dress code for men was introduced,
stipulating that national costumes were to be worn only on national
holidays. In September the King gave the first formal reception of his
reign on the occasion of the ninth anniversary of the proclamation of
the Monarchy. Over 300 people attended this event, including the entire
diplomatic corps, the heads of Albanian religious bodies, Cabinet Ministers, former ministers, representatives from Parliament, high ranking
civil and military officials and a number of prominent foreign visitors. It
was the first time the King had entertained on such a scale and the entire
evening apparently went off very well.[39]

Zog was so pleased with the festivities that he repeated the entire spectacle a little over one month later on the occasion of the twenty-five
anniversary of the declaration of Albanian independence. The celebrations began with a military review on November 25 when practically the

whole of the Albanian army marched past the King. Three Princesses led a detachment of young women, and were smartly attired in breeches while their followers wore skirts. The festivities included two large receptions at the palace and a large government dinner on November 27.

All of Zog's efforts to achieve stability through slow Westernization were not quite so superficial. Before the year was out, the King had concerned himself with a number of schemes for raising the consciousness of Albanian women to a higher level. Considerable effort was put into the organizing of courses for teaching weaving and child welfare. By December the King claimed that hundreds of such courses had been arranged in different parts of the Kingdom and since the first was started, the attendance had increased a hundredfold. Zog was hopeful that infant mortality would decrease significantly as a result of the courses.[40]

The most signficant step which the King took in an effort to insure stability during the late 1930s was his marriage to the Countess Geraldine Apponyi in April 1938, a step which had been long hoped for by those who welcomed the continuation of Zog's regime. The establishment of a dynasty, many felt, would offer Albania a degree of political certainty and in the process discourage the occasional armed revolt. It would also allow Zog to be somewhat less fearful of the assassin's bullet, something which concerned him less during the 1930s, but could never have been far from his thoughts.

While the King remained without a successor, Albania could have been thrown into chaos by his sudden removal from the scene. With an heir, the chances of this happening would at least have been decreased. To the King, his supporters and all those who by this time had tired of Albania's political turmoil or the threat thereof, the marriage constituted a wise political step as well as a joyous moment.

Why Zog had waited so long is not entirely clear but was most likely the combination of an attempt to find the right person both amourously and in terms of station, along with the King's roving eye. Zog had been something of a ladies' man in his younger days and his relationship with women often found their way onto the pages of Europe's less reputable press. Although he was generally discreet, a public figure, particularly a young handsome unmarried Balkan King, was closely watched for signs of amorous involvements.

The King's first well publicized affair involved a young Austrian dancer named Franciska Janko whom Zog had met either in Belgrade or Vienna in 1924.[41] She was said to sport a pair of "twinkling" legs, a slim body, a snap of light-chestnut-colored hair and a pair of brown mischievous eyes.[42] Given his weakness for things Austrian, Zog could not resist and offered the young lady a position in Tirana as his "protege." Miss Janko accepted and with her sister along as a chaperone moved to Tirana, where the President installed her in a house next to the palace.

Apparently Zog attempted to keep her as much a secret as possible, particularly from his mother who was very old fashioned and still energetic enough to throw the woman out. As a result, the unfortunate mistress, whom Zog made a baroness once he assumed the throne, was permitted to leave her house only on the occasion of her yearly bathing trip to some undisclosed foreign country every summer.[43] The only exception to this routine, apparently, was Zog's trip to Vienna in 1931 where his mistress was permitted to meet him, something which the King eventually regretted considering the rather extensive press coverage their relationship received while they were in Austria.[44]

In June of 1934 a strange story emerged from Athens involving a certain Baroness Dorothes de Ropp, who had committed suicide in late May. According to a moderately reliable newspaper account, she was a German who had married a Russian in Riga. She left Russia after the revolution and in 1920 was divorced from her husband. In 1930 she appeared in Tirana, where she became the mistress of Zog and at the same time of Kemal Messare Bey, then Master of Ceremonies, later the Albanian Minister in Athens. She appears to have been engaged in espionage for Italy and later for Yugoslavia while she was conducting these affairs.

In June of 1933 she left for Athens and upon her arrival got in touch with the communists as a Soviet agent but soon abandoned them for the Italian and Yugoslav secret services. When Messare Bey came to Athens some time afterwards, she betrayed to him all she knew of the Italian and Yugoslav services. Her double dealing eventually caught up with her for letters found on or near the body indicated that one of these services had threatened to inform Messare Bey of her past activities against Albania, that he had abandoned her to destitution and that she had therefore decided to kill herself.

The Albanian Minister informed *Hellenikon Mellon* that the woman in question had only been at the legation once, and added that photographs of King Zog which were found in her room could have been bought at any shop in Albania. The newspaper addressed a letter to him pointing out that this statement was not true, that the photographs were undoubtedly personal gifts and that one bore King Zog's signature dated 1933.[45]

All of this was too much for Zog and his advisors who seemed to agree that the time had come for the King to dispense with his mistresses and take a wife. In late 1934 the Baroness Janko, who the press was now referring to as the "Albanian Lupescu," was sent off to Vienna, where, it was reported, King Zog had purchased a small palace for her costing some twenty-six thousand pounds.[46]

It was not the first time that Zog had thought seriously of marriage. Legend has it that in his youth he had pledged never to marry after his first love, the beautiful daughter of a rival chieftain was killed by her own father who objected to Zog—the liegeman Zog sent to abduct the girl returned with her dead body.[47] Early in his political career Zog did become engaged to the daughter of Albania's wealthiest landowner, Shevket Bey Verlaci, probably as much for political and economic reasons as for love. His desire for her seemed to diminish in direct proportion to the broadening of his political horizons. Many of Zog's advisers, notably his brother-in-law Ceno Bey, suggested that he delay the marriage pending the settlement of Albania's outstanding political questions. Once it became clear to Zog that he was to be king, the Verlaci match lost all remaining attraction.

Zog finally broke the engagement off in 1927 by attempting to have her father killed, apparently the only honorable way to extricate himself from such delicate arrangements. The Italians also became involved here since they too were against the match, primarily because they had chosen Verlaci as a successor to Zog and hoped to use the old Bey to control the President. In an attempt to wreck the proposed marriage, Rome apparently sent a young lady to seduce Zog.[48] Whether she succeeded or not is unimportant considering that the young President had already decided to jetison the daughter of the landowner and eventually look for someone who was better placed.

There was, naturally, frequent speculation as to who the lucky lady would be and most every interested group had its preferences. The question received considerable prominence during the Albanian-Italian negotiations concerning the construction of a monarchy, at which time Rome hinted that there might even be an Italian Princess in the bargain for Zog.

This being out of the question considering Victor Emmanuel's attitude towards Zog, Mussolini suggested that the King might marry a less Italian, a proposal which Zog strenuously refused.[49]

Although the rumors abounded, the only ones given any credence were those connecting Zog with ladies from Austria or Hungary, since his preferences were widely known.[50] In late 1933 there were rumors afloat that definite negotiations were in progress looking to the marriage of the King to the Princess Adelaide, the nineteen-year-old daughter of ex-Emperor Karl of Austria, who was then living in Belgium with Empress Zita. The rumors eventually died down and the plan, if one did exist, probably foundered on the fact that Zog was a Moslem whereas the Habsburg-Lorraine house was one of the most devoutly Catholic in all Europe.[51]

By 1936 the search was going on in earnest and the King had by this time added a concrete stipulation: the future queen of Albania must be young and attractive. Late that year the first serious candidate fitting all the requirements was found. The lady in question, the Countess Hanna Mikes a Hungarian, had come to Tirana in a party headed by Baron Villani, the Hungarian Minister in Rome who was also accredited to Albania. The Countess was the twenty-five year old Calvinist daughter of Countess Bethlen, the sister of the former Prime Minister, and Count Armond Mikes, a Catholic belonging to an important family in Transylvania.

After her fourth meeting with Zog, rumors of a forthcoming engagement announcement began to abound. In early 1937, however, both personal and diplomatic problems began to appear. The Rumanian Minister let it be known that his country was very much opposed to the match because the Countess was politically identified with Hungarian irredentism in regard to Transylvania and her father's persistence in asserting claims to ancestral property had made him a thorn in the side of the Rumanian government.[52]

Zog eventually also had difficulties with the Countess herself, who was described as having a resolute and energetic character, as well as with Count Bethlen who was apparently personally involved with the various arrangements. Zog insisted that children of the marriage be brought up as Moslems, a position which caused further delay. The Count eventually became impatient with the entire affair and sent an ultimatum to Zog demanding that he definitely declare his intentions by January 15, 1937.

Zog failed to react to this deadline and finally informed the Yugoslav Minister in late February that he would not marry the Countess.[53]

The Italians apparently had something to do with this decision since they eventually turned against the match, after having initially supported it. Their primary motive here seems to have been a last effort to persuade Zog to take an Italian wife. Rome came up with two prospects, including a member of the Cenci-Bolgnetti family as well as the daughter of Count and Countess Cereana Mayneri, neither of which Zog was willing to seriously consider. The King made a final request for a member of the House of Savoy which the Italians apparently ignored. In January of 1938 Count Ciano, the Italian Foreign Minister, made one last suggestion, either of the Devini daughters, but by this time the King was already enamored with his wife to be.[54]

Near the end of 1937 Zog was seen in the company of another Hungarian, the Countess Teleki, but soon it became clear that she had come to Albania basically to test the waters for her close friend the Countess Geraldine Apponyi, a celebrated beauty known as the White Rose of Hungary.[55]

The future queen, born in 1915, was the daughter of Count Julius Apponyi whose ancestors were, according to Geraldine, among the seven tribunes of Attilla.[56] Count Julius met his wife to be, Gladys Stewart of Maryland, the daughter of a diplomat, at an Austro-Hungarian Embassy gathering in Geneva in 1912 and the two were married in 1914, a few days after the outbreak of the war. The Count took his wife's rather substantial fortune and invested it all in Hungarian war bonds, a move which contributed to his early death in 1924.

Geraldine's mother soon afterwards married a Frenchman named Giron and they settled in Belgium and in the south of France. Geraldine, in the meantime, had spent most of her early years travelling from one European country to another, leaving Hungary abruptly with the rise of Bela Kun for Switzerland and then France where she attended school in Mouton. Staying with her mother until she was twelve, Geraldine eventually entered the Sacre Coeur near Vienna and studied there until she was seventeen, whereupon she returned to Hungary where she was supported by her father's family. Considerably impoverished, she was eventually granted a small post in the Budapest National Museum in order to support herself.[57]

Once Zog had become serious about finding a wife, he asked his Minister in Vienna to send him photographs of Austrian and Hungarian women who might make suitable brides. The King fell in love with Geraldine's photograph and asked to meet her. The young Countess, who thought the idea rather odd, initially refused. She was not persuaded until the King had sent a representative to speak with her guardian and tutor, who called a meeting of the family. They all concurred that Geraldine should go. She was packed off on a plane to Brindisi and from there by boat to Albania. Her family, in an effort to protect her from the rumors associated with earlier candidates, kept her trip rather secret and claimed that she had simply gone off into the mountains as she did every year to nurse her weak lungs.[58]

Zog, who was still very handsome and debonaire, swept the young Countess away and she immediately fell in love, in what must have seemed a fairy tale to Geraldine. From her arrival in late December, she continually remained within the Royal circle. She danced with the King at the New Year's reception. Zog's engagement to the Countess Apponyi was officially announced on January 31, 1938, and was generally well received. Even Shkodër and the Bektashi reacted favorably. Krossi, who still served as the unofficial spokesman for the northern tribal chieftains was very pleased. His attitude indicated that no opposition could be expected from the clans. The Orthodox community was naturally delighted at the prospect of a Christian queen. The British Minister, Andrew Ryan, reported that his butler, a member of the Orthodox faith, threatened to shoot anyone who questioned the beauty of the King's betrothed.[59]

Even those who were initially somewhat skeptical were soon won over by the young Countess's easy charm. Zog was careful to show off his prospective bride by taking unprecedented drives in the country with her, as well as organizing form gala evenings, including one for the immediate family, one for the diplomatic corps and one for the mountaineers. The Countess, tall and graceful, combined great physical attractiveness with gracious manners. Although early reports from Rome referred to her as having "no ideas in her head beyond clothes and domesticity"; as being in fact "a perfect harem lady," these were soon proven incorrect.[60] Geraldine was well educated and an accomplished linguist, learning Albanian in just a few months, something which naturally further endeared her to the Albanians.

There was no foreign reaction except from the two countries directly involved. Baron Villani and the Hungarians were of course extremely pleased although the Baron would have been happier if Zog had chosen Countess Mikes since he had personally handled the negotiations. The Baron expected that Hungarian prestige would increase and possibly trade as well, something which Hungarian merchants would probably welcome considering that Albania, when it paid its debts, was one of the last nations to still use gold in international trade.[61]

Although the Italian press greeted the engagement in a friendly manner, it is clear that Rome was less than pleased that its project of providing Zog with an Italian wife had failed. Their clandestine opposition to the match often lacked subtlety. They even sent a number of attractive young men to Budapest in an attempt to compromise Geraldine. Although this tactic failed with her, it had apparently succeeded with at least one of the ladies initially under consideration.

Zog seemed very aware of the threat of Italian political intrigue and once Geraldine had arrived in Tirana, he took steps to insure that as few opportunities as possible remained open to them. The King refused, for example, to allow his prospective bride to be served by Albanian ladies in waiting. He recognized how easily they could be bought and possibly used to wreck the marriage. Instead, the Countess brought with her from Hungary, her grandmother, her governess the Baroness Reuling, a maid and a hairdresser.[62] Zog was willing to put up with Italian displeasure but would not allow Rome to undermine his marriage plans.

In an effort to gloss over these growing problems, once the date was decided on, the King asked Count Ciano to be a witness at the wedding, an invitation which the Foreign Minister gladly accepted. The Count was forever interested in raising the prestige of the Italians in Albania. In further pursuance of this aim, Ciano seems to have had a hand in choosing Victor Emmanuel's representative. Initially the Italian King had hoped to send his cousin the Duke of Spelato to represent the crown but Ciano reacted negatively. He complained that ". . . it is tiresome because it is unexpected and because Tirana is not London and to keep this great boozy Spelato creature in order is not easy."[63] Ultimately Victor Emmanuel sent the Duke of Bergamo, a short wooden type who showed few social qualities and could not outshine the rather vain Count.

Apart from the formidable Italian contingent, the guests included five non-resident Ministers who brought the heads of foreign missions up to seventeen, including Franco's representative, the bride's American mother and grandmother with numerous relatives and friends of hers, mostly Hungarian. With the posse of journalists, photographers and various sensation-hunters, added to the rest of the foreign contingent, Tirana's rather meager offerings in terms of accommodations were severely strained. There were only two relatively good hotels in Tirana, both of which were commandeered for the more exalted guests, while everyone else had to make due with the remainder.

The festivities began with a reception at the palace on the evening of April 23, attended primarily by Albanian dignitaries. All members of the diplomatic body and many other foreigners, including the Hungarians, were invited to a second reception on the evening of the 25th, the first day of general rejoicing in Tirana and other towns.

Numerous parties were held in honor of the event, offering Count Ciano the opportunity to dance strenuously and flirt outrageously as was his style. Geraldine remembers taking an immediate dislike to Ciano. She considered him to be most obnoxious and seems rather proud of the fact that she refused to dance with him.[64]

The wedding took place in the gardens of the palace on April 27. A large tent-like structure of thin wood had been built for the occasion, richly decorated with oriental rugs, Albanian costumes and arms. Several hundred guests and a battery of photographers watched as the King, wearing a uniform, entered the hall with his bride, to the strains of the Royal march. Ciano noted that Geraldine looked radiant and that the ceremony, presided over by the Vice-President of the Parliament, went off with a good deal of dignity.[65]

Following the rather brief ceremony, the King and Queen entertained their guests at a luncheon and then took a short tour of Tirana in an open car. The city presented a scene of great animation on the wedding day and throughout the festivities. Much of the activity was naturally organized by the authorities but it is also clear that the wedding excited a good deal of popular enthusiasm. Later the same day, the Royal couple set out by car for Durrës to begin an eight-week honeymoon. The road was carefully but not ostentatiously guarded and at a few frequented points simple but good preparations had been made to welcome the King and Queen as they passed. A long procession of other cars followed the Royal couple, in accordance with the Albanian passion for being in at the death of such occasions.

The marriage was generally well received abroad and expensive gifts were in abundance. Admiral Horthy of Hungary sent a coach with old Hungarian harness and two silver-grey purebred horses, even providing a Hungarian coachman who remained on as a member of Geraldine's servant staff. The Turks sent carpets, the French porcelain and Chancellor Hitler sent a Mercedes. The Italians outdid them all by promising the Royal couple a yacht.[66]

Religious difficulties proved to be the only problem in an otherwise well planned and executed affair. Geraldine came from a strongly Catholic family and continued to practice her religion, including a daily mass in Tirana, after her engagement. Soundings from Rome as to the attitude of the Holy See resulted in the publication in the *Observatore Romano* on February 15 and 16 of a long article defining the practice and doctrine of the Church regarding mixed marriages. It recognized that such marriages, although always repugnant, might take place by dispensation subject to the condition that no religious ceremony should take place other than the Catholic and that all the children should be brought up in the faith.

Zog was willing to make various concessions since he personally was little concerned with religion; he would not, however, consent to have his children raised as Catholics. Some 70 percent of all Albanians were still Moslems and the King had no intention of antagonizing the majority of his population. Geraldine's confessor, who happened to be an Italian Jesuit, addressed a preemptory warning to the future queen in early April and gave such offense to the palace circles that he immediately left for Italy. Geraldine still maintains that he was in actuality an Italian spy relating the contents of her confessions to the Italian government. As the priest warned, the Vatican refused to recognize the marriage and advised Geraldine that she was living in a state of technical concubinage and would be refused communion. It was not until five years later that the Queen was able to straighten out the problem.[67]

Another successful step towards the Westernization and political stability of Albania had been taken. Zog had tied himself to Western aristocracy while at the same time he further secured his personal position by moving towards the creation of a dynasty. Most Albanians seemed to breathe a little easier; Zog began to act more like a Western statesman moving among his people. The Royal couple took occasional trips into the countryside including a visit to Zog's ancestral home at Mati as well as a much more politically important visit to Vlorë in August, the King's first official visit to the south since his elevation to the throne. Queen Geraldine recalls that they were initially somewhat anxious about the visit since Zog had never been very popular in Vlorë. After a short speech, however, the assembled multitudes broke into cheers and went so far as to carry the Royal couple in their car through the streets of the city.[68]

The wedding clearly helped to raise the image of the Monarchy and of Zog himself. Despite grinding poverty, a despised and corrupt administration and the continuing economic morass, Albania was reasonably stable and the gap between the King and the people had narrowed somewhat. Zog was also finally showing some wisdom as a ruler, abjuring some of the recklessness in administrating which had characterized his early career. The future looked a little brighter. The harried King was left with little time to take advantage of these positive developments, however, since difficulties coming his way from across the Adriatic would soon swamp Zog and his regime.

CHAPTER TWELVE

ZOG AND ALBANIA,
THE LAST VICTIMS OF APPEASEMENT

In June of 1936, only four months after the official normalization of Italo-Albanian relations, Count Galeazzo Ciano took over at the Palazzo Chigi, the Italian Foreign Ministry. The new Foreign Minister was responsible not only for infusing the Foreign Ministry with a new aggressive spirit but also with developing and carrying out a new approach to what the Italians were beginning to refer to as "the Albanian problem."

The Count was not particularly well suited for the job, being inexperienced and rather irresponsible. He was something of a playboy, not a hard worker, and some Ambassadors found him hard to take seriously for he could not seem to concentrate on any one problem for more than a few moments. His lapses of taste and manners alienated even Hitler who referred to him as "that disgusting boy."[1] Indeed, he gained the respect of few in the diplomatic field chiefly because of his exhibitionism, vanity and lack of discretion. One of Ciano's girlfriends frequently passed important facts immediately to Lord Perth the British Ambassador, and the Count's favorite haunt, the Roman golf club, was well-known to journalists as about the best place in Europe for leaks of information.[2]

Why Mussolini chose Ciano is somewhat unclear, except that he was married to the Duce's daughter and that he basically did what he was told. Ciano was less subtle and less clever than Mussolini, but showed deference

263

to the Duce as one would to a superior being. The Count was so taken with Mussolini that he copied his mannerisms, his deportment and even his handwriting. The sound of the Duce's voice on the radio would bring him to tears.

This emulation naturally carried over into the conduct of foreign affairs, where the Count not only followed his orders to the letter but worked to instill the Ministry with Mussolini's spirit or the "tona fascista." Like the Duce, who had personally run the Ministry since the dismissal of Grandi in 1932, Ciano disliked reading despatches, relying instead on newspapers and spies for the information upon which to conduct policy. He kept his Ambassadors completely in the dark, to the point where Grandi, who became the Italian Minister in London, looked to the British Foreign Office for clues as to the direction of Italian foreign policy.

Although like Mussolini, the Count was rather flippant and inconsistent in terms of policy, he was able to find one project which held his interest and which he eventually came to consider as his private reserve: Albania. Ciano's Albanian fixation began shortly following his first trip to Tirana in April of 1937.

The visit itself was rather uneventful, except as an indication of the Count's style and his boundless energy. Again in an attempt to ape Mussolini, the Count dramatically flew his own four-motored airplane to Tirana taking with him a bevy of foreign ministry officials. During his three-day stay, the Count had numerous audiences with Zog, attended a myriad of banquets, placed a wreath on the tomb of the Queen Mother, laid cornerstones and visited villages.[3] More significantly, it was during and immediately after this visit that Ciano's plans for Albania began to gel.

The Count's initial actions were quite tame, not knowing exactly what he wanted out of Albania except that a greater Italian presence must be the first step. In August of 1937 Ciano wrote:

> I have persuaded the Duce to give sixty millions to Albania over the next four years, for works of various kinds. My visit to Tirana convinced me of the necessity for taking good care of this sector of the front. We must create stable centers of Italian influence there. Who knows what the future will have in store? We must be ready to seize the opportunities which will present themselves.

The Count then added significantly,

> We are not going to withdraw this time, as we did in 1920. In the south (of Italy) we have absorbed several hundred thousand Albanians. Why shouldn't the same thing happen on the other side of the Adriatic?[4]

By the beginning of 1938, Ciano seems to have decided that even waiting for opportunities was no longer a reasonable approach; opportunities had to be created. The Foreign Minister noted that,

> Our penetration is becoming steadily more intense and more organic. The programme which I traced after my visit is being carried out without a hitch. I am wondering whether the general situation, particularly the Anschluss, does not permit us to take a step towards more and more complete domination of this country which will be ours.[5]

It was while he was in Albania attending the wedding of Zog and Geraldine that Ciano finally decided that "a radical solution" to the Albanian problem was needed.[6] Zog was too clever to fall into a political protectorate through economic pressure; the only way Albania would ever truly become an indivisible part of Mussolini's resurrected Roman Empire was through invasion. Having come to this irrevocable conclusion, Ciano and a large staff of advisers and experts drew up an extensive plan while still in Tirana, to be presented to the Duce for his approval.

The report, discussed on May 10, was a well planned, detailed analysis of Italy's historical role in Albania as well as what Italy could expect to gain from the action proposed by Ciano. In his report the Foreign Minister took advantage of the Duce's weakness for flattery, appealed to him on a rational basis and played on his worst fears.[7]

The report began by presenting Albania as a worthwhile objective for Italian expansion, based upon highly dubious economic figures. The Count described vast opportunities in agriculture, livestock raising, forestry, the fishing industry and mineral deposits. The Count also noted that in ancient times Albania had been heavily populated; now it was practically uninhabited, but with proper Italian organization and management the country could provide a home for up to two million Italians.[8]

Ciano maintained that the Italians would be welcomed in Albania because of the unpopularity of Zog's regime, which was described as money-grubbing and riddled with nepotism. The flashy extravagence of the Royal sisters and the massive expense of the Royal wedding were much resented and clearly emphasized the vast division between the rich and the poor and the court and the people.

The Count contrasted the ill feelings which most Albanians harbored for Zog with the popularity of the Italians. Apart from the pro-Zog faction at court, Ciano maintained that:

> it is worthwhile to underscore that the people of the capital, of the ports and whoever comes in contact with us, are instead in every class and without reticence, pro-Italian. Also in the army, with a few exceptions, the sympathies are with Italy.[9]

On what he based this absurd analysis, remains a mystery.

Next, the Count raised the spector of German hegemony in the Balkans, one of Mussolini's greatest fears. It was known that the Hungarians had shown interest in Albania and the Count pointed out that it ought not be forgotten that Budapest had often been the avant-garde of Germanism. He further noted that it would be a mistake to overlook the strong traces of former Austrian influence in Albania and the danger that Germany, reinforced by the Anschluss, presented. Germany might attempt to take and expand the political and economic position which Imperial Austria once had.[10]

Ciano was careful to play upon Mussolini's need for glory, with several references to Italy's poor military record, and speculated on how Mussolini was about to bury these bad memories with the proposed action in Albania. The Count argued that

> In Albania, which belonged to us every so often in history, we seek and we find the natural road to our expansion in the Balkans. . . . In the sixteen years of Mussolinian policy it has been newly joined to Italy by bonds of great importance. This work . . . must find at the opportune moment its culmination in the annexation of Albania by Italy.[11]

Ciano concluded by presenting three options. First Italy could continue to tighten its economic ties but the Count suggested that the goal of political dominance could not quickly be achieved by this method. The second solution which the Count considered personally unsatisfactory was the partition of Albania among her neighbors. The third, and clearly his choice, was outright annexation which could be easily achieved by playing on the dissensions between the crown and the masses, fomenting a rebellion or internal crisis and moving in to restore order.[12]

Ciano maintained that Mussolini immediately agreed about the necessity for a radical solution and noted that the Duce was prepared even to go to war as long as Albania was secured for Italy. Ciano had done well, the spector of Germany frightened the Duce and the Count's theatrics had appealed to him. At one point Ciano had handed the Duce a specimen of copper ore from the mines at Alessio, with the words "here are the Carthagenian figs."[13] Mussolini was forced to take Ciano's word concerning Albania's vast mineral wealth since in all they years that Italy had been involved there, no one had bothered to conduct a proper geological survey.

Full approval of this plan, however, required a major decision, something from which Mussolini always shied away. He would rather make small unimportant decisions for these would not leave him paralyzed by doubt. The Duce, then, seems to have approved the plan in principle and waivered when a final irrevocable decision concerning implementation was called for. While Mussolini agonized over whether or not to invade, Ciano moved ahead with plans to subvert the Albanian government.

In order to reduce the possibility of armed resistance once the full plan was set in motion, the Count initiated a program designed to rapidly and substantially increase Italian control over every facet of Albanian life. First, the number of Italian military instructors was to be discreetly increased "with the specific mission to create annexationist cells in the Albanian army."[14] Under the direction of the Italian Minister Jacomoni and a certain Giovanni Giro who was sent to Albania to organize Albanian youth on a fascist model, economic and cultural infiltration was also to be intensified. The number of Albanians on the Italian payroll was to be increased and the most important people, particularly the tribal chieftains, were to be won over "on a personal basis with expressions of mutual interest, with promises and with corruption."[15]

By June Giro reported that he had a considerable element of the country under his control. He added that public opinion was steadily rising against the King and that Italian intervention in the event of a disturbance would meet with no opposition. The common people, Giro continued, would welcome with joy any improvement in material conditions and the Italians could expect to destroy the desire to resist within three days.[16]

Overjoyed by this news, and not bothering to check the authenticity of this extremely overoptimistic information, Ciano proceeded to draw up the next phase of the plan with characteristic fascist vigor. The physical removal of Zog played a key role in this phase. Ciano's first attempt may have been an effort to kidnap both the King and Queen. In early December the Royal couple put to sea along with the Minister of Foreign Affairs and other high officials of the government. Zog had promised Geraldine a short honeymoon trip and felt secure enough to leave the country for a short time so they decided to sail to Venice. The vessel and the crew were Italian, something which the Count had been very adamant about supply for Zog in June so as to "guarantee the impossibility of his escaping in any eventuality."[17]

Soon after they left the harbor, Geraldine, who was already with child, became ill because of the bad weather and the doctor who was attending her strongly recommended that the ship return immediately to Durrës. The Queen, who was in her cabin, remembers that a good deal of noise and commotion on deck followed this decision and that Zog himself became very nervous. Geraldine maintains that it became known afterwards within the Royal circle that the Italians had hoped either to murder the King on board or to keep both of them in Italy.[18]

Although no strong evidence exists to support Geraldine's contentions, it is clear that Ciano and Jacomoni did come up with a detailed plan for the assassination of Zog. An anonymous individual who the Count described as being an old friend of the King's who felt neglected, was found to carry out the deed for ten million lire. Ciano met with this person on numerous occasions to finalize the plan.[19]

After Zog was dead, so Ciano's senario ran, the Italians would provoke street fighting and the rebellion of the mountain tribes. The population would call to Italy to restore order and in gratitude offer the crown to Victor Emmanuel. Following the offer, Ciano planned to finalize the annexation by conducting a plebiscite, similar to the one conducted by Hitler in Austria at the time of the Anschluss. Jacomoni guaranteed that all of this could take place at a month's notice.[20]

The plan was so perfectly prepared that Ciano longed to put it into operation. The Foreign Minister presented the scheme to Mussolini for final approval in early December. The Duce again approved of it in principle but out of rationality or doubt, put a temporary lid on the over-zealous Count. The international ramifications of such an act did not escape Mussolini. He knew that if the plan were carried out Italy would most likely drive Yugoslavia into the waiting arms of the Germans. Ciano was forced to slow down and turn his efforts to working out some kind of a partition deal with the Yugoslav Prime Minister Milan Stojadinovic.

Although Jacomoni reported after the war to the High Court of Justice that Ciano let the idea of assassination drop at this point, the Queen recalls two separate attempts during this period which she insists were inspired by the Italians. Sometime in early 1939 she was told of an incident where a rifle had been found on the roof of one of the buildings which lined the park behind the palace. On another occasion a well-placed Albanian with strong Italian connections had apparently bribed Geraldine's Hungarian cook.

The rather shaken women immediately informed the King who told her to keep the money. Zog thereupon apparently invited the offender to lunch and had the cook make one of Geraldine's least favorite dishes, something on the order of cabbage strudel. The Queen took a bite and gasped, whereupon the unfortunate Albanian jumped up demanding to known what they had eaten. The King, who had not lost his taste for manipulation, exposed the culprit.[21]

Zog announced that a plot to overthrow the government and kill the King had been discovered and that the leader, Giovanni Giro, had been asked the leave the country. Giro, who was still unsuccessfully trying to organize an Albanian youth organization on Italian lines, had long made no secret of his hostility to the regime. It came to the attention of the government that he had also been organizing those who were disaffected with the Monarchy as well as corresponding with certain Albanian emigres in Paris, including Zog's old opponent Mustafa Kruja.[22]

At the same time, an accomplice of Giro's named Koci (more than likely Geraldine's poisoner) left the country with the King's permission. Four Italophile Albanians were arrested and gendarmes were dispatched to various areas throughout Albania including Tepelenë and Shkodër. As a final gesture the King called out the army reservists and loyal tribesmen.

By this time, of course, the King was growing somewhat alarmed and agitated, having noticed that his relations with Italy had taken a turn for the worse. This is not to say that the two countries had been on friendly terms since the rapprochement of 1936. Following the new agreements, the normal level of tension in Italo-Albanian relations had been reconstitued. Rome continued to sabotage or strictly direct the loans which had been made to the Albanians, while Zog obstructed the Italians at every turn. By the end of 1938 little progress had been made on the tobacco monopoly and the further organization of the port of Durrës. Zog was using Italian money to buy goods from the Japanese and as Mussolini had feared, the King had asked the Germans why their economic drive had overlooked Albania.[23]

All of this was more or less routine, however, so when Ciano's personal policies began making themselves felt, Zog knew the Italians were up to something and quickly moved to stop them. Zog reasoned that if the Italians were indeed trying to kill him they would eventually succeed and therefore recognized that his only alternative was to attempt to placate them. The King called in Jacomoni and declared that he wished to reestablish the most cordial relations with Italy. The Italian Minister reported to Ciano that he felt this was just a maneuver to gain time to permit the King to come to some sort of understanding with third powers.

This is, of course, exactly what the King had planned. He mentioned to Ryan, in confidence, that he was thinking of turning to the Germans.[24] Geraldine maintains that Zog, soon thereafter, sent personal envoys to Hitler on two occasions and was told each time that only through Mussolini could Zog expect to maintain a free Albania. Aware that he was running out of options, the King, in anger, accused Hitler of not be a patriot, "for no patriot would tell another patriot to go and sell his country."[25] Ciano was concernd about Zog's agitation and wanted to move more quickly, particularly since by the middle of February circumstances had allowed him to return to his favorite plan of annexing Albania outright, with no compensation for her neighbors.

Following Mussolini's suggestion, the Count had gone to Stojadinovic during the middle of January. Ciano had hoped to convince the Yugoslav leader of the advantages of an Italian takeover of Albania, a plan which included a number of corrections in the northern frontiers. He argued that after such an action Albania would cease to be the focus of nationalism thereby reducing the problems concerning Kosovo. The Count also was prepared to promise a military alliance and Italian support for any move Yugoslavia might make against Salonica to assure itself an outlet to the Mediterranean.[26]

Stojadinovic, who had been forewarned of Ciano's purpose by Bosko Hristic the Yugoslav Minister in Rome, was unhappy with talk of "correction of frontiers," he wanted partition. He spoke specifically and covetously of Shkodër, Shëngjin and Yugoslav access to the sea, which would be made possible only by cession of the northern provinces and the completion of a railroad line.[27]

When the Yugoslav Regent, Prince Paul, discovered that his Prime Minister was treating with Ciano about the partition of Albania, he was incensed. He was appalled that neither the cabinet nor the Regent had been included on such a critical matter, something which would have definitely put Yugoslavia in the Axis camp. More importantly, Paul, like King Alexander before him, had no desire to increase the size of the Albanian population in Yugoslavia. "We already have so many Albanians inside our frontiers and they give us so much trouble," Prince Paul complained, "that I have no wish to increase their number."[28]

Stojadinovic was quickly forced out and replaced by Dragisa Cvetkovic who was not only much closer to the Regent and his foreign policy, but more significantly, was not known for his friendly attitude toward Italy. After the dust had settled, Ciano was forced to reevaluate his position. He came to two conclusions: first, "to go ahead just the same, with Stojadinovic, partition of Albania between us and Yugoslavia; without Stojadinovic occupation even against Yugoslavia."[29] The Count also decided that it was now imperative to move as quickly as possible on this Albanian project and he hoped to institute the program by the first week in April.

Ciano's new urgency stemmed primarily from the knowledge that the Yugoslavs now knew the plan and the fear that rumors regarding the undertaking would spread far and quickly. The Count also feared that the new pro-Western Cvetkovic might move closer to Britain and France and might even attempt to come to some understanding with the Albanians.

Jacomoni presented additional reasons for quick action, including the increased demands for payments from tribal chieftains with which he was being beseiged. The Italian Minister also suggested that the local leaders might become suspicious of Italian hesitation and use the knowledge of their subversive activities to force Zog to change his mode of government. Finally, Jacomoni argued that a number of exiles were about to be allowed back into Albania and Italy should move before they could effectively build a patriotic movement of resistance against the Italians.[30]

Mussolini agreed with Ciano's assessment concerning the Yugoslavs but would not be hurried into the Albanian project. The Duce would not move without the successful conclusion of the Spanish Civil War and the signing of a pact with the Germans. Mussolini's decision must have come as another disappointment not only because his plan was again delayed but also because by mid-February rumors of some impending Italian move were becoming rather widespread, causing Ciano no little embarrassment. To counter these stories the Foreign Minister decided that "... we must spread the most varied rumors; like the octopus we must darken the waters."[31]

Ciano could do little else but to wait for another opportunity to convince the Duce that to hesitate any longer was not in the best interests of the Italian Empire. The German occupation of Prague on March 15, 1939, finally offered the Count another chance. Mussolini's initial reaction to the German move was a combination of uncertainty and fear.

Ciano on the other hand, perceived the German move as a cause to take Albania. Germans in Prague led the Count to one of his first outbursts in indignation against Berlin, asking rhetorically at one point "is it worthwhile to deal loyally with such people?" He added, "it is useless to hide that all this bothers and humiliates the Italian people. It is necessary to give them satisfaction and compensation: Albania."[32]

By March 23 the Count had finally convinced the Duce to support an immediate drastic change in Italy's relationship with Albania. Ciano was able to do this by resurrecting the spector of the German menance as well as by presenting him with notes of a meeting between Zog and Jacomoni in which the King implied that he might be willing to grant Rome further concessions.

The last remaining holdout to Ciano's "final solution" was Victor Emmanuel. The Italian King informed Mussolini quite frankly that he was not in agreement with the new policy on Albania since he did not see the point of risking such a venture in order to "grab four rocks." Perhaps the King simply did not approve of the dethroning of another king, even though Victor Emmanuel had always considered Zog to be an upstart unworthy of a member of the House of Savoy for a wife. Either way, the Duce, who was now confimed in his decision, ignored the King, informing Ciano that "if Hitler had had to deal with a nincompop of a King he would never have been able to take Austria and Czechoslovakia."[33]

Although Mussolini had finally agreed to Ciano's basic idea for a solution, he would not support unadulterated annexation. He hoped instead to attempt to subordinate Albania by the construction of irreversible political, economic and military bonds between the two countries. The Duce himself drew up the form of the ultimatum to Zog which Ciano described as "very brief consisting of three dry clauses which gave it more of an appearance of a reprieve than of an international pact."[34] The Count, in conjunction with Leonard Vitelli, Director-General of the Office of General Affairs in the Foreign Ministry, came up with his own proposal which had the advantage of being couched in courteous terms, and the Duce eventually approved.

The Count's document consisted of eight major sections including: 1) a rigorous defensive alliance; 2) the promise of Italian military aid in case of any external threat to Albanian territory; 3) permission for the Italian government to intervene to restore public order; 4) the concession to Italy of free use of ports, air fields and communication lines; 5) the elevation of the status of the Italian legation to Embassy; 6) provision for Italian financial and technical assistance in each Albanian Ministry; 7) the dismantling of customs barriers between the two nations; and 8) the extension of the rights of Italian citizenship to Albanians and vice versa. Ciano further mentioned concessions regarding fascist organizations in Albania as well as the introduction of Italian organizers for the gendarmerie.[35]

Meanwhile in Albania, because of the continuing rumors of troop movements and ultimatums, Zog and his government were confronted with ever increasing requests for information, primarily from the diplomatic corps. The government denied that the situation was serious, most of them did so honestly since Zog handled these negotiations personally. As late as March 30, the Albanian Minister of Foreign Affairs would not admit that there were any serious problems between Albania and Italy or that Albania was menaced. He would not even speak of financial difficulties. Jacomoni informed Ryan that although financial difficulties existed, Italy's best course would be to respect the forms of Albanian independence and to work with and through the Albanian regime.[36]

The King, too, probably for reasons of fear, had become much quieter since his complaints against Italy and Giro in particular, in February. On March 25 during a formal audience with Ryan, he said only that he intended to pursue a "good" policy towards Italy, subject to two things, independence and integrity.[37]

This was, of course, exactly what Ciano hoped to deprive Albania of with his ultimatum. Zog could not accept and yet he feared Italian reaction if he had not. The King fell back upon one of his favorite tactics; playing for time. On March 28 Zog informed Ciano that he supported the demands but his Ministers refused to go along, an obvious ruse which did not fool even Ciano. By March 31 the Italian Foreign Minister decided that Zog had indeed refused to sign.[38]

The Count, however, was prevented from initiating his long hoped for hostilities by military considerations of which he became aware on March 31. Military preparations had begun shortly before the ultimatum was presented to Zog. Four regiments of bersaglieri (specially trained mountain infantry), one regular infantry division, air force detachments and all of the first naval squadron had been ordered mobilized and concentrated at Puglia. Soon thereafter an additional division as well as a battalion of tanks were ordered mobilized at the suggestion of Marshal Badoglio.

Despite the impressive numbers, the deficiencies of this force soon became clear to both Ciano and Jacomoni after talks with General Pariani, the Chief of Staff, and Alfredo Guzzoni, who was to command the occupation forces. It appeared that the Italian military was unable to put together a battalion of trained motorcycle troops. Unforeseen problems with disembarcation further complicated the enterprise and forced Ciano to take another look at the entire undertaking.[39]

Apprehensive about the possibility of either an unsuccessful or a badly executed landing, Ciano moved closer to the option of taking Albania with Zog rather than against him. In conjunction with the Duce, the Count drew up a new set of conditions which Zog was expected to accept since thy supposedly allowed the King to save face. These new demands were somewhat less onerous that the last set and included: 1) control of all ports, communications, roads and airfields in the event it appears that Albanian independence is in danger; 2) an Italian organizer in each Albanian Ministry who would have the rank of Minister ranking immediately below the Albanian Minister; 3) Italians in Albania would have equal civil and political rights with the Albanians; 4) the raising of the Italian legation in Tirana and the Albanian legation in Rome to the rank of Embassies.[40]

Following the presentation of these demands, Jacomoni made it clear to Zog that the situation was now extremely serious. The King was given a simple choice. If he accepted the demands Ciano would go to Tirana to attend the solemn ceremony of signing the treaty, accompanied by a strong squadron of planes to emphasize the new relationship. If he refused, disorders would break out on the 6th, followed by the landing of Italian forces on the 7th.[41]

The King, recognizing that the Italians had taken a step backward, or perhaps fearing that the time had come for international help, finally broke the silence, informing the American Minister not only of the Italian demands but of his specific reaction to these demands. In regard to the first demand, Zog had informed the Italian Minister that only after previous agreement and in case he, the King, requested it, would he agree to the landing of Italian troops in Albania. Zog refused the second demand and as to the third, agreed only to extend civil rights to the Italians. He would not consent to allow Italians to be elected to Parliament or to own land. The King saw no difficulty with the fourth point. Zog further mentioned, however, that since some of his Ministers had asked that he reconsider, he had asked Jacomoni for more time.[42]

The tense situation had, in the meantime, slowly made itself felt among the population of Tirana. On the evening of April 1 there was a demonstration in Tirana, nationalist and anti-Italian. On the night of the 2nd, a larger probably less spontaneous and more definitely pro-Zog and anti-Italian disturbance took place. The King had clearly decided by this time that Italy meant to invade and he hoped that the demonstrations would result in substantial nationalist resistance to the invader. Within two days, the King ordered general mobilization and the evacuation of the Durrës civilian population, something which apparently was never fully achieved.

Although somewhat pessimistic about the possibility of a negotiated settlement, Zog nevertheless intended to keep all possible channels open and worked feverishly to come up with an acceptable set of counterproposals. Motivated by the new slim hope of saving Albania and by the fact that Queen Geraldine was on the verge of giving birth to his heir, Zog presented Ciano with a revised plan on April 2, incorporating the few acceptable points of the Italian ultimatum. The King agreed to certain demands but still refused to accept any proposal which he deemed incompatibel with the independence and integrity of Albania. Finally, the King asked that General Pariani, the only Italian who had ever gained the respect of the Albanians, be sent to Albania to discuss the question at issue.

Zog's proposals were ignored. For Ciano the die had been cast despite the military difficulties and it only remained to create the proper impression internationally. In the pursuance of this end, the Foreign Minister directed that all Italian civilian personnel and their families prepare to leave Albania. Ciano announced to the world that such a move had become necessary because Italian lives were in danger, a claim so blatantly ridiculous that it was greeted with nothing but scorn by the diplomatic community in Tirana. The Duce shared Ciano's impatience with Zog and as a result decided on April 2, to proceed with the invasion if Zog remained intransigent.

In international terms, the time was right for Mussolini; Madrid had fallen and although he had not yet concluded his pact with the Germans, von Mackensen, the German Ambassador in Rome, reacted favorably when informed of the invasion plans.[43] British Prime Minister Chamberlain's actions in March and early April confirmed Mussolini's ideas concerning Western inertia. On March 23 the Duce received a letter from the Prime Minister expressing concern and requesting the Duce's aid in maintaining international peace. Chamberlain's statements to Parliament on April 6 served to signficantly build the confidence of the fascist leadership.

The Prime Minister noted that with regard to Albania, the British government had "no direct interest, but a general interest in the peace of the world."[44] Despite reports that were now arriving from many quarters concerning Italian mobilization, Chamberlain did not feel that it was a propitious time to draw the attention of the Italian government to the fact that the occupation or annexation of Albania would violate the Anglo-Italian agreement of 1938 which called for the maintenance of the status quo in the Mediterranean. To emphasize his lack of concern, the Prime Minister left on the evening of the 6th for a ten-day vacation in Scotland.

That same morning Zog had been presented with a personal telegram from Mussolini fixing the expiration of the ultimatum at noon. The King refused to accept but referred the matter to his Ministers and a committee of Parliament. The Italians gave him six more hours. While he waited, he granted the American Minister an audience which had been set up some time before. Zog seemed by this time to have resigned himself to his fate. He referred with bitterness to the fact that the Italians decided to launch their offensive at the very moment when his wife was giving birth to a child. Grant noted that the King gave the impression of a man who felt bitter disappointment for what he considered a gross betrayal by the Italians as well as the rest of the world. On April 5, he had appealed to the democracies and on April 6, to the Balkan Entente, to no avail.[45]

During the course of the day warships appeared off Durrës and Vlorë to pick up the last of the Italians. In the afternoon dozens of Italian planes passed over Tirana dropping leaflets instructing the population to refuse obedience to their government and not to resist the Italians. The leaflets added that Italian forces would remain as long as was necessary for the re-establishment of peace, order and justice. While the planes were flying overhead a tremendous demonstration by a crowd of several thousand Albanians was staged in the principal square of Tirana. Hundreds of young men cried for arms with which to defend their country. In the evening a special cabinet and parliamentary meeting voted to reject the Italian demands and to resist with force the landing of Italian troops, while at the same time appealing to the Italians for further talks.[46] But the atmosphere was one of gloom. Independence would be lost either way.

Mussolini, who continued to vacillate, had not yet given up hope for a negotiated settlement although it could now only be achieved after the initial landing. The Duce told Zog to send his negotiator to Guzzoni once the Italian force had landed in Albania. Late on the 6th he sent the following orders to Guzzoni:

> If tomorrow morning a spokesman for Zog presents himself at the moment of disembarkation, listen to him and notify me by telegram. If instead no one asks to confer with you, execute the disembarkation smashing whatever resistance.[47]

Meanwhile, the general was ordered to proceed with the invasion.

At 5:30 on the morning of April 7, Good Friday, forty to fifty thousand troops supported by some 400 aircraft and dozens of warships attacked Durrës, Vlorë, Shëngjin and Sarandë. The major fighting seems to have taken place at Durrës where townspeople and a small contingent of troops which had been sent from Tirana, opposed the invasion. The defenders, led by Abbas Cupi, the Durrës gendarmerie commander, although vastly outnumbered and limited to fifty rounds of ammunition per man, managed to beat back the Italians.

After the invaders had retired, the ships opened fire using shrapnell to disperse the resistance. Cupi and his men, instead of retreating, moved forward and lined a parapet closer to the water's edge. Their courage was to no avail, however, since the attackers landed again in larger numbers with a flanking party. Cupi and his men were overcome by sheer weight of numbers and after inflicting a good many casualties, retreated into the town.

For two or three hours street fighting occurred throughout Durrës, although it was soon brought to an abrupt end after a transport disembarked a large number of small tanks. By nine o'clock all effective resistance in Durrës had ended and the Albanian survivors were either having coffee in civilian clothes in the cafes or making their way along the road out of the town to Tirana in the hopes of finding somewhere a few more rounds of ammunition with which to shoot another Italian or two before the inevitable end.[48]

Reports as to the number of casualties differed rather significantly. The townspeople of Durrës maintained that the Italians lost four hundred dead. Although Roman propaganda claimed that Italy lost only twelve men in the entire invasion, it is clear that approximately 200 Italians were killed at Durrës alone, and the Albanians may have lost even more.

There was no important resistance in the port of Vlorë, but Italian cyclists were ambushed on the road outside the town and suffered many casualties. A party of some forty men opposed the landing at Shëngjin with no more than six or seven casualties on each side. The road to Tirana was open on all sides.

During the afternoon, however, Guzzoni's triumphant march ground to a halt and had to be delayed for six hours, much to the chagrin of Mussolini and Ciano. The serious weaknesses in the Italian military machine had made themselves felt and it became clear to all involved, including the Duce, that had it not been for the lack of any organized resistance the Italians might have been faced with a military disaster. As Ciano's chief assistant, Filippo Anfuso, who accompanied the Count on his flight over the battle zone for campaign metals, put it, "if only the Albanians had possessed a well-armed fire brigade, they could have driven us back into the Adriatic."[49]

The organization of the entire expedition had been inadequate, partially because the commanders were given very little time to prepare. Pariani was told on March 29 that Albania would most likely be invaded and the operational commander, General Guzzoni, was not told until late on March 31. Even more remarkable, the air force did not receive their orders until two days before the invasion. As a result of these serious oversights, once the Italians reached Albania, they were seriously handicapped by badly trained men who were inadequately equipped and poorly led.

Guzzoni was forced to mobilize his own corps during a hurried train trip down to Brindisi and as a result, the conscripts to be used were given no more than a few hours notice, not enough time to learn how to use the weapons which they were expected to use. Many conscripts were attached to motorcycle companies without knowing how to ride while others joined signal units without knowing the Morse Code.

A paucity of important information both before and during the invasion added to the difficulties. Although the Italians had built the port installations at Durrës, the naval commanders were not told that the main harbor could not accommodate deepwater ships. Radio communications were so defective that the senior air force officer had to fly back and forth between Albania and Italy carrying messages to explain what was going wrong. He reported with astonishment on the lack of unity of command adding that if the authorities had remembered to use air reconnaissance first, the Italians would have learned that little resistance was to be expected.[50]

The Italian propaganda machine was thrown into action to mask the blunders. Official accounts reported that the attack would remain in history as a classic masterpiece of efficiency, organization, power, courage and political sense. Colonel Emilio Canevari, the best known of the military commentators, reported the brilliant attack by non-existent motorized formations in close contact with the air force and explained that all observers were impressed by the clockwork precision of a carefully studied and brilliantly executed plan.[51]

All of this naturally came as a pleasant surprise to operations commanders who might have expected courtmartials. They were delighted to learn that fascism expected no better of them. Many people were aware of the bungling, however, and Mussolini was forced to make a frank statement to the leadership explaining that the expedition had nearly failed because the organization and the people at his disposal were so defective. In one sense at least the bungled invasion did the fascist leadership a great service, it made clear to them how totally unprepared Italy was to fight a major war.

Fortunately for the Italians, their mistakes were met with inactivity on the part of Zog and his government. No serious preparations for resistance were made, no leadership was offered. Zog behaved less than well in this final crisis. The King's first concern on that fateful day was for the safety of his family. Initially it had been suggested by members of Geraldine's family that the Queen and her two-day-old son, Crown Prince Leka, seek refuge in the American Legation. Hugh Grant, the United States Minister, was approached and readily gave his consent if the King requested refuge.[52] There was some question as to her health since she had not fully recovered from the caesarean which was required to facilitate the birth of Leka.

At the last moment Geraldine was pronounced healthy enough to travel and was sent off in an ambulance at 4:00, 1½ hours before the invasion. The caravan of cars which accompanied the Royal family wound its way slowly through southern Albania towards the Greek frontier.

After the Queen was safely away, Zog moved to his Prime Minister's house and from there broadcast a radio message to his subjects urging them to continue to fight until every bit of blood was exhausted. Few owned radios so few heard the appeal. In the meantime, he made a final effort to come to a negotiated settlement with the Italians, sending emissaries to Guzzoni as Mussolini had suggested. Close to noon, Zog sent R. Gera, Minister of National Economy as well as a certain Colonel Samikoko to talk to the Italians. After these last talks proved fruitless, the King made a fateful decision; he would follow his wife into exile.

The Queen maintains that Zog had planned to withdraw into the hills to continue resistance activities on a guerrilla warfare level, despite the suggestion on the part of the government that he save himself by leaving the country. The King eventually was persuaded to abandon the idea, however, once the Yugoslav position had been made clear. According to the Queen, Belgrade informed Zog that if he withdrew into the hills they would not only block his retreat but would actually step in to stop Albanian nationalist agitation on their borders.[53]

Although Geraldine may have overstated the case somewhat, the dubious attitude of the Yugoslav government certainly played a role in the King's decision. Knowing that organized resistance could be sustained for only a short while, the King would eventually be forced to escape into Yugoslavia. If Belgrade closed its borders, which was likely, the King and his supporters would easily have been rounded up.

The fact that Albania was capable of little more than token resistance must also have been considered by Zog. The army, because of the substantial Italian influence and the fact that Rome had always emphasized numbers rather than quality, could not be counted on to be of any use to either side. Indeed, the military seems to have played only a minor role in the entire encounter.

This left only the tribesmen to carry on the fight, many of whom Zog had disarmed and who would have been, as a result, not only outnumbered but also vastly outgunned. Although they might have fought for Zog, it soon became clear, given the handicaps for which Zog himself was primarily responsible, that the severe shortage of guns, ammunition and organization would have quickly crippled Albania's resistance capabilities. Finally, it is conceivable that Zog, after fifteen years of sparring with the Italians, with no help in sight, simply did not have enough energy to carry on the fight. Clearly he was not dedicated to the idea of resistance. While this decision certainly saved a great many lives, it created a good deal of controversy.

The King's critics have roundly condemned him for his flight to Greece, accusing him of deserting his country. It is clear that whatever popularity he had was lost by this somewhat uncharacteristic act. Had he remained and appeared for example at Durrës, or had he put up some token resistance in the hills, he might have welded the Albanians together. Although he would have been overcome in the end by the numerical superiority of the Italians, King Zog would certainly have made a more positive impression on Albanian history. As it was, with their country invaded, their King gone, most Albanians resigned themselves to the inevitable.

The disappearance of the King and the collapse of resistance allowed the Italians to take Tirana on the morning of the 8th, basically without firing a shot. At about 10:30 Italian soldiers on motorcycles followed by small tanks entered the Tirana square. There were few people in the streets and even fewer in the various Ministries since most of the government had left with the King. Only the doorkeepers and a few subordinate officers, who did not try to conceal their bitterness, remained behind awaiting the invaders.

As soon as it was deemed safe, Ciano flew to Tirana eagerly expecting the festive welcome that he had been guaranteed by one of his personal agents. He was disappointed, for only a few turned out to welcome him. Ciano, accompanied by General Sereggi, King Zog's chief aide and the last Albanian Minister in Rome, arrived at Tirana City Hall at noon and was met by Dr. Mihsherko, Secretary General of the Albanian Ministry of Foreign Affairs as well as Xhafer Bey Ypi, the former Prime Minister and Chief Inspector of the Court. The former archbishop of the Albanian Orthodox Church, Vissar, made a short speech to a small crowd gathered in front of the city hall and urged cooperation with the Italians. His talk was coldly received.

Italian propaganda reported that the Albanians were wildly enthusiastic about the Italian invasion, an idea that had no foundation in fact, although there were some Albanians, including those who met Ciano on his arrival, who deserted their country in its hour of need. Other notable examples of treachery include the case of the ex-prefect of Durrës, Marco Khodeli, who fled to Bari to broadcast statements condemning Zog and calling for the welcoming of Italy and its Duce.[54] Khodeli returned to Albania on the day of the invasion as an officer in the Italian army. The King's own aide, General Sereggi, resigned his post shortly before the invasion and returned to Albania on the 7th in the company of Ciano. Sereggi had been promised a significant role in the Italian puppet state.

There were also, of course, many petty opportunists who saw the coming of the Italians as a means to make a few lire. A particularly distressing example of this sort of individual must be the Durrës tailor Reuf Xhuli whom Andrew Ryan discovered making Italian flags out of calico on the day the Italians marched in.

There were, of course, as many examples of individual heroism as well. Abbas Cupi, who was never a staunch supporter of Zog, not only led the resistance at Durrës but went on to organize a respectable guerrilla movement which the Italians were never able to completely destroy. Showing equal bravery but in another way, the ex-Prime Minister Mehdi Bey Fras-heri took it upon himself to broadcast scathing attacks against the invasion as well as address a remonstrance to Mussolini. Following the departure of the government from Tirana, he urged young men with revolvers to dis-tribute themselves to preserve order. When the invading troops were at the gates he sought asylum in the Turkish legation, continuing to refuse to sign a declaration supporting the Italians. His personal courage impres-sed even the German Minister who successfully appealed to Rome to allow Frasheri to return home unmolested.[55] Despite Italian guarantees, he was soon arrested and interned in Italy.

Apart from these few exceptions, general public opinion varied from indifference to open resentment. Many Albanians may have opposed Zog's regime but it does not follow that they would welcome foreign rule, particularly since one of their general grievances had always been that Zog had given too much away to the Italians. Privately, Ciano was not oblivious to the attitude of the Albanians noting in his diary,

> . . . there is a certain amount of coolness, especially among the high school students. I see that they dislike raising their arms for the Roman salute and there are some who openly refused to do it even when their companions urge them. . . . I see the eyes of some patriots flaming with anger and tears running down their faces. Independent Albania is no more.[56]

Upon his arrival in Tirana, Ciano did indeed see to the dismantling of the Albanian state apparatus. His solemn public assurances to protect the independence of Albania turned out to be just as hollow as his last cate-gorical denial, on April 5, that Italy was planning an invasion. The Count's first act was to set up a provisional governing committee composed of under-secretaries in the Albanian Ministries and headed by Xhafer Bey Ypi. Within four days this body gave way to an improvised Constituent Assembly consisting of some of the deputies who had remained in Tirana, augmented by a number of local citizens.

This group, working quickly under close Italian supervision, abolished the late dynasty and the constitution of 1928 and expressed the "unani-mous" wish of the whole population for the King of Italy to become also the King of Albania in a personal union of the crowns. Ciano, in private, liked to say that local opinion would have actually preferred him as king but either modesty or Mussolini restrained him from pursuing this point.[57] The makeshift Assembly finished its work by setting up a new government under the longtime Italian puppet, Shevket Bey Verlaci. Zog's onetime prospective father-in-law achieved his final revenge.

Victor Emmanuel accepted the Albanian throne and the former Italian Minister, Jacomoni, was appointed Viceroy to rule in his place. To make this task easier, Albania was presented with a new constitution on entirely fascist lines under which Italians assumed direct control of Albanian foreign affairs, and the Albanian armed forces including the gendarmerie were merged into those of Italy. A customs union was created and a special convention gave Italians in Albania and Albanians in Italy the same civil and political rights as they enjoyed in their own country. This exchange of civil rights was made possible by the remarkable discovery by Italian racial experts that the hitherto much despised Albanians were actually another Nordic race like the Italians.

All that remained of Albanian independence was its name, a separate flag, a separate language and the right to print separate postage stamps. Mussolini later though he had been wrong to allow even this degree of freedom because he realized, as did others, that there was little truth in the constant pronouncements that the Albanians welcomed with joy their new union with Italy.[58]

Motivated at least in part by this realization, Ciano and Jacomoni were careful to remove all traces of Zog, recognizing that many Albanians either supported him directly or at least equated the memory of the King with an independent Albania. Streets called after the King were given new names, often after Italian personages. Shortly before the Italian invasion, the Albanian government had renamed the southern port of Sarandë, "Zogai." Ciano, who treated the country as a kind of family property, was most gratified when the new Council of Ministers, instead of restoring the old name, solemnly decided that it should be called "Porto Edda" in honor of Ciano's wife and Mussolini's daughter. The Count even went so far as to rename the remaining members of Zog's family.[59]

The Italians also seemed to feel that it was to their advantage to occasionally rail against Zog in the controlled Albanian press. Immediately following the invasion, Rome spread the story in Albania that Zog had personally started the rumor that Tirana was to be bombed on the night of April 7, a story which caused considerable uneasiness at the time, in order to screen his own departure. In July the Italians launched another verbal outburst against the King to coincide with the sequestation of his property.[60]

Attacks on Zog naturally played a significant role in the Italian press which was left with the difficult task of justifying the invasion. Virginio Gayda, Mussolini's unofficial mouthpiece, argued in his paper, the *Giornale d'Italia* that,

> . . . more and more the King governed like a feudal lord, inconsiderate of the most elemental needs of the people, greedy of money for his personal whims, ambitious, irresponsible and fomenting both internal discord and international intrigue. The implacable enemy of all Albanians not members of his political clientele, he had in large measure, transformed the generous Italian policy of financial and economic assistance into a quasi-exclusive preserve to be doled out again by way to his personal exchequer.
>
> Notwithstanding the treaties and the frequent Italian complaints the Albanian people were the last to profit from Italian generosity. The protests of Albanian patriots and the attempts at revolt of the poor and needy populace were alike silenced by the threat of arms.
>
> A general discontent ranged around the royal house at Tirana. In these last days King Ahmed Zog had requested from the Italian Government new gifts as well as personal protection and the dispatch of troops to garrison certain points in Albania. But at the last moment, the Italian Government learned that these forces were intended to serve for a foolish coup de main of the king against Kosovo with the evident intent of disturbing the tranquility and cordiality of Italo-Yugoslav collaboration . . . .[61]

The editor of the *Lavoro Fascista* attempted to rationalize the invasion on the basis of state security arguing that,

> . . . at a time when all the democracies are extending and attempting to extend their frontiers in all the regions of Europe and Africa, where no real and natural interests calls them, Italy could not neglect for her safety's sake, the adjacent coast.[62]

In the same vein, the *Popolo di Roma* commented that

> . . . it is enough to look at a map of Italy to understand what supreme
> necessity of legitimate defense obliges Italy to take her precautions
> in the Adriatic. . . . In the case of war against anyone, the sure mili-
> tary possession of the Albanian coast is for Italy a question of life
> and death.[63]

Italy's official explanation, as presented by Ciano in a forty-minute
speech before the Chamber of Fasces and Corporations on April 15,
merely restated the comments of the press. In the presence of the German
Reichsminister Hermann Göring as well as a number of Albanian delegates,
the Count traced the historical ties between the Italian and Albanian
people beginning with Roman times. Relations were described as very
friendly until the advent of Zog. In spite of Zog's constant animosity,
Mussolini had been good enough to continue the flow of goods, services
and goodwill to the evergrateful people of Albania. The Count was careful
to itemize the various benefits which Rome had bestowed on Tirana.[64]

Ciano argued that it was Zog himself who, realizing that disorder and
dissension within the country had reached too great a level, had asked the
Fascist government for troops and arms to quell the unrest. Popular opinion, not Italian soldiers, had forced Zog to flee, according to the Count.
Less than a week earlier Ciano had tried to convince Lord Perth that Zog
had asked Rome for aid in order to launch an attack on Yugoslavia.[65]

None of this was of course taken very seriously and the only support
that Ciano received, both for his speech and for his invasion, came from
quarters from which little else could be expected. The Hungarian press
took a purely Italian view of events in Albania. *Pester Lloyd* even went
so far as to comment that Zog bore a heavy responsibility for the fate of
his unhappy Hungarian wife.[66]

The Germans lent Italy full support, despite Italian attempts to conceal
the operation from Berlin until the last minute. An editorial in the *Völkis-
cher Beobachter* on April 8 accused Zog of ill-treatment of his people and
the exploitation of Italian generosity. Much was made of the story that
Zog was planning to use Italian troops in a move against Yugoslavia.

The official German communique released on the same day noted that,

Germany has the fullest understanding for the protection of Italian interests in this area and would not be able to understand or approve if the Democratic Western Powers, who have no interest there, should wish to interfere in the juridically unexceptional position and action of our Axis partners.[67]

Albania's Balkan neighbors, although less willing to accept Italian explanations, were basically too frightened to offer open opposition. Yugoslavia was given twelve hours notice and took the time to ready two divisions but remained quiet during and after the invasion, seemingly satisfied with the Duce's pledge that Italy was disinterested in the Albanians of Kosovo. The Greek Minister in London, M. Simopulos, refused to accept any of Ciano's explanations, expressing complete skepticism as to the stories of Zog's project to attack Yugoslavia and that important Albanian chieftains had asked Mussolini to intervene.[68] Because the Greek government was concerned about Corfu, however, no strong reaction was forthcoming.

Only the Turks refused to accept the new situation and continued to grant the usual diplomatic privileges and immunities to the Albanian Minister and his staff. The Turkish government took the view that Zog's rule had only been interrupted since he had not abdicated. Apart from Turkey, the invasion was met with little more than gloom and misgivings in the Balkans.

In the West, the denunciation of the Italian action was widespread and noisy. Newspapers of the Right, Center and Left alike condemned with extreme severity the attack on Albania. Without exception they considered it a brutal and cynical act of unprovoked aggression in direct violation of the Italo-Albanian Agreement of 1927 as well as the Anglo-Italian Agreement of 1938.

In Paris the situation created was considered a menace both to France and Great Britain, especially for the latter in view of the Anglo-Italian Agreement. As a result, both the newspapers and the government showed, as they had in the past, a definite tendency to look to London for some sort of a lead. Several papers, including the Social Radical *Ere Nouvelle* criticized Great Britain for its complacent attitude towards Italy in the Mediterranean.[69]

This criticism was not misplaced for London proved that Mussolini's lack of concern for the reaction of the democracies was well founded. The official Foreign Office reaction turned out to be a good deal milder than the indignation expressed in the Western press. Both Lord Perth and the Foreign Secretary, Viscount Halifax, advised against a strong reaction, fearing that Italy would only be driven into greater reliance on Germany as a result.[70] The Prime Minister, who had hurried back from Scotland for the occasion, approved this attempt to appease Mussolini and as a result allowed the Anglo-Italian Agreement to remain in force without even denouncing Italy's violation of it. As a final step in Britain's acceptance of the Italian annexation of Albania, London applied to the Italian government for an executor for a new Consul-General on October 31, 1939, and thereby gave defacto recognition to the Italian annexation.[71]

Although the Italian invasion violated the sovereignty of Albania, guaranteed by the League of Nations Covenant, the reaction of this body to the outrage made it amply clear how completely impotent the League had become. Since no nation complained to the League, the issue was not even discussed until the Albanian Charge d'Affaires in Paris, Mehmed Abid, who had been instructed to do so by Zog, sent a letter denouncing the aggression and requested an immediate meeting of the Council of the League to decide with regard to the aid to be given Albania.

The Secretary-General, Joseph Avenol, answered that because the request had not come either from the Albanian government itself or through its accredited representative in Geneva, he could not consider it as an appeal under the Covenant. On May 13, the Secretary received a letter from King Zog who asked for help in the reestablishment of Albanian independence. Avenol read the letter to the Council of the League and "added that the reading of the letter constituted the action he intended to take with reference thereto."[72]

Despite this widespread complacency, Zog and the Albanian people seem to have been the last victims of appeasement, for the West drew a line at this point. A few days after the invasion President Roosevelt made his first serious intervention into European politics by inviting Hitler and Mussolini to give assurances that they would not attack a list of twenty-nine countries for ten years. More importantly, Britain and France immediately moved to guarantee Greece and Rumania against aggression. In Athens the British Ambassador delivered to the Greek government unconditional guarantees that London would not allow Corfu or any other part of Greece to be taken by the Italians.

Ten days later the British announced the introduction of compulsory military training, a move which seemed to mark a fundamental change in London's foreign policy. Soon after this significant development, London signed a pact with Ankara. In a sense, then, events in Albania marked an important stage in the process by which a coalition gradually built up to destory fascism.[73] It can be argued that Zog's and Albania's sacrifice was not in vain, although the King and his people would not have been consoled by the knowledge.

EPILOGUE

THE YEARS IN EXILE

Queen Geraldine, who had not yet fully recovered from childbirth, arrived safely in Florina, Greece on April 8, after having almost bled to death on the difficult journey. Zog, haggard and worn, along with a large group of Albanian officers and most of the top officials in the government, joined her late the same day to begin their difficult years in exile.

As with most unwanted political exiles, Zog's problems began almost immediately. The Greek dictator, John Metaxas, was greatly embarrassed and annoyed and immediately took steps to minimize the ill effects that Zog's presence on Greek soil might have. Fearing the wrath of the Italians, Metaxas promptly informed Rome that the King and his party of 113 would not be allowed to participate in any political activity while in Greece.[1]

The next step, of course, was to get him out of the country as quickly as possible. The Greek government must have applied considerable pressure for by April 10, Zog expressed his intention of leaving Greece within four days. The King would have done so had it not been for the illness of Geraldine. King George of Greece intervened and permitted the Royal party to stay as long as the Queen needed from complete recovery. During these weeks Metaxas insured that they were kept incommunicado at the home of an Albanian near Larrissa, far from the frontier. On May 2, much to the relief of the Greek Government, the Royal family, accompanied by some eighty followers, left Greece by special train for Turkey.[2]

290

The King's stay in Turkey proved to be much more agreeable. The Turks, as fellow Moslems, were on the whole a good deal more hospitable and treated Zog with courtesy. The King found a great many supporters in Istanbul whom he was allowed to see since the Turks had less to fear from the Italians than had the Greeks. The Albanian Minister in Turkey was so attentive to the Royal couple that the soon to be dissolved Albanian Foreign Ministry requested his immediate resignation.

Even Turkish hospitality had its limits however. Despite the fact that the government had never recognized the Italian annexation and had allowed Zog's legation to remain open, President Ismet İnönü made it very clear to Zog that he would prefer that the King refrain from visiting Ankara.

The Queen hoped that Zog would remain in Istanbul, basically because he felt so much at home there. The King spoke excellent Turkish and was still familiar with the environs from the days of his youth. Geraldine recalls Zog showing her around the city pointing out where Skanderbeg had grown up and where he himself had spent time while studying in the Ottoman capital.[3]

Zog seemed content and yet he was determined to leave Turkey soon after his arrival. One factor that might have been important in his decision was the prevailing rumor, which the Turkish government took very seriously, that two Albanians had been delegated by the Italians to go to Istanbul and kill the King.[4] More importantly, Zog hoped eventually to retrieve his throne, something which would only be possible with the help of a major power. Despite his frequent disappointments with British policy, Zog turned again to London, the only country which in his eyes had even shown any altruistic interest in the well being of Albania and in his own personal welfare.

In one sense his decision was of course naive, given the nature of British foreign policy in the 1930s and the fact that London had openly recognized the change of Albania's political status. On the other hand, to a certain extent it can be considered far-sighted and indicates that his years as King had finally taught him something about international affairs. Zog had for some time been convinced of the inevitability of war in Europe, a conflict which he felt Germany and her allies would lose.[5] Zog hoped to be considered on the winning side and as such, he informed the British Ambassador in Ankara of his wish to leave for London. The King's request was granted in mid-June, after he had agreed to refrain from political activity while in England.

In order to avoid travelling near Italy or through Germany, Zog and his party were forced to take a rather long tour through Eastern and Central Europe which included stops in Rumania, Poland, Latvia, Finland and Sweden. Finally, in August, the party arrived in Paris where Zog hoped to remain for a time to see if he might not be able to convince the French government to allow him to organize against the Italians. The King duly requested that the French Foreign Minister, Pierre Bonnet, allow him to become politically involved.

Bonnet, who made certain that Zog agreed to refrain from politics before entering France, refused to allow the King any privileges whatsoever, for a number of reasons. As with the British, the French government seems to have told the Italians that Zog would scrupulously refrain from political activity and neither country was willing to break faith with Rome. Probably more important as a determining factor in Zog's treatment was the personal attitude of the French Prime Minister Edouard Daladier. The Prime Minister considered "Zog to be an appalling gangster who had been paid by Italy to clear out of Albania."[6]

Despite Daladier's vow not to allow Zog to say in France for any length of time and despite the generally hostile environment, Zog remained in Paris until shortly before the German invasion. During this period he seems to have done very little, owing to French restrictions on his activities. He did make one appeal to King George of England, complaining that the attitude of the British gave the impression that London was essentially condoning the action of the Italians. The British made it clear at this point, without offending Italy, that they were not altogether without sympathy for him in his unfortunate position. As a result of this attitude, when Zog asked for evacuation in June the British agreed to help, recognizing that Zog stood a good chance of being killed if he remained.

The flight from France was nevertheless extremely harried with the Royal party getting out of Paris only eight hours before the arrival of the German troops. The group of thirty travelled south to Bordeaux in twelve cars, lacking food and dodging bombs along the way. Once there, no boat was to be found to carry them to England so they appealed to General Franco to be allowed to enter Spain. The Spanish dictator refused his permission, leaving the Royal party stranded in southern France. Finally on June 27, passage was arranged on the *SS Etrick* which carried wounded to Plymouth from St. Jean de Luc. Geraldine remembers that it was on this trip that Zog began to break down for the first time.[7]

Once in England the King, who was recognized only as a private citizen by the government, was immediately confronted with another crisis. British hospitality, like that in Turkey, had its limits and various elements in the Foreign Office were anxious to shuttle the King out of England as quickly as possible. In a meeting with the Foreign Office attended by Andrew Ryan, it was decided that Zog should be asked to leave because it was determined that the King was discredited and that the people associated with him were unpopular. While Zog was still deemed influential among his own tribesmen, the Foreign Office concluded that even if it were thought desirable to use him for the purpose of rallying these tribesment near the Yugoslav border, Belgrade was at that point too frightened to permit such activity to be carried on from Yugoslav territory. It was agreed that any attempt to run a pro-Zog campaign in England would lead to counter-propaganda by the Italians.[8]

The Foreign Office was further confirmed in its decision by the odd collection of people and equipment which Zog brought with him to the Ritz Hotel in Piccadilly, where he stayed while in the capital. Of the thirty-four people Zog had with him six were listed as "H.M. Ordinance Officers," but turned out to be his personal bodyguards made up of Albanian tribesmen carrying sawed-off shotguns. Since the gun was illegal in England, Scotland Yard was most anxious to have these weapons or their owners removed.

Finally, the Treasury Department was disturbed over the large quantity of money which Zog seemed to be carrying around with him. Because no financial records seem to have been kept, the question of how much money Zog brought out of Albania was the subject of considerable speculation. One postwar writer had estimated that Zog made off with a bucket of rubies and emeralds as well as part of the gold reserves of the state bank, all of which was valued at about ten million dollars. Those Albanians who opposed Zog in London (apart from the King's party there were only six Albanians in England) maintained that Zog was in possession of between one and four million pounds.[9]

Whatever the final figure, it is clear that Zog entered England with a large quantity of gold and jewels. Geraldine recalls that the King left

Albania with 100 sacks of gold, money which he had received from the Italians for the lease of forest land around Mati, money which Zog had always kept in his office. The Queen also mentioned a quantity of jewels which provided her with a living after the King's death.[10]

All of this money came to the attention of the British Treasury in September 1940 when Zog's man, Sotir Martini, asked if the Foreign Office would arrange facilities for transport to Canada of seven cases containing money.[11] Apparently the King was worried about the safety of his fortune. Permission was never given and the gold was never shipped, but its very existence seems to have bothered the Treasury for some time.

Based on these considerations, the Foreign Office instructed Andrew Ryan, who became its unofficial liaison, to inform Zog that for reasons of politics and of safety, the British government recommended that he leave for the United States. At the same time the Counsellor of the U.S. Embassy was asked to provide visas for Zog and his party. Not wishing to take responsibility for such a move, the Counsellor suggested that the British Ambassador in Washington, Lord Lothian, explain to the American government why this was necessary.

Abruptly, after many of the arrangements had been made, Zog and his party were allowed to stay. This change of policy was effected partially by the arguments of Zog's secretary Qazin Kastrat who, obviously encouraged by the King, argued that the British would be making a serious mistake in expelling Zog. Kastrat maintained that all Albanians, including formerly implacable exiles from the Zog regime, were willing to support the King's wartime leadership and if he left Europe their cohesion would be destroyed and their usefulness crippled. Only Zog had sufficient status to induce Albanians in their own country to take the risks involved in embarrassing the Italians. Finally, Kastrat argued that Zog possessed great assets in his good relations with the Turkish government and in the high regard which the people of Islam had for the only Moslem king in Europe.

The Foreign Office began to reconsider, fearing that His Majesty's Government might be faced with criticism along the lines that they had lost an opportunity of pursuing the war more vigorously against the Italians if Zog went. It was feared that Zog might spread stories of inhospitality in the United States. The earlier decision was finally reversed after the Foreign Secretary, Lord Halifax, decided that if Zog was going to mobilize his friends in his defense, he should be allowed to stay. Further, Halifax was unwilling to ask the United States to receive people like Zog who would not do any harm in England. The Foreign Secretary decided to reserve that option for those the government desperately wanted out of England.[12]

Once allowed to stay, Zog immediately set about attempting to insure his position after the war. While none of the allies were willing to recognize him as a co-belligerent, primarily because the British had officially recognized Italy's annexation of Albania in October of 1939, he nevertheless offered his assistance in orchestrating an uprising in Albania. The King was motivated by nationalism and the knowledge that if the British used his services he would gain legitimacy with regard to a post-war settlement.

Zog argued that he could be of use to the war effort based upon support for the Monarchy both in Albania and among the Albanian communities abroad. Zog claimed that he could rally some 30,000 supporters in northern Albania who could be equipped with the 10,000 rifles which the King maintained were hidden in the country. Zog told the British that he was in continual contact with not only his supporters but also some of the leaders of the other northern tribes, including Mark, chief of the Mirditë.[13]

With regard to Albanians abroad, Zog claimed to have support among the Albanians in the United States, Bulgaria, Egypt and particularly among the large colony in Istanbul where Juka, Krossi, Aranitas and Cupi remained after their flight from Albania. The King produced a series of telegrams which he had received from Istanbul requesting that he come to Turkey where a fighting force of some 14,000 could be raised.[14]

Based on this support, Zog came up with a plan to organize and train this force in Greece. Once in Greece the King also planned to direct an extensive uprising in all parts of Albania. His main effort, of course, was to be in the north where he hoped to lead a frontal attack against the Italian defenses with the support of the twenty officers at this disposal.

In the south Zog hoped to use the few organized bands not to stir up an uprising, because they were basically too weak, but to harry the Italians as much as possible particularly in the Korcë area. With regard to the Kosovars, the King maintained that the tribesmen there were ready to rise and had sent him a deputation while he was in Istanbul. Although a

good deal of their dissatisfaction was of course directed against the Yugoslav government, Zog was convinced that their efforts could be turned
against the Italians.

The British government initially refused to consider using Zog in any
capacity but began to reconsider this decision once the Italians had launched their invasion of Greece on October of 1940. Both the Foreign Office
and the War Office reversed their decision following testimony from Sir
J. Percy and Sir Andrew Ryan. Percy argued that Zog could be of use
in the war effort. Ryan, who was impressed by the closeness with which
the King followed the course of events affecting the Balkans, maintained
that Zog's plan was constructive enough to be worth considering. Ryan
concluded that with proper financing Zog could direct a united Albanian
effort sufficient to at least embarrass the Italians.[15]

Although the government accepted the idea to use Zog along the lines
that he had suggested in principle, before final arrangements could be
made the British hoped to determine the attitude of the various governments involved, and the true extent of Zog's popularity inside Albania.
The entire project was called into question almost immediately by the
uncompromising attitude of General Metaxas. The general argued that
under no circumstances could he allow Zog to operate on Greek soil,
claiming that the King's unpopularity would actually help the Italians.

Neither Zog nor the British were taken in by Metaxas, who was interested in occupying and retaining part of southern Albania for himself
and realized that if he allowed the King any role in the operations he
would run the risk of committing himself to the restoration of an independent Albania under Zog's rule. Metaxas did, however, react favorably
to the suggestion on the part of the Istanbul Albanians who hoped to
form a legion in Greece. Since the offer was not made dependent on
Zog's leading it, Metaxas commented that he would welcome their participation provided that they could equip themselves.[16]

The British government still believed that Zog could be useful and even
before discovering the attitude of the other nations involved, on the spur
of the moment, on the night of November 23, offered to fly him to
Cairo as the first step in carrying out his plan. It apparently had dawned
on someone in the Foreign Office that November 28 was Albanian independence day and that it would be a good public relations move to begin
operations on that day.

Zog would not be hurried in such a manner, however, at least not before he had been able to see either Churchill or Lord Halifax. The King was of course keenly aware that the government was unwilling to recognize him as anything but an Albanian chieftain and would make absolutely no commitment regarding the future of Albania. The King hoped that a meeting with either the Prime Minister or the Foreign Secretary would at least give him some measure of credibility which might later be useful.

As it turned out, Zog made a wise decision in not rushing off to Cairo. Queen Geraldine maintains that the plane which would have taken him was shot down enroute. Even if he had arrived in Egypt he would have been unable to carry out his plans for a few days after the Foreign Office suggested Zog should go, telegrams began coming in advising that the King should be kept in England.

Unfortunately for Zog, every government or British office slated for some sort of participation in the project reacted negatively to the plan. The Turkish Government made it clear that they would not agree to have Zog go to Istanbul. Of the other possible staging areas, Cyprus was disqualified because of Greek objections and Palestine was rule out after the Colonial Office pointed out that it would be a mistake to admit a non-Jew.

Ambassador Campbell in Belgrade reported that the Yugoslav Minister of War had been informed by the general commanding the Third Yugoslav Army on the Yugoslav-Albanian frontier that the Albanians whom he was secretly in contact with were united in their opposition to Zog.

The project was finally finished off by reports from Cairo and from the Commander-in-Chief, Middle East. The Commander-in-Chief, after soliciting a report from Colonel Stirling head of the commander's Albanian mission in Istanbul, strongly advised against the project. Ambassador Lampson in Cairo concurred, adding that he felt it most unwise to send Zog to Cairo since he doubted whether the Court or the government would relish his presence. Lampson mentioned that since Cairo was filled with so many doubtful legations, Zog's every move would be spied upon and reported to the enemy.[17] On the basis of these various reports, the British government decided to abandon the idea of using the King, yet he was not to be cold-shouldered in the event that he might prove useful in the future. Zog was to be kept in "warm-storage."[18]

Zog, of course, reacted with disappointment particularly with regard to the Turkish government. The King maintained that Ismet Pasha had promised that if there was trouble in the Balkans he would be allowed to organize the Albanians in Turkey. Regardless, the King felt himself unsuited for storage of any kind and did all in his power to convince the British government to reverse its decision.

In January 1941, Zog informed Ryan that he had expanded his contact within Albania to include many of his staunchest erstwhile opponents as well as some Albanians who had initially cooperated with the Italians. Most prominent among this group was Gani Bey who had finally decided to work with Zog. The King also mentioned that he was in contact with Malik Bushati, who was not only a longtime opponent but had become the Minister of the Interior in Shevket Verlaci's post-invasion cabinet. The British could not be moved, however, particularly in light of the successful Greek push into southern Albania. Zog's fate had been sealed.

Somewhat discouraged by the government's refusal to allow him to participate in the war effort and by the unwillingness of Churchill, Halifax or Eden to receive him, Zog moved his family to the relative safety of the countryside in May 1941. Prince Leka, then eighteen months old, had been suffering from convulsions induced presumably by the persistent German bombing which London was forced to endure during May. Geraldine, who had been anxious to move the family, finally found a suitable villa in Sunningdale near Ascot.

Life in the country, although somewhat safer, was certainly as hectic as life in London had been. While few financial problems presented themselves, there was still a matter of procuring provisions for the large group, a task which seemed to fall mostly to Geraldine. Zog felt strongly about the men in his entourage refraining from any work, arguing that they had given up everything to be with him. As a result, Geraldine, particularly after the entire party moved to Parmoor at Henley-on-Thomas near the end of 1941, was forced to cultivate the huge kitchen garden by herself. To complete the picture, Zog gave the Queen chickens for Christmas. The eggs were of course welcome but unfortunately it fell to the Queen to clean out the coup.[19]

Rather than adopt the life of an English country squire, Zog actually stepped up his political activities during the years at Parmoor. Having been rebuffed by the government, the King devised various schemes in order to convince it to change its policy toward him. Lack of recognition remained.

his biggest problem so most of his efforts were aimed at legitimizing his position as leader of the Albanian people.

In pursuance with this goal he scrupulously maintained contact with as many Albanians in and out of Albania as he could. His first claim to legitimacy consisted of his legations in Turkey and Egypt, his mission in Washington and some four consular posts. These received top priority in terms of contact and more importantly, in terms of funds. Zog sent thousands of pounds for the maintenance of these last vestiges of official credibility.

The King's contact within Albania were also maintained. Although Gani Bey and Bushati remained prominent among his list of correspondents, his most useful contact was Abbas Cupi, who returned to Albania in 1942 to organize resistance against the Italians.

Zog, in the meantime, had reverted back to classic Balkan politics and hoped to play the allies off against each other. At a London conference in 1942 he appealed for Canadian, American, Belgian and Czech help in gaining recognition. Although he received a sympathetic reply from the Belgians and a cordial one from Dr. Benes, the Czech leader, nothing came of this attempt. Shortly thereafter, Zog sent a telegram to President Roosevelt, routed through Istanbul declaring Albanian support for the twenty-six power declaration, but the British quickly stepped in and informed Washington that Zog was in England as a private citizen and that Albania did not count among the allies.

The King's most ambitious plan to achieve recognition was stimulated by a group known as the "Balkan Committee," with Lord Noel-Buxton as President and Sir Edward Boyle as Chairman. The group, which was pro-Bulgarian and anti-Greek, counted Sir J. Percy as well as Sir R. Hodgson, the former Minister to Albania, among its members. These two suggested to Zog that both the Albanian cause and his own position would best be served if the King organize some sort of national committee and then appeal to Washington for recognition in light of the Atlantic Charter.[20]

Zog decided to go even further and attempt to organize a national government in exile consisting of four or five cabinet ministers and a small assembly elected by the colonies. In order to do this Zog saw the necessity of creating some kind of a united front among the Albanians abroad, no mean feat considering the myriad of splinter groups that had emerged.

Although division existed among the Albanians in Istanbul as well, the most serious split and hence the greatest obstacle to the plan appeared in the United States. Three groups had emerged led by Faik Konitza, Fan Noli and Kosta Chekrezi respectively. They seemed to have temporarily united only in their opposition to Zog.

The King set to work on these groups and by sending them money and offering to convene a constituent assembly after the war to decide on the future of the Monarchy, he seems to have convinced them to soften their positions. The active participation of Boyle in these negotiations also played a role. At the beginning of July 1942, it was reported that the Albanian organization in Boston, "Vatra," had passed a resolution favoring a united front. Konitza and Noli were willing to work with Zog while Chekrezi, who found it difficult to forget the time he spent in jail under Zog's regime, remained skeptical.

In a last effort to convince him, the King circulated rumors in Washington that the British were on the verge of recognizing Zog. Whether this had any bearing on Chekrezi's decision is unclear, but he does seem to have eventually given in.[21]

All of this came to naught, however, once the British government was informed of Zog's activities. Ironically, it was the King himself who appraised them of his plans, laying the whole scheme out for Ryan in an attempt to gain British approval. Once the plans were out in the open, the Foreign Office moved quickly to put a stop to them. Officials were sent to Boyle instructing him to stop encouraging Zog. The King was told that the government would not allow such activity on its soil and that he had violated his pledge not to become involved in politics.

Zog, genuinely shocked by the British reaction, complained bitterly that Albania was being discriminated against and that he needed to do something since he was being criticized by some Albanians in Istanbul for his inactivity. Further, Zog argued, a small government was necessary as a focal point for the legations still open, for the Albanians in the colonies and for those who had remained loyal in Albania proper.[22]

The unfortunate Ryan was left to explain British policy to the embittered King. The government continued to withhold recognition ostensibly because they had legally acknowledged the invasion and because Zog had not run a democratic government. Ryan also mentioned that Britain intended to preserve liberty of action, indicating that its commitment to Albania's territorial integrity was somewhat weak. One of the more significant determining factors in the British attitude at this point was not communicated to Zog. London had been informed that the principal resistance activities within Albania as of the summer of 1942 were being conducted by Muharrem Bajraktari, one of Zog's old opponents.[23] Considering the general state of allied fortunes at that point, the British were unwilling to jeopardize any resistance movement no matter how small.

After this severe rebuff, Zog's chances for recognition and an active role in the war effort essentially disappeared. He refused to give in, however, and continued to correspond with and send money to the Albanian communities in the United States and Turkey. As he became more desperate his schemes became less and less plausible. In January of 1944 in an interview with members of the Anglo-Jewish Association the King offered to sponsor a plan for a Jewish settlement in Albania if the Jews consented to help him regain his throne.[24]

One last glimmer of hope presented itself shortly after the Jewish scheme. In the beginning of February 1944, the Foreign Office was notified by agents in the Balkans that Abbas Cupi had finally managed to build his band into a large and powerful group. Information was also received that Cupi was to demand British recognition for Zog as head of a provisional government and that all further collaboration was to be dependent on this recognition.

Before the British would commit themselves to recognition, they planned to send a senior officer, Lt. Colonel Maclean, into Albania to determine the actual strength of Cupi's movement. Maclean took with him verbal messages to Zog's followers from the King to unite with other resistance movements. This last glimmer quickly faded when it was learned that Cupi's strength had been overestimated. Several months later, it was discovered that Cupi had fled to Bari and that Enver Hoxha, the communist leader, was in control of much of Albania.[25]

Soon after the end of the war, Zog decided that the time had come to leave England and he began to search for a more permanent place of residence. Since plans were already made to ease the King out of the country, the British government was delighted. The British recognition of the Hoxha government in November 1945 confirmed Zog in his decision and he informed Ryan shortly thereafter that King Faruk of Egypt, who was of Albanian descent, had given firm assurances that the Albanian party was welcome in Cairo. Zog was returning to his own world, for as much as he attempted to identify with the West, as much as he attempted to become a Western monarch, his roots remained in the East.

In February 1946, after five and one-half years in England, the Royal party, consisting of twenty-three people, sailed for Alexandria. Because the one hundred sacks of gold which Zog had brought to England were still basically intact upon his departure, a comfortable villa was procured once the group arrived in Egypt.

Despite the pleasant surroundings, if the years in England represented disappointment then the years in Egypt represented tragedy. It was in Egypt that Zog first became aware that he was suffering from cancer of the stomach, brought on, according to Geraldine, by the bleeding ulcer that the King refused to have removed in 1931. It was in Egypt that Zog suffered the first in a series of heart attacks.

The unstable political situation in Egypt merely compounded the problem faced by the Royal family. Fearing a disaster, Zog travelled to the United States in 1951 and purchased a villa on Long Island in case a hasty retreat from Cairo became necessary. Zog's political sense had not failed him for in 1952, King Faruk was overthrown and forced into exile. Unfortunately for the Royal party, however, Zog suffered a serious hemmorage at about the same time and therefore could not be moved.

It was not until the summer of 1955 that the King was able to travel safely. During these years the Royal family found itself in a rather precarious position particularly after the rise of Abdul Nasser. Because of Zog's close connection with Faruk, the new Egyptian leader quickly closed Zog's legation and sequestered all of the gold which had been deposited in an Egyptian bank. These were times of uncertainty and fear. On several occasions Zog's residence was surrounded and searched. The Queen recalls many tense situations involving Egyptian soldiers and Zog's bodyguards.[26]

Low on funds and with some thirty people in tow, the Royal family fled to Cannes in July of 1955. At that time French doctors informed Zog that he had no more than three months to live. The King managed to cling to life for another six years, filled with little more than pain and suffering. During the years in France, Geraldine recalls that life was dominated by twenty-four hours of illness. Zog was never able to sleep for more than a few hours a night despite the use of sleeping drugs. The King never left the house and the Queen left only rarely, fearing that Zog might suffer some sort of an attack in her absence.

Continued physical degeneration eventually prevented him from keeping abreast of the world political situation. In the early years in France Geraldine maintains that Zog was very active and apparently was somehow involved in the Kim Philby spy scandel as well as the Seuz crisis.[27] By the late 1950s, however, with disease sapping his energy, Zog seemed to become increasingly apathetic and melancholy. Geraldine tried to convince him to write but he had always suffered from an inability to put his thoughts down on paper. Once he was no longer able to remain politically informed, he seemed to lose interest in life. There was little else left.

Geraldine, who had by this time become chief adviser and had long since taken over the King's finances, found it difficult to deal with the ever-increasing misfortune which plagued the Royal party. Added to the King's illness and the tight financial straits, she recalls that she even received a number of anonymous assassination threats during this period, which she successfully kept from the ailing King.

In the beginning of 1961, Zog, a skeleton of his former self, entered the hospital Foch just outside of Paris where he spent the last months of his life. During the final days, after the disease had finally broken his spirit completely, Zog asked his wife to provide him with a revolver. Frightened, she gave him one but refused to provide the ammunition. Since he had contracted jaundice by this time, the King was too weak to pick up the gun in any case. Within a few days, on April 5, Leka's birthday, Zog went into a coma. Four days later he died.

The King was mourned by only a few. His failure had been profound. Yet in many respects, it was understandable for he had remained a child of his environment. He began his political career as the younger son of a small tribal leader with an inadequate education. He very naturally developed into a capricious Balkan chieftan spending most of his time engaged in war or intrigue. His natural talent in this regard and his intimate knowledge of his Albanians allowed him to quickly outmaneuver his rivals, who proved to be no match for the energetic, clever young man from Mati.

Once in power, however, it seemed as if his talents were no longer as useful. The first British Minister to Albania commented that Zog was much better suited to be Minister of the Interior than Prime Minister for he was not a good judge of men and did not know whom to trust. Because of his inability to choose competent advisers, younger more able men were kept in the background and the population suffered under the yoke of unreconstructed Ottoman bureaucrats.

Once Zog became King, his personal shortcomings became even more prominent; it seemed as if the vital period of activity had passed. He seemed to become mentally sloppy, still capable of determined and obstinate action but no longer capable of thoughtful consideration of ways and means to deal with resulting difficulties. While he did show signs of having learned something during his last years, by then it was too late. Because of his limited constructive talent, his inability to grasp economics and his failure to comprehend the true magnitude of the peasant problem in Albania, Zog seemed unable to effect any real material progress.

The result of all this by 1939 was, of course, a desperate situation. The population was still overwhelmingly peasant oriented with industry in 1938 accounting for only 4.4 percent of the national income.[28] Agriculture and stock-breeding methods remained primitive as well because what little capital Albania had was not used efficiently. Transportation and communication was still very difficult. In 1939 there were no railroads and only 500 miles of roads, generally in a state of disrepair.

Because of Albania's primitive transportation system and the negative effect this had on agriculture and industry, extensive importing was necessary. Not only did Albania import all of the needed manufactured goods but signficant quantities of agricultural produce was still needed as well. In 1939 large quantities of wheat, corn and rice were still being imported to meet the basic needs of the people. Export values still had not exceeded 50 percent of the import costs. Trade per capita was 2½ times greater in Bulgaria, 1 3/4 times greater in Yugoslavia, 7½ times greater in Greece and thirty-one times greater in Britain.[29] Zog clearly failed in his attempt to create economic stability in Albania. While this was not his only failure, it certainly was his most serious.

Social conditions remained almost as primitive as the economic conditions. Impoverished peasants were still ruled by feudal Moslem landlords. Only three towns, Tirana, Durrës and Vlorë, in any way resembled a European city. General living conditions were poor everywhere; the people suffered from a bad diet making them vulnerable to disease. Public health services were non-existent and education was still rudimentary. In 1939, 85 percent of the population was still illiterate. the highest rate in Europe.[30] While some small improvement was made, serious social problems remained. With more time Zog might hae been able to accomplish more in this regard.

Despite grinding poverty and Albania's primitive social conditions, Zog must still be considered one of the most important political forces in modern Albanian history. He was almost single-handedly responsible for the creation of conditions, though perhaps intangible, which made it possible for Albania to survive as a state. In the 1920s Zog was one of the only Albanian politicians who thought in terms of a modern state. Considering that his single experience with a modern state structure was with Austria-Hungary before World War I, it is perhaps not surprising that Zog eventually constructed a monarchy.

He was clever enough to realize, however, that he could not simply copy political forms which might have been applicable elsewhere without taking indigenous political realities into consideration. Zog's experiences in Albania during the early 1920s certainly reinforced this point. Drawing on his own political dualism, he eventually created a system composed of a combination of eastern and western political ideas, perhaps more western in form and eastern in substance. In practical terms he divised an inefficient non-absolutist dictatorship not unlike the governments of the other Balkan states during the interwar period and not unlike many of the governments of developing nations in Asia and Africa in the 1970s and 1980s. But Zog was not a tyrant for he was without the means and possibly without the inclination to be overtly oppressive.

Despite its flaws, Zog's curious state provided him with the centralization necessary to forcably reduce the chaotic lawlessness of the highlands and bring the divergent elements of the country together. The independence which the northern tribes had enjoyed for centuries was for the most part curtailed. Many gave up their weapons, significantly reducing brigandage and the blood feud. By the 1930s the central government was recognized in all parts of the country, allowing Zog's administration to collect taxes and draft recruits for the army, something which would have been considered impossible immediately following World War I. Here Zog must be considered successful. Regardless of his serious lack of administrative ability, a situation which he was beginning to remedy by the late 1930s, Zog was able to provide Albania with a certain political stability.

One of the most positive results of this unique political stability, and without a doubt one of Zog's most important contributions, was the creation of an environment ideal for the growth of an Albanian national con-sciousness. Before the advent of the King, local pride was the only form of nationalism existent in most of the country. When Zog left in 1939 the process towards creating a rudimentary form of modern state nation-alism had begun.

But the construction of a state apparatus which could produce centrali-zation was not the only important consideration in the creation of the desired environment. Zog's foreign policy also made a significant contri-bution. In his struggle against the foreigners the King provided a continu-ing focus for national hostility. His relentless resistance to Italian attempts to violate Albanian political sovereignty and territorial integrity demon-strated not only his will to survive but also indicated the level of his own patriotism. Although he was often forced to make concessions, he denied the Italians a customs union, the influx of large numbers of settlers, the renewal of the first Treaty of Tirana, repayment of the SVEA loan and the dismissal of the English gendarmerie officers. That the Italians eventu-ally came to the conclusion that invasion was the only means by which they could completely control Albania is ironically, evidence of Zog's success in keeping them at bay. Most Albanians were able to sympathize with Zog in this struggle. Had he remained to lead the people during the final onslaught, he would have been remembered in a more positive light.

Zog's contribution, then, was of considerable importance. Those who succeeded him as rulers and completed the construction of a modern national state had their task made somewhat simpler as a result of the foundation of nationalism for which Zog was responsible.

NOTES

Notes to Chapter One

1. USDS 875.001 ZOG/86: Tirana (No. 886), 9 October 1933.
2. FO 371/15149 (C6736/6736/90): Durazzo, 25 August 1931.
3. USDS 875.001 ZOG/86: Tirana (No. 886), 9 October 1933.
4. Ekrem Bey Vlora, *Lebenserinnerungen Band II* (München: R. Oldenbourg Verlag, 1973), p. 131.
5. Christo A. Dako, *Zogu the First, King of the Albanians* (Tirana: Kristo Luarasi Printing Press, 1937), p. 28.
6. FO 371/12844 (C1351/146/90): Durazzo, 3 February 1928.
7. Joseph Swire, *Albania the Rise of a Kingdom* (London: Unwin Brothers Limited, 1929), p. 30.
8. FO 371/13560 (C1343/367/90): Durazzo, 11 February 1929.
9. Mary E. Durham, *High Albania* (London: Arnold, 1901), p. 125.
10. Marcel W. Fodor, *Plot and Counterplot in Central Europe* (Boston: Houghton Mifflin Co., 1937), p. 96.
11. Robert Busch-Zanter, *Albanien, Neues Land in Imperium* (Leipzig: W. Gould, 1939), p. 94.
12. Conversations with Queen Geraldine, July 1981, Costa del Sol, Spain.
13. Ibid.
14. FO 371/15149 (C6736/6736/90): Durazzo, 25 August 1931.

15. *Deutsche Allgemeiner Zeitung,* 21 August 1928 and USDS 875. 001 ZOG/86: Tirana (No. 886), 9 October 1933.

16. Stavro Skendi, *The Political Evolution of Albania* (New York: Mid-European Studies Center of the National Committee for a Free Europe, Mimeographed Series, March 8, 1954), p. 1.

17. Ibid., p. 3.

18. Swire, *Albania, the Rise of a Kingdom,* pp. 183-184.

19. Vlora, *Lebenserinnerungen,* p. 134.

20. *Vossische Zeitung,* 14 September 1928.

21. Swire, *Albania, the Rise of a Kingdom,* p. 208.

22. Ibid., p. 215.

23. Ibid.

24. Swire, *Albania, the Rise of a Kingdom,* p. 229.

25. George M. Self, *Foreign Relations of Albania,* (University of Chicago: Unpublished Doctoral Dissertation, 1943), p. 63.

26. Mary E. Durham, *Twenty Years of Balkan Tangle* (London: Allen and Unwin, 1920), p. 48.

27. Swire, *Albania, the Rise of a Kingdom,* p. 238.

28. Alan Palmer, *Gardeners of Salonika* (New York: Simon and Schuster, 1965), p. 158.

29. Swire, *Albania, the Rise of a Kingdom,* p. 260.

30. Ibid., p. 261.

31. Self, *Foreign Relations of Albania,* p. 72.

32. Prince Ludwig Windischgrätz, *My Memoirs* (London: 1921), p. 97.

33. Charles Fenyvesi, *Splendor in Exile* (Washington, D.C.: New Republic Books, 1979), p. 232.

34. Dako, *Zogu the First,* p. 78.

35. Fenyvesi, *Splendor in Exile,* p. 232.

36. Faik Konitza, *Albania, the Rock Garden of Europe* (Boston: G. M. Panarity, 1957), p. 138.

37. FO 371/7330 (C1599/818/90): Durazzo, 18 January 1922.

38. FO 371/11209 (C929/929/90): Durazzo, 16 January 1926 and FO 371/7330 (C1599/818/90): Durazzo, 18 January 1922.

Notes to Chapter Two

1.   Giovanni Zamboni, *Mussolinis Expansionspolitik auf dem Balkan* (Hamburg: Helmust Buske Verlag, 1970), p. XXXI.

2.   Swire, *Albania, the Rise of a Kingdom*, p. 312.

3.   FO 371/7330 (C818/818/90): Durazzo, 10 January 1922.

4.   Ibid.

5.   USDS 875.001 ZOG/86: Tirana (No. 886), 9 October 1933.

6.   FO 371/7330 (C1599/818/90): Durazzo, 18 January 1922.

7.   Vlora, *Lebenserinnerungen*, p. 128.

8.   Ibid.

9.   Swire, *Albania, the Rise of a Kingdom*, p. 320.

10.   Leften Stavrianos, *The Balkans Since 1453* (New York: Holt Rinehart and Winston, 1958), p. 713.

11.   Herbert Monath, "Die politisch-völkerrecktliche Entwicklung Albaniens 1913-1939," *Zeitschrift für Völkerrecht*, v. 24, no. 3 (1940), p. 299.

12.   Swire, *Albania, the Rise of a Kingdom*, p. 325.

13.   "European Economic and Political Survey," *Reference Service on International Affairs of the American Library in Paris* (Vol. 4, No. 1, September 15, 1928), p. 4.

14.   FO 371/7330 (C1599/818/90): Durazzo, 18 January 1922.

15.   Daniel Ravani, "Zogu I., König der Albaner," *Zeitschrift für Politik* (November 1931), p. 497.

16.   Swire, *Albania, the Rise of a Kingdom*, p. 339.

17.   Vlora, *Lebenserinnerungen*, p. 140.

18.   Dako, *Zogu the First*, p. 102.

19.   Stavro Skendi, *The Political Evolution of Albania* (New York: Mid-European Studies Center of the National Committee for a Free Europe, Mimeographed Series March 8, 1954), p. 6.

20.   FO 371/7330 (C818/818/90): Durazzo, 10 January 1922.

21.   FO 371/8535 (C17798/1380/90): Durazzo, 5 October 1923.

22.   Joseph Roucek, "Characteristics of Albanian Politics," *Social Science* (January 1935), p. 78 and Vlora, *Lebenserinnerungen*, pp. 140-144 and FO 371/7330 (C818/818/90): Durazzo, 10 January 1922.

23.   FO 371/7330 (C818/818/90): Durazzo, 10 January 1922.

24.   Skendi, *The Political Evolution of Albania*, p. 7.

25. FO 371/7332 (C6726/6726/90): Durazzo, 1 May 1922.
26. AA Politische Abteilung II, PO Bd. 1: Belgrade, 22 June 1921.
27. FO 371/8535 (C17798/1380/90): Durazzo, 5 October 1923.
28. Ibid.
29. FO 371/7330 (C818/818/90): Durazzo, 10 January 1922.
30. FO 371/5736 (C23786/580/90): Durazzo, 12 December 1921.
31. Ibid.
32. Fodor, *Plot and Counterplot in Central Europe,* p. 100.
33. FO 371/5736 (C23786/580/90): Durazzo, 12 December 1921.
34. FO 371/5736 (C23785/580/90): Durazzo, 9 December 1921.
35. Fodor, *Plot and Counterplot in Central Europe,* p. 100.
36. FO 371/7330 (C818/818/90): Durazzo, 10 January 1922.
37. Ibid.
38. Ravani, "Zogu I., König der Albaner," p. 34.
39. USDS 875.001 ZOG/90: Tirana (No. 11), 15 December 1933.
40. Vlora, *Lebenserinnerungen,* p. 159.
41. Ibid., p. 156.
42. FO 371/7330 (C11405/818/90): Durazzo, 30 July 1922.
43. Ibid.
44. FO 371/7330 (C12535/818/90): Durazzo, 23 August 1922.
45. FO 371/7332 (C16192/14109/90): Durazzo, 12 November 1922.
46. Ibid.

Notes to Chapter Three

1. T. Zavalani, "Albanian Nationalism," in Sugar and Lederer, *Nationalism in Eastern Europe* (Seattle: University of Washington Press, 1969), p. 56.

2. FO 371/10654 (C217/52/90): Durazzo, 5 January 1925.

3. Margaret Hasluck, "The Nonconformist Moslems of Albania," in *The Contemporary Review* (May 1925), pp. 604-606.

4. Stavro Skendi, "Religion in Albania during the Ottoman Rule," Südöst Forschungen (Vol. 15, 1956), p. 327.

5. Maxwell Blake, "Economic Conditions in Albania," *United States Department of Commerce Reports* (April 1923), p. 2.

6. Swire, *Albania, the Rise of a Kingdom,* p. 31.

7. T. Karajowow, "Albanien, Ein Politischer und Wirtschaftlicher Überblick," *Südöstliche Warte* (1929), p. 157.

8.   Wayne S. Vucinich, "Some Aspects of the Ottoman Legacy," in *The Balkans in Transition* edited by Charles and Barbara Jelavich (Hamden: The Shoe String Press, 1974), p. 89.

9.   Stavro Skendi, *Albania* (New York: F. Praeger, 1956), p. 152.

10.   E. Gasser, "The Present Position of the Dairying Industry in the Different Countries: Albania," *International Review of Agriculture* (April 1936), p. 146.

11.   Stavrianos, *The Balkans Since 1453,* pp. 140-141.

12.   Fodor, *Plot and Counterplot in Central Europe,* p. 95.

13.   Blake, "Economic Conditions in Albania," p. 6.

14.   Holmes and Jordan, "Economic Developments in Albania," *United States Bureau of Foreign and Domestic Commerce Reports* (August 1930), p. 373.

15.   Zamboni, *Mussolinis Expansionspolitik,* pp. XLV-XLVI.

16.   Leften Stavrianos, "The Influence of the West on the Balkans," in *The Balkans in Transition* edited by Charles and Barbara Jelavich (Hamden: The Shoe String Press, 1974), p. 205.

17.   Blake, "Economic Conditions in Albania," p. 3.

18.   Ibid., p. 4.

19.   Ibid., p. 6.

20.   *Official Journal of the League of Nations* (May 1923, 4th Year, No. 5), p. 504.

21.   United Nations Relief and Rehabilitation Administration *Operational Analysis Papers,* "Economic Rehabilitation in Albania," (London, 1947), p. 41.

22.   Self, *Foreign Relations of Albania,* p. 119.

23.   Ibid.

24.   Hermann Gross, "Wirtschaftsstruktur und Wirtschaftsbeziehungen Albaniens," *Weltwirtschaftliches Archiv* (Vol. 38, No. 2, 1933), p. 531.

25.   *Official Journal of the League of Nations* (January 1924, 5th Year, No. 1, Part 2), p. 164.

26.   Swire, *Albania, the Rise of a Kingdom,* p. 408.

27.   FO 371/8535 (C21309/1380/90): Durazzo, 1 December 1923.

28.   Ibid.

29.   FO 371/7330 (C1599/818/90): Durazzo, 18 January 1922.

30.   FO 371/8535 (C21308/1380/90): Durazzo, 20 November 1923.

31.   FO 371/8535 (C21309/1380/90): Durazzo, 1 December 1923.

32. Ibid.
33. Ibid.
34. Ravani, "Zogu I., König der Albaner," p. 498.
35. FO 371/9639 (C3411/28/90): Durazzo, 20 February 1924.
36. Vlora, *Lebenserinnerungen*, p. 167.
37. Ibid., p. 179.
38. Ibid., p. 180.
39. Skendi, *The Political Evolution of Albania*, p. 8.
40. FO 371/9639 (C4698/28/90): Durazzo, 8 March 1924.
41. Ibid.
42. Swire, *Albania, the Rise of a Kingdom*, p. 430.
43. FO 371/9639 (C9654/28/90): Durazzo, 10 June 1924.

Notes to Chapter Four

1. Stavrianos, *The Balkans Since 1453*, p. 717.
2. FO 371/7330 (C11405/818/90): Durazzo, 30 July 1922.
3. FO 371/8535 (C12760/1380/90): Durazzo, 20 July 1923.
4. FO 371/8535 (C15153/1380/90): Durazzo, 26 August 1923.
5. Swire, *Albania, the Rise of a Kingdom*, p. 434.
6. FO 371/10658 (C4115/4115/90): Durazzo, 8 March 1925.
7. Zamboni, *Mussolinis Expansionspolitik auf dem Balkan*, p. LIII.
8. *La Gazzetta di Puglia*, 24 June 1924.
9. Zamboni, *Mussolinis Expansionspolitik auf dem Balkan*, p. LIII.
10. Vlora, *Lebenserinnerungen*, p. 196.
11. Self, *Foreign Relations of Albania*, p. 151 and T. Karajowow, "Albanien, Ein Politischer und Wirtschaftlicher Überblick," p. 223 and *Vossische Zeitung*, 23 August 1928.
12. Alan Cassels, *Mussolini's Early Diplomacy* (Princeton: Princeton University Press, 1970), p. 243.
13. Zamboni, *Mussolinis Expansionspolitik auf dem Balkan*, p. LIV and Cassels, *Mussolini's Early Diplomacy*, p. 243.
14. Zamboni, *Mussolinis Expansionspolitik auf dem Balkan*, p. LV and P. Pastorelli, *Italia e Albania, 1924-1927. Origni diplomatiche del Trattato di Tirana del 22 novembre 1927* (Firenze: 1967), p. 55-57.
15. AA Politische Abteilung IIBPol. 5, Bd. 1: Tirana, 9 December 1924.

16. FO 371/9640 (C18496/28/90): Belgrade, 8 December 1924 and FO 371/9640 (C18627/28/90): Belgrade, 10 December 1924 and AA Politische Abteilung IIB Pol. 5, Bd. 1: Berlin zu Tirana, 11 December 1924.

17. Swire, *Albania, the Rise of a Kingdom,* p. 445. J. Swire maintains that the figures, which were approximate only, were obtained from an unquestionable British source. He adds that he has pictures of the troop movements.

18. FO 371/10658 (C4115/4115/90): Durazzo, 8 March 1925.

19. FO 371/9640 (C17661/28/90): Durazzo, 16 November 1924.

20. FO 371/9640 (C14533/28/90): Durazzo, 21 August 1924.

21. Zamboni, *Mussolinis Expansionspolitik auf dem Balkan,* p. LVIII.

22. AA Politische Abteilung IIB Pol. 5 Bd. 1: Tirana, 17 December 1924 and AA Politische Abteilung II B Pol. 5, Bd. 1: Tirana, 28 December 1924.

23. FO 371/10658 (C4115/4115/90): Durazzo, 8 March 1925.

24. FO 371/10654 (C809/52/90): Tirana, 30 December 1924.

25. Vlora, *Lebenserinnerungen,* p. 200 and FO 371/10654 (C809/52/90): Tirana, 30 December 1924.

26. AA Politische Abteilung II B Pol. 5, Bd. 1: Tirana, 28 December 1924.

27. FO 371/10654 (C809/52/90): Tirana, 30 December 1924.

28. Ibid.

29. FO 371/9640 (C18934/28/90): Tirana, 16 December 1924 and FO 371/10654 (C809/52/90): Tirana, 30 December 1924.

30. FO 371/10654 (C808/52/90): Tirana, 29 December 1924 and FO 371/10654 (C809/52/90): Tirana, 30 December 1924.

31. FO 371/10654 (C808/52/90): Tirana, 29 December 1924.

32. Zamboni, *Mussolinis Expansionspolitik auf dem Balkan,* p. LX.

33. FO 371/10654 (C188/52/90): Rome, 30 December 1924.

34. Ibid.

35. FO 371/10654 (C816/52/90): Tirana, 9 January 1925 and FO 371/10654 (C188/52/90): Rome, 30 December 1925.

36. AA Politische Abteilung II Pol. 2, Bd. 1: Tirana, 6 March 1925.

37. Skendi, *The Political Evolution of Albania,* p. 9.

38. FO 371/11209 (C929/929/90): Durazzo, 16 January 1926 and AA Politische Abteilung II B Innere Verwaltung 2, Bd. 1: Tirana, 2 March 1925.

39.   FO 371/10654 (C5306/52/90): Durazzo, 29 March 1925.
40.   T. Zavalani, "Albanian Nationalism," p. 86.
41.   Vlora, *Lebenserinnerungen,* p. 218 and H. C. Luke, "Albania's Latest Capital," *The Near East and India* (September 1927), p. 361.
42.   FO 371/15148 (C1412/1412/90): Durazzo, 24 February 1931.
43.   Vlora, *Lebenserinnerungen,* p. 218.
44.   FO 371/11209 (C929/929/90): Durazzo, 16 January 1926.
45.   FO 371/10656 (C1865/1062/90): Durazzo, 27 January 1925 and Vlora, *Lebenserinnerungen,* p. 213.

Notes to Chapter Five

1.   Cassels, *Mussolini's Early Diplomacy,* p. 246.
2.   Self, *Foreign Relations of Albania,* p. 153.
3.   Christo Dako, *Albania* (Boston: E. L. Grimes and Company, 1919), p. 104 and E. L. P. Dillion, "Albania," *Contemporary Review* (July 1914), p. 125.
4.   Stavro Skendi, *The Albanian National Awakening, 1878-1912* (Princeton: Princeton University Press, 1967), p. 217.
5.   Alfred Pribram, *The Secret Treaties of Austria-Hungary* (Cambridge: Harvard University Press, 1920), p. 109.
6.   Ibid., p. 196.
7.   Zamboni, *Mussolinis Expansionspolitik auf dem Balkan,* p. XXIII.
8.   Ibid., p. XXVI.
9.   Swire, *Albania, the Rise of a Kingdom,* pp. 369-370.
10.   Cassels, *Mussolini's Early Diplomacy,* pp. 255-259.
11.   Lothar Loose, *Die völkerrechtlichen und politischen Beziehungen Albaniens zu Italien* (jur. Dissertation, Leipzig, 1936), p. 142 and Herbert Monath, "Die politisch-völkerrechtliche Entwicklung Albaniens," *Zeitschrift für Völkerrecht,* pp. 305-306 and Zamboni, *Mussolinis Expansionspolitik auf dem Balkan,* p. XLVIII.
12.   FO 371/9639 (C3588/28/90): Durazzo, 15 February 1924 and Zamboni, *Mussolinis Expansionspolitik auf dem Balkan,* p. LIV.
13.   Cassels, *Mussolini's Early Diplomacy,* p. 243.
14.   DDI, VII, Vol. III, Document 654.
15.   Cassels, *Mussolini's Early Diplomacy,* p. 247.
16.   Zamboni, *Mussolinis Expanionspolitik auf dem Balkan,* pp. LXIV-LXV.

17. Ibid., p. LXVI.

18. Vandeleur Robinson, *Albania's Road to Freedom* (London: George Allen and Unwin, 1941), p. 72.

19. Luke, "Albania's Latest Capital," p. 362.

20. FO 371/11209 (C929/929/90): Durazzo, 16 January 1926 and Swire, *Albania, the Rise of a Kingdom,* p. 462 and Self, *Foreign Relations of Albania,* p. 155 and Zamboni, *Mussolinis Expansionspolitik auf dem Balkan,* p. LXVII.

21. Zamboni, *Mussolinis Expansionspolitik auf dem Balkan,* p. LXVIII and Self, *Foreign Relations of Albania,* p. 157.

22. Eugene Stanley, "Italy's Financial Stake in Albania," *Foreign Affairs* (June 1932), p. 85.

23. FO 371/12845 (C7016/150/90): Durazzo, 7 September 1928 and Self, *Foreign Relations of Albania,* p. 168.

24. Zamboni, *Mussolinis Expansionspolitik auf dem Balkan,* p. LXXI.

25. Cassels, *Mussolini's Early Diplomacy,* p. 320 and Zamboni, *Mussolinis Expansionspolitik auf dem Balkan,* p. LXXIII.

26. Zamboni, *Mussolinis Expansionspolitik auf dem Balkan,* p. LXXVIII.

27. Ibid.

28. DDI, VII, Vol. 6, Document 457, footnote 3.

29. FO 371/12068 (C473/473/90): Durazzo, 1, January 1927.

30. HHStA, Z. 68/pol. 14023 pr: 14 VIII1926; Konstantinopel, 26 July 1926 and FO 371/11209 (C10245/925/90): Durazzo, 9 September 1926 and Zamboni, *Mussolinis Expansionspolitik auf dem Balkan,* p. XC and Swire, *Albania, the Rise of a Kingdom,* p. 473 and Self, *Foreign Relations of Albania,* p. 158 and Skendi, *The Political Evolution of Albania,* p. 10.

31. Zamboni, *Mussolinis Expansionspolitik auf dem Balkan,* p. XCI.

32. Skendi, *The Political Evolution of Albania,* p. 10.

33. Zamboni, *Mussolinis Expansionspolitik auf dem Balkan,* p. XCII.

34. DDI, VII, Vol. 4, Document 376.

35. HHStA, Z. 68/pol. 14023 pr:14 VIII1926: Konstantinopel, 26 July 1926.

36. Th. Jonima, "Die neueste Phase der italienisch-albanischen Beziehungen," *Zeitschrift für Politik* (Vol. 22, 1932-33), p. 548.

37. DDI, VII, Vol. 4, Document 383.

38.   FO 371/11210 (C8881/8881/90): Durazzo, 6 August 1926.

39.   DDI, VII, Vol. 4, Document 444 and Zamboni, *Mussolinis Expansionspolitik auf dem Balkan,* pp. 5-6. After Chamberlain briefed the general secretary of the French Foreign Ministry on his Livorno conversations, General Secretary P. J. L. Berthelot came to basically the same conclusion.

40.   DDI, VII, Vol. 4, Document 443 and Zamboni, *Mussolinis Expansionspolitik auf dem Balkan,* p. 6.

41.   DDI, VII, Vol. 4, Document 443 and Zamboni, *Mussolinis Expansionspolitik auf dem Balkan,* pp. 3-4 and Denis Mack Smith, *Mussolini's Roman Empire* (London and New York: Longman, 1976), p. 14.

42.   G. Salvemini, *Prelude to World War II* (New York: Doubleday and Co., 1954), p. 107.

43.   FO 371/12847 (C2191/2191/90): Durazzo, 5 March 1928.

44.   Zamboni, *Mussolinis Expansionspolitik auf dem Balkan,* p. 10.

45.   Ibid., p. 16.

46.   *League of Nations Treaty Series,* Vol. LX, 1927, pp. 16-21.

47.   Jonima, "Die neueste Phase der italienisch-albanischen Beziehungen," p. 549 and Swire, *Albania, the Rise of a Kingdom,* p. 479.

48.   Eugen Kogon, "Albanien. Zum italienisch-jugoslawischen Gegensatz," *Zeitschrift für Politik* (Vol. 17, 1927), p. 156 and Zamboni, *Mussolinis Expansionspolitik auf dem Balkan,* p. 19.

49.   Zamboni, *Mussolinis Expansionspolitik auf dem Balkan,* p. 25.

50.   AA Politische Abteilung 11B, Pol. 5, Bd. 1: Tirana, 1 February 1927.

Notes to Chapter Six

1.   Rene MacColl, "Albania and the British Mission," *Quarterly Review* (October 1938), p. 311.

2.   FO 371/13562 (C6428/3383/90): Durazzo, 12 August 1929.

3.   FO 371/13560 (C2310/2310/90): Durazzo, 26 March 1929.

4.   FO 371/12848 (C9228/4052/90): Durazzo, 5 December 1928 and FO 371/13562 (C6428/3383/90): Durazzo, 12 August 1929.

5.   FO 371/12844 (C1351/146/90): Durazzo, 3 February 1928.

6.   FO 371/12847 (C2557/2557/90): Durazzo, 27 March 1929 and FO 371/12844 (C1351/146/90): Durazzo, 3 February 1928.

7.   FO 371/11209 (C9292/929/90): Durazzo, 16 January 1926.

8. FO 371/12069 (C7363/946/90): Durazzo, 26 August 1927.

9. FO 371/11208 (C4762/925/90): Durazzo, 31 March 1926 and FO 371/13560 (C2310/2310/90): Durazzo, 26 March 1929.

10. FO 371/12069 (C1605/1605/90): Durazzo, 14 September 1926 and 5 February 1927.

11. FO 371/11209 (C929/929/90): Durazzo, 16 January 1926.

12. FO 371/12069 (C1605/1605/90): Durazzo, 14 September 1926 and 5 February 1927.

13. Ibid.

14. FO 317/12847 (C2210/2210/90): Durazzo, 6 March 1928 and FO 371/12069 (C1605/1605/90): Durazzo, 14 September 1926 and 5 February 1927 and AA Politische Abteilung IIB, Pol. 7, Bd. 1: Tirana, 7 May 1927.

15. USDS 875.001 ZOG/8: Tirana (No. 469), 16 July 1928.

16. DDI VII, Vol. V, Document 681.

17. USDS 875.001 ZOG/39: Tirana (No. 156), 31 December 1930 and Vlora, *Lebenserinnerungen,* p. 222.

18. USDS 875.001 ZOG/39: Tirana (No. 156), 31 December 1930 and USDS 875.001 ZOG/80: Tirana (No. 11), 15 December 1933.

19. FO 371/10654 (C12551/52/90): Durazzo, 23 September 1925.

20. FO 371/11208 (C2235/925/90): Durazzo, 14 February 1926 and FO 371/11209 (C929/929/90): Durazzo, 16 January 1926.

21. FO 371/10654 (C12551/52/90): Durazzo, 23 September 1925.

22. *Das Deutsche Tageblatt,* 26 September 1925.

23. FO 371/110654 (C14141/52/90): Foreign Office Minute, 5 November 1925 and FO 371/11208 (C4913/925/90): Foreign Office Minute, 4 April 1926.

24. FO 371/11208 (C925/925/90): Durazzo, 9 January 1926.

25. FO 371/11208 (C3011/925/90): Durazzo, 23 February 1926 and FO 371/11209 (C9662/925/90): Durazzo, 31 August 1926 and FO 371/11209 (C9741/925/90): Durazzo, 4 September 1926.

26. Zamboni, *Mussolinis Expansionspolitik auf dem Balkan,* pp. 14-15.

27. Swire, *Albania, the Rise of a Kingdom,* p. 475.

28. FO 371/12068 (C2074/946/90): Durazzo, 25 February 1927.

29. USDS 875.00/259: Tirana (No. 492), 15 August 1928.

30. USDS 875.001 ZOG/80: Tirana (No. 11), 15 December 1933.

31.   AA Politische Abteilung II, Pol. 2, Bd. 1: Tirana, 18 August 1927 and FO 371/12068 (C7362/946/90): Durazzo, 26 August 1927.

32.   AA Politische Abteilung II, Pol. 2, Bd. 1: Tirana, 26 August 1927.

33.   FO 371/12068 (C7362/946/90): Durazzo, 26 August 1927.

34.   FO 371/12069 (C7577/946/90): Durazzo, 3 September 1927 and AA Politische Abteilung II, Pol. 2, Bd. 1: Tirana, 1 September 1927.

35.   FO 371/12073 (C8384/8384/90): Prague, 15 October 1927.

36.   FO 371/12848 (C9158/9158/90): Prague, 3 December 1928.

37.   Ibid.

38.   FO 371/12073 (C9153/8384/90): Tirana, 27 October 1927.

39.   *Vossische Zeitung,* 12 May 1927 and Zamboni, *Mussolinis Expansionspolitik auf dem Balkan,* p. 341.

40.   Zamboni, *Mussolinis Expansionspolitik auf dem Balkan,* p. 348.

41.   Ibid., pp. 347-348.

42.   AA Politische Abteilung II, Pol. 2, Bd. 1. Tirana, 7 December 1927 and FO 371/12069 (C10397/946/90): Durazzo, 13 December 1927 and DDI VII, Vol. V, Document 681.

43.   HHStA, Albanien 2/12 Polizeidirection in Wien, Pr. ZI. IV-656/ 26: 3 February 1928 and *Tagliche Rundschau,* 4 February 1928.

44.   FO 371/12847 (C5305/1355/90): Durazzo, 2 July 1928 and USDS 875.001 ZOG/6: Tirana (No. 475), 21 June 1928.

45.   USDS 875.001 ZOG/8: Tirana (No. 480), 16 July 1928.

46.   Ibid.

47.   AA Politische Abteilung IIB, Pol. 5, Bd. 2: Tirana, 25 June 1928 and USDS 875.001 ZOG/8: Tirana (No. 480), 16 July 1928 and USDS 875.001 ZOG/6: Tirana (No. 475), 21 June 1928 and USDS 875.00/259: Tirana (No. 492), 15 August 1928.

48.   USDS 875.00/259: Tirana (No. 492), 15 August 1928 and AA Politische Abteilung II, Pol. 5, Bd. 2: Tirana, 10 July 1928.

49.   USDS 875.001 ZOG/80: Tirana (No. 11), 15 December 1933.

50.   FO 371/12847 (C2907/1356/90): Belgrade, 10 April 1928.

51.   MacColl, "Albania and the British Mission," p. 304 and Vlora, *Lebenserinnerungen,* p. 222 and *Kreuzzeitung,* 4 January 1929.

52.   USDS 875.001 ZOG/80: Tirana (No. 11), 15 December 1933.

53.   FO 371/12846 (C7017/1090/90): Durazzo, 8 September 1928 and AA Politische Abteilung IIB, Pol. 2, Bd. 1: Tirana, 15 October 1929.

54. USDS 875.001 ZOG/6: Tirana (No. 475), 21 June 1928.

55. AA Politische Abteilung II, Pol. 5, Bd. 2: Tirana, 10 July 1928 and USDS 875.001 ZOG/96: Tirana (No. 180), 22 July 1936.

56. Zamboni, *Mussolinis Expansionspolitik auf dem Balkan,* p. 34.

57. Alfred Rappaport, "Der Tirana-Vertrag, Seine Vorgeschichte und seine Tragweite," *Europäische Gepräche* (Vol. 5, 1927), p. 105.

58. DDI VII, Vol. V, Document 41.

59. Zamboni, *Mussolinis Expansionspolitik auf dem Balkan,* p. 277.

60. FO 371/13560 (C2310/2310/90): Durazzo, 26 March 1929.

61. Zamboni, *Mussolinis Expansionspolitik auf dem Balkan,* pp. 386, 393. For the full text of the pact see: Swire, *Albania, the Rise of a Kingdom,* pp. 509-512.

62. Zamboni, *Mussolinis Expansionspolitik auf dem Balkan,* pp. 386, 393.

63. FO 371/10656 (C13155/763/90): Tirana, 8 October 1925.

64. Zamboni, *Mussolinis Expansionspolitik auf dem Balkan,* p. 106.

65. FO 371/12846 (C3295/1119/90): Durazzo, 19 April 1928 and FO 371/12846 (C3296/1119/90): Durazzo, 21 April 1928.

66. Swire, *Albania, the Rise of a Kingdom,* p. 507.

67. FO 371/12846 (C3295/1119/90): Durazzo, 19 April 1928.

68. FO 371/12846 (C3295/1119/90): Durazzo, 19 April 1928 and Swire, *Albania, the Rise of a Kingdom,* p. 506.

69. DDI VII, Vol. V, Document 170 and Zamboni, *Mussolinis Expansionspolitik auf dem Balkan,* pp. 307-312.

70. FO 371/12069 (C7363/946/90): Durazzo, 26 August 1927.

71. DDI VII, Vol. V, Document 439.

72. FO 371/12845 (C2197/150/90): Durazzo, 12 March 1928 and T. Karajowow, "Albanien, Ein Wirtschaftlichen und Politischen Überblick," pp. 225-226.

73. Zamboni, *Mussolinis Expansionspolitik auf dem Balkan,* p. 380.

74. Ibid., p. 318.

Notes to Chapter Seven

1. *National-Zeitung,* 14 September 1928.

2. *Deutsche Allgemeine Zeitung,* 21 August 1928.

3. Friedrich Wallisch, *Neuland Albanien,* (Stuttgart: Fanckhsahe Verlagshandlung, 1931), p. 29.

4.   *National-Zeitung,* 14 September 1928.

5.   Conservations with Queen Geraldine, July 1981. Costa del Sol, Spain.

6.   Faik Konitza, *Albania, The Rock Garden of Europe* (Boston: G. M. Panarity, 1957), p. 96.

7.   Vlora, *Lebenserinnerungen,* pp. 212-213.

8.   FO 371/12845 (C6245/1090/90): Durazzo, 14 August 1928.

9.   Vlora, *Lebenserinnerungen,* p. 213.

10.   Wallisch, *Neuland Albanien,* p. 60.

11.   See page 1 of this work.

12.   *Berliner Tageblatt,* 22 August 1928 and Wallisch, *Neuland Albanien,* p. 43.

13.   *Berliner Tageblatt,* 22 August 1928.

14.   See page 94 of this work.

15.   Zamboni, *Mussolinis Expansionspolitik auf dem Balkan,* p. 318.

16.   Ibid., p. 334.

17.   Ibid., p. 336.

18.   For material on the Verlaci assassination attempt see page 116 of this work. On *Telegraph* article see AA Politische Abteilung II, Pol. 12, Bd. 1: 15 October 1928.

19.   Zamboni, *Mussolinis Expansionspolitik auf dem Balkan,* pp. 460-461.

20.   AA Politische Abteilung II, Pol. 12, Bd. 1: 10 January 1928.

21.   FO 371/13560 (C2310/2310/90): Durazzo, 26 March 1928.

22.   FO 371/12845 (C1090/1090/90): to Durazzo, 16 February 1928.

23.   Ibid.

24.   FO 371/12845 (C6346/1090/90): Durazzo, 20 April 1928.

25.   FO 371/15148 (C1412/1412/90): Durazzo, 24 February 1931.

26.   USDS 875.00/260: Tirana, (No. 491), 15 August 1928.

27.   FO 371/12845 (C6346/1090/90): Durazzo, 20 April 1928.

28.   Ibid.

29.   Ibid.

30.   Richard Busch-Zantner, *Albanien, Neues Land in Imperium* (Leipzig: W. Gould, 1939), p. 151.

31.   FO 371/13560 (C2310/2310/90): Durazzo, 26 March 1929.

32.   FO 371/12845 (C6346/1090/90): Durazzo, 15 August 1928.

33. AA Politische Abteilung IIB, Pol. 5, Bd. 2: Berlin, 7 September 1928.

34. AA Politische Abteilung II, Pol. 2, Bd. 1: Tirana, 14 December 1927.

35. FO 317/12847 (C4051/1355/90): Durazzo, 18 May 1928.

36. Ibid.

37. Zamboni, *Mussolinis Expansionspolitik auf dem Balkan*, p. 464.

38. Ibid., p. 466.

39. Zamboni, *Mussolinis Expansionspolitik auf dem Balkan*, pp. 472-477 and DDI VII, Vol. VI, Document 611.

40. DDI VII, Vol. VI, Document 406 and Zamboni, *Mussolini Expansionspolitik auf dem Balkan*, p. 463.

41. *Deutsche Tageszeitung,* 17 August 1928.

42. Roucek, "Characteristics of Albanian Politics," p. 73 and *The Times,* London, 14 December 1928. The hatred and fear of the President and Shevket Verlaci for each other notwithstanding, the government had to concede a seat in the Constituent Assembly to Verlaci. This was necessary to assure the support which the government had by this time acquired among some of Verlaci's supporters. The old gentleman had not been in Tirana since the attempt against him in December. His only extended trip had been to Rome at the beginning of August, accompanied by two bodyguards. Upon landing in Vlorë, he was met by twenty additional guards, each wearing a large revolver strapped on a belt. For more on Verlaci see USDS 875.00/260: Tirana, (No. 491), 15 August 1928.

43. USDS 875.00/260: Tirana, (No. 491), 15 August 1928.

44. *Telegraph,* 5 August 1928.

45. *Popolo d'Italia,* 25 August 1928.

46. *Tribuna,* 26 August 1928.

47. USDS 875.00/260: Tirana, (No. 491), 15 August 1928.

48. FO 371/12846 (C7017/1090/90): Durazzo, 8 September 1928.

49. Robinson, *Albania's Road to Freedom,* p. 54.

50. USDS 875.00/260: Tirana, (No. 491), 15 August 1928.

51. Ibid.

52. FO 371/12845 (C6609/1090/90): Durazzo, 29 August 1928.

53. Ibid.

54. FO 371/12846 (C7017/1090/90): Durazzo, 8 September 1928.

55. International Affairs of the American Library in Paris, "European Economic and Political Survey, Albania," p. 8.

56. FO 371/12846 (C7017/1090/90): Durazzo, 8 September 1928.

57. FO 371/12846 (C7017/1090/90): Durazzo, 8 September 1928 and *Berliner Tageblatt,* 5 September 1928.

58. *Berliner Tageblatt,* 5 September 1928.

59. FO 371/12846 (C7017/1090/90): Durazzo, 8 September 1928.

60. Ibid.

61. Wallisch, *Neuland Albanien,* p. 30.

62. FO 371/12846 (C7017/1090/90): Durazzo, 8 September 1928.

63. Zamboni, *Mussolinis Expansionspolitik auf dem Balkan,* p. 469 and FO 371/12846 (C7018/1090/90): Durazzo, 10 September 1928.

64. FO 371/13560 (C2310/2310/90): Durazzo, 26 March 1929.

65. FO 371/12846 (C7017/1090/90): Durazzo, 8 September 1928 and FO 371/12846 (C7018/1090/90): Durazzo, 10 September 1928.

66. FO 371/12846 (C6974/1090/90): British Delegation at the League, 7 September 1928.

67. For order of recognition see FO 371/12846 (C7735/1090/90): Durazzo, 25 September 1928.

68. International Affairs of the American Library in Paris, "European Economic and Political Survey, Albania," p. 9.

69. Swire, *Albania, the Rise of a Kingdom,* p. 462.

70. *Giornale d'Italia,* 24 August 1928.

71. *Impero,* 5 September 1928.

72. FO 371/12845 (C6734/1090/90): Foreign Office Minute, 4 September 1928.

73. FO 371/12846 (C8804/1090/90): Durazzo, 20 November 1928.

74. FO 371/12846 (C8052/1090/90): Durazzo, 23 October 1928 and FO 371/12846 (C8372/1090/90): Constantinople, 1 November 1928 and FO 371/12846 (C8804/1090/90): Durazzo, 20 November 1928.

75. FO 371/12846 (C8052/1090/90): Durazzo, 23 October 1928.

76. *The Times,* London, 25 August 1928.

77. AA Politische Abteilung II, Pol. 11, Bd. 1: 15 January 1931.

78. AA Politische Abteilung IIB, Pol. 5, Bd. 2: Tirana, 29 August 1928.

79. *The Times,* London, 1 and 2 September 1928.

80. Federal Writers Project, *The Albanian Struggle in the Old World and the New* (Boston: The Writers Inc., 1939), p. 80 and The New York *Times,* 7 September 1928.

81. Ibid.

82. FO 371/12846 (C7017/1090/90): Durazzo, 8 September 1928 and *Vossische Zeitung,* 21 August 1928.

83. USDS 875.00/266: Tirana, (No. 542), 22 October 1928.

84. AA Politisch Abteilung II, Allgemeines, Bd. 1: Tirana, 23 January 1929.

Notes to Chapter Eight

1. *The New York Times,* 14 December 1928.

2. USDS 875.001 ZOG/90: Tirana, (No. 11), 15 December 1933.

3. Ibid.

4. FO 371/14304 (C5425/5425/90): Durazzo, 30 June 1930.

5. Skendi, *Albania,* p. 98.

6. USDS 875.001 ZOG/90: Tirana, (No. 11), 15 December 1933.

7. FO 371/12847 (C8805/1359/90): Durazzo, 26 November 1928.

8. Robinson, *Albania's Road to Freedom,* p. 110.

9. Vlora, *Lebenserinnerungen,* p. 220.

10. FO 371/15148 (C1412/1412/90): Durazzo, 24 February 1931 and FO 371/15149 (C6736/6736/90): Durazzo, 25 August 1931.

11. Robinson, *Albania's Road to Freedom,* p. 110.

12. Ibid.

13. AA Politische Abteilung IIB, Pol. 5, Bd. 2: Tirana, 5 December 1928.

14. Konitza, *Albania, The Rock Garden of Europe,* p. 106.

15. USDS 875.001 ZOG/28: Tirana, (No. 682), 10 October 1929 and AA Politische Abteilung IIB, Pol. 2, Bd. 1: 15 October 1929 and AA Politische Abteilung IIB, Pol. 2, Bd. 1: 7 October 1929.

16. AA Politische Abteilung IIB, Pol. 2, Bd. 1: 10 October 1929 and USDS 874.001 ZOG/28: Tirana, (No. 682), 10 October 1929.

17. USDS 875.00/404: Tirana, (No. 94), 10 October 1929.

18. Ibid. Herman Bernstein the American Minister described the proceedings as follows:

> Uncle Tom was a reddish blond with a long mustache like a French gendarme of 25 years ago and his master was a bald individual with a beard like Tartaran de Tarascon in a blue business suit who walked about his own house carrying a derby hat and a pair of brown gloves.

Little Eva was apparently 'Little Adam' as a boy played the part. Topsy was a strapping youth of 20 and was carried on the program as 'Popsy.' Eliza was a huge male in a skirt and a white lace apron who embraced everybody in the place and spoke in a deep bass voice. The police wore broad, bright green hats and carried in their belts wooden daggers with hilts six inches long. It was altogether the most ludicrous affair imaginable and some members of the legation staff experienced difficulty in maintaining proper decorum.

19.   Konitza, *Albania, The Rock Garden of Europe,* p. 36.

20.   Josef März, "Das albanische Problem," *Zeitschrift für Politik* (October 1931), pp. 494-495.

21.   FO 371/14302 (C6755/175/90): Durazzo, 1 September 1930.

22.   FO 371/12845 (C2197/150/90): Durazzo, 19 March 1928.

23.   Ibid.

24.   Ibid.

25.   Gross, "Wirtschaftsstruktur und Wirtschaftsbeziehungen Albaniens," pp. 529-531.

26.   Royal Institute of International Affairs, *The Balkan States I, Economic* (New York: Oxford University Press, 1936), p. 114.

27.   Gross, "Wirtschaftsstruktur und Wirtschaftsbeziehungen Albaniens," pp. 529-539 and Royal Institute, *The Balkan States I,* p. 96.

28.   This was a considerable underestimate since many of the weapons sold to Albania during this period were done so on credit.

29.   Holmes and Jordan, "Economic Developments in Albania," p. 373.

30.   Gross, "Wirtschaftsstruktur und Wirtschaftsbeziehungen Albaniens," p. 530.

31.   Herman Gross, "Albanien, ein Land im Umbruch," *Erwachendes Europa* (1934), p. 281.

32.   Holmes and Jordan, "Economic Development in Albania," p. 374 and Royal Institute, *The Balkan States I,* pp. 139-140.

33.   FO 371/13562 (C6005/3279/90): Durazzo, 30 July 1929.

34.   *Daily Telegraph,* 12 October 1928.

35.   FO 371/12847 (C9721/1355/90): Durazzo, 18 December 1928.

36.   Vlora, *Lebenserinnerungen,* p. 219.

37.   FO 371/13560 (C2310/2310/90): Durazzo, 26 March 1929.

38.   FO 371/14304 (C5425/5425/90): Durazzo, 30 June 1930.

39. FO 371/15148 (C1412/1412/90): Durazzo, 24 February 1931.

40. Ibid.

41. Skendi, *The Political Evolution of Albania,* p. 12.

42. FO 371/13560 (C2310/2310/90): Durazzo, 26 March 1929.

43. Ibid.

44. FO 371/13561 (C1988/565/90): Belgrade, 13 March 1929.

45. Ibid.

46. Robinson, *Albania's Road to Freedom,* p. 98.

47. FO 371/15147 (C478/478/90): Durazzo, 13 January 1931.

48. USDS 875.51/59: Tirana, (No. 167), 14 January 1931 and FO 371/15147 (C478/478/90): Durazzo, 13 January 1931.

49. USDS 875.51/51: Tirana, (No. 167), 14 January 1931.

50. Antoinette de Szinyei-Merse, *Ten Years, Ten Months, Ten Days* (London: Unwin Brothers Limited, 1945), p. 81.

51. Robinson, *Albania's Road to Freedom,* p. 67 and Skendi, *Albania,* p. 157.

52. L. Stavrianos, *The Balkans Since 1453,* p. 724.

53. Skendi, *Albania,* p. 160.

54. FO 371/14302 (C6755/175/90): Durazzo, 26 August 1930. The article was attributed to Faik Konitza, the Albanian Minister in Washington.

55. FO 371/15148 (C1412/1412/90): Durazzo, 24 February 1931.

56. *The Times,* London, 24 April 1930.

57. FO 371/14302 (C6755/175/90): Durazzo, 26 August 1930.

Notes to Chapter Nine

1. AA Politische Abteilung II, Pol. 2, Bd. 1: Tirana, 11 May 1925.

2. AA Politische Abteilung II, Pol. 2, Bd. 1: Tirana, 24 January 1931.

3. Conservations with Queen Geraldine, July 1981, Costa del Sol, Spain.

4. *Kreuzzeitung,* 4 January 1929 and AA Politische Abteilung II, Pol. 2, Bd. 1: Tirana, 1 January 1929.

5. USDS 875.00 ZOG/39: Tirana, (No. 156), 31 December 1930 and AA Politische Abteilung II, Pol. 2, Bd. 1: Tirana, 24 January 1931.

6. USDS 875.00 ZOG/39: Tirana, (No. 156), 31 December 1930.

7.   Ibid.

8.   FO 371/15146 (C4392/475/90): Durazzo, 11 June 1931.

9.   USDS 875.00 ZOG/39: Tirana, (No. 156), 31 December 1930.

10. USDS 875.001 ZOG/44: Tirana, (No. 186), 28 January 1931.

11. HHStA, Albanien 1/1 Nieder osterreichische Landesamtsdirection, PR. II-636/1: 11 February 1931.

12. HHStA, Pol. 1, 20587 Pr. 2 II1931: Tirana, 27 January 1931 and USDS 875.00/316: Tirana, (No. 209), 12 March 1931.

13. *Die Stunde,* 24 February 1931 and USDS 875.00/316: Tirana, (No. 209), 12 March 1931.

14. AA Politische Abteilung II, Pol. 2, Bd. 1: Tirana, 27 February 1931 and *Die Stunde,* 24 February 1931 and USDS 875.00/316: Tirana, (No. 209), 12 March 1931.

15. USDS 875.001 ZOG/49: Tirana, (No. 195), 12 February 1931 and USDS 875.001 ZOG/52: Tirana, (No. 204), 26 February 1931 and HHStA, Albanien 1/1, Z 112: Berlin, 31 January 1931.

16. Dr. Terenzio Tocci, former Secretary General to Zog, maintained to the contrary that he was told by one of the King's physicians, Dr. Osman, that the King had been suffering from a serious intestinal ailment, that the Vienna specialists had advised an operation but that the King refused to undergo any operation. Tocci further stated that Dr. Osman believed that Zog was suffering from an ailment which was developing into cancer. USDS 875.00/317: Tirana, (No. 225), 26 March 1931.

17. USDS 875.00/316: Tirana, (No. 209), 12 March 1931 with enclosed report No. 12376 Military Attache Rome, 4 March 1931.

18. FO 371/15147 (C1349/480/90): Vienna, 24 February 1931 and USDS 875.00/266: Tirana, (No. 542), 22 October 1928 and USDS 875.00/317: Tirana, (No. 225), 26 March 1931 and *Wolff's Telegraphisches Büro,* 21 February 1931 and USDS 875.00/316: (No. 209), 12 March 1931 with enclosed report No. 12375, Military Attache Rome, 4 March 1931 and HHStA, Albanien 1/1 Polizeidirection in Wien, Pr. Z1. IV-5 Exp.: Wien, 21 February 1931.

19. HHStA, Albanien 1/1 Polizeidirection in Wien, Pr. 11-636/2: 21 February 1931.

20. Ibid.

21. HHStA, Albanien 1/1 Polizeidirection in Wien, Pr. Z1.IV-5 Exp.: 21 February 1931 and FO 371/15147 (C1349/480/90): Vienna, 24 February 1931.

22. HHStA, Albanien 1/1 Polizeidirection in Wien, Pr. Z1. IV-1004/31:22 September 1931 and HHStA, Albanien 1/1 Polizeidirection in Wien, Pr.Z1.IV-1004/50/31: 7 July 1931 and HHStA, Albanien 1/1 Polizeidirection in Wien, Pr.Z1.IV-1004/64/31: 11 September 1931.

23. HHStA, Albanien 1/1 Polizeidirection in Wien, Pr. Z1.IV-1004/31: 4 March 1931.

24. FO 371/15147 (C7636/480/90): Vienna, 5 October 1931 and FO 371/15147 (C3293/480/90): Durazzo, 4 May 1931 and FO 371/15147 (C6190/480/90): Durazzo, 6 August 1931.

25. FO 371/15147 (C7636/480/90): Vienna, 5 October 1931.

26. *Reichpost,* 24 February 1931 and *Freiheit,* 24 February 1931 and HHStA, Albanien 1/1 Polizeidirection in Wien, Pr. Z1.IV-1004: 22 February 1931 and HHStA, Albanien 1/1 Polizeidirection in Wien, Pr. Z1. IV-1141/31: 4 March 1931 and HHStA, Albanien 1/1 Polizeidirection in Wien, Pr.Z1.IV-1004/31: 11 March 1931.

27. FO 371/15147 (C7336/480/90): Vienna, 12 October 1931 and FO 371/15147 (C1917/480/90): Vienna, 18 March 1931.

28. USDS 875.001 ZOG/52: Tirana, (No. 204), 26 February 1931 and USDS 875.00/317: Tirana, (No. 225), 26 March 1931.

29. *Neue Freie Presse,* 12 March 1931.

30. USDS 875.001 ZOG/52: Tirana, (No. 204), 26 February 1931.

31. USDS 875.00/317: Tirana, (No. 204), 26 February 1931.

32. AA Politische Abteilung II, Pol. 2, Bd. 1: Belgrade, 10 May 1931 and AA Politische Abteilung IIB, Pol. 2, Bd. 2: Belgrade, 4 March 1931.

33. USDS 875.00/317: Tirana, (No. 225), 26 March 1931.

34. USDS 875.001 ZOG/52: Tirana, (No. 204), 26 February 1931 and FO 371/15147 (C8338/474/90): Durazzo, 10 November 1931.

35. FO 371/15148 (C2806/1418/90): Durazzo, 21 April 1931.

36. USDS 875.001 ZOG/52: Tirana, (No. 204), 26 February 1931.

37. USDS 875.001 ZOG/49: Tirana, (No. 195), 12 February 1931.

38. FO 371/15148 (C2113/1418/90): Durazzo, 25 March 1931 and FO 371/15887 (C1030/1030/90): Durazzo, 28 January 1932.

39. USDS 875.001 ZOG/49: Tirana, (No. 195), 12 February 1931.

40. USDS 875.00/334: Tirana, (No. 373), 26 October 1931.

41. USDS 875.00/317: Tirana (No. 225), 26 March 1931.

Notes to Chapter Ten

1. Royal Institute, *The Balkan States I*, p. 22 and FO 371/15887 (C1030/1030/90): Durazzo, 28 January 1932.

2. FO 371/15146 (C3389/475/90): Durazzo, 4 May 1931.

3. FO 371/15887 (C1030/1030/90): Durazzo, 28 January 1932.

4. Stanley, "Italy's Financial Stake in Albania," p. 85 and Royal Institute, *The Balkan States I*, p. 34.

5. Skendi, *Albania*, p. 114.

6. Ibid., p. 203.

7. FO 371/15148 (C1412/1412/90): Durazzo, 24 February 1931 and Joseph Swire, *King Zog's Albania* (New York: Arno Press, 1941), p. 216.

8. FO 371/15148 (C1412/1412/90): Durazzo, 24 February 1931.

9. Ibid.

10. Ibid.

11. Ibid.

12. Ibid.

13. FO 371/15147 (C6456/475/90): Durazzo, 5 August 1931.

14. FO 371/15146 (C475/475/90): Durazzo, 13 January 1931.

15. FO 371/15147 (C6452/475/90): Durazzo, 5 August 1931.

16. FO 371/15887 (C1030/1030/90): Durazzo, 28 January 1932 and USDS 875.001 ZOG/76: Tirana, (No. 421), 31 December 1931.

17. Jonima, "Die neueste Phase der italienisch-albanischen Beziehungen," pp. 550-551.

18. USDS 875.001 ZOG/76: Tirana, (No. 421), 31 December 1931 and USDS 875.001 ZOG/74: Tirana, 29 December 1931.

19. FO 371/16623 (C1383/1383/90): Durazzo, 7 February 1933.

20. FO 371/16624 (C2873/2873/90): Durazzo, 21 March 1933.

21. FO 371/18338 (R3775/67/90): Durazzo, 6 July 1934.

22. FO 371/16624 (C2873/2873/90): Durazzo, 21 March 1933.

23. Ibid.

24. FO 371/16623 (C1383/1383/90): Durazzo, 7 February 1933.

25. FO 371/18341 (R2465/2465/90): Durazzo, 3 April 1934 and FO 371/16623 (C1383/1383/90): Durazzo, 7 February 1933.

26. FO 371/18341 (R2465/2465/90): Durazzo, 3 April 1934.

27. Self, *Foreign Relations of Albania*, p. 172.

28.   FO 371/18341 (R2465/2465/90): Durazzo, 3 April 1934.

29.   FO 371/16625 (C3805/3420/90): Durazzo, 19 April 1933.

30.   FO 371/16625 (C3805/3420/90): Durazzo, 19 April 1933 and FO 371/18341 (R2465/2465/90): Durazzo, 3 April 1933.

31.   "Albania," *The Near East and India* (May 1933), p. 355 and FO 371/18341 (R2465/2465/90): Durazzo, 3 April 1934.

32.   FO 371/19477 (R3822/113/90): Durazzo, 10 June 1935 and Self, *Foreign Relations of Albania*, p. 172.

33.   FO 371/18341 (R2465/2465/90): Durazzo, 3 April 1934.

34.   FO 371/18338 (R3775/67/90): Durazzo, 6 July 1934.

35.   FO 371/16623 (C1383/1383/90): Durazzo, 7 February 1933.

36.   FO 371/19478 (R1515/1515/90): Durazzo, 23 February 1935 and FO 371/18338 (R3775/67/90): Durazzo, 6 July 1934.

37.   FO 371/19478 (R1515/1515/90): Durazzo, 23 February 1935.

38.   FO 371/18339 (R4791/67/90): Durazzo, 24 August 1934 and Gross, "Albanien, ein Land im Umbruch," p. 284 and Monath, "Die politisch-völkerrechtliche Entwicklung Albaniens," p. 316.

39.   USDS 875.001 ZOG/87: Tirana, (No. 892), 10 October 1933.

40.   FO 371/18338 (R319/67/90): Durazzo, 9 January 1934.

41.   FO 371/18839 (R3477/168/90): Durazzo, 13 June 1934 and Robinson, *Albania's Road to Freedom*, p. 75.

42.   FO 371/19478 (R1515/1515/90): Durazzo, 23 February 1935 and FO 371/18341 (R2465/2465/90): Durazzo, 3 April 1934.

43.   FO 371/2112 (R709/709/90): Durazzo, 27 January 1937.

44.   FO 371/18338 (R319/67/90): Durazzo, 9 January 1934.

45.   Ibid.

46.   Royal Institute, *The Balkans I,* p. 22, figures on foreign trade in millions of gold francs.

	Exports	Imports
Average 1922-1930	11.8	25.7
1931	7.5	29.5
1932	4.5	22.8
1933	5.7	15.9
1934	4.3	12.3
1935	6.0	14.2

47.   FO 371/16624 (C2873/2873/90): Durazzo, 21 March 1933 and FO 371/18341 (R2465/2465/90): Durazzo, 3 April 1934.

48. FO 371/18341 (R2465/2465/90): Durazzo, 3 April 1934 and Gross, "Albanien, ein Land im Umbruch," p. 285.

49. Gross, "Albanien, ein Land im Umbruch," p. 285.

50. FO 371/18338 (R3770/39/90): Paris, 2 July 1934 and FO 371/18338 (R4189/39/90): Belgrade, 23 July 1934.

51. FO 371/15887 (C1030/1030/90): Durazzo, 28 January 1932.

52. FO 371/18339 (R479/67/90): Durazzo, 24 August 1934.

53. Ibid.

54. FO 371/16624 (C2872/2872/90): Durazzo, 20 March 1933.

55. FO 371/19478 (R1515/1515/90): Durazzo, 23 February 1935.

56. FO 371/20358 (R1532/1532/90): Durazzo, 11 March 1936.

57. Self, *Foreign Relations of Albania*, p. 172.

58. FO 371/20358 (R1532/1532/90): Durazzo, 11 March 1936.

59. FO 371/19477 (R4321/878/90): Durazzo, 3 July 1935.

60. FO 371/20357 (R2378/502/90): Durazzo, 21 April 1936.

61. FO 371/19477 (R7682/878/90): Durazzo, 17 December 1935.

62. Ibid.

63. USDS 875.0011/13: Tirana, (telegram), 11 January 1936.

64. FO 371/21112 (R709/709/90): Durazzo, 27 January 1937.

65. Zamboni, Mussolinis Expansionspolitik auf dem Balkan, p. 482 and footnote 53.

66. FO 371/21112 (R709/709/90): Durazzo, 27 January 1937 and FO 371/23710 (R724/724/90): Durazzo, 23 January 1939.

67. FO 371/20357 (R2378/502/90): Durazzo, 21 April 1936.

Notes to Chapter Eleven

1. HHStA, Albanien 1/1 Polizeidirection in Wien, Pr.Z1.IV-2801/3/32: 26 October 1932 and HHStA, Albanien 1/1 Polizeidirection in Wien, Pr.Z1.IV-2801/1/32: 13 October 1932 and AA Politische Abteilung IIB, Pol. 5, Bd. 3: Tirana, 14 September 1932 and FO 371/16623 (C1383/1383/90): Durazzo, 7 February 1933.

2. FO 371/15887 (C7735/2552/90): Durazzo, 7 September 1932.

3. In February 1935, ten of those convicted received reduced terms while the rest were completely pardoned.

4. USDS 875.001 ZOG/78: Tirana, (No. 594), 7 October 1932 and FO 371/15887 (C7370/2552/90): Durazzo, 25 August 1932 and FO 371/16623 (C1383/1383/90): Durazzo, 7 February 1933.

5. See pp. 229-230 for earlier attempts. For Prishtina's role in the 1931 attempt see HHStA, Albanien 1/1 Polizeidirection in Wien, Pr.Z1. IV-1004/31: 26 March 1931.

6. FO 371/16623 (C7704/88/90): Durazzo, 21 August 1933 and HHStA, Albanien 1/1 Polizeidirection in Wien, Pr.Z1. IV-3859/5/32: 17 August 1933.

7. FO 371/15887 (C8874/4715/90): Durazzo, 19 October 1932.

8. FO 371/16623 (C1383/1883/90): Durazzo, 7 February 1933.

9. Ibid.

10. Fitso Bey had taken Iljas Bey Vrioni's position in early 1929 after the old gentleman expressed a desire to have his old post in Paris back. AA Politische Abteilung II, Pol. 7, Bd. 1: Tirana, 16 January 1929.

11. FO 371/18341 (R2465/2465/90): Durazzo, 3 April 1934.

12. See page 212 of this work.

13. USDS 875.001 ZOG/89: Tirana, (No. 923), 16 November 1933.

14. FO 371/19478 (R1515/1515/90): Durazzo, 23 February 1935.

15. HHStA, Pol. 1 30384 1411935: Athens, 5 January 1935.

16. FO 371/20358 (R1532/1532/90): Durazzo, 11 March 1936 and FO 371/19478 (R1515/1515/90): Durazzo, 23 February 1935. Embassies abroad reported to their governments that the incident was indeed a serious crisis as evidenced by the Austrian Minister's report from Athens. See HHStA, Pol. 1 30384 1411935: Athens, 5 January 1935.

17. FO 371/19476 (R5163/80/90): Durazzo, 19 August 1935.

18. FO 371/20358 (R1532/1532/90): Durazzo, 11 March 1936.

19. AA Politische Abteilung IIB, Pol. 5, Bd. 3: Tirana 13 September 1935 and FO 371/19476 (R5936/80/90): Durazzo, 26 September 1935.

20. FO 371/19476 (R5936/80/90): Durazzo, 26 September 1935 and AA Politische Abteilung IIB, Pol. 5, Bd. 3: Tirana, 26 September 1935.

21. FO 371/19476 (R6152/80/90): Belgrade, 14 October 1935 and FO 371/19476 (R6180/80/90): Durazzo, 14 October 1935 and FO 371/19476 (R6479/80/90): Durazzo, 23 October 1935.

22. FO 371/20358 (R1532/1532/90): Durazzo, 11 March 1936 and AA Politische Abteilung IIB, Pol. 5, Bd. 3: Tirana, 26 September 1935.

23. FO 371/20358 (R1532/1532/90): Durazzo, 11 March 1936.

24. Robinson, *Albania's Road to Freedom,* p. 100.

25. FO 371/20358 (R1532/1532/90): Durazzo, 11 March 1936.

26. Ibid.

27.   FO 371/21112 (R709/709/90): Durazzo, 27 January 1937.

28.   Robinson, *Albania's Road to Freedom,* p. 105 and FO 371/20358 (R1532/1532/90): Durazzo, 11 March 1936.

29.   FO 371/21112 (R709/709/90): Durazzo, 27 January 1937.

30.   FO 371/22307 (R1285/1285/90): Durazzo, 31 January 1938.

31.   USDS 875.001 ZOG/106: Tirana, (No. 343), 12 March 1937.

32.   Ibid.

33.   Ibid.

34.   USDS 875.0011/31: Tirana, (No. 333), 1 March 1937.

35.   FO 371/22307 (R1285/1285/90): Durazzo, 31 January 1938.

36.   Andrew Ryan, *The Last of the Dragomans* (London: Geoffrey Bles, 1951), p. 322 and *The Times,* London, 19 May 1937 and FO 371/22307 (R1285/1285/90): Durazzo, 31 January 1938.

37.   FO 371/22307 (R1285/1285/90): Durazzo, 31 January 1938.

38.   Ibid.

39.   USDS 875.001 ZOG/109: Tirana, (No. 478), 2 September 1937.

40.   FO 371/22307 (R1285/1285/90): Durazzo, 31 January 1938.

41.   *Daily Express,* 28 August 1934 and AA Politische Abteilung II, Pol. 2, Bd. 1: Tirana, 1 January 1929..

42.   *Daily Express,* 28 August 1934.

43.   AA Politische Abteilung II, Pol. 2, Bd. 1: Tirana, 5 October 1934 and USDS 875.001 ZOG/90: Tirana, (No. 11), 15 December 1933.

44.   See page 182 of this work.

45.   FO 371/18341 (R3490/3490/90): Athens, 8 June 1934.

46.   *Daily Express,* 28 August 1934 and AA Politische Abteilung II, Pol. 2, Bd. 1: Tirana, 5 October 1934 and HHStA, Albanien 1/1 Z1.4/Pol. 34.650/13/37: Athens, 15 January 1937.

47.   Fenyvesi, *Splendor in Exile,* p. 233.

48.   FO 371/12069 (C10397/946/90): Durazzo, 13 December 1927 and FO 371/13562 (C3666/3666/90): Durazzo, 17 May 1929.

49.   AA Politische Abteilung II, Pol. 2, Bd. 1: Tirana, 21 October 1928.

50.   Zog employed three drivers, three chambermaids, one manservant, one hairdresser and a cook all from Austria or Hungary, which lends some credence to this argument. HHStA, Albanien 1/1 Z1.4/Pol. 34.650/13/37: Athens, 15 January 1937.

51.   USDS 875.001 ZOG/38: Tirana, (No. 922), 14 November 1933.

52. USDS 875.001 ZOG/105: Tirana, (No. 334), 1 March 1937 and FO 371/22307 (R1285/1285/90): Durazzo, 31 January 1938.

53. USDS 875.001 ZOG/105: Tirana, (No. 334), 1 March 1937 and HHStA, Albanien 1/1, Z1.4/Pol. 35.661/13/37: Rome, 9 February 1937.

54. HHStA, Albanien 2/3, Z1. 219/Pol.: Rome, 4 December 1937 and Ryan, *The Last of the Dragomans,* p. 326 and USDS 765.75/366: Rome, (No. 349), 4 May 1937 and FO 371/22307 (R1285/1285/90): Durazzo, 31 January 1938 and Count Galeazzo Ciano, *Ciano's Hidden Diary 1937-1938* (New York: Dutton, 1953), p. 59.

55. Fenyvesi, *Splendor in Exile,* p. 233.

56. Conversations with Queen Geraldine, July 1981, Costa del Sol, Spain.

57. FO 371/22306 (R742/103/90): Budapest, 25 January 1938 and Conversations with Queen Geraldine, July 1981, Costa del Sol, Spain.

58. Conversations with Queen Geraldine, July 1981, Costa del Sol, Spain.

59. FO 371/22306 (R1346/103/90): Durazzo, 9 February 1938.

60. FO 371/22306 (R1291/103/90): Rome, 8 February 1938 and FO 371/22306 (R1960/103/90): Durazzo, 22 February 1938.

61. HHStA, Albanien 1/1, Z1.15/Pol. 51290: Rome, 3 February 1938.

62. FO 371/22306 (R1291/103/90): Rome, 8 February 1938 and Conversations with Queen Geraldine, July 1981, Costa del Sol, Spain.

63. Ciano, *Ciano's Hidden Diary,* p. 98.

64. Conservations with Queen Geraldine, July 1981, Costa de Sol, Spain and FO 371/22306 (R4641/103/90): Durazzo, 30 April 1938.

65. Ciano, *Ciano's Hidden Diary,* p. 106.

66. de Zzinyei-Merse, *Ten Years, Ten Months, Ten Days,* pp. 114-115.

67. Conservations with Queen Geraldine, July 1981, Costa del Sol, Spain and FO 371/22306 (R4637/103/90): Holy See, 6 May 1938 and FO 371/23710 (R724/724/90): Durazzo, 23 January 1939.

68. Conservations with Queen Geraldine, July 1981, Costa del Sol, Spain.

Notes to Chapter Twelve

1.   Mack Smith, *Mussolini's Roman Empire*, p. 141.

2.   Ibid.

3.   USDS 765.75/366: Rome, (No. 349), 4 May 1937.

4.   Ciano, *Ciano's Hidden Diary*, p. 4.

5.   Ibid., p. 94.

6.   Ibid., p. 107.

7.   Marcia Fishel Lavine, *Count Ciano: Foreign Affairs and Policy Determination in Fascist Italy, January 1939-June 1940* (Unpublished doctoral dissertation: Vanderbilt University, 1977), p. 17.

8.   Malcolm Muggeridge, ed., *Ciano's Diplomatic Papers* (London: Idhams Press, 1948), p. 207 and Lavine, *Count Ciano: Foreign Affairs and Policy Determination,* p. 17 and Mack Smith, *Mussolini's Roman Empire,* p. 150.

9.   Lavine, *Count Ciano: Foreign Affairs and Policy Determination,* p. 17.

10.   Muggeridge, *Ciano's Diplomatic Papers,* p. 207 and Lavine, *Count Ciano: Foreign Affairs and Policy Determination,* p. 17.

11.   Lavine, *Count Ciano: Foreign Affairs and Policy Determination,* p. 18.

12.   Ibid., pp. 18-19.

13.   Ciano, *Ciano's Hidden Diary,* p. 107.

14.   Muggeridge, *Ciano's Diplomatic Papers,* p. 204.

15.   Ibid.

16.   Ciano, *Ciano's Hidden Diary,* p. 125.

17.   Ibid., p. 114.

18.   Conversations with Queen Geraldine, July 1981, Costa del Sol, Spain.

19.   Ciano, *Ciano's Hidden Diary,* p. 202.

20.   Ibid., pp. 184-185, 205.

21.   Conversations with Queen Geraldine, July 1981, Costa del Sol, Spain.

22.   FO 371/12710 (R725/725/90): Durazzo, 23 February 1939 and FO 371/23710 (R1273/725/90): Durazzo, 22 February 1939 and FO 371/23714 (R4454/1335/90): Durazzo, 18 May 1939.

23.   FO 371/23711 (R2065/725/90): Durazzo, 16 March 1939 and Mack Smith, *Mussolini's Roman Empire,* p. 149.

24.   Count Galeazzo Ciano, *The Ciano Diaries, 1939-1943* (New York: Doubleday, 1945), p. 31 and FO 371/23711 (R2065/725/90): Durazzo, 16 March 1939.

25.   Conversations with Queen Geraldine, July 1981, Costa del Sol, Spain.

26.   Muggeridge, *Ciano's Diplomatic Papers*, p. 271.

27.   Lavine, *Count Ciano: Foreign Affairs and Policy Determination*, p. 23.

28.   Jacob Hoptner, *Yugoslavia in Crisis 1934-1941* (New York: Columbia University Press, 1962), p. 126.

29.   Ciano, *The Ciano Diaries*, p. 23.

30.   Lavine, *Count Ciano: Foreign Affairs and Policy Determination*, p. 26 and Mack Smith, *Mussolini's Roman Empire*, p. 151.

31.   Ciano, *The Ciano Diaries*, p. 28.

32.   Lavine, *Count Ciano: Foreign Affairs and Policy Determination*, p. 29 and Ciano, *The Ciano Diaries*, p. 47.

33.   Ciano, *The Ciano Diaries*, p. 53.

34.   Ibid., p. 51.

35.   Lavine, *Count Ciano: Foreign Affairs and Policy Determination*, p. 33.

36.   FO 371/23714 (R4454/1335/90): Durazzo, 18 May 1939.

37.   Ibid.

38.   Ciano, *The Ciano Diaries*, pp. 54, 56.

39.   Ibid., pp. 51, 55, 56.

40.   USDS 765.75/444: Tirana, (telegram, sec. 1), 6 April 1939.

41.   Ciano, *The Ciano Diaries*, p. 57.

42.   USDS 765.75/444: Tirana, (telegram, sec. 1), 6 April 1939.

43.   The Germans actually became aware of the plan even before the Italian army was informed.

44.   David B. Funderburk, "Anglo-Albanian Relations, 1920-1939," *Revue Etudes Sud-Est Europeenes* (XIII, 1, 1975), p. 6.

45.   USDS 765.75/444: Tirana, (telegram, sec. 2), 6 April 1939 and FO 371/23714 (R2951/1335/90): Durazzo, 11 April 1939.

46.   USDS 765.75/444: Tirana, (telegram, sec. 2), 6 April 1939 and FO 371/23714 (R2951/1335/90): Durazzo, 11 April 1939 and American Council on Public Affairs, *The Greek White Book, Diplomatic Documents relating to Italy's Aggression Against Greece* (Agence D'Athenes: 1943), p. 25.

47.   Lavine, *Count Ciano: Foreign Affairs and Policy Determination*, p. 37.

48.   FO 371/23713 (R2953/1335/90): Rome, 13 April 1939.

49.   Mack Smith, *Mussolini's Roman Empire*, p. 153.

50.   Ibid., p. 152.

51.   Ibid., pp. 152-154.

52.   USDS 765.75/459: Tirana, (telegram), 8 April 1939.

53.   Conservations with Queen Geraldine, July 1981, Costa del Sol, Spain. Zog himself maintained on more than one occasion that Yugoslavia was prepared to invade Albania, see FO 371/22110 (R1799/867/90): 14 March 1942.

54.   FO 371/23713 (R2657/1335/90): Rome, 8 April 1939.

55.   FO 371/23713 (R2755/1335/90): Durazzo, 11 April 1939 and FO 371/23713 (R2927/1335/90): Durazzo, 16 April 1939.

56.   Ciano, *The Ciano Diaries*, pp. 64-65.

57.   Mack Smith, *Mussolini's Roman Empire*, p. 154.

58.   Ibid., p. 155.

59.   Ryan, *The Last of the Dragomans*, p. 337.

60.   FO 371/23715 (R10774/1335/90): Durazzo, 21 November 1939.

61.   Self, *Foreign Relations of Albania*, p. 178.

62.   *The Times*, London, 7 April 1939.

63.   Ibid.

64.   *The New York Times* estimated that Italian investments in Albania during the interwar period approached one billion lire. *The New York Times*, 4 April 1939.

65.   Lavine, *Count Ciano: Foreign Affairs and Policy Determination*, pp. 42-43 and FO 371/23717 (R2333/1335/90): Rome, 4 April 1939.

66.   FO 371/23713 (R2759/1335/90): Budapest, 11 April 1939.

67.   FO 371/23712 (R2447/1335/90): Berlin, 8 April 1939 and FO 371/23712 (R2449/1335/90): Berlin, 8 April 1939.

68.   FO 371/23712 (R2484/1335/90): Foreign Office Minute, 8 April 1939.

69.   FO 371/23712 (R2487/1335/90): Paris, 8 April 1939.

70.   FO 371/23785 (R2473/1/22): Rome, 8 April 1939 and CAB 23/98 18A, 19 April 1939.

71.   Funderburk, "Anglo-Albanian Relations, 1920-1939," p. 7.

72. FO 371/23711 (4816/725/90): League of Nations, Events in Albania: Various communications addressed to the Secretary-General. A.14. 1939, VII, 10 June 1939.
73. Mack Smith, *Mussolini's Roman Empire*, p. 156 and USDS 741. 68/28 GDG: Athens, (telegram), 10 April 1939.

Notes to Epilogue

1. FO 371/23712 (R2446/1335/90): Athens, 8 April 1939.
2. USDS 875.001/ZOG/43: Tirana, (telegram), 10 April 1939 and USDS 765.68/218: Athens, (telegram), 3 May 1939 and Conversations with Queen Geraldine, July 1981, Costa del Sol, Spain.
3. Conversations with Queen Geraldine, July 1981, Costa del Sol, Spain.
4. USDS 875.00/511: Tirana, (telegram), 18 May 1939.
5. USDS 123 GRANT, HUGH G./80: Tirana, (No. 268), 23 December 1936 and USDS, Memorandum on conversation of Minister Grant and King Zog at Durazzo, 5 August 1936.
6. FO 371/23714 (R5445/23/90): Paris, 4 July 1939.
7. Conversations with Queen Geraldine, July 1981, Costa del Sol, Spain.
8. FO 371/24868 (R6817/6586/90A): Foreign Office Draft Memorandum, 23 July 1940.
9. Fenyvesi, *Splendor in Exile*, p. 234 and FO 371/24868 (R6712/6586/90): Foreign Office Memorandum, 25 August 1940 and FO 371/24868 (R8236/6586/90): Censorship, 26 October 1940.
10. Conversations with Queen Geraldine, July 1981, Costa del Sol, Spain.
11. FO 371/24868 (R7622/6586/90): Foreign Office Minute, 16 September 1940.
12. FO 371/24868 (R6817/6586/90): Foreign Office Minute, 12 July 1940.
13. FO 371/24867 (R8881/503/90): Greek Minister Simopoulos to O. Sargent, 5 December 1940 and FO 371/24868 (R6586/6586/90E): Ryan conversation with Zog, 3 July 1940.
14. FO 371/24868 (R8270/G) in (R8270/6586/90): to Athens, 9 November 1940.

15.   FO 371/24868 (R8270/6586/90): Ryan conservation with Zog, 8 November 1940 and FO 371/24868 in (R6817/6586/90): Foreign Office Minute from Major Kenyon M.I.R. War Office.

16.   FO 371/24868 (R8270/6586/90): Athens, (telegram), 4 November 1940, and (telegram), 23 November 1940.

17.   FO 371/24868 (R8639/6586/90): Cairo, (telegram), 29 November 1940, and Belgrade (telegram), 4 December 1940.

18.   FO 371/24868 (R8639/6586/90): Foreign Office Minute, 11 December 1940.

19.   Conversations with Queen Geraldine, July 1981, Costa del Sol, Spain.

20.   FO 371/33109 (R4190/390/90): Foreign Office Minute, 25 June 1942.

21.   FO 371/29709 (R5733/390/90): Washington, 24 August 1942 and FO 371/22110 (R4497/867/90): Washington, 8 July 1942 and FO 371/33109 (R4470/390/90): Foreign Office Minute, 3 July 1942.

22.   FO 371/33110 (R4493/867/90): Ryan conversation with Zog, 6 July 1942.

23.   FO 371/33110 (R4990/876/90): Foreign Office Minute, 27 July 1942.

24.   FO 371/43559 (R1219/616/90): Foreign Office Minute, 21 January 1944.

25.   FO 371/43559 (R5595/616/90): Foreign Office Minute, 8 February 1944 and FO 371/43559 (R7439/616/90): Foreign Office Minute, 8 May 1944 and FO 371/43559 (R21222/616/90): Ryan conversation with Zog, 12 December 1944.

26.   Conversations with Queen Geraldine, July 1981, Costa del Sol, Spain.

27.   Ibid.

28.   Nicholas Pano, *The Peoples' Republic of Albania* (Baltimore: Johns Hopkins Press, 1968), p. 13.

29.   Stavrianos, *The Balkans Since 1453*, p. 729.

30.   Ibid., p. 730.

BIBLIOGRAPHY

I. Archival Sources

Austria. Haus-Hof und Staatsarchiv, Wien.

Germany. Akten aus dem Archiv des Auswärtigen Amtes, Bonn.

—————. Bundesarchiv, Koblenz.

Great Britain, Foreign Office Archives, Public Record Office, London.

—————. Cabinet Papers, Public Record Office, London.

United States. U.S. Department of State, Records of the Department of State, National Archives, Washington, D.C.

II. Interviews

Conversations with Her Majesty Queen Geraldine of the Albanians, July 22-July 27, 1981, Casa Ponderosa, Costa del Sol, Spain.

III. Published Documents

Ciano, Galeazzo. *Ciano's Diplomatic Papers: Being a record of nearly 200 conservations held during the years 1936-1942*. Edited by Malcolm Muggeridge. Translated by Stuart Hood. London: Odhams Press Limited, 1948.

Greece. *The Greek White Book: Diplomatic Documents Relating to Italy's Aggression Against Greece*. The American Council on Public Affairs. Washington: Agence D'Athenes, 1943.

Italy. Ministero degli Affair Esteri. Commissione per la pubblicazione dei documenti diplomatici. *I documenti diplomatici italiani*. Settima serie: 1922-1935. Rome: La libreria dello stato, 1967.

League of Nations. *League of Nations Treaty Series: Publication of Treaties and International Engagements registered with the Secretariat of the League.* Lausanne: Imprimerie Reunies SA.

Pribram, Alfred. *The Secret Treaties of Austria-Hungary.* Cambridge: Harvard University Press, 1920.

IV. Secondary Sources

Avramovski, Z. "Italijanska ekonomska penetracija u Albaniju," *Istorija XX Veka*, Zbornik Radova, V, Belgrad, 1963.

Bell, E. A. "Albanian Heavy Oil," *World Oil*, July 1940.

Blake, Maxwell, "Economic Conditions in Albania," *United States Department of Commerce Reports*, April 1923.

de Bosdari, Graf Alessandro, "Italien Jugoslawien und Albanien," *Nord und Süd*, V. 50, 1927.

Busch-Zanther, Richard, *Albanien, Neues Land in Imperium*, Leipzig: W. Gould, 1939.

————, "Beitrage zur Wirtschaftsgeographie Albaniens," *Erde und Wirtschaft*, V. VII, 1933.

Carr, E. H., *International Relations between the Two World Wars*, New York: Harper and Row, 1947.

Cassels, Alan, *Mussolini's Early Diplomacy*, Princeton: Princeton University Press, 1970.

Ciano, Count Galeazzo, *Italy's Foreign Policy*, Roma: Editoriale degli Agricoltori SA, 1937.

————, *Ciano's Hidden Diary, 1937-1938*, New York: Dutton, 1953.

————, *The Ciano Diaries, 1939-1943*, New York: Doubleday, 1945.

Claar, Maximilian, "Italien und Osteuropa," *Zeitschaft für Politik*, V. 22, 1932.

Craig and Gilbert, *The Diplomats, 1919-1939*, Princeton: Princeton University Press, 1953.

Dako, Christo A., *Albania*, Boston: E. L. Grimes, 1919.

————, *Zogu the First, King of the Albanians*, Tirana: Kristo Luarasi Printing Press, 1937.

Dillion, E. L. P. "Albania," *Contemporary Review*, July 1914.

Durham, M. E., *Twenty Years of Balkan Tangle*, London: Allen and Unwin, 1920.

————, *High Albania*, London: Arnold, 1909.

"European Economic and Political Survey: Albania," Paris: Reference Service on International Affairs of the American Library in Paris, September 15, 1928.

Federal Writers Project, *The Albanian Struggle in the Old World and the New,* Boston, The Writers Inc., 1939.

Fenyvesi, Charles, *Splendor in Exile,* Washington, D.C.: New Republic Books, 1979.

Fodor, M. W., *Plot and Counterplot in Central Europe,* Boston: Houghton-Mifflin, 1937.

Frasheri, Kristo, *The History of Albania,* Tirana: Naim Frasheri Publishing, 1964.

Funderburk, David B., "Anglo-Albanian Relations, 1920-1939," *Revue Etudes Sud-Est Europeennes,* V. XIII, 1975.

Fusoni, Alan E., "An Experiment in Foreign Agricultural Education in the Balkans," *East European Quarterly,* January 1975.

Gasser, E., "Albania's Dairying Industry," *International Review of Agriculture,* April 1936.

Gegaj and Krasniqi, *Albania,* New York: Free Albania Committee, 1964.

Glasgow, George, "Italy, Albania and the Mediterranean," *The Contemporary Review,* May 1939.

Gross, Hermann, "Wirtschaftsstruktur und Wirtschaftsbeziehungen Albaniens," *Weltwirtschaftliches Archiv,* V. 38, 1933.

————, "Albanien, Wirtschaftlage und Wirtschaftsbeziehungen," *Wirtschaftdienst,* V. 18, 1933.

————, "Albanien, ein Land im Umbruch," *Erwachendes Europa,* 1934.

von Handel-Mazzetti, P., "Die geopolitischen Probleme des Adriatischen Meeres," *Zeitschrift für Geopolitik,* V. 8, 1931.

Hasluck, Margaret, "The Nonconformist Moslems in Albania," *The Contemporary Review,* May 1925.

Heymann, Egon, "Balkan 1935, von Belgrad aus gesehen," *Zeitschrift für Politik,* V. 25, 1935.

Hiltebrandt, Philipp, "Grundzüge der italienischen Aussenpolitik," *Erwachendes Europa,* May 1934.

Hito, Sadik, *An Albanian Letter,* New York: Cocce Press, 1941.

Holmes and Jordan, "Economic Developments in Albania," *United States Bureau of Foreign and Domestic Commerce,* August 1930.

Hoptner, J. B., *Yugoslavia in Crisis,* New York: Columbia University Press, 1962.

The Institute of Marxist-Leninist Studies at the Central Committee of the Party of Labor of Albania, *History of the Party of Labor of Albania,* Tirana: The Naim Frasheri Publishing House, 1971.

Jacomoni di San Savino, Francesco, *La Politica dell'Italia in Albania,* Rocca San Casciano: Cappelli Editore, 1965.

Jacques, Edwin, "Islam in Albania," *Moslem World,* July 1938.

Jelavich and Jelavich, *The Balkans in Transition,* Hamden: The Shoe String Press Inc., 1974.

Jokl, Norbert, "Die Bektaschis von Naim Be Frasheri," *Balkan-Archiv,* V. II, 1926.

Jonima, Th., "Die neueste Phase der italienisch-albanischen Beziehungen," *Zeitschrift für Politik,* V. 22, 1932-1933.

Karajowow, T., "Albanien, ein politischen und wirtschaftlicher Überblick," *Südostliche Warte,* 1929.

Keefe, K. E., *Area Handbook for Albania,* United States Government Printing Office, 1962.

Kempner and Rotta, "Albaniens Staatsverfassung," *Jahrbuch des öffentlicher Rechts der Gegenwart,* V. 14, 1926.

Kennedy, Phineas, "Politics and Religion in Albania," *Missionary Review of the World,* July 1939.

Kirkpatrick, Ivone, *Mussolini, A Study in Power,* New York: Hawthorn Books, Inc., 1964.

Kogen, Eugen M., "Albanien zum italienisch-jugoslawischen Gegensatz," *Zeitschrift für Politik,* V. 17, 1927.

Konitza, Faik, *Albania,* Boston: G. M. Panaritz, 1957.

Körber, A., "Rückblick und ausschau auf den Balkan," *Zeitschrift für Geopolitik,* V. 5, 1928.

Lavine, Marcia Fishel, *Count Ciano: Foreign Affairs and Policy Determination in Fascist Italy,* Vanderbilt University: Unpublished doctoral dissertation, 1977.

von Lindeiner-Wildau, H. E., "Der Kampf um die Vorherrschaft auf dem Balkan," *Zeitschrift für Geopolitik,* V. 3, 1927.

Logoreci, Anton, *The Albanians, Europe's Forgotten Survivors,* Boulder: Westview Press, 1977.

Lohr, Karl, "Die volkischen Minderheiten Albaniens," Petermanns geographische mitteilungen aus Justus Perthes' *Geographischer Anstalt,* V. 76, 1930.

Loose, Lothar, *Die völkerrechtlichen und politischen Beziehungen Albaniens zu Italien,* Würzburg: jur. Diss. Leipzig, 1936.

Lowe and Marzari, *Italian Foreign Policy, 1870-1940,* London and Boston: Routledge and Kegan Paul, 1975.

Lukacs, John, *The Great Powers and Eastern Europe,* New York: American Book Company, 1953.

Luke, H. C., "Tirana, Albania's Latest Capital," *The Near East,* V. 32, 1927.

MacCartney and Cremona, *Italy's Foreign and Colonial Policy, 1914-1937,* London: Oxford University Press, 1938.

MacColl, Rene, "Albania and the British Mission," *Quarterly Review,* October 1938.

Mack Smith, Denis, *Mussolini's Roman Empire,* London and New York: Longman, 1975.

März, Josef, "Das albanische Problem," *Zeitschrift für Politik,* October 1931.

Monath, Herbert, "Die politische-völkerrechtliche Entwicklung Albaniens," *Zeitschrift für Völkerrecht,* V. 24, 1940.

The Near East (London), "The Minerals of Albania," March 1923.

————, "Albania," May 1933.

Newman, Bernard, *Albania's Backdoor,* London: Herbert Jenkins, 1936.

Nowack, Ernst, "Albaniens bergwirtschaftliche Möglichkeiten," *Internationale Bergwirtschaft,* V. III, 1928.

Official Journal of the League of Nations, May 1923, 4th Year, No. 5; January 1924, 5th Year, No. 1 (Part 2).

Palmer, Alan, *The Gardeners of Salonika,* New York: Simon and Schuster, 1965.

Pano, Nicholas, *The People's Republic of Albania,* Baltimore: Hopkins Press, 1968.

Papenhusen, Friedrich, "Das politische Problem der Balkanhalbinsel," *Zeitschrift für Geopolitik,* V. 2, 1925.

Pastorelli, P., *Italia e Albania, 1924-1927. Origni diplomatiche del Trattato di Tirana del 22 novembre 1927.* Firenze: 1967.

————, *L'Albania, Nella Politica Estera Italiana, 1914-1920,* Napoli: Editore Jovene, 1970.

Rappaport, Alfred, "Albaniens Werdegang," *Die Kriegeschuldfrage Berliner Monathefte,* September 1927.

————, "Die Tirana-Vertrag, seine Vorgeschichte und seine Tragweite," *Europäische Gespräche*, V. 5, 1927.

————, "Der zweite Tirana-Vertrag und die Unabhängigkeit Albaniens," *Europäische Gespräche*, V. 6, 1928.

Rathjens, Carl, "Die Politik Albaniens seit dem zweiten Balkankrieg," *Zeitschrift für Politik*, V. 14, 1924.

Ravani, Daniel, "Zogu I., König der Albaner," *Zeitschrift für Politik*, V. 12, 1931.

Robinson, Vandeleur, *Albania's Road to Freedom*, London: George Allen and Unwin, 1941.

Royal Institute of International Affairs, *The Balkans, I Economic*, New York: Oxford University Press, 1936.

Roucek, Joseph, "Characteristics of Albanian Politics," *Social Science*, January 1935.

Ruches, P., *Albania's Captives*, Chicago: Argonaut Press, 1965.

Ryan, Andrew. *The Last of the Dragomans*, London, Geoffrey Bles, 1951.

Salvemini, G., *Prelude to World War II*, New York: Doubleday and Co., 1954.

Seifert, Günther, "Grundzüge italienischer Aussenpolitik," *Zeitschrift für Geopolitik*, V. 3, 1927.

Self, George M., *Foreign Relations of Albania*, University of Chicago: Unpublished doctoral dissertation, 1943.

Skendi, Stavro, *Albania*, New York: Praeger, 1956.

————, *The Political Evolution of Albania*, New York: Mid-European Studies Center of the National Committee for a Free Europe, Mineographed Series, March 1954.

————, *The Albanian National Awakening, 1878-1912*, Princeton: Princeton University Press, 1967.

————, "Religion in Albania during the Ottoman Rule," *Südost Forschungen*, V. 15, 1956.

————, "Albanian Political Thought and Revolutionary Activity, 1881-1912," *Südost Forschungen*, V. 13, 1954.

Stadtmüller, Georg, "Die albanische Volkstumsgeschichte als Forschungsproblem," *Leipziger Vierteljahrsschrift für Südosteuropa*, V. 5, 1941.

Stanley, Eugene, "Italy's Financial Stake in Albania," *Foreign Affairs*, June 1932.

Stavrianos, Leften, *The Balkans Since 1453*, New York: Holt, Rinehart and Winston, 1958.

Sugar and Lederer, *Nationalism in Eastern Europe,* Seattle: University of Washington Press, 1969.

Swire, Joseph, *Albania, the Rise of a Kingdom,* London: Unwin Brothers Limited, 1929.

————. *King Zog's Albania,* New York: Arno Press, 1941.

de Szinyei-Merse, Antoinette, *Ten Years, Ten Months, Ten Days,* London: Unwin Brothers Limited, 1941.

Tittoni, Thomas, *Italiens Aussenpolitik,* München: Südost Verlag Adolf Dresler, 1928.

Toptani, Esad Pasha, "My Policy for Albania," *The Balkan Review,* June 1919.

United Nations Relief and Rehabilitation Administration, "Economic Rehabilitation in Albania," *Operational Analysis Papers,* London: 1947.

Villari, Luigi, *Foreign Policy under Mussolini,* London: Deven-Adair, 1956.

————, *The Expansion of Italy,* London: Deven-Adair, 1956.

————, "The Italian Loan to Albania," *The Near East,* January 1928.

Vlora, Ekrem Bey, *Lebenserinnerungen,* München: R. Oldenbourg Verlag, 1973.

Wallisch, Friedrich, *Neuland Albanien,* Stuttgart: Franckhsche Verlagshandlung, 1931.

Windischgrätz, Prince Ludwig, *My Memoirs,* London: 1921.

"Control of Albanian Oilfields Assures 4% of Italy's Crude Requirements," *World Petroleum,* May 1939.

Zamboni, Giovanni, *Mussolinis Expansionspolitik auf dem Balkan,* Hamburg: Helmut Buske Verlag, 1970.

V. Newspapers

Albania
 Arbenia, Besa, Telegraph
Austria
 Die Stunde, Freiheit, Kreuzzeitung, Neue Freie Presse, Reichpost
France
 Ere Nouvelle
Germany
 Berliner Tageblatt, Deutsche Allegemeine Zeitung, Deutsche Tageszeitung, Hamburger Nachrichten, National-Zeitung, Tägliche Rundschau, Välkischer Beobachter, Vossische Zeitung, Wolff's Telegraphisches Büro

Great Britain
  Daily Express, Daily Telegraph, The Times
Greece
  Hellikon Mellon
Hungary
  Pester Lloyd, Pesti Naplo
Italy
  Gazeta Shqipetare, Giornale d'Italia, Impero, La Gazzetta di Puglia
  Lavoro Fascista, Mondo, Popolo d'Italia, Popolo di Roma, Tribuna
United States
  Dielli, The New York Times, The Republic
Vatican
  Observatore Romano
Yugoslavia
  Novosti

INDEX